THE CHANGING FACE OF THE SUBURBS

The Changing Face of the Suburbs

Edited by Barry Schwartz

The University of Chicago Press
Chicago and London

This volume is sponsored by the American Journal of Sociology and the Center for Policy Study.

The University of Chicago Press, Chicago 60637
The University of Chicago Press, Ltd., London

International Standard Book Number: 0-226-74218-0
Library of Congress Catalog Card Number: 75-7221

CONTENTS

Preface

A critical new balance in the organization of the American metropolis has been struck. This development has made especially visible during the past several years the accumulated product of decades of gradual, sometimes imperceptible, change. That evolution seems now to contain an almost revolutionary promise.

During the 1960s, when the problems of the cities commanded so much of our attention, city populations were for the first time met and actually surpassed by the population of the suburbs. Presently there are over 13 million more people in the suburban rings than in the cities which they surround, and this gap promises to widen during this and at least part of the next decade. At the same time, there appears to have been no basic change in the social organization of the suburbs. Metropolitan territory beyond the core city remains as fragmented as ever, partitioned into small independent communities, each with its own network of ordinances and institutions. A growing demographic force thus seems to be colliding with a relatively static social structure.

From this sociological contradiction at least three interrelated questions come to mind. First, how did the demographic change come about in the first place? What are the underlying conditions of suburbanization and what kinds of people have been affected by them? Second, what kinds of problems await a fragmented social structure which is not presently geared to the demands of massive populations? Third, does suburbanization involve a mere spatial extension of existing cultural modes or will it level these diverse forms and effect a basic transformation of the ways of life that are brought to it? This volume will be organized around these three very broad questions.

The first set of papers, brought together in Part I under the heading of "Master Trends," deals with two principal developments. The investigations by Reynolds Farley, Larry Long and Paul Glick, and Leo Schnore and his associates chart the magnitude of suburban growth over past decades; they identify the sectors of the population which have contributed most to that growth and specify the regions in which it has been most and least pronounced. Papers by John Kasarda and Gary Tobin, relating as they do to the diffusion of metropolitan business, industry, and transportation networks, describe the major structural changes which accompany and reinforce this centrifugal population movement. Finally, Thomas Guterbock's investigation seeks to measure the extent to which suburban growth is determined by the push of social conditions within the city as opposed to the pull of expanding opportunities outside the city.

While Part I treats the suburban ring as an undifferentiated whole, Part II, titled "Institutional and Behavioral Ramifications," brings to the fore the issues of social organization and social interaction. The first paper, written by Basil Zimmer, shows that the growing populations of the suburbs are being absorbed by a highly differentiated system of politically autonomous communities; it then explores suburbanites' readiness to delegate the institutional functions served by these communities to regional or centralized authorities. Taking fragmentation and resistance to metropolitan integration as their point of departure, Ann and Scott Greer show how the circumscribed territory and functions of the suburban community help bring about its unique governmental and political climate. Both of these papers are relevant to the question of how suburbs control the direction of their own growth. However, Brian Berry's (and associates') treatment of racial segregation confronts this issue in a direct way, unveiling the "sorting mechanisms" by which new arrivals to the suburbs are "tagged" and residentially organized. In addition, William Newman, in his article, demonstrates the impact of suburbs' population control and recruitment policies on the social functions and internal dynamics of religious institutions.

We turn next to the social psychological aspects of suburban life, which are explored in the last two papers. Claude Fischer and Robert Jackson show how the broader organization of the suburb helps structure informal contacts among its residents. And Scott Donaldson, in characteristically bold strokes, portrays the social climate and life-style which emerge from the separate developments treated by the preceding writers.

The concluding statement, which I have given myself to write, attempts to make the contents of this volume theoretically intelligible by placing them in the context of two models, each of which contains its own special vision of the sociological meaning of suburbanization. In doing this, I try to bring to the volume's point of describing and explaining metropolitan change a counterpoint which stresses ultimate limits to that change.

This volume is unique in two very important respects. It is the first book on the suburbs ever produced which consists of original papers on predefined themes. The volume is also a collective statement rather than a collection of independent investigations. This is true in a very literal sense. On June 17–19, 1974, approximately one year after all invitations to submit documents were accepted, 10 contributors, each supplied with a first draft of all articles, met in Chicago to voice comments on others' work and to listen to criticisms of his own. This very intensive conference, made possible by the Center for Policy Study of the University of Chicago, allowed participants to organize and refine their own papers in terms of the remarks and special intent of others, thus giving the total enterprise a color and coherence it would not have otherwise had.

These proceedings were graced and enriched by the presence of Bennett Berger who, besides taking part in the working meetings, presented his own paper, "American Pastoralism, Suburbia, and the Commune Movement," during a banquet offered for contributors and other guests by the Center for Policy Study.

I believe this volume brings the current state of knowledge on the suburbs to high expression. For this, many people deserve thanks. Above all, there is Charles Bidwell, editor of the *American Journal of Sociology*, who not only gave this project administrative approval but also took an active part in its management. He was of assistance to me in developing a topical outline for the book, in choosing contributors, and in organizing the June 1974 conference, over which he agreed, at my request, to preside. The meetings themselves would not have been possible without the direct encouragement and support of D. J. R. Bruckner, vice-president of Public Affairs and director of the Center for Policy Study. The Fellows of the Center played an equally supportive role. To Jean Entwistle, assistant to the director, goes credit for the achievement of setting up the conference. The Ford Foundation and Illinois State Department of Transportation deserve the gratitute of everyone for sponsoring it.

Besides Charles Bidwell and Bennett Berger, a number of other people joined the authors and made valuable contributions to the consideration of their drafts. These are Charles Winick of the Ford Foundation, William E. Barrows, Mark E. Hovind, and Steven Scaife of the Illinois State Department of Transportation, and Dorothy B. Holleb of the Center for Urban Studies of the University of Chicago.

BARRY SCHWARTZ

PART I
Master Trends

1 Components of Suburban Population Growth

Reynolds Farley
University of Michigan

I. INTRODUCTION

Numerous suburban trends are frequently reported in the press. Even the casual observer knows that suburban areas have grown rapidly, that few blacks reside in American Suburbs, and that the more elegant new homes tend to be built in the suburbs. Tables of data documenting these trends may be assembled ad nauseam. There are many deviations from these patterns, and we can identify rapidly growing central city areas with high-status populations as well as deteriorating suburbs which have the problems alleged to prevail in central cities.

In considering why people are interested in suburban growth, I realize that, on one hand, geographers, economists, and sociologists wish to describe how cities grow and how groups differentiate themselves by place of residence. On the other hand, in both the scholarly literature and popular press there are assertions that something is seriously awry about the distribution of population within American metropolises. The most frequently espoused view contends that cities house the poor, the elderly, and the economically unsuccessful ethnic groups. Other commentators note the physical deterioration of older cities and the location of new employment in suburbia. Presumably the quality of life in large cities has fallen and will continue to decline unless new policies are adopted.

One paper cannot address all the issues worthy of investigation or challenge many popular misconceptions. This paper has the following specific aims:

A. To describe patterns of population growth, specific for race, in large urbanized areas since the end of World War II.

B. To ascertain whether the populations of central cities and their suburban rings have become increasingly differentiated with regard to socioeconomic status.

A grant from the center for Population Research of the National Institute of Child Health and Human Development, NIH-71-2210, "The Distribution and Differentiation of Population within Metropolitan Areas," supported this research.

C. To analyze patterns of migration within large metropolitan areas and their effects on city-surburban differentiation.

D. To examine, in an exploratory manner, data from one large urbanized area to see if population distribution may be better described by data pertaining to local areas.

II. POPULATION GROWTH IN CENTRAL CITIES AND SUBURBAN RINGS SINCE WORLD WAR II

Before describing suburbia, we must define the term. Several definitions have been popular within sociology. Most focus upon the location of residences away from the center of a metropolis, although many sociologists describe suburbia in terms of low-density housing, the presence of strong family ties, or the absence of ethnic minorities. (For a discussion, see Schnore 1965, pp 137–50; Glenn 1973; or Dobriner 1963, chap. 1.) In this paper, the term "suburban" means the area which is urban in its demographic character but outside the large central cities. Suburbia is defined, then, in geographic terms.

A trend toward population growth at the periphery of the settled area is in no way a post–World War II innovation. Wirt (1972), for instance, begins his book on suburbia with comments about suburbanization in Mesopotamian cities, and Weber (1899, pp. 36–38) documents 19th-century suburbanization in American Cities. If we are interested in data for a recent period, we can examine the findings of two major studies which assessed suburban growth. Amos Hawley, working with metropolitan areas as defined in 1950, showed that from 1900 to 1920 population was concentrating, but that during the three decades following 1920 deconcentration occurred. The first period witnessed rapid growth of central cities combined with slower growth of satellite areas. This was followed by a centrifugal process in which outlying areas grew much faster than central cities (Hawley 1956, chaps. 2 and 10).

Irene Taeuber assembled data concerning population in central cities and in the rings surrounding them but within the corresponding Standard Metropolitan Statistical Areas (SMSA). These tabulations referred to the 208 SMSAs defined by the Bureau of the Census in the conterminous United States in 1960 (Taeuber and Taeuber 1971, chap. 15; Taeuber 1972; U. S. Bureau of the Census 1963). Her findings corroborate and extend those of Hawley. Since the end of World War I suburban rings have grown faster than central cities. In 1910, 65% of the nation's metropolitan population lived within these central cities, but by 1970 this fell to 47% (Taeuber 1972, table 19).

The decade of the 1960s was differentiated from previous decades in two important ways. First, although the growth rate of whites within central cities declined over time, the 1960s was the first period in which the number of whites in these cities failed to increase. Second, the 1960s was the first decade in which the black population of suburban rings grew faster than the white.

Preliminary data for the 1970s reveal a continuation of these trends. The white population of central cities, as defined for the census of 1970, declined between 1970 and 1973 while the black population of cities grew, albeit at a slower rate than in the 1960s. In the suburban rings the white and black populations both increased (U.S. Bureau of the Census 1974*b*).

To more thoroughly analyze city-suburban differences since 1950, a few specific areas were selected. Investigations of suburbanization in the United States are constrained by the availability of census tabulations. Ideally, demographic data would be available for small areal units identified by geographic coordinates so that investigators could assemble data as they wish. Instead, tabulations are available for political units and for enumeration areas classified according to Census Bureau criteria. For analyzing city-suburban trends, an investigator typically must select either urbanized areas or SMSAs. There is a convenience in using SMSAs since they are composed of entire counties, and county boundaries seldom change. However, SMSAs now contain many people who hardly fit the common notion of suburbanites. In 1970 more than one-quarter of the population within SMSAs but outside central cities was classified as rural (U.S. Bureau of the Census 1972*b*, table 47). For this reason, urbanized area data are used. The Census Bureau employed a similar definition in 1950, 1960, and 1970: An urbanized area includes a central city or cities of 50,000 or more and the densely populated contiguous areas (Shryock and Siegel 1971, pp. 160–61). The areal units forming a particular urbanized area may change from one decade to the next, but the functional unit remains the same.

A second decision concerns which areas should be considered. As Leo Schnore's work convincingly demonstrates, generalizations about cities and suburbs derived from older northern areas often do not accurately describe smaller, southern, or newly emerging metropolises (Schnore 1972, chap. 3). Optimally, an investigator would calculate data for all urbanized areas and discuss the effects of size, age, and region. Since that is beyond the scope of this report, this analysis is limited to the 15 largest urbanized areas in 1970. In that year, these locations with their 60 million residents contained over one-half of the nation's total population living within urbanized areas (U.S. Bureau of the Census 1971*a*, table 20).

Table 1 shows the population of central cities and their rings for the three most recent census dates. In those places where the Census Bureau defined more than one central city, data are aggregated for all central cities, a practice followed in subsequent tables. No control has been made for annexations. This is not a problem in most locations since few cities annexed areas in this

TABLE 1

Total Population of Urbanized Areas and Decennial Growth Rates, 1950–70

Urbanized Area	Total Population (Thousands)			Decennial Growth Rates (%)					
				Total		Whites		Nonwhites	
	1950	1960	1970	1950–60	1960–70	1950–60	1960–70	1950–60	1960–70
New York:*									
City	8,891	8,743	8,820	−2	+1	−8	−10	+52	+61
Ring	3,405	5,372	7,387	+58	+38	+57	+35	+85	+88
Los Angeles:*									
City	2,221	2,823	3,175	+27	+12	+19	+4	+98	+56
Ring	2,147	3,666	5,177	+70	+41	+20	+36	+167	+149
Chicago:*									
City	3,897	3,898	3,697	0	−5	−11	−18	+65	+38
Ring	1,024	2,061	3,017	+101	+46	+100	+45	+117	+82
Philadelphia:									
City	2,072	2,003	1,949	−3	−3	−13	−13	+41	+25
Ring	851	1,633	2,073	+92	+27	+93	+26	+78	+48
Detroit:									
City	1,850	1,670	1,496	−10	−10	−23	−29	+60	+35
Ring	810	1,867	2,475	+131	+33	+135	+31	+58	+62
San Francisco:*									
City	1,160	1,158	1,077	0	−7	−10	−22	+70	+51
Ring	862	1,273	1,911	+48	+50	+47	+47	+56	+86
Boston:									
City	801	697	641	−13	−8	−17	−17	+60	+70
Ring	1,432	1,716	2,015	+20	+17	+20	+16	+39	+93
Washington:									
City	802	764	757	−5	−1	−33	−39	+47	+30
Ring	485	1,045	1,725	+115	+65	+117	+58	+83	+207

	TOTAL POPULATION (THOUSANDS)			DECENNIAL GROWTH RATES (%)					
				Total		Whites		Nonwhites	
URBANIZED AREA	1950	1960	1970	1950–60	1960–70	1950–60	1960–70	1950–60	1960–70
Cleveland:									
City	915	876	751	−4	−14	−19	−26	+69	+16
Ring	469	909	1,209	+94	+33	+93	+29	+269	+413
Saint Louis:									
City	857	750	622	−12	−17	−24	−32	+40	+19
Ring	543	918	1,261	+69	+37	+72	+35	+37	+66
Pittsburgh:									
City	677	604	520	−11	−14	−15	−18	+23	+6
Ring	856	1,200	1,326	+40	+10	+41	+10	+26	+22
Minneapolis:*									
City	833	796	744	−4	−7	−6	−9	+69	+69
Ring	283	581	960	+105	+65	+105	+65	+233	+250
Houston:									
City	596	938	1,233	+57	+31	+53	+26	+73	+51
Ring	104	202	445	+93	+120	+93	+131	+91	+35
Baltimore:									
City	950	939	906	−1	−4	−16	−21	+45	+30
Ring	212	480	674	+126	+40	+134	+41	+23	+38
Dallas:									
City	434	680	844	+56	+24	+45	+14	+129	+66
Ring	105	253	494	+141	+96	+189	+96	−65	+93
Average:									
City	1,797	1,823	1,815	+1	0	−7	−12	+58	+42
Ring	906	1,545	2,143	+71	+39	+70	+36	+76	+91

SOURCE.—U.S. Bureau of the Census, *Census of Population: 1950*, vol. 2, table 33; *Census of Population: 1960*, vol. 1, table 20; *Census of Population: 1970*, vol. 1, table 24 (Washington, D.C.: Government Printing Office, various).

*More than one central city in these urbanized areas.

interval. Houston and Dallas are exceptions since they annexed large outlying areas between 1950 and 1960 (U.S. Bureau of the Census 1961, table 9).

During the 1950s the national population grew by 19% (U.S. Bureau of the Census 1972*b*, table 48). Among these 15 central cities, only Los Angeles, Houston, and Dallas grew in excess of the national rate. However, each suburban ring increased more rapidly than the national population, reflecting the trend toward growth at the periphery of the settled area.

Between 1960 and 1970 the nation's population grew by 14% (U.S. Bureau of the Census 1972*b*, table 48), but only two of the cities—Houston and Dallas—recorded such a large gain and 11 of the cities lost population. The suburban rings grew rapidly, and in every location but Pittsburgh the rings increased more rapidly than the national population.

Since the end of World War II the nation's largest cities are assumed to have attracted blacks and lost whites. Growth rates specific for color are shown in table 1. The generalization is borne out, since in both decades 12 of the cities lost whites and gained blacks. Los Angeles, Dallas, and Houston are the exceptions as both their white and black populations grew.

Gross changes in population reflect natural increase and migration. The lack of appropriate tabulations of vital events prevents a decomposition of growth into these components for urbanized areas. However, net changes in population specific for age, sex, and race may be estimated for central cities and their suburban rings. Selected results are presented in table 2 and figure 1.

National census survival rates were applied to the population of each city and ring—specific for age, sex, and color—as enumerated in 1950 and 1960 (U.S. Bureau of the Census 1965, table 1; 1972*d*, table 1). This yielded estimates of the population which would have been present 10 years later in the absence of change. The difference between the expected and actual population in the latter year—1960 or 1970—represents net change in population size. If the areal units were fixed, as was the case in most central cities, the number represents net migration. For suburban rings, however, the number includes migration and change attributable to shifts in the boundaries of urbanized areas.

Table 2 shows, for example, that the city of Detroit lost 327,000 whites between 1960 and 1970. The rate of losses was 31 per 100 expected in 1970. The city's nonwhite population, however, showed an increase through migration of 64,000, a rate of 14 per 100 residents expected in 1970.

Looking at table 2, we observe, first, that most central cities lost white population in both decades. In some places the volume and rate of white population loss were high. In Saint Louis and Washington, for example, there were more than 30 net out-migrants per 100 whites expected in 1970. With the exception of the two cities whose 1950–1960 growth was inflated by annexation, the patterns of change for whites in central cities were much the same in both decades. There is no evidence of an accelerated out-migration of whites.

Second, during the 1950s there were very high rates of nonwhite in-migration to these central cities. In many cities the patterns for nonwhites in the 1960s are rather different than they were in the previous decade. In all cities except New York and Boston the rate of nonwhite in-migration was lower during the 1960s than in the 1950s. Three cities—Cleveland, Pittsburgh, and Saint Louis—switched from gaining to losing nonwhites.

Third, the in-migration of nonwhites to these cities does not offset the loss of whites. In the 1960s the typical city lost about 189,000 whites but gained only 62,000 nonwhites. Even after the natural increase of blacks is taken into account, we find that the rise in nonwhite population was generally smaller than the loss of white, and thus the aggregate population of these cities declined (U.S. Bureau of the Census 1971b, table 3).

Fourth, suburban rings showed increases for both white and nonwhite population. There were changes from one decade to the next. The growth rate of the suburban white population slowed while that of nonwhites increased. Between 1960 and 1970 the growth rate of the nonwhite suburban population, as assessed here, exceeded that of the white suburban population in 12 of these 15 areas. High growth rates for the suburban nonwhite population should not be misinterpreted. In many areas there were small numbers of suburban blacks both at the beginning and end of this span. Indeed, in only six of the areas did the Negro suburban population exceed 25,000 in 1970.

Rates of population change vary by age. To illustrate how cities and suburbs differ in this regard, figure 1 presents rates of change for specific age groups. Data for all cities and for all suburban rings were summed and used to calculate these rates.

Nationally, migration rates are highest among people in their late teens and twenties and generally decline with age (U.S. Bureau of the Census 1974a, table 1). The growth rates of figure 1 reflect this phenomenon. Both in the 1950s and 1960s these central cities, in the aggregate, lost white population and gained black. Central cities experienced the greatest rates of loss among whites who were 30–40 at the end of the decade, undoubtedly the result of many couples' preference for suburban living as they formed their families. Central cities—including New York and Washington—which in the aggregate lost large numbers of whites, gained whites who were 20–30 at the end of the decade. The presence of colleges and employment opportunities probably accounts for this. For suburban whites, the peak growth rates were recorded at ages 30–40 in both decades.

Within cities and suburbs the highest growth rates for nonwhites were for people aged 25–35 at the end of the decades. Both cities and suburbs apparently attract young nonwhites who are starting careers and forming

9

TABLE 2

Net Population Change Estimated by Census Survival Rates and Ratio of Net Change to Population Expected at End of Decade for Cities and Suburban Rings by Color

| | CITY | | | | RING | | | |
| | White | | Nonwhite | | White | | Nonwhite | |
URBANIZED AREA	Number (Thousands)	Ratio	Number (Thousands)	Ratio	Number (Thousands)	Ratio	Number (Thousands)	Ratio
New York:*								
1950–60	−1,034	−14	+218	+27	+1,055	+35	+75	+60
1960–70	−842	−13	+408	+32	+1,047	+23	+241	+57
Los Angeles:*								
1950–60	+198	+11	+129	+65	+1,115	+70	+63	+134
1960–70	−28	−1	+121	+30	+685	+22	+145	+97
Chicago:								
1950–60	−582	−19	+151	+30	+609	+67	+21	+75
1960–70	−584	−22	+99	+11	+494	+27	+28	+46
Philadelphia:								
1950–60	−309	−20	+57	+16	+458	+63	+24	+45
1960–70	−208	−16	+24	+5	+170	+12	+21	+22
Detroit:								
1950–60	−442	−31	+75	+27	+597	+83	+9	+21
1960–70	−327	−31	+64	+14	+210	+12	+10	+13
San Francisco:*								
1950–60	−155	−17	+46	+37	+217	+29	+14	+23
1960–70	−107	−14	+64	+29	+306	+27	+50	+52
Boston:								
1950–60	−160	−23	+12	+32	+73	+6	+2	+22
1960–70	−102	−18	+22	+34	+113	+7	+11	+67
Washington:								
1950–60	−163	−35	+54	+21	+322	+74	+11	+45
1960–70	−105	−35	+41	+10	+348	+37	+67	+142

| | CITY | | | | RING | | | |
| URBANIZED AREA | White | | Nonwhite | | White | | Nonwhite | |
	Number (Thousands)	Ratio	Number (Thousands)	Ratio	Number (Thousands)	Ratio	Number (Thousands)	Ratio
Cleveland:								
1950–60	−189	−27	+48	+35	+275	+65	+5	+210
1960–70	−173	−31	−8	−3	+135	+16	+30	+330
Saint Louis:								
1950–60	−187	−30	+17	+12	+196	+43	+4	+8
1960–70	−149	−32	−2	−1	+155	+20	+21	+32
Pittsburgh:								
1950–60	−125	−23	+3	+4	+156	+21	+1	+4
1960–70	−87	−20	−8	−9	+12	+1	+1	+4
Minneapolis:*								
1950–60	−112	−15	+5	+35	+262	+183	+1	+765
1960–70	−83	−12	+8	+33	+186	+34	+3	+162
Houston:								
1950–60	+113	+26	+41	+36	+45	+51	+5	+45
1960–70	+71	+11	+42	+20	+155	+91	+2	+9
Baltimore:								
1950–60	−163	−25	+31	+15	+165	+88	<0	−2
1960–70	−123	−23	+19	+6	+102	+24	+3	+17
Dallas:								
1950–60	+83	+24	+43	+82	+103	+130	−13	−72
1960–70	+18	+4	+38	+30	+142	+61	+4	+54
Average:								
1950–60	−215	−14	+62	+26	+377	+49	+15	+43
1960–70	−189	−15	+62	+17	+285	+21	+42	+57

SOURCE.—Same as for table 1.
*Data for these locations refer to more than one central city.

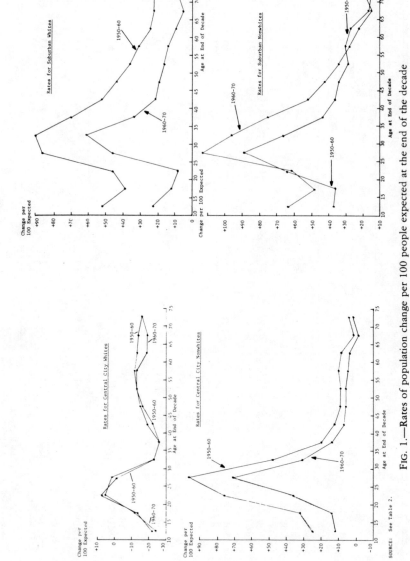

SOURCE: See Table 2.

Fig. 1.—Rates of population change per 100 people expected at the end of the decade

their families. In central cities all the age-specific growth rates for nonwhites were lower in the 1960s than in the 1950s. In the suburbs the higher age-specific rates were registered for the 1960s.

We next examined the effects of the age-specific migration trends —shown in figure 1—upon city-suburban differences in age composition. To do this, we calculated the average age of the population of cities and their suburban rings, specific for race, for 1950 and 1970. Selected results appear in table 3. The first two columns show the average age of the total population. The next three columns indicate city-suburban differences in average age for the total, white, and nonwhite populations.

First, we observe that in 1950 in all areas except Cleveland city residents were older than suburban residents. The maximum difference was found in Minneapolis, a difference of six years. Between 1950 and 1970 the average age of the city population increased in some locations but decreased elsewhere. Within the suburban rings decreases in age were more common than increases, and thus the aggregate city-suburban difference which was 1.7 years in 1950 grew to 2.5 years in 1970.

Second, columns 4 and 5 of table 3 indicate that city-suburban differences in age were greater among whites than among nonwhites. In Chicago in 1970, for instance, whites in the suburbs were on the average five years younger than city whites, but suburban nonwhites were only one year younger than city nonwhites. The increase between 1950 and 1970 in the city-suburban age difference is primarily accounted for by changes occurring among whites.

The index of dissimilarity was used to further assess the similarity of city and suburban age distributions. If central cities and suburbs had identical age compositions, the index would equal its minimum value, zero. If city and suburban residents were grouped so that the age distributions did not overlap at all, the index would take on its maximum value, 100. These measures appear in columns 6–8.

In most urbanized areas, and in both years, there was an extensive overlap of city and suburban age distributions, as revealed by the generally small values of the indexes of dissimilarity. Between 1950 and 1970 the indexes for the total population increased in most areas, reflecting modest rises in city-suburban age differentiation. The indexes for whites typically increased during this interval while in the majority of locations they decreased for nonwhites.

We conclude that the effects of migration and natural increase produced modest changes in the age compositions of cities and their suburbs. Whites in cities are now an average of about five years older than suburban whites, whereas in 1950 this difference was two years. Among nonwhites, city and suburban age distributions have become somewhat more similar, and at both dates nonwhites in cities were only an average of one year older than those in the suburbs.

TABLE 3

AVERAGE AGE OF POPULATION OF CITIES AND RINGS, CITY-RING DIFFERENCES BY COLOR, AND MEASURES OF CITY-RING DISSIMILARITY, 1950 AND 1970

URBANIZED AREA	AVERAGE AGE OF TOTAL POPULATION			CITY-RING DIFFERENCES BY COLOR		INDEX OF DISSIMILARITY		
	City (1)	Ring (2)	Diff. (3)	White (4)	Non-white (5)	Total (6)	White (7)	Black (8)
New York:								
1950	34.7	33.7	−1.0	−1.4	+0.5	3	5	4
1970	34.9	32.9	−2.0	−4.6	+0.7	8	11	2
Los Angeles:								
1950	35.6	33.2	−2.4	−2.8	−1.4	5	5	5
1970	33.8	31.1	−2.7	−3.6	−2.9	6	8	8
Chicago:								
1950	34.1	32.7	−1.4	−1.9	+0.4	4	5	4
1970	33.2	30.7	−2.5	−5.4	−0.8	7	12	3
Philadelphia:								
1950	34.1	33.0	−1.1	−1.7	−0.4	3	3	5
1970	34.4	32.0	−2.4	−4.6	−0.9	7	9	3
Detroit:								
1950	32.6	29.5	−3.1	−3.5	−4.0	7	8	11
1970	33.8	29.9	−3.9	−7.8	−1.2	10	17	3
San Francisco:								
1950	36.2	30.9	−5.3	−5.8	−3.1	11	12	7
1970	36.7	31.6	−5.1	−8.0	−2.0	10	18	5
Boston:								
1950	34.5	34.4	−0.1	−0.3	+0.9	2	2	10
1970	34.0	33.6	−0.4	−2.1	+2.5	7	10	6
Washington:								
1950	33.7	29.1	−4.6	−6.5	−1.5	11	15	5
1970	32.7	29.7	−3.0	−12.1	−3.9	8	29	11
Cleveland:								
1950	33.8	33.8	...	−0.7	+2.8	5	6	9
1970	32.9	32.5	−0.4	−2.6	−2.2	5	9	8
Saint Louis:								
1950	35.1	32.3	−2.8	−3.2	−1.7	6	5	6
1970	35.4	31.4	−4.0	−7.9	−2.3	10	17	5
Pittsburgh:								
1950	33.8	32.7	−1.1	−1.4	−1.9	3	4	5
1970	36.1	34.0	−2.1	−3.2	−1.1	8	10	2
Minneapolis:								
1950	34.5	28.7	−5.8	−5.8	−0.2	15	15	12
1970	34.8	27.4	−7.4	−7.9	+0.3	19	20	10
Houston:								
1950	30.6	26.8	−3.8	−4.2	−1.8	7	7	9
1970	29.8	28.0	−1.8	−2.9	+0.4	5	8	5
Baltimore:								
1950	33.0	29.0	−4.0	−4.9	−3.1	10	12	8
1970	33.0	31.5	−1.5	−5.8	+2.1	6	14	6

TABLE 3 (*Continued*)

URBANIZED AREA	AVERAGE AGE OF TOTAL POPULATION			CITY-RING DIFFERENCES BY COLOR		INDEX OF DISSIMILARITY		
	City (1)	Ring (2)	Diff. (3)	White (4)	Non-white (5	Total (6)	White (7)	Black (8)
Dallas:								
1950	32.1	29.9	−2.2	−1.6	−4.8	11	5	11
1970	31.1	27.3	−3.8	−5.6	+0.5	10	14	2
Average:								
1950	34.3	32.6	−1.7	−2.1	−1.1	4	5	5
1970	34.0	31.5	−2.5	−4.6	−0.9	7	11	3

SOURCE.—U.S. Bureau of the Census, *Census of Population: 1950*, vol. 2, table 33; *Census of Population: 1970*, PC(1)-B, table 24 (Washington, D.C.: Government Printing Office, various).

III. CITY-SUBURBAN DIFFERENCES IN SOCIOECONOMIC STATUS

Suburban rings grew rapidly, while central cities lost whites but gained blacks. This gave rise to speculations that cities and their suburbs became less alike in socioeconomic status as well as in racial composition. The concept of the suburbanization of cities has been described. That is, all who can leave the central city do so, and in the future cities will house only those who cannot afford the suburbs (Downes 1973, p. 289).

To ascertain whether the populations of cities and their rings became increasingly differentiated since 1950, data concerning income, education, and occupation were examined. Tables 4 and 5 and figure 2 describe city-suburban differences.

Table 4 shows family income, in 1960 and 1970, for each central city and its suburbs. Three aspects of these data should be noted. First, the 1960 figures refer to whites and nonwhites, while the 1970 data refer to Negroes and non-Negroes. Second, to adjust for inflation, the dollar amounts are shown in constant dollars, that is, in 1969 dollars. Third, the data indicate the mean income of families. A Pareto curve was fitted to the reported income distribution to ascertain the mean of the open-ended upper income category, and this was then used to compute the overall mean (Miller 1966, pp. 215–20).

In each city and ring real income rose during the 1960s, and at the end of the decade the typical family had a purchasing power almost $3,000 greater than at the beginning. The rise in income in the suburbs was somewhat greater than in the cities. That is, in cities mean family income rose 27% from $9,200 to $11,700, while in the suburbs the increase was 35% from $11,300 to $15,200.

TABLE 4

AVERAGE INCOME OF FAMILIES IN CITIES AND RINGS, CITY-RING DIFFERENCES
BY RACE AND MEASURES OF CITY-RING DIFFERENCES, 1960 AND 1970

URBANIZED AREA	AVERAGE FAMILY INCOMES FOR TOTAL FAMILIES ($ THOUSAND)			CITY-RING DIFFERENCES IN INCOME BY RACE* ($ THOUSAND)		INDEX OF DIFFERENTIATION†		
	City (1)	Ring (2)	Diff. (3)	White (4)	Black (5)	Total (6)	White (7)	Black (8)
New York:								
1960	9.3	12.9	3.6	3.4	1.2	25	22	15
1970	12.1	16.2	4.1	3.5	1.9	27	24	17
Los Angeles:								
1960	10.8	10.8	0	−0.6	0.7	5	2	9
1970	13.4	13.8	0.4	−0.4	1.4	8	3	13
Chicago:								
1960	9.9	13.7	3.8	3.7	0.9	26	20	12
1970	12.0	16.8	4.8	3.9	1.5	31	24	13
Philadelphia:								
1960	8.4	11.3	2.9	2.4	0.3	24	19	5
1970	10.9	14.6	3.7	3.0	0.7	25	19	7
Detroit:								
1960	9.0	11.1	2.1	1.1	0.2	22	13	4
1970	11.6	16.0	4.4	3.4	0.1	29	21	1
San Francisco:								
1960	10.0	11.2	1.2	0.7	0.4	13	5	10
1970	12.7	14.9	2.2	1.5	0.8	18	14	8
Boston:								
1960	8.3	10.8	2.5	2.3	2.1	21	19	19
1970	10.8	14.7	3.5	3.3	3.1	26	21	28
Washington:								
1960	10.1	14.7	4.6	−0.8	−0.4	30	10	−4
1970	12.8	16.9	4.1	−2.5	1.3	31	−2	14
Cleveland:								
1960	8.2	12.6	4.4	4.0	1.0	35	29	11
1970	10.2	15.8	5.6	4.9	2.9	37	31	28
Saint Louis:								
1960	7.5	10.6	3.1	2.8	−0.6	30	26	−10
1970	9.6	14.3	4.8	4.1	0.5	34	29	4
Pittsburgh:								
1960	8.4	9.6	1.4	0.7	0.1	14	9	3
1970	11.2	12.5	1.3	0.6	0.2	16	11	7
Minneapolis:								
1960	9.2	11.0	1.8	1.7	‡	20	19	‡
1970	12.0	15.5	3.5	3.3	‡	27	26	‡
Houston:								
1960	9.6	9.0	−0.6	−0.1	−0.2	10	4	−6
1970	12.4	13.3	0.9	−0.3	−0.3	13	3	−2
Baltimore:								
1960	8.4	10.3	1.9	0.8	0.7	25	14	13
1970	10.6	14.3	3.7	2.3	2.3	31	22	21

TABLE 4 (*Continued*)

	Average Family Incomes for Total Families ($ Thousand)			City-Ring Differences in Income by Race* ($ Thousand)		Index of Differentiation†		
Urbanized Area	City (1)	Ring (2)	Diff. (3)	White (4)	Black (5)	Total (6)	White (7)	Black (8)
Dallas:								
1960	9.3	10.1	0.8	−0.1	−0.2	12	3	−7
1970	13.2	13.9	0.7	−0.7	−0.5	14	3	−3
Total:								
1960	9.2	11.3	2.1	1.5	0.6	20	15	8
1970	11.7	15.2	3.5	2.7	1.2	26	19	13

SOURCES.—U.S. Bureau of the Census, *Census of Population: 1960*, PC(1)-C, tables 76 and 78; *Census of Population: 1970*, PC(1)-C, tables 89 and 94 (Washington, D.C.: Government Printing Office, various).
*Data for 1960 refer to nonwhites and whites. Data for 1970 refer to Negroes and non-Negroes.
†This is the Gini index computed from a 12-category income distribution.
‡Fewer than 500 black families.

As anticipated, suburban rings generally contained richer population than cities. City-suburban differences in average family income are shown in columns 3–5 of table 4. The differences were greatest in Cleveland and Saint Louis, where suburban families reported average incomes 50% above those of city families. In 1960 there were two areas—Los Angeles and Houston—in which the average income of ring families was as low or lower than that of city families. In 1970 ring families had the higher average income in all 15 urbanized areas.

The magnitude and direction of city-suburban differences depend upon the measure employed. Average family income is useful since it assesses purchasing power, but it is sensitive to the mean assigned to the upper income category. One other measure of the similarity of city and suburban populations—the Gini index—is presented in table 4. The measure compares the distribution of city and ring residents on any ordered variable such as income or years of schooling. If the city and ring have similar distributions, the index assumes its minimum absolute value, zero. Large positive values of the indexes, as computed here, indicate that suburban residents are in higher status categories than city residents. The maximum value, 100, occurs if all suburban residents are in higher status categories than any city residents. It is possible for a suburban area to contain a less prestigious population than a city, in which case the Gini indexes will have negative values.

Columns 6–8 of table 4 present the Gini indexes comparing the income distributions of cities and their suburbs. In all cases the indexes for the total population are positive, indicating that family income levels are higher in the suburbs. Between 1960 and 1970 the Gini indexes rose in all locations, reflecting the increasing city-suburban differentiation. Most of the changes, however, were small; from 26 to 31 in Chicago and from 25 to 27 in New York.

Aggregate city-suburban differences reflect areal differences in the distribution of population by race. The concentration of blacks in central cities and their small representation in suburbs maximizes city-suburban income differences. This is revealed by the race-specific data in table 4. When urbanized areas are combined, we see that the average income of ring families exceeded that of city families by $3,500 in 1969. Among whites, however, the difference was $2,700; among nonwhites, only $1,200. In four urbanized areas—Los Angeles, Washington, Houston, and Dallas—data for the total population reveal that average family income was higher in the suburbs, but in these locations central city white families had higher average incomes than suburban white families. The race-specific Gini indexes tell a similar story. Controlling for race indicates a smaller city-suburban difference than is implied by the aggregate figures.

Comparable data regarding educational attainment for the interval 1950 to 1970 are presented in table 5. Educational attainment has risen in both cities and their suburbs, but the increase in the suburbs slightly exceeded that in cities, producing a larger city-suburban difference. In 1950 the suburban population averaged about nine-tenths of a year more schooling than did city residents; in 1970, the difference was 1.1 years. In most urbanized areas the city and suburbs became more dissimilar in educational attainment as measured by either the difference in average attainment (cols. 3–5) or the Gini index (cols. 6–8). In Los Angeles, however, the city and its suburbs were quite alike in socioeconomic composition at all dates, and city-suburban differences in Houston were smaller in 1970 than a score of years earlier. Aggregate city-suburban differences in attainment are greater than the race-specific differences.

A different manner for analyzing these data is to consider the representation of socioeconomic groups in suburbia. Borrowing from Leo Schnore, we use representation to mean the relative proportion of a group living in the suburbs (1964, p. 166). Suppose that 30% of the total families in an urbanized area reside within the suburbs but that 60% of the families with incomes exceeding $25,000 live in the suburbs. We would contend that the well-to-do are overrepresented in suburbia.

Figure 2 presents summary measures of suburban representation. Among whites in 1960, 48% of the adult population of these urbanized areas lived in the suburbs, but the proportion varied by educational attainment. Among those with an elementary school education, 35% were found in the suburbs; among those with a college education, 60%. A similar pattern obtained among whites in 1970.

The proportion of nonwhites in the suburbs is much smaller than the proportion of whites, and among nonwhites there was almost no variation by education in suburban representation. In 1960, at all educational levels, about 14% lived outside the central city. Comparing the suburban representation of the races reveals that proportionally fewer college-educated blacks than grammar-school-educated whites lived in the suburbs. This illustrates that the absence of blacks from the suburbs is not simply a function of their socioeconomic status (Hermalin and Farley 1973, pp. 601–3).

Figures such as this one do not indicate the variety of suburban representation patterns found in large urbanized areas. Schnore demonstrated the inappropriateness of generalizing that suburban representation increases directly with socioeconomic status (1972, pp. 57–68). In some areas, such as Los Angeles, groups at both the top and bottom of the educational distribution were overrepresented in the city. Data analyzed for this paper corroborate Schnore's findings. In Los Angeles, Houston, and Dallas, higher-income white families in 1970 were substantially overrepresented within the central city. The small white population of Washington has higher socioeconomic status—as indexed by income, occupational prestige, or educational attainment—than the large suburban white population.

After reviewing these data concerning city and suburban status, we conclude, first, that assertions that socioeconomic levels are decreasing in cities are unfounded. Income, educational attainment, and the proportion of workers with prestigious jobs have increased in these large central cities just as they have nationally. Cities now have wealthier and more extensively educated populations than they used to, although they are smaller populations.

Second, for these major indicators of status the rises were somewhat greater in most suburban rings than in central cities, producing slightly greater city-suburban differences.

Third, aggregate city-suburban differences result, in part, from differences in the distribution of the races. Blacks in the suburbs differ less from blacks in cities and whites in suburbs differ less from whites in cities than the total suburban population differs from the total city population.

Fourth, among whites suburban representation tended to increase with socioeconomic status, although exceptions such as Los Angeles, Houston, Dallas, and Washington can be noted. Among nonwhites there is little evidence that the likelihood of living in suburbia increased with socioeconomic status.

IV. THE EFFECTS OF MIGRATION UPON POPULATION DISTRIBUTION AND CITY-SUBURBAN DIFFERENCES

The previous section reported that socioeconomic status increased somewhat more within suburbs than in central cities. This may have occurred because long-term residents of suburbia experienced greater upward mobility than city residents or because of selective migration. The large volume of migra-

TABLE 5

AVERAGE YEARS OF SCHOOL FOR POPULATION 25 AND OVER IN CITIES AND RINGS, CITY-RING DIFFERENCE BY RACE, AND MEASURES OF CITY-RING DIFFERENTIATION, 1950, 1960, AND 1970

URBANIZED AREA	AVERAGE YEARS OF SCHOOL FOR POPULATION 25 AND OVER			CITY-RING DIFFERENCES IN EDUCATION BY RACE*		INDEX OF DIFFERENTIATION†		
	City (1)	Ring (2)	Diff. (3)	White (4)	Black (5)	Total (6)	White (7)	Black (8)
New York:								
1950	9.5	10.4	+0.9	...	...	15	...	...
1960	9.8	10.9	+1.1	+1.1	+0.1	16	16	1
1970	10.5	11.6	+1.1	+1.1	+0.2	18	17	4
Los Angeles:								
1950	10.8	11.0	+0.2	...	...	3	...	...
1960	11.1	11.2	+0.1	0	0	1	−1	1
1970	11.6	11.7	+0.1	+0.1	+0.4	1	−1	7
Chicago:								
1950	9.7	10.9	+1.2	...	...	18	...	...
1960	9.9	11.3	+1.4	+1.4	0	24	23	0
1970	10.5	12.0	+1.5	+1.6	+0.2	27	25	2
Philadelphia:								
1950	9.3	10.5	+1.2	...	...	19	...	...
1960	9.5	10.9	+1.4	+1.3	−0.2	22	21	−4
1970	10.3	11.6	+1.3	+1.2	+0.2	24	22	4
Detroit:								
1950	9.7	10.3	+0.6	...	...	9	...	...
1960	9.8	10.9	+1.1	+0.9	−0.2	18	16	−2
1970	10.3	11.5	+1.2	+1.1	−0.2	21	19	−2
San Francisco:								
1950	10.6	11.3	+0.7	...	...	12	...	...
1960	10.7	11.5	+0.8	+0.5	+0.8	12	10	10
1970	11.4	12.2	+0.8	+0.7	+0.5	11	8	7
Boston:								
1950	10.2	10.9	+0.7	...	...	11	...	...
1960	10.4	11.3	+0.9	+0.9	+1.0	15	14	17
1970	11.0	12.0	+2.0	+0.9	+0.9	17	16	16
Washington:								
1950	10.8	12.1	+1.3	+0.7	−1.0	21	11	−16
1960	10.8	12.3	+1.5	+0.6	−0.6	23	8	−9
1970	11.4	12.8	+1.4	−0.1	+0.6	23	−5	11
Cleveland:								
1950	9.3	11.3	+2.0	...	...	32	...	...
1960	9.5	11.4	+1.9	+1.6	+0.3	32	32	4
1970	10.1	11.9	+1.8	+1.8	+1.3	34	33	24
Saint Louis:								
1950	9.2	10.0	+0.8	...	...	15	...	...
1960	9.3	10.6	+1.3	+1.3	−0.6	22	23	−11
1970	9.8	11.4	+1.6	+1.6	+0.1	28	29	2
Pittsburgh:								
1950	9.5	9.8	+0.3	...	...	5	...	...
1960	9.9	10.5	+0.6	+0.4	−0.3	10	9	−5
1970	10.7	11.3	+0.6	+0.5	−0.1	12	10	−1

TABLE 5 (*Continued*)

URBANIZED AREA	AVERAGE YEARS OF SCHOOL FOR POPULATION 25 AND OVER			CITY-RING DIFFERENCES IN EDUCATION BY RACE*		INDEX OF DIFFERENTIATION†		
	City (1)	Ring (2)	Diff. (3)	White (4)	Black (5)	Total (6)	White (7)	Black (8)
Minneapolis:								
1950	10.7	11.2	+0.5	. . .	. . .	10	. . .	. . .
1960	10.9	11.8	+0.9	+0.9	+1.0	18	17	18
1970	11.5	12.5	+1.0	+1.0	+2.1	20	20	37
Houston:								
1950	9.9	10.7	+0.8	+0.6	−1.1	11	9	−16
1960	10.5	10.9	+0.4	+0.4	−0.8	7	4	−11
1970	11.2	11.5	+0.3	+0.1	−0.6	5	0	−9
Baltimore:								
1950	8.9	10.2	+1.3	+0.9	+0.6	20	15	11
1960	9.3	10.5	+1.2	+1.0	+0.2	21	16	3
1970	9.8	11.2	+1.4	+1.1	+0.7	23	19	10
Dallas:								
1950	10.6	10.5	−0.1	+0.2	−1.0	1	7	−16
1960	10.7	11.4	+0.7	+0.4	−1.0	11	6	−16
1970	11.3	11.9	+0.6	+0.3	−0.8	9	4	−14
Total:								
1950	9.7	10.6	+0.9	. . .	. . .	15	. . .	. . .
1960	10.0	11.0	+1.0	+0.9	+0.1	17	15	2
1970	10.6	11.7	+1.1	+1.0	+0.4	18	16	7

SOURCES.—U.S. Bureau of the Census, *Census of Population: 1950*, vol. 2, tables 34 and 36; *Census of Population: 1960*, PC(1)-C, tables 73 and 77; *Census of Population: 1970*, PC(1)-C, tables 83 and 91 (Washington, D.C.: Government Printing Office, various).
*Data for 1950 and 1960 refers to nonwhites and whites. Data for 1970 refer to Negroes and non-Negroes.
†This is the Gini index computed from nine-catetory education distributions.

tion, as indicated in table 2, suggests that population movement played an important role. The Taeubers' (1964) study of 1960 data measured the impact of selective migration upon city-suburban status differences.

The census of 1970 asked a sample of the population where they lived five years previously. People may then be classified by their previous residence, their present residence, and their current socioeconomic status. As the Taeubers observed, migration data are more problematic than other census tabulations. First, nonresponse rates concerning place of residence are high and apparently rose from 2% in 1960 to 5% in 1970 (U.S. Bureau of the Census 1963, table 164; 1973a, table 196). Second, there apparently is a tendency to inaccurately report previous place of residence. County names may be confused or people may report a large city rather than their specific suburban location (Taeuber and Taeuber 1965, p. 434). Third, most migra-

Proportion Living in
Suburban Ring

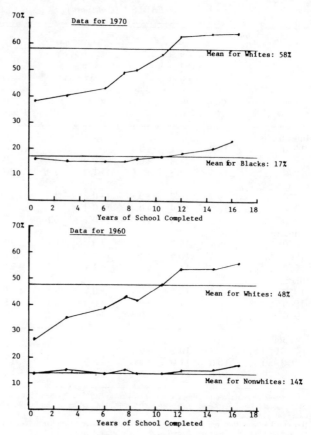

SOURCE: See Table 4.

FIG. 2.—Proportion of adults living in suburban rings specific for educational attainment and race, 15 urbanized areas, 1960 and 1970.

tion data pertain to counties, making it impossible to precisely compare cities and their suburbs as the terms have been defined in this paper. Finally, undercount affects these data. The census of 1970 apparently missed 2% of the white and 8% of the black population. The undercount rates were unusually high for nonwhite males at the ages of peak migration. The census may have enumerated only 82% of the black males 25–44 (Siegel 1974, tables 3 and 5). These migration data must be interpreted cautiously.

Data in tables 6 and 7 refer to those SMSAs which most nearly correspond to the urbanized areas in previous tables. For some locations, such as Cleveland, the urbanized area and the SMSA include much the same population. In other places, such as Baltimore, the SMSA includes outlying coun-

TABLE 6

POPULATION AGE FIVE AND OVER IN 1970, NUMBER OF MIGRANTS BY PLACE OF RESIDENCE IN 1965, AND MEASURE OF SUBURBAN SELECTION, STANDARD METROPOLITAN STATISTICAL AREAS

SMSA	CENTRAL CITY OR CITIES			REMAINDER OF SMSA						CITY TO RING MOVERS PER 100 RING TO CITY MOVERS (9)
		Migrants from:			Migrants from:					
	Total Pop. (Thousand) (1)	Ring (Thousand) (2)	Elsewhere in U.S.A. (Thousand) (3)	Total Pop. (Thousand) (4)	City (Thousand) (5)	Elsewhere in U.S.A. (Thousand) (6)	% of Total Pop. in Ring (7)	% of In-Migrants Going to Ring (8)		
New York:										
Whites	5,790	61	171	3,185	329	136	35	44		541
Blacks	1,489	6	45	194	14	11	12	19		234
Los Angeles:										
Whites	2,456	191	299	3,317	279	386	57	56		146
Blacks	466	19	52	213	53	21	31	29		271
Chicago:										
Whites	2,102	72	97	3,178	290	318	61	77		403
Blacks	979	23	40	115	12	10	11	21		51
Philadelphia:										
Whites	1,202	26	54	2,460	126	235	67	81		484
Blacks	588	4	21	170	7	14	22	40		152
Detroit:										
Whites	790	42	43	2,357	193	183	75	81		455
Blacks	589	16	49	86	9	7	13	13		60
San Francisco:										
Whites	809	36	106	1,772	97	282	69	73		269
Blacks	199	7	20	98	9	13	33	39		119
Boston:										
Whites	500	34	53	1,924	59	173	79	77		172
Blacks	91	5	8	20	2	3	18	24		34
Washington:										
Whites	211	7	39	1,764	48	349	72	91		662
Blacks	486	3	29	145	31	19	23	40		1,095
Cleveland:										
Whites	423	23	30	1,167	95	112	73	79		420
Blacks	260	6	15	40	17	4	13	21		297

TABLE 6 (*Continued*)

SMSA	CENTRAL CITY OR CITIES			REMAINDER OF SMSA			% OF TOTAL POP. IN RING (7)	% OF IN-MIGRANTS GOING TO RING (8)	CITY TO RING MOVERS PER 100 RING TO CITY MOVERS (9)
	Total Pop. (Thousand) (1)	Migrants from:		Total Pop. (Thousand) (4)	Migrants from:				
		Ring (Thousand) (2)	Elsewhere in U.S.A. (Thousand) (3)		City (Thousand) (5)	Elsewhere in U.S.A. (Thousand) (6)			
Saint Louis:									
Whites	346	18	22	1,480	73	157	81	88	398
Blacks	228	4	10	110	14	7	32	42	378
Pittsburgh:									
Whites	390	20	23	1,680	69	109	81	83	341
Blacks	96	3	4	58	4	2	38	40	105
Minneapolis:									
Whites	660	33	65	957	103	138	59	68	310
Blacks	26	<1	17	2	<1	<1	7	2	95
Houston:									
Whites	835	26	163	622	96	124	43	43	370
Blacks	280	9	23	59	6	4	17	14	66
Baltimore:									
Whites	453	21	27	1,004	85	122	69	82	402
Blacks	377	9	13	63	6	6	14	32	72
Dallas:									
Whites	583	33	118	609	58	146	51	57	173
Blacks	184	10	16	33	1	3	15	15	12
Average:									
Whites	1,170	43	87	1,633	133	198	58	69	309
Blacks	423	8	24	94	12	8	18	25	150

SOURCE.—U.S. Bureau of the Census, *Census of Population: 1970*, PC(2)-2C, table 15 (Washington, D.C.: Government Printing Office).

TABLE 7

PERCENTAGE OF POPULATION AGE 25 AND OVER WITH ONE OR MORE YEARS OF
COLLEGE COMPLETED BY MIGRATION STATUS AND RACE, STANDARD
METROPOLITAN STATISTICAL AREAS

| | CENTRAL CITY OR CITIES | | | REMAINDER OF SMSA | | |
| | | Migrants from: | | | Migrants from: | |
SMSA	Non-migrants	Ring	Else-where in U.S.A.	Non-migrants	Ring	Else-where in U.S.A.
New York:						
Whites	19	46	64	27	34	59
Blacks	10	19	22	12	26	26
Los Angeles:						
Whites	31	35	43	27	31	39
Blacks	20	23	24	23	26	26
Chicago:						
Whites	17	32	51	27	30	54
Blacks	13	15	21	11	18	25
Philadelphia:						
Whites	12	37	52	21	27	49
Blacks	7	15	19	9	22	27
Detroit:						
Whites	14	25	37	20	25	46
Blacks	10	9	19	8	11	16
San Francisco:						
Whites	28	53	59	32	40	50
Blacks	16	29	29	20	29	32
Boston:						
Whites	16	33	64	27	34	60
Blacks	10	10	20	20	23	53
Washington:						
Whites	45	69	79	37	39	61
Blacks	16	16	36	12	30	46
Cleveland:						
Whites	9	21	27	25	20	50
Blacks	9	9	16	20	20	40
Saint Louis:						
Whites	17	19	40	19	20	48
Blacks	10	14	16	9	20	25
Pittsburgh:						
Whites	14	26	59	16	25	47
Blacks	7	8	29	6	17	18
Minneapolis:						
Whites	21	31	38	28	34	51
Blacks	18	*	38	*	*	*
Houston:						
Whites	29	30	49	21	30	39
Blacks	13	12	24	9	12	15
Baltimore:						
Whites	13	23	51	19	23	50
Blacks	8	10	22	10	27	35

TABLE 7 (*Continued*)

| | | CENTRAL CITY OR CITIES | | | REMAINDER OF SMSA | |
| | | Migrants from: | | | Migrants from: | |
SMSA	Non-migrants	Ring	Else-where in U.S.A.	Non-migrants	Ring	Else-where in U.S.A.
Dallas:						
Whites	27	33	48	23	31	40
Blacks	11	11	25	5	5	16
Average:						
Whites	15	34	42	23	30	47
Blacks	11	15	21	12	24	30

SOURCE.—Same as for table 6.
*Fewer than 500 blacks.

ties which are not in the urbanized area. In New York and Los Angeles the urbanized area encompasses a much larger area than the SMSA.

Table 6 shows the total population in 1970 of central cities and their suburban rings, that is, the part of the SMSA lying outside the city. Migrants, as defined for these tables, are divided into movers who switched from the city to the ring, or vice versa, between 1965 and 1970 and migrants from elsewhere in the United States who moved into either the city or ring. These data do not include migrants from abroad (U.S. Bureau of the Census 1972c, table 82).

The proportion of adults who have completed one or more years of college is used as the measure of social status for migrants and nonmigrants. This was selected since most people finished their education prior to 1965. If an index were based upon income or occupation, it could be argued that changes in place of residence were linked to the income or occupation reported in 1970.

Table 6 illustrates, first, that whites who migrate to metropolitan areas are very likely to select suburban locations. The rings accounted for 58% of the total white population of these SMSAs (col. 7), but they attracted 69% of the in-migrants from elsewhere in the United States (col. 8).

Second, although numerous whites move from suburbs to cities—72,000 in Chicago; 61,000 in New York—this stream is small compared with the stream going in the opposite direction. Columns 2 and 5 report these migration streams, while the final column shows the number of city-to-ring movers per 100 going from the suburbs to the city. In New York and Washington there were five or more city-to-ring movers for each person heading in the opposite direction and, overall among whites, the ratio was three to one.

Turning to table 7, which concerns educational attainment, we find that white migrants are more extensively educated than nonmigrants, a finding congruent with previous observations about the selectivity of migration (Lee 1964, pp. 128–31; Taeuber and Taeuber 1964, p. 728). The two streams of migrants coming to cities—those from the suburban ring and those from elsewhere in the country—both report greater educational attainment than the nonmigrant population. This is also true for the streams of migrants entering suburban rings. Both local movers and in-migrants report greater attainment than the nonmigrant suburban population.

We anticipated that data for specific areas would reveal that the greater the educational attainment of a city resident in 1965, the more likely the person would be to move to suburbia before 1970. Similarly, we expected that low-status white in-migrants to an SMSA would select city residences while higher-status in-migrants would go to the suburbs. Such a pattern may be found in some SMSAs, but deviations and inversions are common. A more accurate generalization is that migrants attracted by cities are relatively high in socioeconomic status and quite similar to those entering suburban rings. The basic difference concerns the volume of migration. Cities attract a small proportion of the high-status white migrants who enter an SMSA and fare poorly vis-à-vis the suburbs on the exchange of local movers.

This has implications for city-suburban differences in status. Cities lose a sizable proportion of their high-status white population to the suburbs and attract a small share of the whites who migrate to the area. Thus the nonmigrant population, which was typically of lower status, became a larger share of the city's total white population, and average socioeconomic levels rose more rapidly in suburban rings.

The migration patterns of blacks are less readily summarized than those of whites since there is greater area-to-area variation. Looking at the characteristics of black in-migrants, shown in table 7, reveals they are typically high in status. Overall in 1970, about 10% of the black population age 25 and over completed some college education (U.S. Bureau of the Census 1973b, table 3). In these areas the stream of black migrants included higher proportions with such an education. For instance, 25% of the blacks migrating into the New York metropolitan area and 24% of those entering Los Angeles completed one or more years of college (U.S. Bureau of the Census 1973c, table 15).

Urban analysts, including Banfield, have argued that urban problems are exacerbated by the in-migration to cities of poorly educated persons who are ill-prepared for urban living, such as blacks coming from the South (1968, chap. 4). Data in table 7 counter this view, for they show that blacks who migrated to these central cities between 1965 and 1970 were not only more extensively educated than the resident black population but often reported greater attainment than the resident white population. In Detroit, for example, 16% of the city's and 23% of the ring's adult whites reported some college education. Among blacks migrating from elsewhere to Detroit, 19%

completed one or more years of college (U.S. Bureau of the Census 1973c, table 15). In 10 of the 15 central cities considered in that table, black in-migrants from other points in the United States reported greater attainment than the nonmigrant white population. This is partially a function of the age structure, since black in-migrants tend to be younger than the resident white population. Nevertheless, the influx of blacks has not necessarily lowered average socioeconomic levels in these cities (see Long 1974; Long and Heltman 1974).

Table 6 demonstrates that the volume of black in-migration to suburbs is very small compared with the volume of white in-migration, and in some areas the suburban black population is so small that it is impossible to draw conclusions about city-suburban migration trends. We can identify several SMSAs which have rapidly growing suburban black populations and in which the stream of city-to-ring movers dominated the opposite flow. A major component of this suburban black growth involves the extension of central city black areas and the emergence of suburban black ghettos. The black area on the east side of Cleveland expanded, and the census of 1970 recorded substantial increases in the black population of East Cleveland and Shaker Heights (U.S. Bureau of Census 1971c, table 29). Near Los Angeles, the suburb of Compton underwent a similar change, and two neighboring suburbs—Westmont and Willowbrook—had principally black populations by 1970 (U.S. Bureau of the Census 1971d, tables 24 and 29). Racial change occurred in several of the older suburbs bordering Saint Louis (Sutker and Sutker 1974). In these and several other areas city-suburban differences in social status and migration among blacks may come to resemble those among whites. That is, as the income of blacks rises, there will likely be a substantial flow of blacks to selected suburban locations where more desirable housing is available. Similar to whites, a large fraction of the intermetropolitan flow of black migrants may directly enter the suburbs.

V. THE DISTRIBUTION OF METROPOLITAN POPULATION IN 1970: AN ANALYSIS OF DETROIT

Tables presented thus far dichotomize areas into central cities and their suburban rings. We report extensive segregation by race in that blacks are more likely to live in cities than suburbs, and moderate segregation by socioeconomic status in that educational levels and incomes are higher in rings than in cities. City-suburban boundaries reflect historical annexation patterns and the peculiarities of local legislation. Additionally, an analysis which treats an entire city or suburban ring as one unit may conceal variations which will appear if the investigation treats smaller areal units.

Data from the census of 1970 were used to determine if residential differentiation could be more adequately described through the use of data for

TABLE 8

MEASURES OF RESIDENTIAL SEGREGATION OF SOCIOECONOMIC GROUPS AND MEASURES OF RACIAL RESIDENTIAL SEGREGATION SPECIFIC FOR SOCIOECONOMIC STATUS, DETROIT URBANIZED AREA, 1970

SOCIOECONOMIC CATEGORIES	RESIDENTIAL SEGREGATION SCORES FOR SOCIOECONOMIC GROUPS*						RESIDENTIAL SEGREGATION SCORE COMPARING BLACKS AND WHITES†		
	Whites			Blacks					
	Total Urbanized Area (1)	City (2)	Ring (3)	Total Urbanized Area (4)	City (5)	Ring (6)	Total Urbanized Area (7)	City (8)	Ring (9)
Education (yrs):‡									
0	41	36	40	35	35	35	86	80	96
Elementary:									
1–4	36	31	33	25	26	21	82	75	91
5–6	30	25	29	21	21	20	84	78	92
7	29	25	29	21	21	21	86	79	93
8	21	16	21	16	15	20	87	78	94
High school:									
9–11	16	13	17	12	12	12	88	78	94
12	14	14	12	16	15	16	91	81	96
College:									
13–15	21	24	18	27	25	35	91	81	95
16	37	37	35	42	42	38	94	78	99
17+	40	44	38	58	58	52	91	70	97
Total	...	...	...	...	...	...	88	77	94
Occupation:‡									
Professionals	26	29	24	38	38	36	92	76	97
Managers	28	27	28	36	36	33	95	81	98
Sales	24	28	23	33	31	44	95	84	98
Clerical	14	15	13	19	18	22	91	82	97
Craftsmen	17	16	17	15	14	20	92	84	95

TABLE 8 (*Continued*)

| | RESIDENTIAL SEGREGATION SCORES FOR SOCIOECONOMIC GROUPS* | | | | | | RESIDENTIAL SEGREGATION SCORE COMPARING BLACKS AND WHITES† | | |
| | Whites | | | Blacks | | | | | |
SOCIOECONOMIC CATEGORIES	Total Urbanized Area (1)	City (2)	Ring (3)	Total Urbanized Area (4)	City (5)	Ring (6)	Total Urbanized Area (7)	City (8)	Ring (9)
Operatives	24	25	23	13	13	15	89	81	94
Laborers	22	23	21	19	19	19	91	83	96
Service	18	16	16	14	13	17	89	82	93
Total	...	...	...	...	...	...	90	80	95
Family income ($):†									
<1,000	38	42	34	26	25	26	85	78	93
1,000–1,999	33	33	31	29	30	26	85	75	95
2,000–2,999	34	26	32	28	29	23	83	76	93
3,000–3,999	32	25	29	25	25	26	85	78	94
4,000–4,999	28	21	26	23	24	23	86	78	96
5,000–5,999	27	23	25	21	21	22	86	78	93
6,000–6,999	25	19	25	19	18	26	87	79	94
7,000–7,999	23	20	23	17	17	20	88	80	94
8,000–8,999	21	17	21	16	16	20	89	81	93
9,000–9,999	19	15	20	18	18	17	90	81	93
10,000–11,999	15	13	15	15	15	19	91	84	96
12,000–14,999	14	13	13	20	20	18	92	84	96
15,000–24,999	19	19	17	27	28	23	93	84	97
25,000+	43	36	44	41	42	35	95	80	98
Total	...	...	...	...	...	...	90	80	95

SOURCE.—U.S. Bureau of the Census, *Public Use Samples of Basic Records from the 1970 Census* (Washington, D.C.: Government Printing Office, 1970).
*Indices of dissimilarity comparing the residential distribution of one socioeconomic group to the residential distribution of all others, using data for census tracts.
†Indices of dissimilarity comparing the residential distributions of blacks and whites in the same socioeconomic category, using data for census tracts.
‡Data for education refer to males 25 and over in 1970. Data for occupation refer to the employed males. Income data refer to all families reporting income.

small areas. This section is based upon 1970 census tract data for the Detroit Urbanized Area (U.S. Bureau of the Census 1973*d*).

The first issue concerned the segregation of racial and socioeconomic groups. Table 8 presents indexes of dissimilarity measuring residential segregation. These were computed specifically for race and separately for the city and ring. The first six columns of figures in the table compare the residential distribution of one socioeconomic group with that of all other groups. The number at the top of column 1, for example, is 41. For the white population of the total urbanized area this compares the residential distribution of adults reporting no years of schooling with the residential distribution of whites reporting other educational attainments. Forty-one percent of this group would have to switch census tracts if they were to be distributed as all other educational attainment groups were. As indicated previously, this index ranges from 0 to 100, with large values indicating extensive residential segregation.

The findings of the Duncans (1955), Uyeki (1964), and Kantrowitz (1973, chap. 3) are confirmed in these figures. Groups at the extremes of the socioeconomic distribution are most highly segregated from other socioeconomic groups, while those at the middle of the continuum are least segregated. Several further inferences may be drawn from this table. First, levels of socioeconomic segregation are no greater in the suburban ring than in the central city. Detroit's suburban ring is relatively new, since 64% of the housing present in 1970 was erected after 1949 while only 16% of the city's housing was built as recently (U.S. Bureau of the Census, 1972*a*, table 43). Despite this city-suburban difference, socioeconomic segregation was of a similar magnitude in each area. An investigation with 1950 and 1960 data found that this was the case in several large areas (Fine, Glenn, and Monts 1971).

Second, when the black and white communities are separately considered, we discover very much the same levels of socioeconomic segregation. Although the housing markets blacks and whites face in the Detroit area are not the same because of racial differences in income and, presumably, because of discriminatory practices, the levels of socioeconomic segregation are similar in the black and white communities.

Census tracts may also be used to assess residential segregation controlling for socioeconomic factors. Figures in columns 7–9 of table 8 compare the residential distributions of blacks and whites in each specific socioeconomic classification. We find that racial residential segregation hardly varied by social status in the Detroit area. Poor black and white families were almost as highly segregated from one another as well-to-do families were. Furthermore, the residential segregation of socioeconomic groups was small compared with racial residential segregation. For instance, the segregation score comparing Detroit area white families with incomes exceeding $25,000 with white families whose incomes were $3,000–$3,999 was 56 (figure not shown in table 8). The segregation score comparing white families in the $25,000 or more bracket with black families in the identical income category was 95.

The degree of racial residential segregation was greater in Detroit suburbs than in the central city. In each comparison the segregation score comparing blacks and whites in the same socioeconomic category was higher in the ring than in the city of Detroit. We conclude that the extent of socioeconomic segregation was no greater in the suburbs than in the city, but racial residential segregation was more pronounced in the suburbs.

Although using census tract data, table 8 employs the city-suburban dichotomy. Most theories of urban growth and population differentiation imply that socioeconomic status in the suburbs exceeds that of cities because urban areas expand in a ringlike fashion. Thus, it is suggested that new and attractive homes are typically added toward the periphery of the settled area and are often occupied by people of similar socioeconomic status. This indicates that distance from the center of a city, rather than the city-suburban dichotomy, may be the important variable.

To investigate this, census tracts in the Detroit urbanized area were coded by distance from the central business district and sorted into rings. The socioeconomic characteristics of the total, white, and black populations of each ring were then considered. Indexes of population composition are shown in table 9. The average educational attainment and the mean family income for residents in every ring are indicated. Then, as a measure of dispersion, the standard deviation of educational attainment and income for the population in each ring is shown. Finally, to test hypotheses about the relationship of distance and the socioeconomic homogeneity of residential areas, the variance in educational attainment and in income in the entire area and in each ring was divided into within-tract and between-tract variance (for a description of a similar analysis, see Kish 1954). Table 9 presents η^2 coefficients (Hays 1973, p. 535). If average socioeconomic levels differ greatly from one census tract to another but within tracts there is very little variation in socioeconomic status, η^2 will approach its maximum value of one. On the other hand, if all census tracts have the same average socioeconomic composition, it will approach its minimum value, zero.

For both blacks and whites average socioeconomic status in the Detroit area tended to increase with distance from the city's center. After reaching a maximum there was a decline in average status levels. The rings housing the most prestigious population differ by race. The peak was in the 18–22-mile ring for whites but in the 8–12 mile ring for blacks. The Detroit suburban ring appeared to contain an inner core of tracts whose population had a higher status than residents toward the outer limits of the urbanized area. There is a fringe population whose status is inferior to that of other suburbanites (Smith 1970).

The standard deviations of these socioeconomic measures do not vary systematically with distance. There is little support for the hypothesis that

TABLE 9

MEASURES OF SOCIAL STATUS AND DECOMPOSITION OF VARIANCE IN SOCIAL STATUS FOR CENSUS TRACTS IN RINGS BY DISTANCE FROM CENTER OF DETROIT

ZONE (DISTANCE IN MILES)	TOTAL POPULATION			WHITE POPULATION			BLACK POPULATION		
	Mean	σ	η^2	Mean	σ	η^2	Mean	σ	η^2
				Mean Years of School Completed					
0–1.9	9.7	4.1	.19	10.3	4.1	.22	8.8	3.8	.16
2–3.9	9.4	3.7	.08	9.9	4.0	.15	9.1	3.5	.04
4–5.9	9.8	3.6	.04	9.7	3.7	.05	9.8	3.5	.05
6–7.9	10.7	3.7	.09	10.9	3.7	.10	10.2	3.5	.05
8–9.9	11.2	3.5	.14	11.2	3.5	.14	11.5	3.5	.13
10–11.9	11.7	3.4	.11	11.7	3.4	.11	11.1	3.7	.14
12–13.9	12.0	3.3	.08	12.0	3.3	.08	10.3	3.0	.16
14–15.9	12.1	3.2	.09	12.2	3.2	.08	10.0	3.5	.06
16–17.9	12.6	3.4	.20	12.6	3.4	.19	8.7	3.7	.10
18–19.9	12.8	3.4	.20	12.8	3.4	.20	8.6	4.2	.20
20–21.9	13.3	3.4	.22	13.4	3.4	.20	9.4	3.7	.09
22–23.9	11.6	3.6	.16	11.8	3.5	.15	9.5	3.6	.02
24+	11.5	3.4	.14	11.6	3.3	.13	9.8	3.5	.08
Total	11.3	3.6	.19	11.6	3.6	.18	9.8	3.6	.10

TABLE 9 (*Continued*)

ZONE (DISTANCE IN MILES)	TOTAL POPULATION			WHITE POPULATION			BLACK POPULATION		
	Mean	σ	η^2	Mean	σ	η^2	Mean	σ	η^2
				Average Family Income					
0–1.9	8.2	7.8	.28	9.9	8.9	.33	6.9	6.5	.22
2–3.9	8.8	6.5	.06	10.2	7.0	.12	8.0	6.1	.03
4–5.9	9.7	6.5	.05	10.5	6.8	.04	9.0	6.3	.06
6–7.9	11.9	7.6	.10	12.4	8.0	.12	10.7	6.6	.04
8–9.9	13.4	8.0	.14	13.4	8.1	.14	13.1	7.5	.18
10–11.9	14.4	8.2	.11	14.4	8.3	.11	12.5	7.1	.13
12–13.9	14.9	8.1	.10	14.9	8.1	.10	11.2	7.7	.09
14–15.9	14.8	8.0	.11	14.9	8.0	.10	10.8	7.2	.06
16–17.9	15.9	8.9	.23	15.9	8.9	.23	10.6	7.4	.23
18–19.9	16.8	9.7	.24	16.9	9.7	.23	9.3	6.5	.26
20–21.9	18.5	10.8	.27	18.9	10.8	.26	9.5	6.2	.09
22–23.9	14.1	8.5	.14	14.7	8.6	.12	9.5	5.7	.03
24+	13.3	7.9	.13	13.6	8.0	.11	9.2	6.2	.11
Total	13.4	8.4	.21	14.2	8.5	.18	9.5	6.6	.12

SOURCE.—Same as for table 8.

the rings lying far from the center of Detroit contain a population which is more homogeneous in socioeconomic status than rings which are near the city center.

The η^2 measures in table 9 suggest that there is relatively little variance in the average socioeconomic status of tracts. These indexes challenge the argument that the Detroit urbanized area is composed of many subareas which are internally homogeneous in status but differ greatly, one from another, in average status level. If that were the case, there would be a large variation in average socioeconomic status between census tracts, and the η^2 indexes would be much larger than they actually are.

Examining η^2 measures for the different distance rings indicates little systematic variation. There is no evidence that the outlying rings, which contain newer housing, exhibit different patterns of social class segregation than the rings close to downtown Detroit.

In this section, census tract data for Detroit have been examined in an exploratory manner to determine if they would better describe population distribution. Many of the observations corroborate previous findings. We find a moderate degree of residential segregation of socioeconomic groups, although both the variance measures and the indexes of dissimilarity suggest that census tracts typically contain a population heterogeneous in socioeconomic status. Status levels in Detroit tended to increase with distance, although the most prestigious population was not at the outer limits of the urbanized area. The extensive racial residential segregation implied by city-suburban comparisons in earlier sections was confirmed by measures based upon Detroit census tracts. Racial residential segregation was much greater than residential segregation of socioeconomic groups. Whites and blacks who share the same education, occupation, or family income were highly segregated by place of residence.

VI. CONCLUSIONS AND OVERVIEW

The findings of this investigation may be summarized as follows:

1. The populations of the larger central cities continue to decline. The net out-migration of whites largely accounts for this. All central cities considered in this paper had growing nonwhite populations, although several experienced a recent net out-migration of nonwhites.

2. Suburban rings had rapidly growing populations. The growth rates of the white suburban populations generally fell between the 1950s and the 1960s while those of suburban nonwhites increased.

3. Age-specific growth rates indicate the continued movement out of central cities and into suburban rings of people in their late twenties and thirties. Many central cities attracted younger people of both races who apparently attended school there or pursued jobs early in their careers. Between 1950 and 1970 city-suburban differences in age composition widened

slightly. By 1970 the average age of suburban whites was five years less than that of central city whites. Among nonwhites, the difference was approximately one year.

4. Following national trends, educational attainment and income rose within both central cities and suburbs. These areas have become slightly more differentiated in status since the increases in status were greater within the suburbs than in the central cities. For example, in 1950 suburban residents averaged 0.9 year more schooling than city residents. By 1970 this difference grew to 1.1 years. In all 15 urbanized areas the suburban population had higher average socioeconomic status than the city population, but part of this difference is attributable to differences in the racial composition of the areas.

5. Migrants tend to be of higher socioeconomic status than people who did not change their residence in the five-year interval preceding either of the two censuses. Among whites, a large proportion of the migrants who entered an area chose suburban rather than city residences. Additionally, suburban rings attracted many high-status residents from their central cities. The whites who moved into a central city from its suburban ring or who migrated directly to the city tended to be high in status but few in number.

We observed at the outset that suburban growth concerned both scholars who wished to describe cities and observers who commented upon urban problems from other perspectives. This paper does not offer suggestions about improved ways to measure metropolitan growth and differentiation. Several persisting problems prevent investigators from precisely summarizing urban demographic trends. One difficulty is the great heterogeneity of patterns we find in urbanized areas. Another problem is that many data are cross-sectional, and since boundaries change from one census to the next it is exceedingly difficult to appropriately describe fluctuations over time. Finally, we note that there are numerous methodologies which describe population distribution in one area at a single point in time, such as factor-analytic investigations or the measures of residential segregation presented in this paper. A thorough analysis of one area is difficult to summarize, and collating and summarizing analyses of many areas at different points in time is extraordinarily problematic.

Turning to the interest in urban problems, we believe the forces producing rapid suburban growth are well established, and the trends outlined in this paper will likely continue. The stock of housing and industrial plants within many of the largest central cities is old, and most new construction will likely occur outside central cities. The investigations cited in this paper, dealing with previous periods, reported moderate levels of residential segregation of socioeconomic groups and high levels of racial residential segregation. It is difficult to imagine abrupt changes in these patterns in the immediate future.

Many of the social problems which are included in the framework of urban problems have an important urban component, but terminating the growth of suburbs and rebuilding cities is unlikely, in itself, to eliminate them. That is, poverty, crime, racial discrimination, and family dissolution may be particularly evident in older central cities. Restructuring the cities might help to conceal these problems. However, they will probably be solved more expeditiously if they are attacked directly.

REFERENCES

Banfield, Edward C. 1968. *The Unheavenly City.* Boston: Little, Brown.

Dobriner, William M. 1963. *Class in Suburbia.* Englewood Cliffs, N.J.: Prentice-Hall.

Downes, Bryan T. 1973. "Problem-Solving in Suburbia: The Basis for Political Conflict." Pp. 281–312 in *The Urbanization of the Suburbs,* edited by Louis H. Masotti and Jeffrey K. Hadden. Urban Affairs Annual Reviews, vol. 7. Beverly Hills, Calif.: Sage.

Duncan, Otis Dudley, and Beverly Duncan. 1955. "Residential Distribution and Occupational Stratification." *American Journal of Sociology* 60 (March): 493–503.

Fine, John, Norvell D. Glenn, and J. Kenneth Monts. 1971. "The Residential Segregation of Occupational Groups in Central Cities and Suburbs." *Demography* 8 (February): 91–101.

Glenn, Norvell. 1973. "Suburbanization in the United States since World War II." Pp. 51–78 in *The Urbanization of the Suburbs,* edited by Louis H. Masotti and Jeffrey K. Hadden. Urban Affairs Annual Reviews, vol. 7. Beverly Hills, Calif.: Sage.

Hawley, Amos H. 1956. *The Changing Shape of Metropolitan America: Deconcentration since 1920.* Glencoe, Ill.: Free Press.

Hays, William L. 1973. *Statistics for the Social Sciences.* 2d ed. New York: Holt, Rinehart & Winston.

Hermalin, Albert I., and Reynolds Farley. 1973. "The Potential for Residential Integration in Cities and Suburbs: Implications for the Busing Controversy." *American Sociological Review* 38 (October): 595–610.

Kantrowitz, Nathan. 1973. *Ethnic and Racial Segregation in the New York Metropolis.* New York: Praeger.

Kish, Leslie. 1954. "Differentiation in Metropolitan Areas." *American Sociological Review* 19 (August): 388–98.

Lee, Everett S. 1964. "Internal Migration and Population Redistribution in the United States." Pp. 123–36 in *Population: The Vital Revolution,* edited by Ronald Freedman. Garden City, N.Y.: Doubleday.

Long, Larry H. 1974. "Poverty Status and Receipt of Welfare among Migrants and Non-Migrants in Large Cities." *American Sociological Review* 39 (February): 46–56.

Long, Larry H., and Lynne R. Heltman. 1974. "Income Differences between Blacks and Whites, Controlling for Education and Region of Birth." Paper presented at the annual meeting of the Population Association, New York, April 19.

Miller, Herman P. 1966. *Income Distribution in the United States.* Washington, D.C.: Government Printing Office.

Schnore, Leo F. 1964. "Urban Structure and Suburban Selectivity." *Demography* 1 (1): 164–76.

———. 1965. *The Urban Scene.* New York: Free Press.

———. 1972. *Class and Race in Cities and Suburbs.* Chicago: Markham.

Shryock, Henry S., and Jacob S. Siegel. 1971. *The Methods and Materials of Demography.* Washington, D.C.: Government Printing Office.

Siegel, Jacob S. 1974. "Estimates of Coverage of the Population by Sex, Race, and Age in the 1970 Census." *Demography* 19 (February): 1–24.

Smith, Joel. 1970. "Another Look at Socioeconomic Status Distributions in Urbanized Areas." *Urban Affairs Quarterly* 5 (June): 423–53.

Sutker, Solomon, and Sara Smith Sutker, eds. 1974. *Racial Transition in the Inner Suburb.* New York: Praeger.

Taeuber, Irene B. 1972. "The Changing Distribution of the Population of the United States in the Twentieth Century." Pp. 31–108 in *Population Distribution and Policy,* edited by Sara Mills Mazie. Commission on Population Growth and the American Future, Research Reports, vol. 5. Washington, D.C.: Government Printing Office.

Taeuber, Irene B., and Conrad Taeuber. 1971. *People of the United States in the 20th Century.* Washington, D.C.: Government Printing Office.

Taeuber, Karl E., and Alma F. Taeuber. 1964. "White Migration and Socioeconomic Differences between Cities and Suburbs." *American Sociological Review* 29 (October): 718–29.

———. 1965. "The Changing Character of Negro Migration." *American Journal of Sociology* 70 (January): 429–41.

U.S. Bureau of the Census. 1961. *Census of Population: 1960.* PC(1)-45A. Washington, D.C.: Government Printing Office.

———. 1963. *Census of Population: 1960.* PC(3)-1D. Washington, D.C.: Government Printing Office.

———. 1965. *Current Population Reports.* Series P-23, no. 15 (July). Washington, D.C.: Government Printing Office.

———. 1971a. *Census of Population: 1970.* PC(1)-A1. Washington, D.C.: Government Printing Office.

———. 1971b. *Census of Population and Housing, 1970,* PHC(2). Washington, D.C.: Government Printing Office.

———. 1971c. *Census of Population: 1970.* PC(1)-B37. Washington, D.C.: Government Printing Office.

———. 1971d. *Census of Population: 1970.* PC(1)-B6. Washington, D.C.: Government Printing Office.

———. 1972a. *Census of Housing: 1970.* (HC)1-B24. Washington, D.C.: Government Printing Office.

———. 1972b. *Census of Population: 1970.* PC(1)-B1. Washington, D.C.: Government Printing Office.

———. 1972c. *Census of Population: 1970.* PC(1)-C Washington, D.C.: Government Printing Office.

———. 1972d. *Current Population Reports.* Series P-23, no. 41 (April). Washington, D.C.: Government Printing Office.

———. 1973a. *Census of Population: 1970.* PC(1)-1D. Washington, D.C.: Government Printing Office.

———. 1973b. *Census of Population: 1970.* PC(2)-1B. Washington, D.C.: Government Printing Office.

———. 1973c. *Census of Population: 1970.* PC(2)-2C. Washington, D.C.: Government Printing Office.

———. 1973d. *Index of 1970 Census Summary Tapes.* Washington, D.C.: Government Printing Office.

———. 1974a. *Current Population Reports.* Series P-20, no. 262 (March). Washington, D.C.: Government Printing Office.

———. 1974b. *Current Population Reports.* Series P-23, no. 48 (July). Washington, D.C.: Government Printing Office.

Uyeki, Eugene S. 1964. "Residential Distribution and Stratification, 1950–1960." *American Journal of Sociology* 69 (March): 491–98.

Weber, Adna Ferrin. 1899. *The Growth of Cities in the Nineteenth Century.* Columbia University Studies in History, Economics, and Public Law, vol. 11. New York: Macmillan.

Wirt, Frederick M., Benjamin Walter, Francine F. Rabinovitz, and Deborah R. Hensler. 1972. *On the City's Rim: Politics and Policy in Suburbia.* Lexington, Mass.: Heath.

2 Family Patterns in Suburban Areas: Recent Trends

Larry H. Long and Paul C. Glick
Population Division Bureau of the Census

Summarizing research on cities and suburbs conducted during the 1960s, Schnore observed (1972, p. 2) that: " . . . city-suburb differentiation simply represents another manifestation of the three principles of segregation according to which American urbanites have long been 'sifted and sorted' in space. These three principles are (1) color or ethnicity, (2) social class, and (3) family type. Evidently, the greatest attention has been given to color and ethnicity and the least to family type." Although many of the popular treatments of suburban living written in the 1950s (and reviewed in Dobriner [1963] and Donaldson [1969]) were at least as concerned with numerous alleged effects of suburban living on women and children and family patterns in general as with ethnic and class differences between cities and suburbs, Schnore is certainly correct in his evaluation of empirical research on cities and suburbs.

This paper focuses on changing family patterns and living arrangements in metropolitan suburbs and their central cities between 1960 and 1970 and presents some new evidence on the contribution of migration to city-suburb differences in family structure and socioeconomic levels in the period since 1970. Many central cities and their suburban rings became increasingly differentiated during the 1950s in terms of socioeconomic status (Taeuber and Taeuber 1964). The concern in the present research is the extent to which the degree of difference between cities and suburbs was maintained during the 1960s. Impressionistic evidence suggests that some differences might have been reduced.

The sections that follow present an analysis of the relative representation of different family types in central cities and their suburban fringe areas in 1960 and 1970. The central question or hypothesis involves the extent to which numerous changes in family patterns noted in the 1960s—the increasing proportion of families headed by women, the increasing proportion of women and mothers participating in the labor force, and other changes in family relations—may have taken place disproportionately in suburban areas.

Another area of investigation is the amount of geographic movement

The authors express appreciation to Kristin A. Hansen and Lynne R. Heltman for their assistance in assembling material for this article.

between cities and suburbs that is associated with different stages in the family life cycle. More specifically, this investigation shows the extent to which central cities may still serve as "staging areas" where people meet and marry before moving to suburbs to raise children. Impressionistic evidence suggests that such "prefamily household formation" may be taking place increasingly in the suburbs, but conclusive studies of this question are non-existent.

Finally, this study examines some new relationships that appear to be developing between metropolitan and nonmetropolitan areas. The differences between cities and suburbs arise not only as a result of the volume and unlike family composition involved in population movement between these parts of metropolitan areas but also as a result of the nature of the movement to and from nonmetropolitan parts of the country. The massive movement from nonmetropolitan areas to metropolitan areas has abated in recent years, and this change will affect future family patterns in cities and suburbs. Some of these population movements are evaluated for the period 1970–73, and new evidence is presented on how rates of movement between cities and suburbs during this period have affected city-suburb differences in family patterns.

MARITAL AND FAMILY STATUS, 1960 AND 1970

A major reason for expecting to find greater heterogeneity in family types in suburban areas in 1970 than in 1960 is the fact that in the 1960s employment in standard metropolitan statistical areas (SMSAs) outside the central cities increased faster than the total population in these areas (U.S. Bureau of the Census 1972, table A). The increase in the number of jobs as compared with population in the balance of SMSAs also represented a wider variety of employment than was available at the beginning of the decade of the 1960s. These trends alone would seem to imply that a wider variety of persons could both live and work in suburban areas. Changes in the availability of different types of housing in the suburbs (proportionately more modern apartments in quieter neighborhoods and fewer old single-family dwellings) would also seem to imply a greater and more attractive variety of household types in metropolitan areas outside the central cities. Moreover, greatly improved highway systems connecting suburbs with central cities have probably increased suburban residence combined with downtown employment more than they have increased the reverse arrangement.

Several measures of family patterns do, in fact, reflect the increasing heterogeneity of households in metropolitan areas living outside the central cities. One of the most straightforward indicators is marital status, as shown in table 1, which compares the distribution of the population by marital status in central cities and the fringe areas of urbanized areas and the rate of change between 1960 and 1970.

The problems in making intercensal comparisons of central cities and their fringe areas (the balance of their urbanized areas) include the change in the number of central cities and annexations made during the decade by central cities as defined at the beginning of the decade. The problem of annexations is reduced somewhat by the fact that cities most likely to be annexing new territory tend to be newer areas where city-suburb differences are small.

Table 1 shows what one would expect: for both central cities and their fringe areas the percentage of persons married and living with their spouses decreased between 1960 and 1970. Concomitantly, increases occurred in both central cities and their fringe areas in the proportion of persons constituting the "singles"—those who were separated from their spouses, or who were divorced, or who had never been married. In central cities the proportion of men 14 years old and over living with their wives decreased from 65.1% to 60.1%; in fringe areas the decrease was from 72.9% to 67.1%. Meanwhile, "singles" increased from 30.8% to 36.5% of the men 14 years and over in central cities and from 24.3% to 30.6% in fringe areas.

Even though the changes in marital status were in the same direction for city and suburban residents, the changes in the proportion of "singles" were more pronounced in the urban fringe areas than in the central cities of urbanized areas. The last two columns of table 1 show the relative changes in each of the marital-status categories for central cities and suburbs. Between 1960 and 1970, the decline in the proportion of persons who were married and living with their spouses occurred at about the same rate for both city and urban-fringe residents (about one-ninth). However, the proportion living as "singles" increased at a notably slower pace for persons in central cities (about one-fifth) than for those in the urban fringe (about one-fourth). Among the "singles," the proportions divorced or never married increased especially rapidly in urban fringe areas.

For different age groups and in individual metropolitan areas, the urban-fringe population may have had a more pronounced tendency to approximate the central-city population in terms of marital-status distribution. Nevertheless, the fringe areas around central cities, in the United States as a whole, now clearly include a smaller proportion than in 1960 of adults living as married couples and a larger proportion living as separated, divorced, or never-married persons.

Another indicator of changes in living arrangements in cities and suburbs is the proportion of household heads who are family heads and the proportion who are primary individuals (persons living alone or with nonrelatives only), as shown in table 2. This indicator needs to be analyzed in the context of the fact that the number of families increased by only 13% between 1960

TABLE 1

MARITAL STATUS BY SEX FOR CENTRAL CITIES AND URBAN FRINGE IN URBANIZED AREAS OF THE UNITED STATES, 1970 AND 1960

MARITAL STATUS AND SEX	CENTRAL CITIES		URBAN FRINGE		1970 AS % OF 1960	
	1970	1960	1970	1960	Central Cities	Urban Fringe
No. of males 14 and over	22,401,000	20,076,000	18,990,000	12,536,000	112	151
% married, except separated	60.1	65.1	67.1	72.9	92	92
% singles, except widowed	36.5	30.8	30.6	24.3	118	126
% separated	2.4	2.2	1.1	1.0	110	115
% divorced	3.7	2.8	2.3	1.7	130	138
% never married	30.4	25.8	27.2	21.6	117	126
% widowed	3.4	4.1	2.3	2.8	83	80
No. of females 14 and over	25,727,000	22,369,000	20,565,000	13,491,000	115	152
% married, except separated	52.4	58.3	62.1	67.9	90	91
% singles, except widowed	33.7	27.8	27.6	21.8	122	127
% separated	3.7	3.1	1.7	1.4	122	121
% divorced	5.4	4.0	3.8	2.6	136	146
% never married	24.6	20.7	22.1	17.8	119	125
% widowed	13.9	13.9	10.3	10.3	100	100

SOURCE.—U.S. Bureau of the Census (1973, tables 96 and 107; 1964, table 49).

and 1970, whereas the number of primary individuals increased by 58%. The rates of change in the percentages (shown in the last two columns of table 2) have in effect been adjusted for this wide difference in growth rates.

The proportion of households including a family was lowest in central cities of SMSAs in both 1970 and 1960, and the proportion of households that were of this type declined most rapidly in central cities in the 1960s. Thus, in 1970 only 74.0% of the households in central cities were maintained by a family head as compared with 84.9% of those in other parts of SMSAs; on the other hand, fully 26.0% of the households had a primary individual as the head in central cities as compared with only 15.1% in the balance of SMSAs. Moreover, the proportion of households that were headed by a primary individual increased during the 1960s by about one-half (from 10% to 15%) outside central cities but by only about one-fourth (from 20% to 26%) inside central cities.

This finding provides additional evidence that married couples came to be more underrepresented in suburban areas during the 1960s than in the preceding decade. To some extent, table 2 suggests greater changes than does table 1, perhaps because table 2 refers to the entire balance of SMSAs whereas table 1 considers only the urban fringe of urbanized areas. (Comparable data for metropolitan and nonmetropolitan areas were not available for 1960 and 1970 for presentation in table 1.)

The rapid increase in recent years in the number of primary individuals is partly the product of increasing affluence, as more and more elderly persons and young persons are able to maintain households of their own apart from their relatives. But an increasing number of primary individuals were separated or divorced persons maintaining a household apart from their spouses (or former spouses). In this context, an underlying question is the extent to which households are increasingly formed in the suburbs rather than in central cities. The traditional view is that substantial numbers of young persons first take up residence in the central city before moving to the suburbs following marriage or as children are born. The increase in the number of primary individuals may represent more persons taking up residence in the suburbs rather than in the central city as they enter the labor force. But other evidence considered in the next section indicates that, to a considerable extent, central cities still perform their traditional function as "staging areas" where young people settle temporarily before moving to the suburbs to raise their families.

An important change in family relations in recent years is the increase in labor-force participation rates among women. As noted above, during the 1960s the number of jobs in SMSAs outside central cities increased faster than population, suggesting, among other things, that labor-force participation rates among women may have increased more in the balance of SMSAs than in central cities. If so, then this would be still another departure from

TABLE 2

Households by Type for the United States, 1970 and 1960

Area	Household Heads Who Were Family Heads			Household Heads Who Were Primary Individuals		
	1970	1960*	1970 as % of 1960	1970	1960	1970 as % of 1960
No. of households in United States	51,169,000	45,128,000	113	12,469,000	7,896,000	158
% of all households	80.4	85.1	94	19.6	14.9	132
% metropolitan	79.6	84.2	95	20.4	15.8	129
% central cities	74.0	79.7	93	26.0	20.3	128
% balance of SMSA	84.9	89.6	95	15.1	10.4	145
% urban	84.2	89.0	95	15.8	11.0	144
% rural nonfarm	87.7	91.2	96	12.3	8.8	140
% rural farm	88.3	92.8	95	11.7	7.2	163
% nonmetropolitan	82.3	86.8	95	17.7	13.2	134

SOURCE.—U.S. Bureau of the Census (1973, tables 96 and 107; 1964, tables 78 and 101).
*Includes the small number (101,000) of secondary family heads (lodgers or resident employees with relatives in the household).

TABLE 3

PERCENTAGE OF WOMEN IN THE LABOR FORCE BY MARITAL STATUS AND
PRESENCE OF OWN CHILDREN UNDER SIX YEARS OLD
FOR THE UNITED STATES, 1970 AND 1960

| | | | MOTHERS OF CHILDREN UNDER 6 YEARS OLD | | | |
| | ALL WIVES | | Wives | | Other Women | |
AREA	1970	1960	1970	1960	1970	1960
United States	39.2	30.7	28.2	19.5	51.0	47.3
Metropolitan	39.6	31.3	27.1	18.7	50.3	48.5
Central cities	41.2	33.2	30.4	21.0	47.0	48.2
Balance of SMSA	38.4	29.4	24.9	16.8	56.1	49.1
Urban	38.9	29.9	24.5	16.7	56.4	50.3
Rural nonfarm	37.6	28.2	26.1	17.3	54.4	44.2
Rural farm	33.2	23.8	24.4	16.1	57.7	55.2
Nonmetropolitan	38.4	29.3	30.5	20.4	52.9	44.9

SOURCE.—U.S. Bureau of the Census (1973, tables 101 and 112; 1964, tables 100 and 101).

the "familism" pattern assumed to be characteristic of suburban areas. Table 3 was designed in order to answer this question. It shows, for 1960 and 1970, the labor-force participation rates for all wives and for mothers of children under six, according to type of residence.

In both 1960 and 1970, wives living in central cities had higher labor-force participation rates than wives living in the balance of SMSAs. In 1970, 41.2% of all wives in central cities were in the labor force—an increase of 8 percentage points, or nearly one-fourth, over the 1960 rate. In the balance of SMSAs, 38.4% of all wives in 1970 were in the labor force—an increase of 9 percentage points, or nearly one-third, over the 1960 rate. Among rural-nonfarm wives in metropolitan areas (including "exurbanites"), labor-force participation rates rose even more, 9.4 percentage points—from 28.2% to 37.6%. Among all wives, therefore, there was a modest tendency for labor-force participation to rise faster among those living in the balance of SMSAs than in central cities.

Among mothers with children under six, labor-force participation rates also rose much more sharply among wives than among other women between 1960 and 1970, but the rates for wives remained far below the rates for other women. Again, rates for married women were higher in both 1960 and 1970 in central cities than in the balance of SMSAs. In fact, the percentage point increase was slightly greater in central cities (9.4%) than in the balance of SMSAs (8.1%); thus, both types of areas shared in this aspect of family change. In central cities, married women with children under six increased their labor-force participation rates from 21.0% to 30.4% between

1960 and 1970, whereas in the balance of SMSAs, married women with children under six increased their labor-force participation rates from 16.8% to 24.9%.

Perhaps the most interesting finding revealed by table 3 concerns changes in labor-force participation of women not living with their spouses but having children under six years old. In the balance of SMSAs, the labor-force participation of such women increased, as might be expected, the change being from 50.3% in 1960 in 56.4% in 1970. But among such women living in central cities, labor-force participation rates decreased slightly, from 48.2% to 47.0%. This decline was somewhat unexpected, since central cities have an increasing proportion of black population, and black women have typically had higher labor-force participation rates than white women. A partial explanation of this decline might be the rapid expansion of Aid to Families with Dependent Children in central cities during the 1960s, which provided many of these women with a viable alternative to labor-force participation (see Levitan, Rein, and Marwick 1972). Again, as pointed out above, the number of jobs was rising faster in the suburbs than in the central cities and was therefore causing a relative decrease in the employment opportunities for unmarried women with young children in central cities.

At any rate, suburban areas came to be characterized by increasing rates of participation in the labor force among married women in the 1960s. Wives in central cities still have higher rates of labor-force participation than wives in suburban areas, but the increases in labor-force participation for suburban wives have been so great that in 1970 they had higher labor-force participation rates than did central-city wives in 1960. Here is another instance in which suburban areas have come to be less representative of the traditional image of "familism."

In fact, on each of these three dimensions—marital status, household type, and percentage of wives (and mothers) who are working—suburban areas (variously defined) have come to reflect a greater heterogeneity of family patterns; yet the evidence indicates that cities and suburbs are coming only slightly or moderately to resemble one another in terms of family patterns. Most of the changes in suburban areas between 1960 and 1970 were reflected also in central cities but generally to a lesser degree. Introducing controls for areal changes in the definition of SMSAs, making allowance for annexation, and making intensive investigation of individual areas might produce more definite conclusions, but it seems warranted to conclude that the changes in family patterns noted above have characterized both cities and suburbs and have preserved a large degree of the differences noted in 1960. One of the most dramatic changes involved the rapid increase in the number of persons living as primary individuals in suburban areas during the 1960s. The next section presents the results of an investigation into the extent to which household and family formation may begin in suburbs (as opposed to cities) and the extent to which city-to-suburb moves (and other types of moves) are associated with different stages of the family life cycle.

FAMILY FORMATION IN CITIES AND SUBURBS

During the 1950s suburban areas around central cities developed a population structure heavily weighted toward parents and their young children, with relatively few persons in their late teens and early twenties and few of retirement age and beyond. Such a bimodal age distribution must result primarily from migration—generally the migration of young married couples from central cities to suburbs. Thus, one would expect to find net migration for cities and suburbs to reflect bimodal patterns of opposite direction. Such a pattern would conform to the traditional image of migrants from nonmetropolitan areas (or from other metropolitan areas) taking up initial residence in the central cities as a place to launch their careers and families. Upon marriage, or with the arrival of children, such young families would be expected to move to a larger home in the suburbs.

In other words, the expected pattern in the suburbs is for the greatest amount of net in-migration to occur among children (say, under 15) and among their parents (say, persons 30–40), with little gain, if any, at other ages. Concomitantly, the expected pattern in central cities is just the opposite, with the greatest losses among persons under 15 and 30–40.

But, if households and families are increasingly formed in the suburbs, the expectation is that patterns became less pronounced during the 1960s, with suburban areas experiencing more in-migration at the 15–24 age group and somewhat less at immediately younger and older ages. Statistics on net migration during the 1950–60 decade are available by age for every county in the United States (Bowles and Tarver 1965); these statistics and similar statistics for the 1960–70 decade from a forthcoming report by the same authors are presented below in graphic form for selected metropolitan counties.

The hypothesis to be tested, therefore, is that suburban counties exhibited a sharply bimodal pattern of net in-migration during the 1950s, with the greatest gains among persons under 15 years old and at ages 30–40 (with central-city counties experiencing their greatest losses at these ages) but that during the 1960s this degree of bimodality decreased. To test this hypothesis, statistics for the white population were assembled for some of the largest central-city counties and selected suburban counties in the United States (see Appendix), and corresponding statistics for 1960–70 for the District of Columbia (a "central city") and adjacent suburban Montgomery County, Maryland, are shown in figure 1.

The data are limited to the white population, because most central-city

47

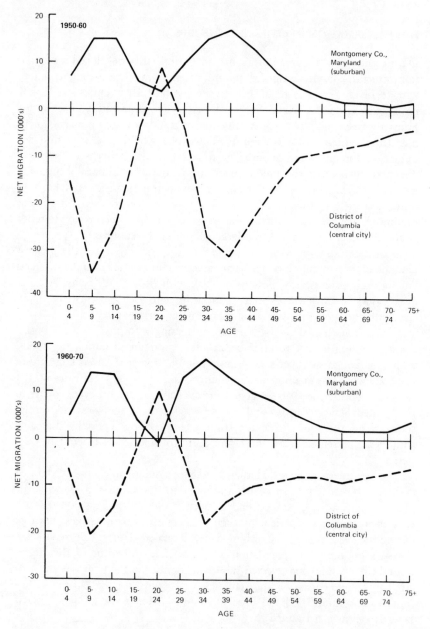

FIG. 1.—Net migration of the white population by age, 1950–60 and 1960–70, for Montgomery County, Md., and the District of Columbia. Source: Bowles and Tarver (1956); Bowles and associates (1975).

counties had net in-migration of blacks at almost all ages and most suburban counties had no appreciable net in-migration of blacks during the 1950s. In each of the 12 areas shown, the expected high degree of bimodality for the 1950–60 decade was immediately evident. For suburban Montgomery County, Maryland, the net gain of children under five was low, but net in-migration was great among children 5–9 and 10–14 (age at end of decade). Net in-migration then declined to a low point at ages 20–24 before rising to a maximum among persons 35–39 years old.

The District of Columbia showed the opposite pattern, with greatest losses among whites at ages 5–9 and 35–39. The District of Columbia actually had net in-migration of whites at ages 20–24, in spite of the fact that net out-migration at other ages resulted in a 40% decline in the white population between 1950 and 1960.

The other 11 central-city and suburban counties shown in the Appendix—representing the Boston, New York City, Philadelphia, Baltimore, Cleveland, Detroit, Chicago, Saint Louis, Atlanta, New Orleans, and San Francisco metropolitan areas—revealed essentially the same basic pattern of migration of whites during the 1950s. For each of the selected suburban counties, net in-migration reached a peak among children under 15 years of age and was also relatively high among persons 30–40 years old. In every case, the central-city counties had some of their greatest losses of whites at these ages and had either net in-migration or one of their smallest losses at ages 20–24. Among large metropolitan areas not shown are Houston and Los Angeles, neither of which is well represented by central-city and suburban counties and neither of which exhibited the bimodal patterns but had their greatest in-migration among persons in their twenties.

Moreover, the degree of bimodality for the District of Columbia and Montgomery County—and for the central-city and suburban counties in several of the other metropolitan areas—actually increased during the 1960s. In this more recent period, Montgomery County and most of the other suburban counties shown in the Appendix experienced slight out-migration of whites 20–24 years old; also, the District of Columbia and most of the central-city counties continued to gain whites in their twenties or to show relatively small losses at that age. The age group 25–29 emerged during the 1960s as one with either heavy growth or with substantial holding power in the central-city counties. This fact may reflect the considerable increase in college enrollment in this period and an associated delay in age at marriage and childbearing.

These data support the conclusion that many of the metropolitan central cities continue to serve as "staging areas," or areas of first residence, for young adults before they move to the suburbs to raise their children. It should be recognized that the suburban counties selected for display in the charts are not representative of suburban areas generally. The suburban counties shown in figure 1 and the Appendix that demonstrate the greatest bimodality in net migration generally have the suburban communities with the highest per capita incomes. Suburban counties with lower per capita incomes generally showed the bimodal pattern less distinctively in the 1950s and had a larger proportion of their net in-migration consisting of persons in their early twenties. For suburban counties of moderate income levels, this tendency may have increased in the 1960s. Suburban counties of high income probably maintained into the 1960s the relative homogeneity of families migrating to them at the same life cycle stage. Any increasing heterogeneity of suburban areas in terms of family types probably took place in suburban counties of relatively low per capita income.

Some further evidence about these relationships between cities and suburbs in terms of family mobility patterns is available for the period 1970–73. This information shows, for the first time, gross and net population exchanges between central cities and the balance of SMSAs for the period 1970–73 in terms of family status in 1973. To the extent that central cities still serve as "staging areas," they would be expected to have net in-migration of young single persons from suburban areas and to lose families to the suburbs. Of course, central cities may also gain population from nonmetropolitan areas, but for the moment the question is whether central cities may still gain young single persons from suburban areas.

For persons living in SMSAs in 1970 and 1973, table 4 shows rates of moving from central cities to the balance or rings of SMSAs and from the rings of SMSAs to central cities. In addition, the net exchange is indicated in the last column, which shows the ratio of the number of city-to-ring movers to the number of ring-to-city movers, a ratio of greater than one indicating net gain to the ring and a ratio of less than one indicating a net gain to central cities.

As can be seen in the last column, central cities do gain young primary individuals from the balance of SMSAs. Between 1970 and 1973 more primary individuals—both male and female—under 25 years old moved to central cities from the balance of SMSAs than moved in the opposite direction. In addition, central cities gained male primary individuals at ages above 35. There is also a tendency for more young female heads (nearly half of whom are separated or divorced) to move from suburbs to central cities than to move in the opposite direction.

Central cities lose most heavily among married couples, particularly at ages 25–44. Over two and one-half times as many married couples with the husband 25–34 moved from central cities to the balance of SMSAs as moved in the opposite direction. At ages 35–44, the differences were even greater: more than three times as many married couples moved from central cities to the balance of SMSAs as moved in the opposite direction. These findings provide additional evidence of the tendency for central cities to attract single

TABLE 4

U.S. Household Heads Living in SMSAs in March 1970 and March 1973—Percentage Who Moved between Central Cities and Rings of SMSAs by Sex, Age, and Type of Head

Sex, Age, and Type of Household Head	% Living in Central Cities in 1970 and in SMSA Rings in 1973	% Living in SMSA Rings in 1970 and in Central Cities in 1973	Ratio of Number of City-to-Ring Movers to Number of Ring-to-City Movers
Male head:			
Under 25 years:			
Married, wife present.........	28.3	22.2	1.30
Primary individual	21.5	33.9	0.88
25–34 years:			
Married, wife present.........	27.8	9.3	2.57
Primary individual	22.7	25.1	1.39
35–44 years:			
Married, wife present.........	13.9	3.0	3.27
Primary individual	8.0	16.8	0.96
45–64 years:			
Married, wife present.........	6.5	2.2	2.16
Primary individual	3.7	14.2	0.42
Female Head:			
Under 25 years:			
Head of primary family	11.8	37.8	0.76
Primary individual	19.2	40.2	0.56
25–34 years:			
Head of primary family	11.0	27.1	0.87
Primary individual	15.0	20.8	1.26
35–44 years:			
Head of primary family	6.1	5.1	1.60
Primary individual	8.5	8.3	2.25
45–64 years:			
Head of primary family	5.6	3.9	2.00
Primary individual	5.3	4.6	1.87

Source.—U.S. Bureau of the Census (1974, table 3).

persons and to lose them as they marry and have children.

Furthermore, the rates of residential mobility between 1970 and 1973 were generally higher on the part of married couples living in central cities in 1970 than on the part of those living in suburban areas in 1970. According to the same source as table 4, among male household heads 25–34 years old with wife present, 64.3% of 1970 central-city residents moved between 1970 and 1973, compared with only 52.7% of those living in the balance of SMSAs. Similar differences prevailed at earlier and later ages. These differences result primarily from the higher rates of city-to-suburb than suburb-to-city moving on the part of married couples.

Do these high rates of city-to-suburb moving among married couples augment or diminish traditional city-suburb income differences? One possibility is that the lower income of central-city families results largely from a higher concentration of relatively low-income migrants from nonmetropolitan areas. However, as shown in figures 2 and 3, movement of families between central cities and the balance of metropolitan areas also tends to affect city-suburb family income differences. These figures also show that the amount of movement both (1) within and between central cities and (2) within and between the balance of SMSAs is greater than the amount of movement (1) from city to suburb or (2) from suburb to city.

Figure 2 shows that the rate of movement from cities to the balance of SMSAs forms somewhat of a U-shaped relationship to income but is always greatest at the highest income interval ($15,000 or more). In sharp contrast, the rate of moving from the balance of SMSAs to central cities is shown in figure 3 to be inversely related to income. The probabilities of moving from the balance of SMSAs to central cities clearly slope downward with income for each age group.

One conclusion to be drawn from figures 2 and 3 is that, for almost every age and income category in the 1970–73 period, the balance of SMSAs gained families from central cities, but the greatest absolute gains to suburbs occurred at the highest income levels. Another conclusion is that, although families moving from cities to suburbs tended to have higher incomes than those moving from suburbs to cities, families moving from cities to suburbs tended to have lower incomes than those living in suburbs at both the beginning and end of the period. The net effect of this movement is to lower the family income levels in both the central cities and in the balance of the SMSAs and, in this process, to increase city-suburb differences in family income.

DISCUSSION

In terms of family status, suburban areas became more heterogeneous during the 1960s, with proportionately more persons in the "singles" category, fewer married couples, more working wives, and more working mothers. But central cities also reflected such changes, and this tendency reduced the extent to which central cities and suburbs became more alike in terms of family status during the 1960s.

Central cities still attract single persons in their early twenties (both black and white) and then lose them to the suburbs as they reach their late twenties or as they enter their thirties. High-income suburbs are still characterized by in-migration of parents in their late twenties or early thirties and their children. Moderate-income suburbs have a higher concentration of in-movers in their early twenties.

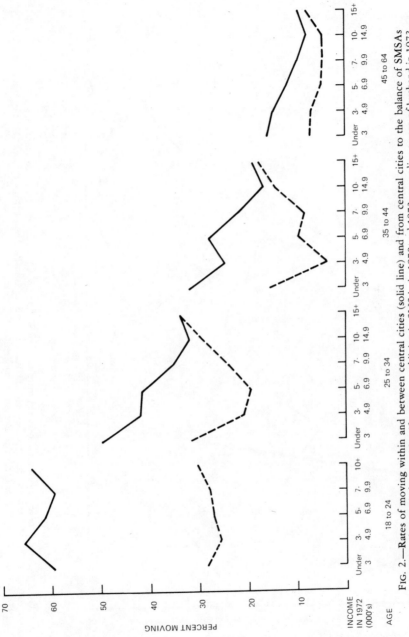

FIG. 2.—Rates of moving within and between central cities (solid line) and from central cities to the balance of SMSAs (broken line) for married men with wife present and living in SMSAs in 1970 and 1973, according to age of husband in 1973 and income in 1972. Source: U.S. Bureau of the Census (1974, table 19).

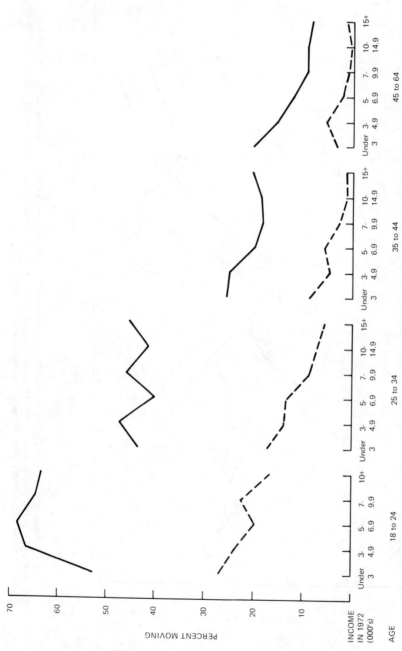

FIG. 3.—Rates of moving within and between the balance of SMSAs (solid line) and from the balance of SMSAs to central cities (broken line) for married men with wife present and living in SMSAs in 1970 and 1973, according to age of husband in 1973 and income in 1972. Source: U.S. Bureau of the Census (1974, table 19).

During the 1950s, when city-suburb differences became so pronounced, metropolitan areas received considerable migration from nonmetropolitan areas, and a great many of the nonmetropolitan migrants settled in central cities, probably adding to the city-suburb differences that resulted from movement directly from cities to suburbs. In the 1960s, however, migration from nonmetropolitan areas was a less important source of metropolitan growth, constituting only about 11% of metropolitan population increase (U.S. Bureau of the Census 1971, table 7). Net movement from nonmetropolitan to metropolitan areas during the 1960s was less than half the volume of the 1950s.

Furthermore, a disproportionate amount of the net in-migration to metropolitan areas during the 1960s consisted of blacks. Metropolitan areas in the northeast and north-central regions actually had net *out*-migration of whites; overall, these SMSAs had net in-migration from nonmetropolitan areas only because the net in-migration of blacks exceeded the net out-migration of whites (U.S. Bureau of the Census 1971, table 7). Most of the black migrants from nonmetropolitan areas settled in central cities of SMSAs.

Since 1970 the pattern characterizing metropolitan areas in the northeast and north-central states may have spread, because SMSAs collectively appear no longer to gain population from nonmetropolitan areas (U.S. Bureau of the Census 1974). Thus, this factor, which has tended to increase city-suburb differences in the past, is now operating with much less force. Future city-suburb differences in family structure and socioeconomic status are increasingly likely to result from population exchanges between cities and suburbs as the volume of movement from nonmetropolitan areas decreases.

APPENDIX

1950–60 and 1960–70 Net Migration by Age for the White Population of Selected Central-City and Suburban Counties

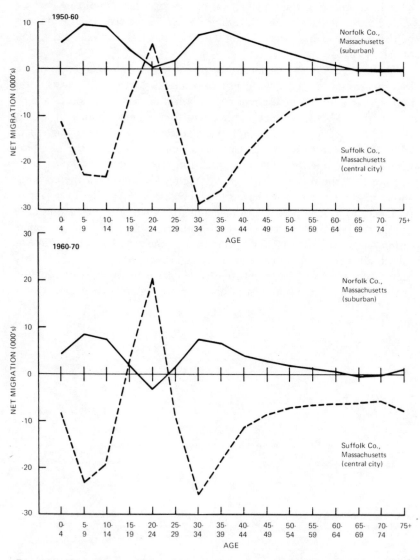

FIG. A1.—Net migration of the white population by age, 1950–60 and 1960–70, for Norfolk and Suffolk Counties, Mass.

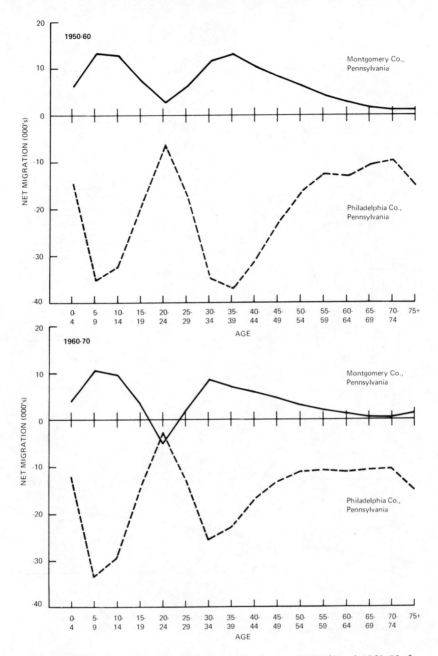

FIG. A2.—Net migration of the white population by age, 1950–60 and 1960–70, for Montgomery and Philadelphia Counties, Pa.

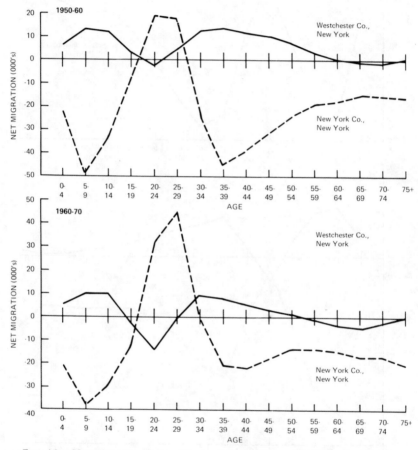

FIG. A3.—Net migration of the white population by age, 1950–60 and 1960–70, for Westchester and New York Counties, N.Y.

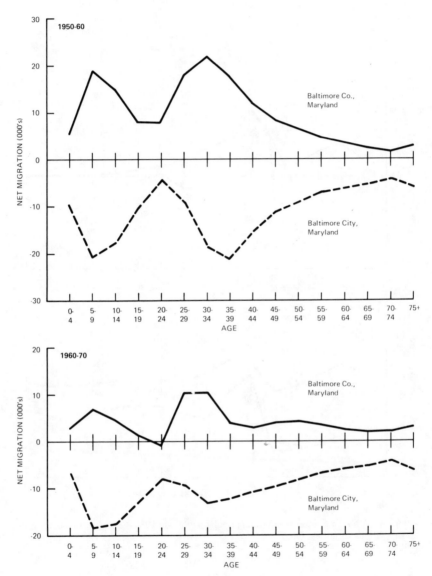

FIG. A4.—Net migration of the white population by age, 1950–60 and 1960–70, for Baltimore County and Baltimore City, Md.

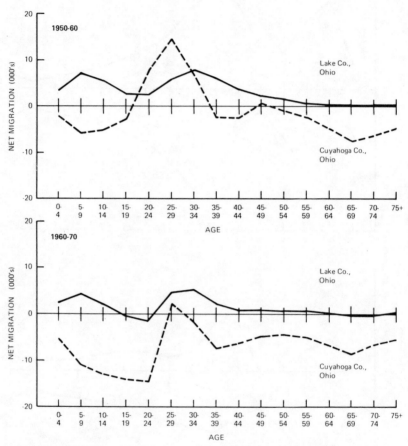

FIG. A5.—Net migration of the white population by age, 1950–60 and 1960–70, for Lake and Cuyahoga Counties, Ohio.

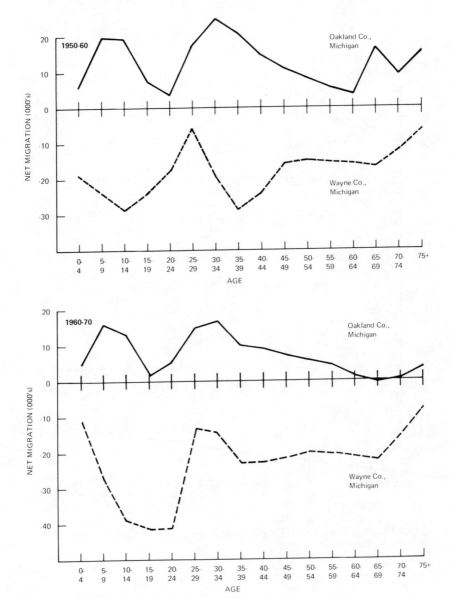

FIG. A6.—Net migration of the white population by age, 1950–60 and 1960–70, for Oakland and Wayne Counties, Mich.

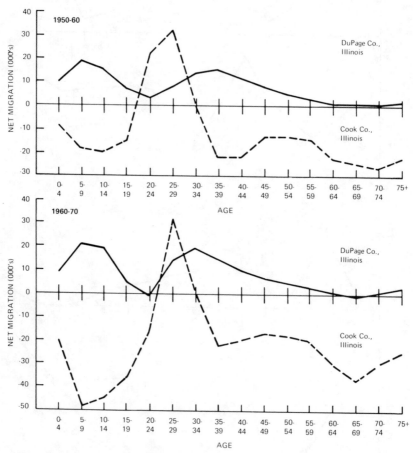

FIG. A7.—Net migration of the white population by age, 1950–60 and 1960–70, for DuPage and Cook Counties, Ill.

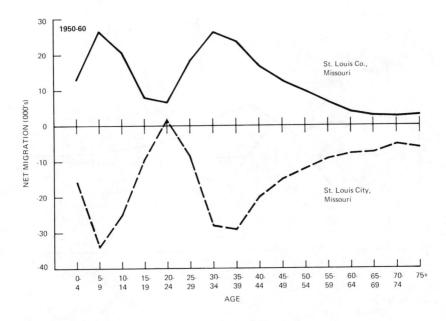

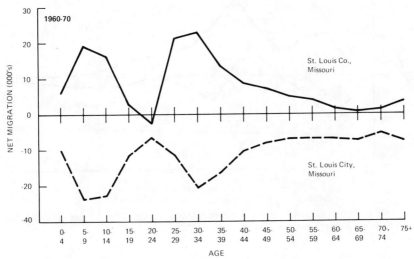

FIG. A8.—Net migration of the white population by age, 1950–60 and 1960–70, for Saint Louis County and Saint Louis City, Mo.

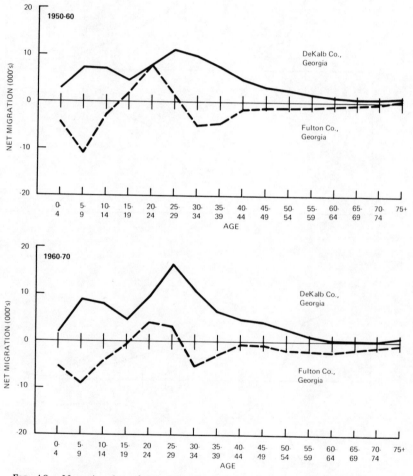

Fig. A9.—Net migration of the white population by age, 1950–60 and 1960–70, for DeKalb and Fulton Counties, Ga.

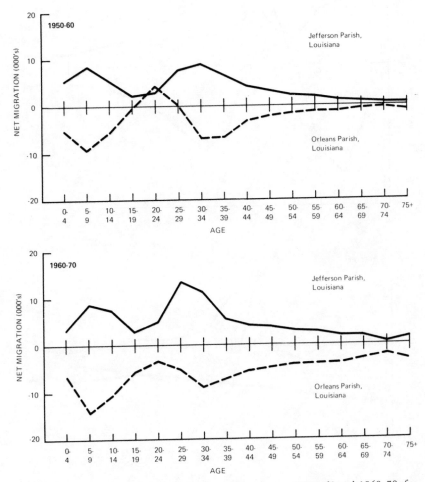

FIG. A10.—Net migration of the white population by age, 1950–60 and 1960–70, for Jefferson and Orleans Parishes, La.

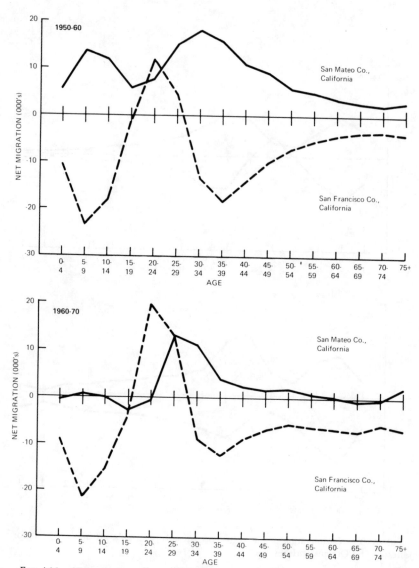

FIG. A11.—Net migration of the white population by age, 1950–60 and 1960–70, for San Mateo and San Francisco Counties, Calif.

REFERENCES

Bowles, Gladys K., and James D. Tarver. 1965. *Net Migration of the Population, 1950–60, by Age, Sex, and Color.* Vol. 1. Washington, D.C.: Government Printing Office.

Bowles, Gladys K., et al. 1975. "Net Migration of the Population, 1960–70, by Age, Sex, and Color." Preliminary unpublished estimates from NSF-RANN Population Redistribution Project. U.S. Department of Agriculture and University of Georgia cooperating. Basic data supplied by U.S. Bureau of the Census.

Dobriner, William M. 1963. *Class in Suburbia.* Englewood Cliffs, N.J.: Prentice-Hall.

Donaldson, Scott. 1969. *The Suburban Myth.* New York: Columbia University Press.

Levitan, Sar A., Martin Rein, and David Marwick. 1972. *Work and Welfare Go Together.* Baltimore: Johns Hopkins University Press.

Schnore, Leo F. 1972. *Class and Race in Cities and Suburbs.* Chicago: Markham.

Taeuber, Karl E., and Alma F. Taeuber. 1964. "White Migration and Socio-economic Differences between Cities and Suburbs." *American Sociological Review* 29 (October): 718–29.

U.S. Bureau of the Census. 1964. *Census of Population: 1960.* Vol. 1. *United States Summary.* Washington, D.C.: Government Printing Office.

———. 1971. *Census of Population and Housing: 1970. General Demographic Trends for Metropolitan Areas, 1960 to 1970, United States Summary.* PHC(2)-1. Washington, D.C.: Government Printing Office.

———. 1972. *Special Economic Reports. Employment and Population Changes, Standard Metropolitan Statistical Areas and Central Cities.* Series ES20(72)-1. Washington, D.C.: Government Printing Office.

———. 1973. *Census of Population: 1970.* Vol. 1. *United States Summary.* Washington, D.C.: Government Printing Office.

———. 1974. *Current Population Reports. Mobility of the Population of the United States March 1970 to March 1973.* Series P-20, no. 262. Washington, D.C: Government Printing Office.

3 Black Suburbanization, 1930–1970

Leo F. Schnore
University of Wisconsin, Madison

Carolyn D. André
University of California, San Diego

Harry Sharp
University of Wisconsin, Madison

Black suburbanization seems to be getting under way in a number of our largest metropolitan areas, but it appears to be a painfully slow process. Our analysis in confined to the 12 largest metropolitan areas and the 40-year interval between 1930 and 1970. The data offer very little support for those investigators who foresee a black surge to the suburbs. What is now needed is a close examination of the *types* of suburb in which blacks have an opportunity to settle. Case studies, in depth, are required. An even greater need is for comparative analysis, giving attention to such variables as size of place, city age, economic makeup, quality of housing, etc.

The subject of black suburbanization has captured public attention on an unprecedented scale in recent years. This has been reflected in all the media: television, radio, newspapers, popular periodicals, and scholarly journals. Comments and research by (1) journalists and (2) university-based scholars (often aiming their books at audiences wider than those composed of their professional colleagues) crowd our libraries in this country.

Examples of the former are to be found in such periodicals as *Business Week, Ebony, Newsweek, Time,* and *U.S. News and World Report.*[1] We have examined a nonrepresentative sample of these materials, and they seem to convey two common themes: (1) "suburbia" is already an extremely hetero-

This research was supported by funds supplied to the Wisconsin Survey Research Laboratory by the University of Wisconsin, Madison, and a grant from the National Science Foundation (no. GS-35306) awarded to Schnore. An abbreviated version, stressing methodological problems, was presented at the annual meeting of the Population Association, New York, April 19, 1974.

[1] See the anonymous (1970, 1971*a*, 1971*b*, 1973) contributions from four of these sources cited in the references. The article in *U.S. News and World Report* is especially informative.

geneous area in terms of population composition, and (2) recent trends—especially during the 1960s—show a substantial movement of blacks into the suburban "rings" of our major metropolitan areas.

But what do the more empirically oriented social scientists have to say of the decade of the 1960s? There are a number of discussions in the literature that draw on 1960 and 1970 census materials. One of the best treatments of the 1960–70 decade is to be found in a work entitled *On the City's Rim: Politics and Policy in Suburbia*, by a group of political scientists (Wirt et al. 1972). We are especially inclined to recommend chapter 4, on "The Black Suburb," even though it tends to overemphasize the Los Angeles experience.[2] Although they do not all draw on 1970 data, other valuable contributions are to be found in the work of economists (e.g., Bradford and Kelejian 1973), sociologists (e.g., Blumberg and Lalli 1966), and geographers (e.g., Rose 1969, 1970, 1971, 1972). It is no surprise, however, to find the most intensive use of census statistics by demographers and ecologists. In a penetrating analysis of the 1930–50 period, Lieberson (1962) analyzed ethnic segregation in cities and suburbs in 10 metropolitan areas. Another outstanding contribution is that by Farley (1970); it used census data for 1900–1960, and employed 1968 data from the Current Population Survey (CPS). He concluded that "in recent years, the growth of the Negro suburban population has accelerated" (Farley 1970, p. 512). Another historically oriented study, however, concluded that there was very limited black suburbanization in the largest metropolitan areas over the 30-year interval between 1930 and 1960 (Sharp and Schnore 1962).

Were the 1960s—an era of changing law and custom—so very different? Unfortunately, there are substantial problems of measurement that must be recognized. We must give some attention to these before presenting our own results.

PROBLEMS OF MEASUREMENT

The CPS—a monthly survey conducted by the Bureau of the Census—has known sources of sampling error and other biases. But the full-scale decennial census also has errors—underenumeration being the major source—and for questions other than those on the "100%" census schedule, sampling errors also enter the picture.[3] We feel that it is preferable to use final-count

---

[2] The references in chap. 4 make an excellent beginning bibliography on the subject.

[3] For a thorough discussion of underenumeration, its causes, effects, and census staff efforts to counteract it, see Parsons (1972). A rough test of the completeness of coverage in the 1970 census in a single state may be found in Sharp and Schnore (1971).

census data on questions of color and residence. One reason is that self-reported ethnic affiliation is one of the "100%" items in the 1960 and 1970 censuses. In other words, it was one of the five questions asked of *all* respondents. But the principal reason for our preference is that use of the full-count census permits disaggregation well below that of the national or regional level. Individual metropolitan areas and suburbs may be examined in detail. The otherwise excellent studies by Farley and by Wirt and his colleagues suffer because, although they are able to discuss a few individual cases, they are otherwise limited to anecdotal treatment of individual metropolitan areas and particular suburbs and are not able to conduct studies of area-by-area variations except along the most gross regional lines. Such variables as population size, age of the city, and its functional composition are also important (Schnore 1965).

The nature of the areal unit employed by all the investigators so far cited must also be critically examined. The Standard Metropolitan Statistical Area (SMSA) is not the most ideal unit for studies of "suburbia." The "ring"—that area outside the officially designated central city or cities—is extremely heterogeneous and in many instances contains rural farm population. To use the phraseology of Gibbs (1961), some are "overbounded" and others are "underbounded," as demonstrated in a detailed analysis of the 1950 Standard Metropolitan Areas (SMAs), the forerunners of the SMSAs used in our study (see Feldt 1965). One of us has already asserted a reasoned preference for the use of Urbanized Areas in studies of "suburbia" (Schnore 1972, chap. 2).

There is also the vexing problem of *annexation*. We have become most sensitive to this matter because we have examined the very substantial effects on comparisons of central city versus ring between 1950 and 1960 and again between 1960 and 1970. To take only the most dramatic example, the Oklahoma City SMSA now contains an area larger than that of the combined states of Rhode Island and New Hampshire. Much of it is "rural" territory. Other difficulties arise in the analysis of data for such places as Indianapolis and Jacksonville, where city-county consolidations have occurred. These make intercensal comparisons between central city and ring virtually impossible. (Some black leaders see annexation as a deliberate political effort on the part of central-city officialdom to dilute the black vote in the cities.) Whatever the "causes," we must turn to our major findings.

CHANGING COLOR COMPOSITION: THE PRINCIPAL RESULTS OF OUR ANALYSIS

We have examined trends over the period 1930–70 in the 12 largest SMSAs. These were the 12 largest metropolitan areas in both 1960 and 1970, although the ranking changed somewhat during the decade. It is important to note that our 1970 data relate to the 12 SMSAs *as they were delineated in 1960*. This facilitates observations and comparisons between 1930 and 1970, and it conforms to the practice employed by Farley, who retrojected the 212 SMSAs delineated for the 1960 census to the year 1900.

In table 1, the aggregate population of the 12 largest SMSAs is shown as a percentage of the total population of the United States for each census year from 1930 through 1970. The data show that over these 40 years there has been a substantial rise in population in the rings, associated with a progressive decrease in population within the central cities. In 1930 the 12 central cities housed over twice as many people as their rings. By 1960 the rings contained almost as many inhabitants as the central cities, and by 1970 the population of the rings surpassed that of the central cities by 3.4 percentage points, or slightly more than 7 million people. While the population of the rings continued to increase rather substantially, the central cities declined from 1930 through 1970. (Hence the widespread comments, particularly among political scientists, regarding "the new suburban majority.")

The color composition of the central cities has changed markedly since the 1930s. Table 1 shows that the proportion of whites who lived in the central cities has fallen steadily since 1930, while the proportion of non-whites has increased dramatically. Of all nonwhites in the United States, the proportion of those living in the central cities of the 12 largest SMSAs has more than doubled since 1930, from 12.5% to 27.9% in 1970. During the same time span, the central cities' white inhabitants decreased by almost half, or from 17.3% to 9.0%. In 1930, whites were more likely to live in the central city than nonwhites; by 1950, there was a reversal; and by 1970, nonwhites in the total population were three times as likely to live in the largest central cities as were whites. On the other hand, the white population in the rings of these 12 metropolitan areas increased steadily and by 1970 had doubled the 1930 figure. The nonwhite population of the rings has also doubled since 1930, but the absolute number of nonwhites has remained relatively small. As of 1970, whites were more than twice as likely to live in the rings as were nonwhites.

Semilogarithmic graphs show a logarithmic scale on the *y*-axis and a plain numerical (or uniform) scale on the *x*-axis. This type of graphic exhibit is especially convenient in representing population growth over a number of years, or (as in this case) a number of census dates at 10-year intervals, when federal censuses have been taken. Growth rates can be readily inferred from the slope of the population sizes represented on the *y*-axis. (See Schmid [1954] for a discussion of this technique.)

The semilogarithmic graphs in figure 1 represent the combined population of the largest SMSAs from 1930 to 1970. Within the 40-year period, the total population of these areas increased by 83.5%. However, the nonwhite population has had a far higher growth rate than the white, as may be seen

TABLE 1

PERCENTAGE DISTRIBUTION BY COMBINED POPULATION OF THE 12 LARGEST SMSAs, CENTRAL CITIES, AND RINGS, BY COLOR, FOR TOTAL U.S. POPULATION, 1930–70

| | DISTRIBUTION (%) BY COLOR, 1930–70 | | | | | | | | | | | | | | |
| | Total Population | | | | | White | | | | | Nonwhite | | | | |
	1930	1940	1950	1960	1970	1930	1940	1950	1960	1970	1930	1940	1950	1960	1970
12 largest SMSAs	24.4	24.6	25.6	26.3	26.2	25.4	25.4	25.7	25.8	25.0	15.5	17.6	24.2	29.7	35.0
Central cities	(16.8)	(16.5)	(15.7)	(13.2)	(11.4)	(17.3)	(16.7)	(15.2)	(11.6)	(9.0)	(12.5)	(14.5)	(20.2)	(24.7)	(27.9)
Rings	(7.6)	(8.1)	(9.9)	(13.1)	(14.8)	(8.1)	(8.7)	(10.5)	(14.2)	(16.0)	(3.0)	(3.1)	(4.0)	(5.0)	(7.1)
Remainder of United States	75.6	75.4	74.4	73.7	73.8	74.6	74.6	74.3	74.2	75.0	84.5	82.4	75.8	70.3	65.0
Total United States	100.0	100.0	100.0	100.0	100.0	100.0	100.0	100.0	100.0	100.0	100.0	100.0	100.0	100.0	100.0

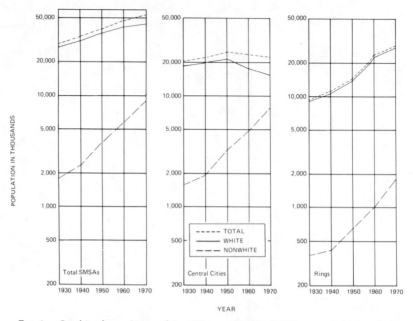

FIG. 1.—Combined population of the 12 largest SMSAs (1960), central cities, and rings, by color, 1930–70.

in the first panel. The nonwhite growth rate between 1930 and 1970 was 362.7% as compared to 58.4% for the white population. (We are aware, of course, that percentage increases from small bases are likely to be extremely misleading.)

The second panel of figure 1, representing the combined population of the central cities, shows quite a different population pattern from that portrayed within the SMSAs as a whole. After only modest growth rates in the 1930s and 1940s, the large cities began to experience a population decline in the 1950s. This drop reflected the significant number of white residents moving out of the central cities and into the surrounding rings. During the same time period, the number of nonwhite central-city residents showed a steady increase.[4] The third panel of figure 1 reveals that outlying nonwhite growth since 1940 has been more rapid than white suburban growth.

In absolute numbers the decline of white central-city residents between 1950 and 1970 in the 12 largest SMSAs represents a loss of over 4.5 million

---

[4] A detailed account of the "components" of change in the 10 largest SMSAs may be found in the anonymous contribution to the *Statistical Bulletin* (1973). In addition, Farley's contribution to this volume should be perused.

74

people, contrasting with an increase in the nonwhite population of almost 4 million. Let us project these observations. *If* the rate of growth of the central-city nonwhite population continues in the future as it has since 1940, and *if* the decrease in the central-city white population continues from the base of 1950, the total number of nonwhites in the combined population of nonwhites in the 12 largest SMSAs will exceed that of the whites before 1990.

The size and color composition of the total SMSAs, 1930–70, are shown in figure 2 for each of the 12 largest metropolitan areas. These graphs look very much like those representing the aggregate of the 12 largest SMSAs. The last three decades have shown a larger total population increase than that between 1930 and 1940. While the white population has generally been increasing, growth has slowed appreciably in the last few decades. In contrast, the nonwhite population has increased much more rapidly than has the white population.

The central-city population for each of the 12 largest SMSAs is plotted separately in figure 3. Again, these graphs generally depict the same patterns previously seen in the aggregate population of the 12 central cities. The rate of growth for whites remained stable between 1930 and 1950 and has declined since the 1950s. The only central city which did not experience this absolute loss in number of white residents between 1950 and 1970 was Los Angeles–Long Beach, and in this dual central city the white growth rate has become nominal.[5]

By contrast, in every one of these huge metropolitan centers the nonwhite population has grown tremendously since 1940 and, in several instances, since 1930. Simultaneously, the absolute number of whites has not increased appreciably over the last 30–40 years and (with the sole exception of Los Angeles–Long Beach) has steadily declined since 1950. Washington, D.C., achieved a majority of nonwhite residents by 1950. The trends discussed here, *if maintained*, will almost certainly produce a similar situation in Detroit, Saint Louis, and Baltimore during the 1970s. In addition, it is also possible that Chicago, Philadelphia, and Cleveland will have nonwhite majorities by 1980.

Figure 4 depicts a growth in the individual rings that is much like the pattern shown in the aggregate totals of the 12 rings. Population increases are evident for both the white and nonwhite populations. However, it must be noted that while the growth rates are similar, the absolute increase of nonwhites is far lower than that of their white counterparts. Cleveland's ring

---

[5] It should be noted that annexations played a large role in producing this deviant pattern. For a general discussion of this factor, see Schnore (1962).

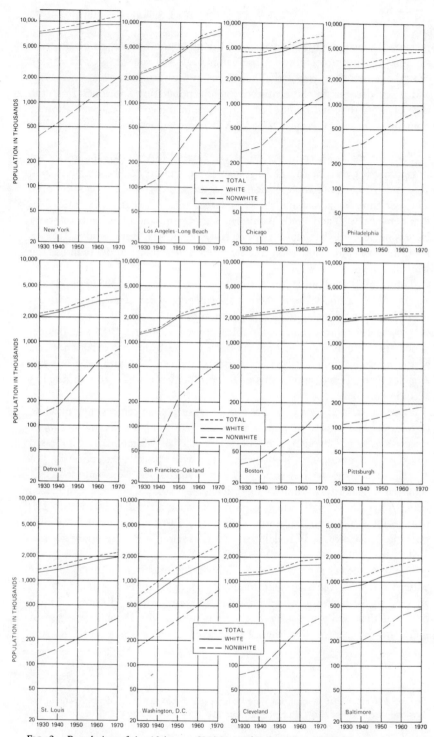

FIG. 2.—Population of the 12 largest SMSAs (1960), by color, 1930–70.

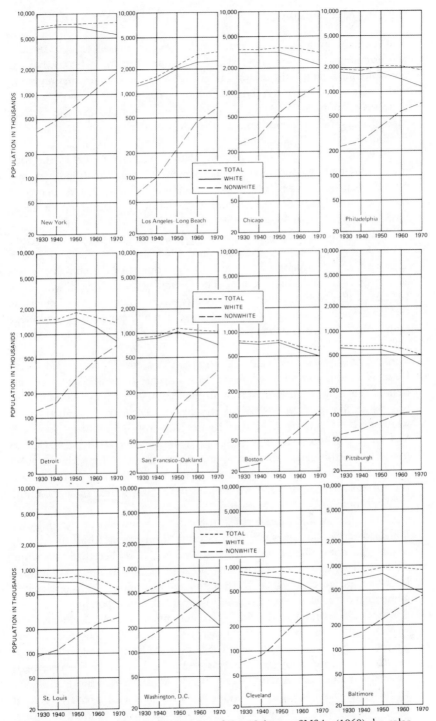

FIG. 3.—Population of the central cities of the 12 largest SMSAs (1960), by color, 1930–70.

is an extreme example of this pattern. In 1960, it housed only 7,328 non-white residents. By 1970, this figure had jumped to almost 48,000, but the nonwhite inhabitants still comprised only 4.8% of the total population living within Cleveland's ring. Overall, nonwhites accounted for no more than 6% of the total population of the 12 metropolitan rings. To cite the extreme cases, the nonwhite population of the individual rings ran from 1.6% in Boston to 9.1% in Washington.

As a result of disproportionate population increases by color, the total metropolitan white population of this country's 12 largest metropolitan communities has decreased by over 6 percentage points since 1930. As shown in the first panel (Total SMSA) of table 2, the white population within the 12 SMSAs dropped from 93.6% of the total in 1930 to 83.2% in 1970.

Of the 12 areas, the Washington SMSA has housed the greatest relative number of nonwhites consistently since 1930. By 1970, Baltimore, with approximately one-quarter of its population comprised of nonwhites, was edging up to the Washington level. The Detroit SMSA followed, with about 19%. Six other SMSAs—New York, Chicago, Philadelphia, San Francisco–Oakland, Saint Louis, and Cleveland—had a white population percentage ranging in the eighties, while the Boston and Pittsburgh SMSAs housed over 90% white residents.

Examining the second panel (Central City) of table 2, we find dramatic losses in the proportion of white residents in central cities. With the exception of Washington, at least 82% of all the central cities' populations in 1930 was white. For example, 82.3% of the city of Baltimore's population was white in 1930, but by 1970 this figure had dropped to little over 50%. Washington presents the most striking picture between 1930 and 1970. Like most of the other cities, the white population loss was minimal in the 1930s and not much more pronounced in the 1940s. By 1950, however, the coming pattern was obvious; by 1970, whites constituted only a little over one-fourth of Washington's central-city dwellers.

Unlike that of the central cities, the color composition of the rings has remained fairly constant since 1930 (see the third panel [Ring] of table 2). While the nonwhite growth rate has been much higher than the white, whites still accounted for at least 90% of each ring's total population in 1970. In several instances, notably Washington and Baltimore, the proportion of whites has actually increased slightly since 1930. Correspondingly, the proportions of nonwhites in the rings have not appreciably changed since 1930. However, there has been a general increase in the absolute number of nonwhites living within the rings over the last decade. Detroit and Baltimore are the exceptions, and both experienced a change of less than a one percentage point. Cleveland, Los Angeles–Long Beach, Washington, and Saint Louis, on the other hand, all showed a nonwhite growth rate of over five percentage points between 1960 and 1970, with Cleveland topping the list with an

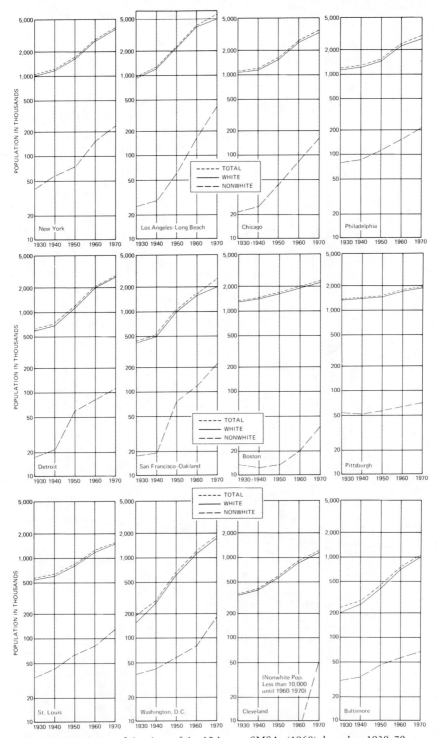

FIG. 4.—Population of the rings of the 12 largest SMSAs (1960), by color, 1930–70.

TABLE 2

PERCENTAGE OF WHITES IN TOTAL POPULATION, CENTRAL CITIES, AND RINGS OF THE 12 LARGEST SMSAs, 1930–70

WHITES (%), 1930–70

12 LARGEST SMSAs	Total SMSA					Central City					Ring				
	1930	1940	1950	1960	1970	1930	1940	1950	1960	1970	1930	1940	1950	1960	1970
All 12 SMSAs	93.6	92.7	89.9	87.1	83.2	92.4	91.0	86.3	78.6	69.2	96.0	96.1	95.6	95.6	94.0
New York	95.2	93.9	91.1	88.0	82.0	95.1	93.6	90.2	85.3	76.6	96.2	95.4	95.5	95.2	93.6
Los Angeles–Long Beach	96.0	95.6	93.7	91.2	87.4	95.0	94.0	90.2	84.7	78.8	97.3	97.7	97.3	95.9	92.6
Chicago	94.1	92.3	89.3	85.2	81.3	92.9	91.7	85.9	76.4	65.6	98.0	97.8	97.1	96.9	95.9
Philadelphia	90.4	89.5	86.8	84.3	81.9	88.6	86.9	81.7	73.3	65.6	93.3	93.4	93.4	93.7	92.9
Detroit	93.6	92.7	88.0	84.9	81.4	92.2	90.7	83.6	70.8	56.0	97.1	97.1	95.0	96.2	96.0
San Francisco–Oakland	95.3	95.6	90.6	87.5	82.9	95.1	95.1	88.2	78.9	67.3	95.9	96.4	93.2	93.2	90.6
Boston	98.3	98.3	97.7	96.6	94.5	97.1	96.7	87.7	90.2	81.8	99.0	99.1	99.2	99.0	98.4
Pittsburgh	94.7	94.6	93.8	93.2	92.7	91.7	90.7	82.0	83.2	79.3	96.2	96.4	96.5	96.6	96.4
Saint Louis	90.7	89.6	87.4	85.5	83.2	88.5	86.6	94.7	71.2	58.7	93.9	93.3	92.7	93.7	92.3
Washington, D.C.	75.0	76.2	76.6	75.1	73.3	72.7	71.5	64.6	45.2	27.7	81.0	86.3	91.3	93.6	90.9
Cleveland	93.9	93.0	89.5	85.5	82.2	91.9	90.3	83.7	71.1	61.0	98.9	99.1	99.2	99.2	98.9
Baltimore	83.2	82.5	80.6	77.8	74.9	82.3	80.6	76.2	65.0	53.0	86.2	88.1	89.8	93.1	93.8

ncrease of 11.3 percentage points. (Here the small-base problem is especially ?vident.) The remaining rings followed with less substantial increases. It must be emphasized, however, that the changes between 1960 and 1970 in :he nonwhite ring population were sizable only when compared to growth during the preceding three decades.

What is most discernible, and has maintained an unbroken pattern since 1930, is the increasing propensity toward living within the rings. Table 3, which presents the ring population as a percentage of the total SMSA, clearly points up this phenomenon. The increases were steady and observable in the 1930s and 1940s and peaked in the 1950s. Between 1960 and 1970 there was a decrease in the rapidity of the change, but the absolute increase remained substantial. In 1930, only Boston and Pittsburgh had a larger population in their rings than in their central cities. Today a larger ring population is the rule rather than the exception. Of the 12 SMSAs under consideration, only New York has a larger population in its central city than in its ring, and even there the decentralization process has been rapid.[6] In the second panel (White) of table 3, eight of the 12 white rings doubled their percentage levels over the 1930–70 interval. Finally, the third panel (Non-white) reveals only three exceptional cases (Philadelphia, Detroit, and Baltimore). In these three rings, nonwhite percentages *fell* between 1960 and 1970.

In addition, the increasing concentration of the white population within the rings is striking. In 1930, of all white residents living in the 12 SMSAs, only those in the Boston and Pittsburgh areas were more likely to live in the rings than in the cities. The pattern of white occupancy of the rings paralleled that of the SMSA population as a whole. Again, New York is the only exception to the rule that whites in 1970 were more likely to live in the rings of the country's largest SMSAs than in the central cities. Thus, while variations existed between the individual SMSAs, an overall pattern is quite obvious. The SMSAs as a whole have been increasing, but only because the rings are growing rapidly enough to offset population losses within the central cities. With the sole exception of Los Angeles–Long Beach, the cities themselves grew slowly between 1930 and 1950 and over the last two decades have suffered considerable losses.

The decline of whites within the central cities has been counterbalanced to a degree by rapid increases within the nonwhite population. These population decreases and increases along color lines have significantly changed

---

[6] Use of the Standard Consolidated Area (SCA), another "metropolitan" areal unit, would yield different results. In the case of New York City, the SCA includes a number of New Jersey counties. For Chicago, the SCA contains northern Indiana counties.

TABLE 3

Percentage of Population, by Color, in Rings of the 12 Largest SMSAs, 1930–70

Population (%) in Rings, by Color, 1930–70

12 Largest SMSAs	Total Population					White					Nonwhite				
	1930	1940	1950	1960	1970	1930	1940	1950	1960	1970	1930	1940	1950	1960	1970
All 12 SMSAs	31.2	33.0	38.5	50.0	56.6	32.1	34.2	40.9	54.9	63.9	19.3	17.8	16.7	17.0	20.3
New York	13.1	14.4	17.4	27.2	31.8	13.2	14.6	18.3	29.5	36.2	10.5	10.8	8.8	10.9	11.3
Los Angeles–Long Beach	40.7	42.8	49.1	58.1	62.4	41.3	43.7	51.0	61.1	66.1	27.1	22.3	21.0	27.3	36.9
Chicago	24.1	25.7	30.1	42.9	51.8	25.1	26.9	32.7	48.8	61.1	8.2	8.2	8.1	9.0	11.3
Philadelphia	37.8	39.6	43.6	53.9	59.6	39.0	41.4	46.9	59.9	67.6	26.4	25.0	21.7	21.6	23.3
Detroit	28.0	31.7	38.7	55.6	64.0	29.0	33.2	41.8	63.0	75.5	12.8	12.7	16.1	14.1	13.8
San Francisco–Oakland	31.9	35.9	48.2	60.2	67.2	32.0	36.2	49.6	64.1	73.4	28.4	28.8	34.8	33.0	37.0
Boston	64.0	65.1	66.8	73.1	76.7	64.4	65.7	67.8	74.9	79.8	37.5	33.3	24.2	22.4	22.9
Pittsburgh	66.9	67.7	69.4	74.9	78.3	67.9	69.1	71.4	77.6	81.5	48.4	47.7	39.5	37.9	38.8
Saint Louis	40.7	44.3	50.2	63.6	73.0	42.2	46.1	53.2	69.7	81.0	26.6	28.3	28.9	27.7	33.6
Washington, D.C.	27.8	31.7	45.2	61.8	72.1	30.0	35.9	53.8	77.0	89.5	21.1	18.3	16.9	16.0	24.5
Cleveland	27.6	30.7	37.6	51.2	60.9	29.1	32.7	41.6	59.5	71.0	4.8	3.8	3.0	2.8	14.1
Baltimore	22.4	24.6	32.4	45.6	53.7	23.2	26.3	36.1	54.6	67.2	18.3	16.7	17.1	14.3	13.3

the color composition of our largest cities. As more whites moved out, the number of nonwhites continued to grow. Concomitantly, there has been a heavy influx of whites into the suburbs. While the nonwhite population has also increased in the rings, it is far lower in terms of absolute numbers than the white growth. Thus, though the cities are becoming increasingly nonwhite, the suburbs appear to be remaining predominantly white.

DETROIT: A CASE STUDY

The experience of the Detroit SMSA as a whole resembles quite closely that of the 12 largest SMSAs combined. By use of census tract data for Detroit, it is possible to follow in more detail the distributional changes that have been occurring since 1930 in this single SMSA. In this analysis, the entire three-county Detroit SMSA (Wayne, Oakland, and Macomb counties) has been divided into a series of seven contiguous, semicircular zones centered at the heart of Detroit's central business district (CBD). As is seen in the map (fig. 5), the central city has been partitioned into four zones on the basis of distance from the center. The city of Detroit has two enclaves—Hamtramck and Highland Park. These two cities are legally separate and incorporated units, but for the remainder of this discussion they are treated as part of the "central city."

The "ring" of the Detroit SMSA has been divided into three zones. The first ring zone borders directly on the central city. The second zone is the tier of townships bordering on the first. The third and outlying zone includes the entire remainder of the three-county Detroit SMSA. This last zone is from 20 to 45 miles from the center of the city.

As with most of the other SMSAs discussed here, the total Detroit SMSA had a relatively small population increase in the 1930s (9.2%) and added about 25% in each of the next two decades. But in the 1960s, the growth rate fell off again to about what it was in the 1930s (11.6%). The central city itself (here treated as including the two enclaves) increased only slightly in the 1930s, grew by 12.5% in the 1940s, and suffered a net decrease of about 10% per decade since 1950. As a result, the city of Detroit in 1970 was actually 6.2% *smaller* than it was 40 years earlier.

The growth patterns of whites and nonwhites in the central city, however, are very different from each other. Whites showed an extremely modest increase between 1930 and 1940, were almost stable in the 1940s, and then declined by about one-quarter in the 1950s. The relative loss was even greater (29.3%) in the 1960–70 decade. As a consequence, 43.4% fewer whites lived in the city of Detroit in 1970 than 40 years earlier. About 672,000 fewer white residents lived in the city in 1970 than in 1930. Over the last 40 years, therefore, Detroit has *lost* almost as many white residents as now live in the city of Milwaukee.

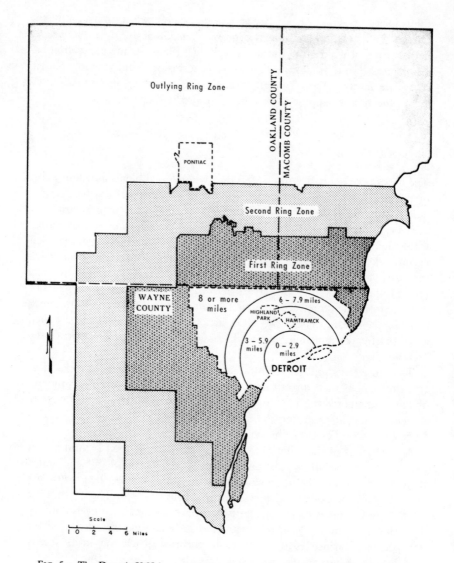

FIG. 5.—The Detroit SMSA organized by rings centered on the city of Detroit's central business district.

The growth rates of the nonwhite population of Detroit are dramatically different from those of the whites. Nonwhites increased by a sizable proportion (22.1%) even in the 1930s and doubled in the 1940s. Their growth rate fell off to 60.1% in the 1950s and declined to 39.2% between 1960 and 1970.

These redistributions over the last 40 years have had a tremendous effect on the color composition of the city of Detroit. Although there were about 672,000 fewer whites in Detroit in 1970 than just 40 years earlier, this large metropolitan center contained almost 570,000 more nonwhites. Whites still outnumbered nonwhites, but the trend is obvious and could be seen at least as far back as the 1930s.

To this point in the discussion we have treated the central city as though it were a homogeneous unit which is undergoing a certain pattern of population redistribution by color. Just as a description of the total SMSA will mask contrasting population flows between the center and the ring, it is reasonable to expect that a description of the city as a whole will not apply equally to its various parts. Figure 6 shows very convincingly that the city of Detroit has not experienced a common population change through its entire area.

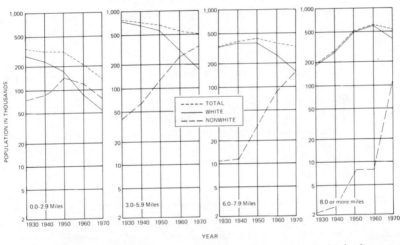

FIG. 6.—Population of the central city and its enclaves of the Detroit SMSA, by distance of residence from the center and by color, 1930–70.

No part of the city as we have categorized it here (by distance from the center) has experienced a common pattern of change by color. All four distance zones declined in total population during the 1960s, but the drop in total population was quite small for the city zone farthest from downtown Detroit. The decrease in total population started as far back as the 1930s for the areas located within six miles of downtown; the zone located six to eight miles from the CBD had little growth until the 1940s; then it too had a slight net loss in population.

The white population living within six miles of the city's core has dropped steadily since 1930. After 1950, those whites living six to eight miles from the CBD also decreased, and the rate of decline has been quite steep over the last 20 years represented in the graph. Only in the outermost zone of the central city did the white population grow rapidly between 1930 and 1950. In the 1950s, the white growth rate in this more distant zone was very small, and a net loss in the number of whites in this zone occurred in the 1960s.

The growth trends of the nonwhite population within the four central-city distance zones also are quite distinctive. In the zone closest to the center, nonwhites increased between 1930 and 1950 and then started a decline in the 1950s that became even steeper during the 1960–70 decade. Between 1960 and 1970, both whites and nonwhites were leaving this zone at about the same rate. The inner city was being deserted by both whites and nonwhites. In 1970, over 100,000 *fewer* persons lived within three miles of downtown Detroit than in 1930. In 1930, about 20% of the total population of Detroit lived this close to the center; by 1970 this proportion had dropped to 8%. As urban historian Jackson (1975, p. 141) has observed, the only new thing about suburbanization in recent years is the virtual abandonment of the core of the city as a residential area:

> I would suggest that fear and the economics of slum housing have created an entirely new form of deconcentration in contemporary America—abandonment. Throughout the nineteenth century, population was forced outward by pressures for more intensive use of land. What we witness now is not simply centrifugal growth, but the desertion of apartments, buildings, and even whole blocks. Abandoning neighborhoods to different ethnic or racial groups is not new, but some blighted areas are now left to the rodents, and some are devoid even of rats.

The two middle zones of the city have shown consistently sharp increases since 1930 in the number of nonwhites who reside there. The greatest relative growth in the nonwhite population has occurred in the zone between six and eight miles from downtown Detroit. It is safe to say that nonwhites now outnumber whites in that part of the city of Detroit which is located within eight miles of downtown.

The zone located eight miles or more from the center displays a pattern of population growth by color which is quite different from those of the inner zones. The white population grew steadily between 1930 and 1960; its growth rate fell off sharply in the 1950s, although the number of whites continued to increase. Between 1960 and 1970, however, the white population suffered a net *decline* of over 100,000 individuals.

The nonwhite population of the fourth city zone showed almost no growth during the 1950s but had an extremely strong increase between 1960 and 1970. In 1970, almost 100,000 more nonwhites lived in this outermost zone than was the case in 1960.

The ring zones surrounding Detroit reveal quite similar growth patterns for both whites and nonwhites (see fig. 7). The fastest rate of growth over the last 40 years has occurred in the zone bordering on the city of Detroit. It is interesting to note, however, that since 1950 nonwhite growth in this first ring zone has been much slower than that of whites.

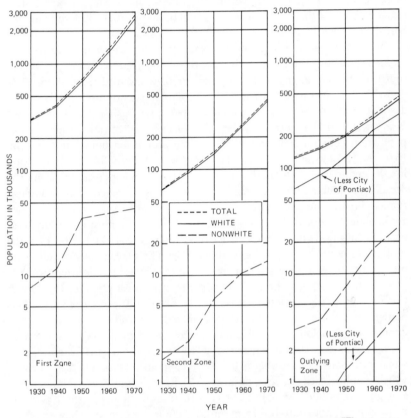

FIG. 7.—Population of the ring of the Detroit SMSA, by distance of residence from the center and by color, 1930–70.

In recent years, the population dynamics of the Detroit SMSA may be summarized as follows: both whites and nonwhites have been leaving the inner city; the white population has failed to maintain its numbers in all sections of the city, but especially in the areas located within eight miles of downtown. Nonwhites have been showing the fastest rate of growth in those parts of Detroit that are six miles or more from the center. The ring has been growing at an extremely fast rate, especially in that part which is adjacent to the central city; in absolute numbers, the overwhelming share of the total population increase in the ring has been due to the addition of whites. Finally, these trends could be discerned at least 30–40 years ago, and most of them have grown stronger during the 1960s.

As for Detroit in the 1960s, table 4 is instructive. It shows the size and color composition of all "urban" municipalities (incorporated places of 2,500 or more inhabitants) that lie within the three-county SMSA. In general, it may be observed that only a handful of "suburbs" contained more than 10% nonwhites, even in 1970.

The exceptions are seven, and we offer brief characterizations of each of them. (1) Ecorse, a relatively old suburb on the Detroit River, just to the south of the central city, is heavily industrial. It dropped from almost 50% nonwhite in 1960 to less than 40% in 1970, apparently as a result of the destruction of old housing in that city. (2) As previously noted, Hamtramck is an enclave of the central city, heavily Polish in ethnic composition; it lost population between 1960 and 1970, and the proportion nonwhite fell from 16.9% to 12.5% over the decade. To put it most bluntly, blacks do not find it a "friendly" city. (3) Another enclave—Highland Park—grew during the decade and doubled its percentage nonwhite. It is of mixed ethnic composition, and blacks are not subjected to the same kind of social pressures as they are likely to experience in Hamtramck. (4) Perhaps the most interesting case of all is Inkster. It had a black majority as recently as 1960, but by 1970 the proportion nonwhite fell to only about 45%. The explanation is quite simple; in the 1960s an undeveloped area north of a major traffic artery was put to residential use, and the new inhabitants were mostly white. (5) Mount Clemens showed a modest increase over the 1960–70 decade (13.3%–16.7% nonwhite) while growing slowly. It is an old city, and its housing stock is quite run down. Only 179 inhabitants were added by a modest annexation during the decade. (6) Pontiac is a very large and old industrial satellite, with a major automobile assembly plant and related ancillary industries, many of which employ blacks in large numbers. (7) River Rouge—like Pontiac—has a major automobile assembly plant (Ford). It grew rapidly in the 1960s, and its proportion nonwhite fell from almost 50% in 1960 to less than one-third in 1970. We have no ready explanation for this dramatic shift. Indeed, these ad hoc "explanations" should be subjected to more rigorous scrutiny than we have suggested here.

CONCLUSIONS AND IMPLICATIONS

If continued, the trends sketched above will certainly have strong implications for our metropolitan communities. Perhaps the most important—and difficult—job of the analyst is to determine why they happen at all. The components of population change must be studied. Color differentials in

TABLE 4

SIZE AND COLOR COMPOSITION OF URBAN MUNICIPALITIES IN THE
RING OF THE DETROIT SMSA, 1960–70

	TOTAL POPULATION		NONWHITE (%)	
MUNICIPALITY	1960	1970	1960	1970
Allen Park	36,874	40,747	*	0.6
Berkley	23,237	22,618	*	0.4
Beverly Hills†	8,644	13,598	*	0.6
Birmingham	25,415	26,170	*	0.5
Bloomfield Hills	2,294	3,672	*	1.9
Center Line	10,161	10,379	*	0.1
Clawson	14,744	17,617	*	0.4
Dearborn	111,863	104,199	*	0.4
Dearborn Heights	Uninc.‡	80,069	...	0.4
Drayton Plains	Uninc.	16,462	...	0.2
East Detroit	45,717	45,920	*	0.3
Ecorse	11,559	17,515	49.9	38.8
Farmington	6,877	13,337	*	0.2
Ferndale	31,206	30,850	*	0.7
Flat Rock†	4,694	5,643	*	0.6
Franklin	2,645	3,344	*	0.3
Fraser	7,026	11,868	*	0.3
Garden City†	37,940	41,864	*	0.4
Gibraltar	2,196	3,325	*	0.3
Grosse Isle	6,284	7,799	*	0.4
Grosse Pointe	6,594	6,637	*	0.5
Grosse Pointe Farms	12,063	11,701	*	0.6
Grosse Pointe Park	15,372	15,585	*	0.5
Grosse Pointe Shores	2,147	3,042	*	0.6
Grosse Pointe Woods	18,558	21,878	*	0.1
Hamtramck§	29,199	27,245	16.9	12.5
Harper Woods	19,968	23,784	*	0.3
Hazel Park	25,582	23,784	*	0.5
Highland Park§	29,900	35,444	27.3	56.9
Huntington Woods	8,634	8,536	*	0.6
Inkster	25,528	38,595	53.1	44.9
Keego Harbor	2,755	3,092	*	0.5
Lincoln Park	53,871	52,984	*	0.4
Livonia	66,562	110,109	*	0.4
Madison Heights	33,257	38,559	*	0.5

TABLE 4 (*Continued*)

MUNICIPALITY	TOTAL POPULATION		NONWHITE (%)	
	1960	1970	1960	1970
Melvindale	13,089	13,862	0.5	0.8
Mount Clemens†	18,549	20,476	13.3	16.7
Northville†	2,973	5,400	*	0.5
Novi†	Uninc.	9,668	...	0.4
Oak Park	36,465	36,762	*	0.6
Pleasant Ridge	3,800	3,989	*	0.2
Plymouth	8,758	11,758	*	0.7
Pontiac†	68,256	85,279	20.5	27.5
Quakertown North	Uninc.	7,101	...	0.3
River Rouge	5,886	15,947	48.0	32.4
River View	7,230	11,342	*	0.5
Rochester	5,431	7,054	*	0.6
Rockwood	2,015	3,119	*	0.2
Roseville	49,457	60,529	*	1.4
Royal Oak	80,470	85,499	*	0.4
Saint Clair Shores	76,424	88,093	*	0.5
South Field	31,435	69,285	*	0.7
Southgate	29,377	33,909	*	0.6
Sterling Heights	Uninc.	61,365	...	0.5
Taylor	Uninc.	70,020	...	0.5
Trenton	18,408	24,127	*	0.3
Troy	19,025	39,419	*	0.5
Utica	1,454	3,504	*	0.5
Walled Lake	3,547	3,759	*	0.3
Warren	89,072	179,260	*	0.5
Wayne†	Uninc.	21,054	...	0.8
Westland	Uninc.	86,749	...	3.1
Wolverine Lake†	2,402	4,301	*	0.4
Woodhaven	Uninc.	3,330	...	0.5
Wyandotte	43,471	41,060	*	0.4

*Less than 0.05%.
†Minor annexations between 1960 and 1970.
‡"Uninc." indicates that the municipality was unincorporated in 1960.
§Enclaves of Detroit, as shown in fig. 5.

birth and death rates certainly explain at least part of the changing population patterns of our cities. The birth rate of nonwhites in the central cities tends to be somewhat higher than that of whites. In addition, many of the white city residents are older and thus have higher death rates. Younger white families are apparently not compensating for these facts by moving into the cities (see Farley's analysis in this volume). The housing stocks of older central areas are deteriorating, despite heroic efforts in some cities, and do not provide attractive living quarters for families with young children.

Thousands of housing units that have deteriorated to the point of being uninhabitable (and that were very likely to have been occupied by nonwhites) have been razed by the wrecking ball and the bulldozer. In their places are raised facilities for the expanding office and business interests in the city or new and costly high-rise apartments. Space devoted to freeways and automobile parking is another factor in destroying old central housing (see Kasarda's contribution to this volume). Many young white couples who either cannot afford expensive central quarters or who prefer suburban amenities move into the rings. Many nonwhites who have not reached the same economic level as whites relocate in other areas of the central city. We are not posing a simple "economic" interpretation, but income differentials by color certainly play a role.

Another possible explanation is that the central cities provide—in a limited sense—the "best" economic and social climate for nonwhites. Until rather recently, when many industries and businesses started moving all or part of their production operations into industrial parks and to other outlying sites, there have been few job opportunities for nonwhites outside the cities. In addition, jobs of a semiskilled or unskilled nature are apparently still abundant in the central cities. We refer to the example of service occupations in the burgeoning hotels and restaurants in or very near the heart of the CBD.

Housing commensurate with modest income is still more readily available in the central cities. For many nonwhites, the cities offer the only housing they can afford. For others who might be in a position to rent or buy elsewhere, the cities provide the social atmosphere in which they can live most comfortably. Housing discrimination, or more subtle varieties of social discrimination, may induce nonwhites to remain in segregated areas so that they and/or their children are not constantly in an uncomfortable minority. (Black city and suburban housing quality in 1970 is ably treated in Pendleton [1973].)

In central-city areas, where neighborhoods are in flux, whites are probably also feeling some discomfort. Fears, both real and imagined, enhance the desire to move to the rings. Cries of decreasing property values with racial turnover are not uncommon, although this has been shown to be fallacious. The streets and even the schools are not safe. The rings offer promises of

better schools, better housing, less crowding, and less crime, although those
promises may not be fulfilled. In addition, with the advent of more and
better highways, rush-hour buses, and commuter trains, the combination of
city work and suburban living is a relatively easy one for millions of white
Americans in our largest metropolitan areas.

But what of the future? Some writers have been led to see black suburbanization as a process that is only now beginning and that will occur on a
more massive scale in coming years. Clawson (1973, p. 3) has said that "a
preoccupation with overall statistics on racial change in the older urban cores
has obscured the significant migration of middle- and upper-income blacks
to the suburbs—a movement that is likely to continue and to accelerate."

Others see or imply portents of a different future. Farley and Taeuber
(1968, p. 955) used tract data for 13 central cities that had special censuses in
the 1960s, and observed that "there is no evidence in these data of an
acceleration or even continuation of the trend toward decreasing segregation
observed for northern cities from 1950–60." Still others project a massive
reversal of the apparently dominant trends. Goldston (1970, p. 110) contends:

> The truth is that people are people, not statistics, and do not necessarily
> behave in predictable ways. Demographers and sociologists witnessing the
> flight to the suburbs of the 1940s and 1950s assumed that those who fled had
> fled for good. Yet such intangible, unmeasurable influences as simple bore-
> dom have caused an unexpected remigration to the city of many of these
> refugees. An inspection, therefore, of the mutual impacts of city and suburb
> and megapolitan environment upon each other is a kaleidoscope of people
> and events in *motion*; today's image may be reversed tomorrow.

In this passage, Goldston is merely echoing the thought expressed some
years earlier by demographer-ecologist Hauser (1960, p. 115):

> The combination of urban renewal in the inner zones of central cities and
> blight and urban sprawl in the suburbs is tending to disrupt the pattern of
> population distribution which has placed the higher income groups farthest
> out from the center of the city. Should these trends continue, the residential
> land use pattern in metropolitan areas would be turned inside out, with the
> newer and more desirable areas located in the rebuilt inner city zones as well
> as in the most distant parts of suburbia.

Our final remarks concern the policy implications of our research. As we
have indicated, Detroit is a fairly typical large northern metropolitan area,
and we examined it rather closely. It is therefore extremely interesting to us
that the historic U.S. Supreme Court decision announced on Thursday, July
25, 1974 should have dealt with Detroit. On a five–four basis, the Court
ruled that mandatory busing between largely black central-city schools and
largely white suburban schools was unconstitutional. As a *New York Times*
writer (Weaver 1974) put it:

To those who had been fighting for school desegregation in the courts for decades, last Thursday looked like the end of an era. For the first time in 20 years, the United States Supreme Court handed down a ruling that will mean less, rather than more, integration. . . . When the Detroit case was decided last week it became apparent that there was a new majority, Potter Stewart and the four Nixon appointees, which still embraced the principle of integrated schools but which could not approve the remedy that a lower court felt was needed to end segregation.

We are inclined to agree with Mr. Justice Thurgood Marshall who, in a dissenting opinion, asserted: "After twenty years of small, often difficult, steps toward this great end, the court today takes a giant step backward."

REFERENCES

Anonymous. 1970. "A New Way to Integrate the Suburbs." *Business Week* (March 28), pp. 168, 172.
———. 1971*a*. "Where Blacks Are Moving—and Moving Up." *U.S. News and World Report* (March 1), pp. 24–26.
———. 1971*b*. "Will the Suburbs Beckon?" *Ebony* 27 (July): 112–13.
———. 1973. "A Decade of Population Change in Leading Metropolitan Areas." *Statistical Bulletin of the Metropolitan Life Insurance Company* 54 (November): 2–4.
Blumberg, Leonard, and Michael Lalli. 1966. "Little Ghettos: A Study of Negroes in the Suburbs." *Phylon* 27 (Summer): 117–31.
Bradford, David F., and Harry H. Kelejian. 1973. "An Econometric Model of the Flight to the Suburbs." *Journal of Political Economy* 81 (May/June): 566–89.
Clawson, Marion. 1973. "Editor's Introduction." Pp. 3–13 in *Modernizing Urban Land Policy*, edited by Marion Clawson. Baltimore: Johns Hopkins University Press, for Resources for the Future.
Farley, Reynolds. 1970. "The Changing Distribution of Negroes within Metropolitan Areas: The Emergence of Black Suburbs." *American Journal of Sociology* 75 (January): 512–29.
Farley, Reynolds, and Karl E. Taeuber. 1968. "Population Trends and Residential Segregation since 1960." *Science* 159 (March 1): 953–56.
Feldt, Allan G. 1965. "The Metropolitan Area Concept: An Evaluation of the 1950 SMAs." *Journal of the American Statistical Association* 60 (June): 617–36.
Gibbs, Jack P. 1961. "Methods and Problems in the Delimitation of Urban Units." Pp. 57–87 in *Urban Research Methods*, edited by Jack P. Gibbs. Princeton, N.J.: Van Nostrand.
Goldston, Robert. 1970. *Suburbia: Civic Denial*. New York: Macmillan.
Hauser, Philip M. 1960. *Population Perspectives*. New Brunswick, N.J.: Rutgers University Press.
Jackson, Kenneth T. 1975. "Urban Deconcentration in the Nineteenth Century: A Statistical Inquiry." Pp. 110–42 in *The New Urban History: Quantitative Explorations by American Historians*, edited by Leo F. Schnore. Princeton, N.J.: Princeton University Press.
Lieberson, Stanley. 1962. "Suburbs and Ethnic Residential Patterns." *American Journal of Sociology* 67 (May): 673–81.
Parsons, Carole W., ed. 1972. *America's Uncounted People*. Washington, D.C.: National Academy of Sciences.
Pendleton, William W. 1973. "Blacks in Suburbs." Pp. 171–84 in *The Urbanization of the Suburbs*, edited by Louis H. Masotti and Jeffrey K. Hadden. Urban Affairs Annual Reviews, vol. 7. Beverly Hills, Calif.: Sage.
Rose, Harold M. 1969. "The Origin and Pattern of Development of Urban Black Social Areas." *Journal of Geography* 68 (September): 327–32.

Schnore, André, and Sharp

———. 1970. "The Development of an Urban Subsystem: The Case of the Negro Ghetto." *Annals of the Association of American Geographers* 60 (March): 1–17.

———. 1971. *The Black Ghetto: A Spatial-Behavioral Perspective.* New York: McGraw-Hill.

———. 1972. "The Spatial Development of Black Residential Systems." *Economic Geography* 48 (January): 43–65.

Schmid, Calvin F. 1954. *Handbook of Graphic Presentation.* New York: Ronald.

Schnore, Leo F. 1962. "Municipal Annexations and the Growth of Metropolitan Suburbs, 1950–60." *American Journal of Sociology* 67 (January): 406–17.

———. 1965. *The Urban Scene: Human Ecology and Demography.* New York: Free Press.

———. 1972. *Class and Race in Cities and Suburbs.* Chicago: Markham.

Sharp, Harry, and Leo F. Schnore. 1962. "The Changing Color Composition of Metropolitan Areas." *Land Economics* 38 (May): 169–85.

———. 1971. "Public Response to the 1970 Census: A Wisconsin Survey." *Demography* 8 (August): 297–305.

Weaver, Warren, Jr. 1974. "Court Puts a Stone Wall before the School Bus." *New York Times* (July 28), sec. E, p. 3.

Wirt, Frederick M., Benjamin Walter, Francine F. Rabinovitz, and Deborah R. Hensler. 1972. *On the City's Rim: Politics and Policy in Suburbia.* Lexington, Mass.: Heath.

4 Suburbanization and the Development of Motor Transportation: Transportation Technology and the Suburbanization Process

Gary A. Tobin
Washington University

The metropolis of the 1970s hardly resembles the city of 1900. It would be even more difficult to liken contemporary urban America to the city of the middle 19th century. In the last 150 years, cities have been the center of rapid industrialization and magnets for foreign immigrants and surplus rural population. As a result, urban areas have experienced radical change in size, spatial structure, and function.[1]

Although 19th- and 20th-century American cities are much different, the process by which they have expanded has not significantly changed. Suburbanization has been primarily a function of four variables: (1) resource availability, (2) social and individual values, (3) institutional structure, and (4) availability of given technologies, including transportation.[2] A change in any of these variables results in a change in the degree and pattern of suburbanization.

The supply and costs of resources have been one determinant of population diffusion. The availability of given resources, particularly fossil fuels and ores, has affected the comparative efficiency and cost feasibility of particular transportation modes. The supply of land has been a second important resource that has influenced movement away from the city center. The consumption of land and transportation has been influenced by the availability of a third resource: individual and institutional income levels. National production and personal income growth have played a significant role in the scale of suburbanization.

Social and individual values have been the second important variable in suburbanization. Values have affected the choices that individual and institutional urban consumers have made in allocating resources to purchase both transportation and urban space. This is not to argue that values can be equated with consumer preference. But within the constraints of their own wealth, the choices made by individuals and groups often have represented a

---

[1] For urban history overviews, see Glaab and Brown (1967), Callow (1969), and McKelvey (1963, 1968).

[2] Much of this thinking originated jointly through a research effort with John Forester at the University of California, Berkeley.

compromise between values and resources within the consumer's control.

Institutional structure has been the third important variable in the suburbanization process. Institutions provide the mechanism for resource allocation and expression of individual and social values. Throughout 19th- and 20th-century American urban history, the private market has been the main institutional structure for the allocation of urban space and transportation.[3]

Technology has been the fourth major factor in the suburbanization process. The use of elevators, telephones, and computers, for example, has affected urban form. Of all technologies, however, transportation has been the most important factor in influencing spatial structure. The cost and time of movement of goods and individuals have set constraints on the location of people and buildings. As a result, urban activity has always occurred within limited geographic space. "Transportation is a device to overcome the 'friction of space: and the better the transportation, the less the friction,' " summarizes one analyst (Alonso 1964, pp. 6–7). Decreased transportation costs have allowed increased dispersal of residences and manufacturing, wholesale, and retail firms.

In this century, the use of motor transportation has increased the geographic area that is conveniently and efficiently within reach of individuals and their enterprises, allowing new ecological relationships to develop. As the degree of suburban growth has increased, so has the use of motor vehicles. In short, the introduction of motor technology at the turn of the century redefined what might be geographically possible in American cities. The availability of resources, values, and institutions has determined to what extent these possibilities have been realized.

Some analysts have argued that transportation technology has determined urban form and that the use of a particular technology has inevitably produced a specific kind of city. This hypothesis has been especially popular among those scholars who believe that the automobile has become an uncontrollable force that has shaped the city, institutions, and social behavior. Suburbanization has been seen as a product of automobile usage, not as a process in which transportation has played a role (see Schneider 1971; Hébert 1972). The history of suburbanization and the growth of the motor-vehicle industry, however, do not support this hypothesis.

The development of motor transportation in America can be divided into four historical periods. The first stage was the "adoptive period."[4] Although motor-vehicle technology was introduced into the urban system and its use increased, alternate transportation modes maintained supremacy as movers of goods and people. Accordingly, motor transportation during this period had

---

[3] This has been true at least since the beginning of the 19th century (see Warner 1968).

[4] For a history of the automobile, see Flink (1971) and Rae (1965).

little influence on the structure of the metropolis. The second stage was the "diffusion period." Motor-vehicle use increased while other modes also increased or stabilized. Both motor technology and other transportation modes had some influence on urban form; however, automobiles and trucks exerted the least influence. The third stage was the "replacement period," when the use of motor technology increased rapidly while use of other modes began to decline. In this period, the metropolis began to develop within the geographic constraints set by the use of motor technology. The fourth stage is the "dominant period." Motor technology becomes the primary mover of people and goods. Other modes serve specific, but limited, functions and no longer play a major role in determining most spatial relationships.

The adoptive period of motor-transportation use occurred between 1895 and 1908. This period included the approximate date of the introduction of motor vehicles and the beginning of Model T mass production. During this period, widespread suburban growth depended upon nonmotor transportation modes. The diffusion stage took place roughly between 1908 and World War I. Use of motor vehicles increased rapidly, but other modes remained dominant. The replacement period occurred between World War I and World War II, with most of the replacement taking place in the 1920s. Urban form then developed primarily within the constraints set by motor transportation. Other modes continued to be widely used but began to experience decline. The fourth stage began after World War II. During this period, suburbanization is tied almost exclusively to expansion of motor transport.

These stages in the history of motor transportation are discussed within three larger periods of suburbanization. The first time frame is 1890 to World War I. Prior to the electrification of street railways, the residential city was tightly packed in an area three to six miles from the city center. Suburban towns were connected to the central city by steam railroads, with most land between left vacant. With the use of electric street railways, spokelike development occurred along the new routes, with some areas built up along crosstown routes. It was in this period that the adoption and diffusion of motor vehicles occurred. Some minor changes in urban spatial structure took place with the use of automobiles and trucks. But residential development was determined primarily by streetcar routes. In addition, the use of horse power and steam railroads kept most industry tied to the city's water and rail connections.

The second period of suburbanization took place between World War I and World War II, with the fastest growth rates in the 1920s. Crosstown streetcar routes, which allowed more interstitial development, were built farther from the city center. This allowed increased development in previously empty areas between the spokes from six to 10 miles away from the city center, often in patchwork form. The replacement period for motor vehicles occurred in this time frame. Horses were almost eliminated from urban use, while the automobile and bus captured larger shares of the riding market. While the construction of crosstown street railway routes continued to be important, the widespread use of motor vehicles was the primary factor in changing spatial structure. Large numbers of interstitial areas not served by street railways were developed in locations accessible only by automobile and truck. In addition, increasing numbers of retail, wholesale, and manufacturing firms were able to abandon water and rail terminals. Residential suburbanization, however, outpaced industrial diffusion. Not until the post–World War II period did rates of industrial suburbanization match the outward movement of people. Clearly, the relocation of a business, regardless of transportation, involves a much larger and more complicated set of decision criteria than the individual choice in settlement.

The third period of suburbanization began after World War II. This was also the dominant period for motor vehicles. Except for specific industries still bound to water and rail terminals, most industries have been able to locate throughout urban areas stretching 30 miles or more from the city center, often in more than one direction. Residential development also has occurred in much the same patchwork form set in 1920s, but over a much larger geographic area. In addition, the metropolis has become multinodal. Shopping centers and industrial and office parks have been constructed throughout an area served primarily by motor transportation vehicles and often having connecting rail spurs.

STAGES IN THE RELATIONSHIP BETWEEN SUBURBANIZATION AND THE DEVELOPMENT OF MOTOR TRANSPORT

In considering the historical relationship between suburbanization and motor transport, four problems must be recognized. First, census definitions of metropolitan areas, satellite cities, and SMSAs have changed over time. In addition, the extent of suburbanization is understated by reason of annexation. Second, depending on size, age, and geography, rates of suburbanization, adoption of different transportation modes, and changes in spatial structure have differed between cities. Discussion of both suburbanization periods and the history of motor transportation depicts general time frames, not absolute historical chronicles for all American cities. Third, the thesis that suburban growth has determined rates of adoption of motor transportation, which in turn has been the primary technological constraint in urban form, is discussed in linear language. But the process has been nonlinear and interactive over time, with influence exerted by other variables as well. Fourth, the proliferation of automobiles has been related primarily to residential patterns, while the use of trucks has been more influential in commercial and industrial location. Although the histories of the automobile and the truck are discussed separately in this essay, the diffusion of people and industry has been interactive and reciprocal, not unidirectional.

We now turn to the first phase of this rather complicated historical process.

1890–WORLD WAR I

Prior to the introduction of electricity on streetcar lines, the residential city was built primarily within the limits of horse power. In addition, suburban towns, some as far as 10 miles from the center, were linked to the city by the steam railroad. Urban space was redefined with the introduction and use of electric power by the street railways. In 1890, 60% of the street railway mileage was still operated by animal power. By 1902, only 273 of 26,429 miles of track were run by horses (Withington 1931, p. 541). By 1912 the transition to electric power was completed: only 57 of over 41,000 miles of street railway were animal powered (U.S. Bureau of the Census 1915, p. 184).

With the electrification of the street railways, "the radius of the densely built-up areas lengthened to 10 miles in cities like Boston and Chicago" (Holt 1972, p. 331). This expansion, however, was primarily from downtown to suburban towns, with development occurring along the streetcar lines. Suburban towns once served only by steam railroads were connected with electric street railways, and so linked to developing settlements in the vacant space between. Areas outside the city, however, were primarily subdivided and developed along streetcar lines.

The decade between 1890 and 1900 was a period of rapid growth both in the central city and in the suburbs. New York grew from a city of 1.5 million to almost 3.5 million inhabitants. Philadelphia, Saint Louis, and Boston all grew by more than 20%. Los Angeles doubled in size to reach more than 100,000 persons in 1900 (U.S. Department of the Interior 1895, abstract).

As the cities grew so did the suburbs. Between 1890 and 1900 the population of the city of Chicago grew from about 1.1 to 1.7 million, a growth of 54.4%. The remainder of Cook County also experienced rapid growth, from 92,000 to 140,000—an increase of 51.6%. Similarly, Warner analyzes diffusion in Boston between 1850 and 1900, showing that in 1850 about 26% of the population of Boston lived in the railroad and streetcar suburbs in a three- to 10-mile radius from the city center. By 1900 this figure had grown to about 39%. The 1900 population of Boston was four times as large as the population in 1850, while the number of inhabitants in the suburbs had grown sixfold (Warner 1962, p. 179).

Suburban development far outpaced central growth in many cities. Between 1900 and 1910 Baltimore grew by 10%, but the satellite areas grew by 46%. Chicago registered a 29% increase between 1900 and 1910, while the area surrounding Chicago experienced an 88% jump in population. Los Angeles more than tripled in size in a single decade, while the suburbs had a 533% increase. Rapid suburban expansion also occurred in New York, Philadelphia, Pittsburgh, and Saint Louis (U.S. Bureau of the Census 1947, pp. 33–45).

Rapid suburban growth continued between 1910 and 1920. As a whole, metropolitan areas grew by 25%. Central cities outpaced suburban development, growing by 28% while the suburbs grew by 20%. As in the previous decade, however, much of the growth inside the city boundaries was accomplished by annexation of previously undeveloped areas. In spite of this, suburbanization was the dominant trend in many areas. Chicago grew by 23%, while the satellite areas jumped by 79%. Pittsburgh registered a 10% increase in its population, but the suburbs grew by 24%. The number of inhabitants in Saint Louis increased by 12%, whereas areas outside the central city grew by 26% (ibid.).

Little industrial decentralization occurred between 1890 and World War I. High costs of hauling kept industry confined to railroad and port terminals. Yet suburban locations were beginning to prove attractive to some types of enterprise. As Adna Weber (1899) points out: "Attention has often been called to another encouraging tendency favoring suburban growth, namely, the transference of manufacturing industries to the suburbs. The local advantages of a suburban town have been pointed out; they include not only a great saving in rent and insurance, but economy in the handling and storing of goods. All carting is avoided by having a switch run directly into the factory; saving to machinery is effected by placing it all on solid foundations on the first floor; and plenty of space is at hand for the storing of fuel and materials, so that these may be bought when the market offers the most favorable terms" (p. 473).

Although firms may have desired a suburban location, few were able to move. Industry remained tied to the city's rail and water links. In 1905, in Cleveland about 94% of the manufacturing establishments were located in the city, in Minneapolis–Saint Paul 99%, in Baltimore 96%, in Saint Louis 95%, and in Philadelphia 91% (U.S. Bureau of the Census 1909, pp. 9–80). Manufacturing located outside the city was primarily in suburban towns along steam railroad lines.

Some diffusion of industry occurred between 1904 and 1914. Baltimore's share of manufacturing establishments declined from 96% to 93%, Saint Louis's from 95% to 90%, and Philadelphia's from 91% to 87%. Other cities saw little or no diffusion of manufacturing establishments. Thus, at the advent of World War I the diffusion of motor vehicles had occurred, but this had little effect on industrial relocation (U.S. Bureau of the Census 1918, pp. 564, 787, 1292).

As noted, public carriers served as the primary movers of people to the new suburbs. The bicycle boom of the 1890s had died by 1902, leaving the horse and buggy as the major means of private transportation (Tobin 1974). However, the horse and wagon were the primary intraurban delivery mode for freight and other goods.

Large-scale production of automobiles *followed* the suburban growth of the 1890s and early 1900s. Although a few automobiles were built in the mid-1890s and some 4,000 vehicles were built in 1900, the first automobile boom began in 1908 with the mass production of the Model T. In 1905 some 24,000 automobiles were built; in 1908 the number jumped to 63,500. Production of trucks and buses did not begin until 1904, although some automobiles were used for hauling before that year. In 1908 only 1,500 trucks and buses were produced (Automobile Manufacturers Association 1967, p. 3).

As the suburbs grew at the beginning of the century, so did the market for more efficient means of hauling and delivery. The adoption of the motor truck began to meet this demand for an efficient delivery mode. However, horses and horse-drawn vehicles continued to operate as the urban setting expanded far beyond the limits of a walking city. Delivery of fire and police services, coal for homes, and other urban services and goods remained mostly dependent on horse and wagon. Yet the maximum efficiency of this particular transportation mode remained static.

The gradual adoption of mechanical power as a substitute for horses occurred for primarily three reasons: safety, health, and efficiency. The health problem was due to the large amounts of waste that the horse deposited on city streets (Tarr 1971; Bolce 1908). Safety was an issue arising from frequent runaways (*New York Times* 1906a, 1906b, 1906c). But it was the horse's inefficiency and high operating costs that made it a rare consumer item in the private-transportation market and a high cost constraint for business. Not only was the mode itself costly; it also generated costs: the necessity of using horses limited location choice of businesses to high rent–high congestion areas.

Most urbanites either walked or used the mass carriers to commute and shop. The automobile was adopted by an urban population that generally disliked, and even despised, public carriers. Mass transit was characterized by crowding, discomfort, and inconvenience. The urban public's dissatisfaction with common carriers was nurtured throughout the 19th century. Each transportation innovation was an improvement, but each advance failed to meet expectations and demands. Modes changed, but the old problems did not disappear. Streetcars remained crowded and dirty, routes were fixed, service was irregular, and unpleasant social intermingling persisted. The commuter was subjected to "suffering and inconvenience" that was "almost inconceivable" (*New York Times* 1903b). The cars were often "pressed to suffocation" (*New York Times* 1903a); people were forced to stand on the running board and on the rear buffer (*New York Times* 1906f). But even those inside endured "physical discomfort, often amounting to little less than real agony" (*New York Times* 1899). The commuter responded to the ride on urban transit with endurance, constant complaining, and an occasional outburst of violence (*New York Times* 1906*d*, 1906*e*).

Private transportation avoided these pathologies. More than the horse and buggy, the automobile embodied a combination of attractive factors. First, the auto was a multipurpose vehicle; it could be used for recreation, commuting, shopping, and carrying. Second, the owner of the automobile could do all of these things with more convenience, speed, and self-scheduling than with public carriers or in a horse and buggy. Third, the vehicle provided social privacy and segregation. Fourth, with the automobile, the owner attained a high degree of mobility and geographic freedom and access to a wide choice of consumer goods, services, and urban amenities. Even though the city expanded geographically, the automobile allowed the owner continued access without loss of time or convenience. Costs were higher than mass transit, but automobile owners were willing to bear them.

At first, the relatively high cost of the automobile and truck kept them out of reach of most individual consumers and small firms (Flink 1971; Casson, Ellis, and Hutchinson 1913). However, a mass diffusion of automobiles and trucks took place between 1908 and World War I. The price of a new automobile became attractive enough for many upper-middle-income buyers. And, as mass production of trucks increased after 1908, the cost of the vehicle decreased. With lower capital investment required, large economies of scale were no longer necessary for the purchase of a motor truck. In addition, growing numbers of used trucks appeared on the market in the price range of smaller firms and individuals.

Between 1908 and 1914 the production of trucks and buses jumped tremendously. Some 1,500 units were produced in 1908. By 1914 nearly 25,000 trucks and buses were manufactured (Automobile Manufacturers Association 1967, p. 3). The total number of trucks in use paralleled production growth. In 1908 a total of 4,000 trucks were registered in the United States; by 1914 the total had reached about 99,000 (Automobile Maufacturers Association 1969, p. 13). The production of automobiles also increased at a rapid rate between 1908 and 1914. In 1908 some 63,000 cars were manufactured; the next year nearly twice that number were produced. By 1914 nearly 550,000 cars were sold—a growth of 775% in six years (Automobile Manufacturers Association 1967, p. 3).

Diffusion of motor vehicles depended on two factors: cost feasibility and convenience for a mass market. Costs decreased substantially between 1908 and 1914 (*American Agriculturist* 1912, p. 343). In 1912 a new Ford runabout cost only $525. Used cars were advertised for as low as $100 in 1909 (*Farm Journal* 1909, p. 247). Clearly, the automobile had come into the price range of many urban upper-middle-class consumers. During this diffusion period, however, the automobile remained a vehicle for the more well-to-do and the adventuresome. Gas stations were few and far between, mechanics were scarce, and the machine was still relatively primitive. But, gradually major improvements were made in brake equipment, tires, and other technological amenities. The major breakthrough came in 1912 with the invention of the electric starter to replace the crank (Rae 1965, pp. 47–48). Still, while many suburban dwellers would have preferred to drive automobiles rather than ride public transit, mass adoption of the automobile did not occur until it was cheaper and even more technologically appealing. The period following World War I saw realization of these conditions, which allowed, in turn, for massive social changes.

BETWEEN THE WORLD WARS

The modern metropolis was shaped in the 1920s. Large-scale suburbanization occurred, bringing widespread adoption of motor vehicles throughout urban America. Residential suburbanization outpaced industrial movement. Some residential areas in the center city experienced population loss, while areas farther from the center and in the suburbs began to grow. These trends were continued throughout the 1930s and, on a smaller scale, during World War II.

The suburban growth of the 1920s was enormous. Central cities grew at a rate of 19.4%, from 29 million to over 34 million inhabitants. The areas outside the central cities, however, grew by 39.2%, from 11 million to over 15 million persons. This accounted for about 44% of the growth within the metropolitan districts over the 10-year period. In 70% of the metropolitan districts, the suburbs grew at a faster rate than the central city (U.S. Bureau of the Census 1932, pp. 6–7). Indeed, many cities experienced rates of suburban growth that would never again be equaled in those urban areas. The central city of Boston grew by 4%, the suburbs by 20%. Cleveland showed a 12% population increase, while its suburbs grew by 126%. New York City gained over 1.5 million inhabitants between 1920 and 1930, some 23%, even as the suburbs gained 400,000 persons, a growth of 67%. Saint Louis grew by 5%, while the population of the suburbs increased by 107% (ibid.).

The rate of suburban growth slowed dramatically between 1930 and 1940. Metropolitan districts grew at a rate of about 7% over the 10-year period. The central city increased in size by about 4%, with the suburbs growing at a rate of over 13%. This rate was substantially lower than the almost 40% increase of the prior decade but still greater than within the central city (U.S. Bureau of the Census 1947, p. 4).

The pattern of central city decline and suburban expansion was firmly established between 1930 and 1940. Major cities such as Cleveland, Boston, Kansas City, Saint Louis, and Philadelphia showed population losses of as much as 3%, while the suburbs grew at rates as high as 23%. In short, although the rates of suburbanization slowed during the 1930s, the trends of the 1920s continued, with new residential construction primarily taking place in the suburbs (ibid., pp. 33–45).

Like population, the movement of industry to the suburbs slowed down in the depression-war years. The total number of the nation's manufacturing establishments located in the central city declined from 51% to 49%, while the ring's share of these firms grew from 14% to 17% of the nation's total (Kitagawa and Bogue 1955, p. 21).

Demand for motor vehicles followed and no doubt subserved prevailing patterns of suburbanization. The growth rate for motor vehicles was characterized by two distinct sections—1918–1929 and the depression-war years. Horse vehicles were replaced by motor trucks primarily during the 1920s, while automobiles began to capture the riding market. The depression slowed the rate of replacement of horses, but by the end of this period the transition was complete. Another motor vehicle, the bus, also began to replace other transit modes, largely during the 1930s.

By 1916 automobile production had grown to over 1.5 million. In 1922 over 2.27 million autos were produced; by 1929 this number had almost doubled to 4.455 million vehicles built in one year. This level was not reached again until 1949 (Automobile Manufacturers Association 1967, p. 13).

In 1916 about 92,000 trucks and buses were built, with about 225,000 units manufactured in 1919. While much of this production was related to World War I, the truck industry began an almost uninterrupted expansion. Between 1919 and 1924 the number of units manufactured almost doubled, to over 416,000 vehicles produced in 1924. Between 1924 and 1929 the production of buses and trucks doubled again, with almost 882,000 units manufactured in 1929. In the 1920s the industry's output quadrupled in size (ibid.). In 1919 under 900,000 trucks were registered; by 1929, the total had about quadrupled to over 3.5 million vehicles (Automobile Manufacturers Association 1969, p. 13).

Slower rates of production took place during the 1930s than in the 1920s, but automobiles and trucks were still built and sold in large numbers. Even in the depth of the depression, 1932, over 1.1 million automobiles were sold. By 1935 the automobile industry again produced more than 3 million cars. Not until the war years, 1943–44, when the industry was converted to war production, did automobile production virtually halt—only 749 cars were built in those two years combined (Automobile Maufacturers Association 1967, p. 3).

Although the depression and war slowed truck production, the decrease was not as large as for the automobile industry. Only 300,000 trucks were added to the total registration between 1930 and 1934. But by 1945 the total number of registered trucks had grown to about 5 million, still a growth of approximately 33% in a period of severe economic constraint (Automobile Manufacturers Association 1969, p. 13).

The replacement of horses by motor trucks occurs throughout the period between 1915 and 1945, primarily in the 1920s. For example, some 50,000 horse-drawn vehicles were registered in Chicago in 1915, with about 7,000 registered motor trucks. In 1920 about 20,000 horse-drawn vehicles were registered, a decrease of 60%, while the number of trucks had grown to nearly 23,000, an increase of over 300%. In 1929 only 11,000 horse-drawn vehicles remained in Chicago, while almost 58,000 trucks were registered. In 1929 then, only 16% of delivery vehicles were horse powered. Replacement continued throughout the next 15 years (McKenzie 1933, p. 272).

Use of the auto in the journey to work became dominant in this period. In 1916, 83% of the persons entering the central business district of Saint Louis came by streetcar, with 17% coming in automobiles. In 1926, 26% used cars, 7% buses, and 57% the streetcar. By 1937, 45% used cars, 12% buses, and only 27% streetcars. As early as 1937 motor vehicles had replaced the streetcar and train as the primary movers of people in Saint Louis, capturing some 57% of the riding market (Queen and Carpenter 1953, p. 200). Of course, displacement patterns vary by city. For example, in 1926 only 19% of the workers entering the Chicago central business district and 32% of those entering the San Francisco central business district used private automobiles. Yet, in 1929, 54.5% of the persons entering the Kansas City central business district and almost 66% of the riders in Washington's central business district used automobiles. In addition, large numbers of riders in each city were using motor buses (McKenzie 1933, p. 282).

POST–WORLD WAR II

Rapid suburbanization of people and businesses began after World War II on a large scale, sometimes served by no other transportation except motor vehicles. Suburban railroad and airport connections for industry have remained important, but the truck has become the primary intraurban mover of goods and freight. Some cities have mass transit that still serves commuters, but the vast majority of urbanites now travel by automobile in the diffused metropolis. Urban areas have become multinodal, connected by vast systems of streets and highways.

The post–World War II suburban boom began in the late 1940s. This rapid diffusion is reflected in the rates of growth within SMSAs (Standard Metropolitan Statistical Areas) between 1940 and 1950. While SMSAs grew as a whole by some 22.6%, central cities grew by only 14.7% while the suburbs grew 35.9% (U.S. Bureau of the Census 1964, p. 98). Nearly all this increase followed the war. Many central cities renewed their growth, which was suppressed during the 1930s, but this reflects the pull of the city for a war-related labor force. In the decade 1940–50, for example, Saint Louis gained 5% in population after registering a loss in the 1930s (U.S. Bureau of the Census 1952, pp. 1, 69, 73). But this brief period during World War II was the last time population increased. Suburban growth completely dominated this, and most metropolitan areas, after 1945.

In terms of absolute numbers, the period between 1950 and 1960 was the decade of greatest suburban expansion in American history. While SMSAs grew at a rate of 26.4%, from 95 to 120 million, central cities grew by only 11.6%, from 54 to 60 million. The suburbs grew by a rate of 45.9%, from 41 to 60 million. Suburbs accounted for over 75% of the population growth for SMSAs between 1950 and 1960. Expansion that did occur in the central city took place primarily in the growing cities of the South and West: Atlanta, Dallas, Denver, Houston, Miami, and San Jose showed large population increases (U.S. Bureau of the Census 1972a, pp. 1, 171, 189). By contrast, the older cities of the East and Midwest experienced rapid decline between 1950 and 1960. Boston lost 13% of its population, while the suburbs grew by 18%; Buffalo lost 8% of its inhabitants, but the suburbs gained 52% more people; Saint Louis city lost 13% of its population, while the areas outside the city gained 51%. Many suburban areas grew by more than 100% or 150% in this single decade (ibid.).

This same pattern was repeated between 1960 and 1970, although the rates were slower and the numbers smaller. Total SMSAs grew by 16.6%, from over 120 to over 139 million. Central cities grew by only 6.4%, from 60 to 64 million inhabitants. The suburbs grew by 16 million, from 60 to 76 million people, an increase of 26.8%. Again, growth outside the central city accounted for 75% of the increase in the SMSAs (ibid.).

This rapid growth of the suburbs has included fast geographic expansion. The central cities of New York, Detroit, Philadelphia, Cleveland, Saint Louis, Washington, Boston, San Francisco, Pittsburgh, and Milwaukee all occupied less than 25% of the total square miles of their respective metropolitan areas in 1960. Chicago and Los Angeles both occupied less than 40% of their metropolitan space. Only the new cities—Houston, San Diego, and Phoenix—occupied most of the land in their metropolitan areas (U.S. Bureau of the Census 1972b, pp. 1–6).

To accommodate an increasingly decentralized population, most residential construction has taken place in the suburban areas. The number of housing units inside SMSAs grew from about 25.6 million in 1950 to over 46 million in 1970. But the location of these new housing units occurred primarily outside the central cities. Of the 21 million additional housing units, only about 7 million were located inside the central city (ibid.). In addition, by 1965, of the 38 million housing units in metropolitan areas, about 26 million were one-unit structures. The differences between the cities and their fringes were substantial. Sixty-one percent of all single-family units were located outside the central city (Ganz 1968, p. 68).

Not only have the suburbs experienced rapid population growth, they have also had increased industrial and commercial expansion. Between 1948 and 1963 the 25 largest metropolitan areas registered tremendous growth. Manufacturing employment grew by 16%, trade by 21%, and selected services by 53%. But the central cities of these 25 metropolitan areas lost an average of 7% in manufacturing employment and 7% in trade employment, while gaining 32% in the selected-service sector. Outside the central city the growth rates were tremendous. Manufacturing employment grew by 61%, trade by 122%, and services by a whopping 135% (ibid., p. 39).

The suburban boom in retail trade and services has been characterized by new planned shopping centers. Shopping centers had always been present in downtowns along streetcar routes, or at line intersections. But contiguous stores built with parking space to accommodate motor transport were an addition of the motor age. The planned shopping center is convenient for use of both trucks and cars. The first planned center was built in 1907 (Jackson 1973, p. 215), but in 1946 there were still only eight in the country. But by 1960 there were an estimated 3,800 such centers, most with a floor area of over 50,000 square feet (Rae 1965, p. 230).

Rapid industrial expansion has also created enormous demand for trucks. This demand was reflected in tremendous growth for the truck industry. Between 1945 and 1955 the number of registered trucks doubled from about 5 million vehicles to over 10 million. Another 5 million were added to the registration lists between 1955 and 1965—a growth of 50%, for a total just under 15 million trucks in 1965 (Automobile Manufacturers Association 1969, p. 13). By 1972 some 21 million trucks were registered in the United States—a growth of 300% since the end of World War II (Automobile Manufacturers Association 1974, p. 22).

The 1947 production of trucks and buses—over 1.2 million units—was about twice the depression-war average. Except at times of recession, production stayed at a steady rate—between 1 and 1.9 million units annually between 1947 and 1968 (Automobile Manufacturers Association 1969, p. 3). Production of trucks reached a new high in 1973: some 3 million trucks and buses were manufactured—two and one-half times the number built in 1947 (Automobile Manufacturers Association 1974, p. 5).

The postwar suburban boom brought with it a demand for automobiles parallel to the growth of the 1920s. In 1946 over 2 million cars were built; by 1953 over 6 million cars were built—a growth of 200%. Production remained between 5 and 7 million from 1953 through 1964, when another large boom occurred. Some 9.3 million cars were built in 1965 (Automobile Manufacturers Association 1967, p. 3), with this figure being fairly constant until the present (Automobile Manufacturers Association 1972, p. 1). Registrations climbed between 1945 and 1955 from 25 to over 51 million in 1955 (Automobile Manufacturers Association 1971, p. 18). Between 1955 and 1973 the number of cars registered doubled again to over 100 million (Automobile Manufacturers Association 1974, p. 18).

THE FUTURE OF MOTOR TRANSPORTATION IN THE METROPOLIS

Although the motor metropolis has experienced geographic diffusion far beyond the restrictions of the streetcar city, the limits of space have remained. The use of motor vehicles has certainly extended these limits but has not removed them. Some individuals may now travel 20–50 miles daily to work or shop but few drive 100 miles, and except for a very few daily airplane commuters, no one travels distances of 500 miles or more each day to work. Clearly, transportation technology has not yet eliminated space as a critical determinant of urban form. Urban functions are still constrained by the cost and speed of transportation.

Sometime in the future, communications innovations may further reduce space constraints for specific functions. But for the immediate future transportation, particularly motor vehicles, will likely continue to be a major factor in the development of metropolitan structure. Suburban development will likely continue within the boundaries set by the outer-belt freeways, and perhaps slightly beyond. Most development will probably continue in the vacant spaces still left within the skeleton of the freeway structure. This land will likely remain cost attractive for both residential and commercial use.

Furthermore, automobiles and trucks will probably remain within the economic reach of most consumers. Of course, the recent "energy crisis" and rising gasoline prices have raised the possiblity that motor transportation might soon be out of the reach of most consumers. This scenario seems unlikely for a number of reasons. First, engines that will use less gasoline are in the process of development. Some predictions are that these engines will be 50% more efficient. Individuals are currently purchasing smaller cars that utilize half the fuel that larger models now use. People are also driving less. In short, consumption of gasoline might drop and efficiency will probably rise. In the near future these factors will partially compensate for rising fuel costs, although private transportation might be somewhat more expensive to purchase. It is also possible that fuel prices will not continue to rise substantially. While it is unlikely that an alternative energy source for private transportation will be developed in the next few years, it is not impossible that major new sources of petroleum will be discovered and distributed, lowering the price of petroleum. In either scenario, the continued dominance of the highway–motor vehicle transport system is most likely in the near future.

In a more distant future, however, supplies of land and fuel might diminish to the point that these resource constraints will begin to alter institutions and values. The ascendance of a new transportation system might occur and, with it, a new urban form. However, these contingencies are entirely matters for speculation.

For the immediate future, then, changes do not seem imminent. The present spatial structure of urban America is, after all, not the unwanted mistake of the widespread use of motor vehicles. Rather it is the product of private markets, social values, institutional supports, and the availability of a convenient transportation mode to meet the demands of the urban consumer. Americans originally adopted motor vehicles because the automobile and truck offered the most appealing transportation alternative for use in the expanding city. Continued use of motor vehicles has depended on their constant superiority as efficient and convenient transportation modes in a diffuse metropolis. Unless urbanites begin to demand reconcentration, or the cost of motor vehicles forces them to choose more-dense urban living, the automobile and truck will not be replaced. The suburban metropolis is likely to remain in its present form for years to come.

REFERENCES

Alonso, William. 1964. *Location and Land Use*. Cambridge, Mass.: Harvard University Press.
American Agriculturist. 1912. 89 (October): 343.
Automobile Manufacturers Association. 1967. *1967 Automobile Facts and Figures*. Detroit: Automobile Manufacturers Association.
———. 1969. *Motor Truck Facts 1969*. Detroit: Automobile Manufacturers Association.
———. 1971. *Automobile Facts and Figures*. Detroit: Automobile Manufacturers Association.
———. 1972. *Automobile Facts and Figures*. Detroit: Automobile Manufacturers Association.
———. 1974. *1974 Motor Truck Facts*. Detroit: Automobile Manufacturers Association.
Bolce, Harold. 1908. "The Horse vs. Health." *Appleton's Magazine* 11 (May): 532–38.
Callow, Alexander B., Jr., ed. 1969. *American Urban History*. New York: Oxford University Press.
Casson, Herbert N., L. W. Ellis, and Rollin W. Hutchinson, Jr. 1913. *Horse, Truck and Tractor*. Chicago: Browne.
Farm Journal. 1909. 32 (May): 247.
Flink, James J. 1971. *America Adopts the Automobile, 1895–1910*. Cambridge, Mass.: M.I.T. Press.
Ganz, Alexander. 1968. *Emerging Patterns of Urban Growth and Travel*. Cambridge, Mass.: M.I.T., Department of City and Regional Planning.
Glaab, Charles A., and A. Theodore Brown. 1967. *A History of Urban America*. New York: Macmillan.
Hébert, Richard. 1972. *The Politics of City Transportation*. Indianapolis: Bobbs-Merrill.

Tobin

Holt, Glen E. 1972. "The Changing Perception of Urban Pathology: An Essay on the Development of Mass Transit in the United States." Pp. 324–43 in *Cities in American History*, edited by Kenneth T. Jackson and Stanley K. Schultz. New York: Knopf.

Hoyt, Homer. 1960. "The Status of Shopping Centers in the United States." *Urban Land* 19 (October): 3–6. Quoted in John B. Rae, *The Road and the Car in American Life*. Cambridge, Mass.: M.I.T. Press, 1971.

Jackson, Kenneth T. 1973. "The Crabgrass Frontier: 150 Years of Suburban Growth in America." Pp. 191–213 in *The Urban Experience: Themes in American History*, edited by Raymond A. Mohl and James F. Richardson. Belmont, Calif.: Wadsworth.

Kitagawa, Evelyn M., and Donald J. Bogue. 1955. *Suburbanization of Manufacturing Activity within Standard Metropolitan Areas*. Oxford, Ohio: Scripps Foundation.

McKelvey, Blake. 1963. *The Urbanization of America*. New Brunswick, N.J.: Rutgers University Press.

———. 1968. *The Emergence of Metropolitan America*. New Brunswick, N.J.: Rutgers University Press.

McKenzie, Roderick D. 1933. *The Metropolitan Community*. New York: McGraw-Hill.

New York Times. 1899. "Topics of the Times." (June 14).

———. 1903*a*. "Another Remedy for Congestion." (January 18).

———. 1903*b*. "Rapid Transit Service to Bath Beach." (November 22).

———. 1906*a* "Horse Caused Two Mishaps." (February 4).

———. 1906*b*. "Runaway Team Dashes through Theatre Crowd." (February 4).

———. 1906*c*. "Nym Crinkles Daughter Killed in a Runaway." (June 4).

———. 1906*d*. "Law and Mob Rule." (August 15).

———. 1906*e*. "More B.R.T. Rows. Trolleys Taken Off." (August 15).

———. 1906*f*. "Watch on Street Can Uphold Complaints." (September 15).

Queen, Stuart A., and David Carpenter. 1953. *The American City*. New York: McGraw-Hill.

Rae, John B. 1965. *The American Automobile*. Chicago: University of Chicago Press.

———. 1971. *The Road and the Car in American Life*. Cambridge, Mass.: M.I.T. Press.

Schneider, Kenneth R. 1971. *Autokind vs. Mankind*. New York: Norton.

Tarr, Joel A. 1971. "Urban Pollution Many Long Years Ago." *American Heritage* 22 (October): 65–70.

Tobin, Gary A. 1974. "The Bicycle Boom of the 1890s: The Development of Private Transportation and the Birth of the Modern Tourist." *Journal of Popular Culture* 7 (Spring): 837–49.

U.S. Bureau of the Census. 1909. *Industrial Districts: 1905. Manufactures and Population*. Bulletin 101. Washington, D.C.: Government Printing Office.

———. 1915. *Central Electric Light and Power Stations and Street and Electric Railways with Summary of the Electrical Industries. 1912*. Washington, D.C.: Government Printing Office.

———. 1918. *Census of Manufactures: 1914*. Vol. 1. *Reports by Streets with Statistics for Principal Cities and Metropolitan Districts*. Washington, D.C.: Government Printing Office.

———. 1932. *Fifteenth Census of the United States: 1930. Metropolitan Districts: Population and Area*. Washington, D.C.: Government Printing Office.

———. 1947. *Population: The Growth of Metropolitan Districts in the United States: 1900–1940*. Washington, D.C.: Government Printing Office.

———. 1952. *Census of Population: 1950*. Vol. 1. *Number of Inhabitants*. Washington, D.C.: Government Printing Office.

———. 1964. *Population Trends in the United States: 1900–1960*. Washington, D.C.: Government Printing Office.

———. 1972*a*. *1970 Census of Population*. Vol. 1. *Characteristics of the Population, Part I: United States Summary, Section I*. Washington, D.C.: Government Printing Office.

———. 1972*b*. *Census of Population: 1970: General Population Characteristics, United States*

Summary. Final Report PC(1)-B1. Washington, D.C.: Government Printing Office.

U.S. Department of the Interior. Census Office. 1895. *Report on the Social Statistics of Cities in the United States at the Eleventh Census: 1890.* Washington, D.C.: Government Printing Office.

Warner, Sam B., Jr. 1962. *Streetcar Suburbs: The Process of Growth in Boston, 1870–1900.* New York: Atheneum.

―――. 1968. *The Private City.* Philadelphia: University of Pennsylvania Press.

Weber, Adna Ferrin. 1899. *The Growth of Cities in the Nineteenth Century.* Ithaca, N.Y.: Cornell University Press.

Withington, Sidney. 1931. "Railroad Electrification of 4,500 Miles." *Railway Journal* 31 (September): 537–41.

5 The Changing Occupational Structure of
the American Metropolis: Apropos the Urban Problem

John D. Kasarda
Florida Atlantic University

The expansion of the compact city of 19th-century America into the diffuse metropolitan community of the present has provided social scientists with a dramatic example of urban ecological change. The Bureau of the Census first recognized the inadequacy of the political area of the city as an ecological unit for measuring urban aggregation in 1910, when they introduced the category "Metropolitan District" to their system of areal classification. Since that time, metropolitan growth has continued without interruption. In every decade between 1910 and 1970, at least two-thirds of the national increase in population occurred within metropolitan areas. By 1974, over 151 million people, or nearly three-fourths of the U.S. population, resided within the 250 metropolitan communities that were designated as Standard Metropolitan Statistical Areas (SMSAs).

Population growth, however, is only one demographic manifestation of the expansion process. Another is deconcentration, or the movement outward from the center of settlement. Deconcentration occurs in a relative sense when suburban areas grow at a faster rate than the central cities. My recent analysis (1974) of demographic change in 247 SMSAs showed that deconcentration began, in metropolitan areas as a whole, at least as far back as 1900 and has accelerated to the present.

The growth and deconcentration of the metropolitan population has been matched by significant changes in the ecological structure of central cities and suburban rings. The dispersion of retail establishments and standard consumer services closely followed the centrifugal drift of metropolitan population. According to the International Council of Shopping Centers, some 14,000 shopping centers have been constructed in this country since 1954— most of them to serve expanding suburban populations.[1] During the same period, there has been a substantial drift of manufacturing activity to the suburban rings. Between 1947 and 1967, the central cities of our 23 largest

---

This research was financed, in part, from funds granted to The University of Chicago Center for Urban Studies by the Ford Foundation and from funds contributed by the Joint Center for Environmental and Urban Problems, Florida Atlantic University. The author is deeply indebted to George V. Redfearn, who furnished substantial computational assistance.

[1] More than one-half of the country's retail sales now take place in shopping centers, compared with 15% at the end of World War II (see *U.S. News and World Report* 1974).

and oldest SMSAs lost an average of 17,370 manufacturing positions, while their suburban rings gained an average of nearly 85,000 positions.

Along with the centrifugal drift of manufacturing activity and establishments offering standard consumer goods and services, there has been a centripetal buildup in the cities of professional, financial, communicative, and specialized business services. The specialized nature of many of these functions requires them to have a median location (Chinitz 1964; Thompson 1965; Vernon 1960). These specialized facilities have been accumulating in the central business districts and have replaced standard goods-and-services establishments that were unable to withstand the increasing land value of a central location.[2]

Another prominent centripetal movement has been in the administrative sector (Armstrong 1972; Berry and Cohen 1973; Cowan et al. 1969). Administrative headquarters rely on large pools of clerical workers and a complement of financial, legal, professional, and technical services which are often available only in the central business districts. The growing demand for centralized office space has stimulated the construction of an increasing number of downtown office complexes. In the central business districts of some of our larger metropolitan areas, the office-building binge has reached staggering proportions (Carruth 1969; Manners 1974; McQuade 1973).[3] As we shall observe later, many of our central cities are becoming occupationally specialized in professional, technical, and clerical office functions.

No doubt, the growth of administrative, professional, and specialized business services in the central cities together with the dispersion of population, manufacturing activity, and establishments providing standard (consumer) goods and services has transformed the structure of the metropolitan community. Through these centripetal and centrifugal movements, an extensive network of territorial interdependences has been fostered within each SMSA (Kasarda 1972b). But the expansion of the metropolitan community has also created serious problems for the viability of our central cities. These problems, which include high unemployment, rising welfare rolls, shrinking tax bases, and growing public-service demands, are direct consequences of movements inherent in the expansion process. Let me elaborate.

[2] The average rental fees that establishments have been willing to pay for space in Manhattan, e.g., have increased from $4.50 per square foot in 1966 to $6.50 per square foot in 1968. In 1969, future 1970–71 space was renting at $10.00 per square foot and for $22.00 per square foot on Fifth Avenue (Carruth 1969).

[3] In downtown Chicago, we have witnessed, during the past three years, the completion of three of the five tallest office buildings in the world (the Sears Tower alone houses over 20,000 employees) along with a plethora of relatively smaller (40–75-story) office structures. Manners (1974) reports that between 1960 and 1972, central business-district office space grew by 52% in Chicago, 74% in New York City, 79% in San Francisco, 82% in Atlanta, and by 100% in Houston. Armstrong (1972), Berry and Cohen (1973), and McQuade (1973) report similar trends in other large central cities.

The centrifugal and centripetal forces of expansion operate on two fundamental sectors of the metropolitan community—the residential sector and the employment sector. In the residential sector, it is well documented that persons with better educational backgrounds who generally hold white-collar jobs have been dispersing to the suburban rings (Guest 1971; Haggerty 1971; Pinkerton 1969; Schnore 1972; Smith 1970). Conversely, persons with weaker educational backgrounds who generally hold blue-collar positions continue to drift to the urban centers (Hawley and Zimmer 1970). The implication of these movements, of course, is that our central cities are becoming the domicile of disproportionately large numbers of less-educated blue-collar workers, while the suburban rings are developing as the residential locus of the better-educated, white-collar worker.

Unfortunately, conflicting movements have been occurring in the employment sector. We noted that jobs having lower educational requirements, such as those in manufacturing and standard consumer trade, are dispersing to the suburban rings, while jobs requiring higher education, such as those in administration, the professions, and specialized business services, are accumulating in the central cities.

The changing distribution of employment opportunities in the metropolis has been especially detrimental to large numbers of lower-class residents of the central cities, particularly poor minority groups. The educational backgrounds of these people are not appropriate for the new (white-collar) functions accumulating in the central cities, and many cannot afford the growing cost of commuting by automobile to blue-collar jobs dispersed throughout the suburban rings. Moreover, suburban zoning restrictions on low-cost housing and discriminatory practices prevent the vast majority of the urban poor from obtaining inexpensive residential sites near expanding suburban industries (Downs 1973; Kain 1968; National Committee against Discrimination in Housing 1970). The outcome is that central-city unemployment is now more than twice the national average and even higher among city residents who have traditionally found employment in blue-collar industries caught in the suburban drift (Friedlander 1972; Harrison 1972; Hosken 1973).[4]

High unemployment rates (and concomitant rising welfare rolls) among central-city residents are only two of the deleterious implications of the changing structure of metropolitan areas. The centrifugal and centripetal movements of expansion have also been instrumental in eroding the tax base of central cities while creating an even greater need for public services in the city. Most of our central cities are plagued with rising debt service, with no apparent reversal of the trend in sight.

---

[4] A survey of Negro areas of nine central cities conducted by the Department of Labor in 1967 showed that 32.7% of their labor force were either unemployed or underemployed (National Commission on Civil Disorders 1968).

It is suggested that four components of the expansion process are at the root of the widening service-resource gap afflicting the central cities. These are: (1) the exodus to the suburban rings of middle- and upper-income families; (2) the large influx into the central cities of poor minority groups, mainly black and brown; (3) the centrifugal drift of commerce and industry beyond the taxing jurisdiction of the central cities and beyond the reach of the urban poor; and (4) the daily flow into the central cities of large numbers of suburbanites who make routine use of central-city public services as part of their journey to work, recreation, and shopping activities.[5] As a consequence of these four interrelated movements, central-city governments are finding themselves in the difficult position of having to meet increased public-service demands with shrinking resource bases. The fundamental problem is not insufficient metropolitan resources to support municipal services but that, in the process of urban expansion, the bulk of these resources has been redistributed to the politically autonomous suburban rings.

In this paper, I shall examine the nature and extent of the redistribution of economic opportunity in the American metropolis since World War II. I will then assess its implications for the separation of home from workplace of different occupational and racial groups. My guiding hypothesis is that the centrifugal and centripetal movements of metropolitan expansion have exacerbated current urban problems by eroding central-city tax bases and by spatially removing employment opportunities from those who need them the most.

DATA AND METHODS

All data that I will analyze come from publications of the U.S. Bureau of the Census. To examine the centrifugal drift of manufacturing employment, data for 245 SMSAs were gathered from the 1947 and 1967 Censuses of Manufacturers. For longitudinal comparability, SMSA boundaries were adjusted to constant areas according to the latest SMSA definitions (National

[5] In the expanded community, the suburban population makes regular use of central-city streets, parks, zoos, museums, and other public facilities. The daily presence of many suburbanites in the central city increases the problems of the sanitation department; it also creates additional fire risks which are reflected in the allocation of funds for fire protection. The routine movement in and out of the central city of a large commuting population leads to traffic congestion on city arteries and is a major factor in the budget of both the police and highway-maintenance departments. Hence, central-city expenditures for such services as police, fire, highway, sanitation, and recreation have been shown to be at least as sensitive to the size of the suburban population (and the commuting population, in particular) as to the size or composition of the central-city population itself (Kasarda 1972a).

Bureau of Standards 1973). Since SMSAs are composed of counties (except in New England, where towns and cities are used), adjustments for peripheral boundary changes were made by adding or deleting appropriate county data at a particular date. In New England, SMSAs were reconstructed in terms of county units to make them definitionally comparable to metropolitan areas in other regions of the nation.

It was also necessary to adjust these data to correct for intrametropolitan boundary changes. Annexation and consolidation systematically understate suburban-ring growth and overstate central-city growth. Adjustments for central-city annexation were made by employing a correction factor based on the proportion of suburban population annexed by central cities between 1950 and 1960 and between 1960 and 1970. Using this correction factor and conventional techniques of extrapolation and interpolation, it is possible to reconstruct all metropolitan manufacturing data in terms of 1950 central-city boundaries.[6]

Along with employment data from the Censuses of Manufacturers, place-of-work data by occupation for the labor force residing in 101 longitudinally comparable SMSA central cities and suburban rings were obtained from the Detailed Characteristic state reports of the 1960 and 1970 Censuses of Population. The sample includes all SMSAs that had 100,000 or more population in 1960 and neither added nor deleted central cities or outlying counties to their definition between 1960 and 1970.[7] The place-of-work data enabled me to construct and compare the occupational distributions within central cities and suburban rings in 1960 and 1970 and to examine their changing occupa-

---

[6] The 1967 data were adjusted to 1950 boundaries by a two-step procedure. First, the 1967 data were adjusted to 1960 boundaries using the formula CCEMP6760 = CCEMP6767 − [(.7 × ANNEX6070/CCPOP6770) × CCEMP6767], where CCEMP6760 is 1967 central-city manufacturing employment in 1960 boundaries, CCEMP6767 is the reported 1967 manufacturing employment in 1967 central-city boundaries, ANNEX6070 is the population annexed by the central city between 1960 and 1970, and CCPOP6770 is the 1967 central-city population in 1970 boundaries (obtained through linear interpolation). The 1967 central-city employment in 1960 boundaries is then adjusted to 1950 boundaries by using the formula CCEMP6750 = CCEMP6760 − [(ANNEX5060/CCPOP6070) × CCEMP6760], where CCEMP6750 is the 1967 central-city employment in 1950 boundaries, ANNEX5060 is the population annexed by the central city between 1950 and 1960, and CCPOP6070 is the 1960 central-city population in 1970 boundaries. Since SMSA boundaries remain constant, 1967 suburban-ring manufacturing employment in 1950 suburban boundaries is obtained by subtracting 1967 central-city manufacturing employment in 1950 boundaries from reported 1967 SMSA employment. We further assumed that central-city annexation of territory containing manufacturing establishments in 1948 and 1949 was negligible.

[7] As a further control, SMSAs whose central cities annexed population between 1960 and 1970 that exceeded 20% of their 1960 population were excluded. Statistical adjustments for occupational annexation by those cities in the sample which did annex population are described in the Appendix.

tional composition. If my working assumptions are correct, we should find central cities becoming increasingly specialized in white-collar functions as blue-collar functions shift to the suburban rings.[8]

Since metropolitan place-of-work data are cross-classified by residence (central city or suburban ring), I will also examine changing commuting patterns of white-collar and blue-collar workers. Furthermore, where longitudinally comparable commuting data are available for both Negroes and whites, their journey-to-work flows will be examined and compared to assess differential changes in separation of residence from workplace. In all cases where longitudinal comparisons of journey-to-work flows are made, appropriate adjustments will be made for possible workplace as well as residential annexation. The techniques for adjusting place-of-work data for annexation by occupation, residence, and race are described in the appendix of this article.

RESULTS

Let us begin with an examination of the growth and redistribution of manufacturing employment in SMSAs since World War II. Table 1 provides an overview.

It is apparent that, adjusting for annexation, recent growth in SMSA manufacturing employment has been due primarily to increases in manufacturing activity in the suburban rings. Between 1947 and 1967, central cities registered a net loss of 293,307 manufacturing jobs, or a 4% overall decline. On the other hand, manufacturing employment in the suburban rings in-

---

[8] Two caveats should be noted here. First, the place-of-work data reported in the Detailed Characteristic tables refer to the resident labor force within each SMSA. Excluded are workers who live entirely outside the SMSA but commute to work in the central cities and suburban rings. Although the vast majority of metropolitan workers do reside within their SMSA of employment, two assumptions must hold for our analysis of these data to be precise. First, the aggregate occupational distribution of workers in the central cities and suburban rings who commute from outside the SMSA is the same as the aggregate distribution of metropolitan residents employed in the central cities and suburban rings. Second, the aggregate numbers of central-city and suburban-ring workers who live outside the SMSAs did not substantially change between 1960 and 1970. Since there are obviously central-city and suburban workers who do commute from outside the SMSA, the absolute figures we report cross-sectionally will be biased downward for both cities and rings. However, the percent distributions, relative differences, and employment changes over time should be representative.

A second caveat is necessary, because place-of-work data in the 1960 census were reported by occupation for employed metropolitan residents 14 years of age and older, while the 1970 place-of-work data were reported by occupation for employed metropolitan residents 16 and older. We do not believe, though, that the exclusion of 14- and 15-year-old metropolitan employees in 1970 will substantially influence our results.

TABLE 1

MANUFACTURING EMPLOYMENT IN 245 SMSAs, THEIR CENTRAL CITIES, AND
SUBURBAN RINGS, 1947–67*

	1947	1967	Change, 1947–67
Central cities	7,356,733	7,063,426	−293,307
Suburban rings	4,141,704	8,044,030	3,902,326
SMSAs	11,498,437	15,107,458	3,609,021

*Constant SMSA boundaries with adjustments for annexation.

creased by 3,902,326, representing a 94% increase in suburban manufacturing employment over a two-decade period. The dramatic growth of manufacturing employment in the suburban rings together with the absolute declines in central cities increased the suburban share of total SMSA manufacturing employment from 36% in 1947 to 53% in 1967.

What are the reasons for this remarkable shift of manufacturing activity to the suburban rings? One important factor is post–World War II changes in production technology, especially capital intensification and new assembly-line techniques which have large single-story space requirements. Many existing central-city factories are of the older multistory design and are thus inappropriate for today's mass-production technology. Numerous manufacturers have found it more efficient and less expensive to build entirely new facilities on relatively cheap suburban land than to redesign and convert their obsolete central-city structures. Likewise, entering industries with extensive areal requirements found it exceedingly difficult to obtain large tracts of central-city land at practical costs, and they have also turned predominately to open space in the suburban rings for their plant sites.

Another factor stimulating the suburban manufacturing drift has been changing modes and improvements in short-distance transportation. The widespread development of suburban highway systems since World War II, pervasive automobile ownership, and increased reliance on trucking for freight shipments have operated concurrently to attract manufacturers to the suburban rings. Many manufacturers recognized that by locating outside the congested centers, yet near a suburban expressway, their transport costs could be substantially reduced, an adequate metropolitan labor supply could be tapped, and problems of limited employee-parking space and freight-transfer areas could be solved. Traffic congestion and lack of sufficient employee-parking space have been particularly troublesome for large manufacturers located in older, more densely settled central cities where street designs were established well before the age of the automobile and truck.

A third, yet no less important, reason for the decentralization of industry has been the spread of public services throughout the suburban rings and the expansion of other external economies. Large industrial facilities require communication and power lines, water supplies, highway services, and police and fire protection. Before World War II, such public services were confined largely to the central cities and their adjacent built-up areas. With the extension of these services throughout the suburban rings, manufacturers have had much greater freedom of location within the metropolitan periphery. At the same time, urban expansion brought numerous subcontractors, local suppliers, and business and repair services to the suburban rings— external economies that, in the past, were available to manufacturers only within the confines of the central cities.

There is no reason to suspect, however, that manufacturing decentralization has exhibited a uniform pattern in all SMSAs. Plant obsolescence, lack of open space, and traffic congestion have been particularly prevalent in larger, older central cities located in the northeastern and north-central states. When we examine average changes of manufacturing employment in central cities and suburban rings by SMSA size, age, and region, we find such characteristics to have substantial effects (see table 2).[9]

By 1950, the large, old central cities in the northeast and midwest had filled up most of their remaining open space, leaving only the suburban ring free for additional industrial development. Younger and smaller SMSA central cities and those located in the south and west typically had more open areas for industrial development. In addition, since most of the latter SMSAs were patterned during the automobile age, they are less congested and have better access routes for freight transfer. The large differences between central-city and suburban manufacturing-employment change within the various types of SMSAs clearly reflect the influence of these factors.

Bearing in mind that, since World War II, the greatest absolute growth of lower-income population has been predominantly in large northeastern and midwestern central cities, we further cross-classified manufacturing employment changes, by region, for SMSAs of 1 million or more population. The results are striking. Adjusting for annexation, central cities of the 16 largest northeastern and north-central SMSAs lost an average of 34,571 manufacturing positions between 1947 and 1967, while their suburban rings gained an average of 86,358 positions. Conversely, central cities of the 17 largest southern and western SMSAs gained an average of 19,756 manufacturing positions, and their suburban rings gained an average of 64,936 positions. The important figures, however, pertain to the 16 largest northeastern

---

[9] The average changes are based on weighted means in 1947 and 1967. It is thus possible to compute absolute changes in manufacturing employment within each category of SMSA by multiplying the mean change by N. All means presented in subsequent tables are also weighted means.

TABLE 2

Mean Change in Manufacturing Employment within 245 SMSAs, Their Central Cities, and Suburban Rings by SMSA Size, Age, and Region, 1947–67*

| | | Mean Change in Manufacturing Employment, 1947–67 | | |
Metropolitan Characteristic	N	SMSAs	Central Cities	Suburban Rings
Size:				
Under 250,000	113	3,457	307	3,150
250,000–500,000	63	7,800	−619	8,419
500,000–1 million	36	12,741	−1,993	14,734
Over 1 million...........	33	68,739	−6,584	75,323
Inception date (age):				
After 1950	80	6,321	659	5,662
1930–50	53	9,846	1,857	7,989
1900–20	63	13,142	1,974	11,168
Before 1900	49	35,785	−11,609	47,394
Region:				
Northeast	42	11,040	−8,216	19,256
North-central	68	11,350	−6,827	18,177
South	98	11,935	2,646	9,289
West	37	32,513	6,939	25,574
Total	245	14,731	−1,197	15,928

*Constant SMSA boundaries with adjustments for annexation.

and north-central SMSAs, where central-city manufacturing employment fell a total of approximately 550,000 positions, or an average *annual* decline of over 1,700 manufacturing jobs per city between 1947 and 1967.

Having focused thus far on the centrifugal drift of manufacturing employment, let us now broaden our analysis to cover recent shifts in the overall occupational structure of central cities and suburban rings. Table 3 presents the mean number of employed persons by occupation for 101 longitudinally comparable central cities and suburban rings in 1960 and 1970.[10]

Central-city employment in all occupational categories, with the exception of professional, clerical, and service functions, declined between 1960 and 1970. The largest declines were in the blue-collar categories—craftsmen and operatives. On the other hand, suburban-ring employment expanded in all occupational categories, with the anticipated exception of farm workers. Like central cities, the largest suburban increases were in professional, clerical,

[10] Since we are reporting weighted means, the total number of employed persons in each occupational category may be obtained by multiplying each mean by 101.

TABLE 3

MEAN NUMBER OF EMPLOYEES BY OCCUPATION IN 101 LONGITUDINALLY
COMPARABLE SMSA CENTRAL CITIES AND SUBURBAN RINGS, 1960–70

OCCUPATIONAL CATEGORY	MEAN N CENTRAL-CITY EMPLOYEES			MEAN N SUBURBAN-RING EMPLOYEES		
	1960	1970*	Change, 1960–70	1960	1970*	Change, 1960–70
Professional and technical	16,015	20,138	4,123	9,392	16,203	6,811
Managers and proprietors	12,458	11,354	−1,104	5,787	8,288	2,501
Clerical workers	26,915	30,002	3,087	10,066	18,411	8,345
Sales workers.........	11,113	9,813	−1,300	5,209	7,921	2,712
Craftsmen...........	18,041	16,043	−1,998	11,684	14,575	2,891
Operatives	25,078	19,838	−5,240	14,263	17,501	3,238
Laborers	5,676	4,668	−1,010	3,649	4,363	714
Service workers.......	15,669	15,713	44	8,393	12,630	4,237
Farm workers	232	203	−29	2,691	1,506	−1,185

*Central-city and suburban employment figures adjusted for annexation between 1960 and 1970.

and service functions. Unlike central cities, however, suburban rings exhibited substantial gains in craftsmen and operatives. Adjusting for occupational annexation, suburban rings of the 101 SMSAs gained an average of 30,264 employees, while the central cities registered an average net loss of 3,427 employees between 1960 and 1970.

It was noted earlier that recent decentralization patterns have been highly selective—removing large numbers of blue-collar functions from the central cities and replacing them with white-collar functions. Table 4 substantiates this contention.

Aggregating central-city and suburban employment into white-collar and blue-collar categories (excluding farm workers), we see that between 1960 and 1970 blue-collar employment in the 101 central cities declined by over 825,000 positions, yet white-collar employment increased by nearly 500,000 positions. This represents a 12.7% reduction in all central-city blue-collar jobs during the decade, with a concurrent 7.2% increase in central-city white-collar positions.

The suburban rings show huge increases in both white-collar and blue-collar functions. Interestingly, however, white-collar employment in the suburbs grew at more than twice the rate of blue-collar employment. Between 1960 and 1970, suburban white-collar jobs increased by 67%, while blue-collar jobs increased by 29%. As a result, in 1970, suburban rings were the locus of more white-collar employment than blue-collar employment.

It is also noteworthy that the overall occupational composition of the

TABLE 4

TOTAL NUMBER OF WHITE-COLLAR AND BLUE-COLLAR EMPLOYEES (EXCLUDING FARMERS) WORKING IN 101 LONGITUDINALLY COMPARABLE SMSA CENTRAL CITIES AND SUBURBAN RINGS, 1960–70

	1960	1970*	Change, 1960–70
Central cities:			
White-collar	6,716,618	7,202,065	485,447
Blue-collar	6,510,906	5,682,649	−828,257
Suburban rings:			
White-collar	3,075,938	5,133,061	2,059,123
Blue-collar	3,836,919	4,956,053	1,119,134

*Central-city and suburban employment adjusted for annexation.

suburban rings in 1970 (i.e., 51% white-collar and 49% blue-collar) was exactly the same as the central-city composition in 1960. Moreover, from 1960 to 1970, differences between central cities and suburban rings declined in terms of total employment, white-collar employment, blue-collar employment, and employment in each of the nine occupational categories. These differences in occupational structure diminished whether measured in terms of absolute number of jobs, percentage of metropolitan jobs, or relative distributions of occupations in central cities and suburban rings. This structural convergence clearly manifests the urbanization of America's suburbs.

Examining selective changes in central-city white-collar and blue-collar employment by SMSA size, age, and region, we observe (see table 5) that the largest and oldest SMSA central cities had the greatest redistribution. Central cities of SMSAs larger than 1 million lost an average of 49,144 blue-collar jobs between 1960 and 1970 but gained an average of nearly 9,000 white-collar jobs. Likewise, central cities that reached metropolitan status before 1900 lost an average of 38,505 blue-collar positions and gained an average of 5,808 white-collar positions. Northeastern and north-central SMSA central cities lost averages of 20,325 and 10,158 blue-collar positions, respectively, compared with average net gains of 171 blue-collar jobs in southern-central cities and 1,649 blue-collar jobs in western-central cities.

The loss of substantial numbers of blue-collar job opportunities in large, old central cities and cities in the northeastern and north-central states is the root of the employment problem facing inner-city residents with limited educational backgrounds. In terms of total numbers of available jobs (and here I believe absolute amounts are the pertinent figures), in just one decade, the 16 largest central cities in our sample lost a total of 786,304 blue-collar jobs; the 21 oldest central cities lost a total of 808,605 blue-collar jobs, and the 59 central cities located in northeastern and north-central states (i.e., the old industrial belt) lost a total of 1,798,497 blue-collar jobs. As noted earlier, it is precisely the same sets of central cities that have experienced the largest influx of minority and other low-income groups since World War II.

Not unexpected is the finding (see table 6) that the largest growth in suburban blue-collar employment has also been in the outer rings of the largest and oldest SMSAs. Note, however, that these suburban rings have shown even greater increases in white-collar employment. Mean growth of white-collar employment in the suburban rings of the largest and oldest SMSAs is more than twice as great as blue-collar employment growth.

Comparison of the differential growth of white-collar employment in the central cities and suburban rings indicates that suburban areas in the largest and oldest SMSAs have been most effective in competing with their central cities for white-collar functions. The reasons for the disproportionate growth of white-collar employment in these suburban rings are many. They include huge increases in their middle- and upper-income population bases, attracting numerous retail establishments along with physicians, dentists, lawyers, and other professionals to serve the massive resident population; management's desire to work closer to their suburban homes; availability of less expensive land for smaller customized office complexes; accessibility to commercial airports; and the push factors of congestion and high crime in large, old central cities.

Another possible push factor is corporate decision making predicated on the changing racial and ethnic composition of resident labor-force pools in our largest and oldest central cities. Although evidence to date is not authoritative, there may be a tendency among some executives to move their companies to outlying suburbs to circumvent hiring workers from central-city resident labor pools that are becoming numerically dominated by persons of minority descent. To illustrate, a high-ranking Detroit insurance executive interviewed by the *New York Times* noted several major corporate moves from the central city because of institutional racism. The executive is quoted as saying: "A vice-president of [he named a prominent organization] told me that they wanted to move for one reason—to get rid of lower echelon workers, like file clerks and typists. These days in Detroit those workers have to be black."[11]

Kenneth Patton, New York City's economic-development administrator, reports that studies conducted by his agency indicated that a major force

[11] This quote and the information that follows on executive decision making regarding suburban corporate moves were drawn from two articles: "Loss of Major Companies Conceded by City Official" (*New York Times*, February 5, 1971); and Richard Reeves, "Concerns in Many Cities Leaving for the Suburbs" (*New York Times*, April 28, 1971). Both articles, along with a plethora of other interesting *New York Times* articles on suburbanization, are reprinted in part in Masotti and Hadden (1974).

TABLE 5

MEAN NUMBER OF WHITE-COLLAR AND BLUE-COLLAR EMPLOYEES IN 101 SMSA CENTRAL CITIES BY SMSA SIZE, AGE, AND REGION, 1960 AND 1970

METROPOLITAN CHARACTERISTIC	N	CENTRAL CITY WHITE-COLLAR			CENTRAL CITY BLUE-COLLAR		
		1960	1970*	Change, 1960–70	1960	1970*	Change, 1960–70
Size:							
Under 250,000	44	14,647	16,648	2,001	16,982	16,209	−773
250,000–500,000	30	25,649	30,520	4,871	26,603	26,436	−167
500,000–1 million	11	58,192	68,378	10,196	64,138	63,873	−265
Over 1 million	16	291,409	300,113	8,704	266,254	217,110	−49,144
Inception date (age):							
After 1950	13	15,035	19,760	4,725	14,640	15,468	828
1930–50	31	23,407	28,067	4,660	23,719	23,705	−14
1900–20	36	31,879	36,257	4,378	34,749	33,915	−834
Before 1900	21	221,327	227,135	5,808	206,397	167,892	−38,505
Region:							
Northeast	27	119,118	124,202	5,084	112,399	92,074	−20,325
North-central	32	62,850	62,298	−552	65,676	55,518	−10,158
South	30	32,598	40,341	7,742	32,240	32,411	171
West	12	47,650	57,397	9,747	39,515	41,164	1,649
Total	101	66,501	71,308	4,807	64,464	56,264	−8,200

*Employment figures adjusted for annexation.

TABLE 6

MEAN NUMBER OF WHITE-COLLAR AND BLUE-COLLAR EMPLOYEES IN 101 SMSA SUBURBAN RINGS BY SMSA SIZE, AGE, AND REGION, 1960 AND 1970

METROPOLITAN CHARACTERISTICS	N	SUBURBAN RING WHITE-COLLAR			SUBURBAN RING BLUE-COLLAR		
		1960	1970*	Change, 1960–70	1960	1970*	Change, 1960–70
Size:							
Under 250,000	44	4,393	6,978	2,585	7,168	8,479	1,311
250,000–500,000 ...	30	11,099	17,933	6,834	16,141	21,160	5,019
500,000–1 million ..	11	26,414	43,958	17,544	39,199	51,743	12,544
Over 1 million	16	141,193	237,780	96,587	162,880	211,188	48,308
Inception date (age):							
After 1950	13	6,095	11,160	5,065	9,311	11,971	2,660
1930–50	31	7,846	15,401	7,555	10,158	15,617	5,459
1900–1920	36	12,336	20,628	8,289	18,098	24,682	6,584
Before 1900	21	109,971	179,426	168,455	130,927	163,229	32,302
Region:							
Northeast	27	63,789	91,257	27,468	79,350	86,657	7,307
North-central	32	25,572	49,336	23,746	31,925	48,809	16,884
South	30	11,693	23,194	11,501	15,494	23,982	8,488
West	12	17,689	37,237	19,548	20,007	32,053	11,976
Total	101	30,455	50,822	20,367	37,989	49,070	11,081

*Employment figures adjusted for annexation.

behind corporate moves to the suburbs is what he termed "social-distance." To quote Mr. Patton: "The executive decision-maker lives in a homogenized ethnic and class community. Increasingly his employees in the city are from communities quite different [from his] in class and ethnicity. . . . The decision-maker can't relate to the city kid, that kid [that] doesn't look the same as him."[12]

According to the *New York Times*, Mr. Patton's analysis was similar to the private view expressed by some city officials, including then Mayor John Lindsay. In discussions with reporters and editors, these officials complained that company presidents move their complexes to the suburbs when they discover that a large percentage of their office help is black or Puerto Rican.[13] If this proposition is sustained by authoritative research, many white-collar employment opportunities, as well as blue-collar jobs, will become even further removed from expanding minority concentrations in our central cities.

THE GROWING SEPARATION OF HOME FROM WORKPLACE

What are the implications of the selective movement of population and economic activity for separation of residence from workplace of different occupational and racial groups? As anticipated, table 7 shows substantial declines between 1960 and 1970 of employees who live and work in the central cities, particularly among blue-collar workers. Concurrently, with the suburbanization of economic activity, commuting streams from city residence to suburban jobs increased across white-collar and blue-collar occupations.

The rapid growth of employment and housing in the suburban rings during the 1960s also contributed to large increments in the number of metropolitan residents living and working in the rings. Still, an increasing number of persons moved to the suburbs while retaining jobs in the central cities, as evidenced by the expansion of blue-collar and white-collar commuting from suburban residence to central-city jobs. Note also that, while there was an average increase of approximately 5,000 blue-collar workers in the 101 SMSAs between 1960 and 1970, there was an average net decline of approximately 2,600 blue-collar workers who lived and worked in the same metropolitan zone.

Examination of the relative distribution of commuting streams provides further documentation of increased crosscutting in journey-to-work flows. Observe that the percentage of metropolitan workers in all four nonlateral

12 Ibid.
13 Ibid.

TABLE 7

Mean Number and Percentage Distribution of Blue-Collar and White-Collar Employees by Place of Residence and Place of Work for 101 Longitudinally Comparable SMSAs, Adjusted for Annexation, 1960 and 1970

		Blue-Collar		White-Collar	
Live	Work	1960	1970	1960	1970
Central city	Central city	50,973	40,096	49,115	47,126
		(47.6)	(35.6)	(48.1)	(36.1)
Central city	Suburban ring	5,690	8,847	3,668	7,080
		(5.3)	(7.9)	(3.6)	(5.4)
Suburban ring	Central city	13,492	15,856	17,387	23,739
		(12.6)	(14.1)	(17.0)	(18.2)
Suburban ring	Suburban ring	32,300	40,563	26,787	44,085
		(30.2)	(36.1)	(26.2)	(33.7)
Suburban ring	Outside SMSA	3,151	4,954	3,540	6,198
		(2.9)	(4.4)	(3.5)	(4.7)
Central city	Outside SMSA	1,525	2,167	1,573	2,485
		(1.4)	(1.9)	(1.5)	(1.9)

Note.—Figures in parentheses are percentages.

commuting streams (i.e., central city–ring, ring–central city, ring–outside SMSA, central city–outside SMSA) has increased among white-collar as well as blue-collar workers. Overall, the percentage of white-collar workers commuting nonlaterally increased from 25.6% in 1960 to 30.2% in 1970. During the same period, blue-collar employees living in different zones from where they worked increased from 22.2% to 28.3% of the blue-collar labor force. Table 7 thus indicates that not only are growing numbers of metropolitan workers commuting across city and suburban boundaries but also that larger proportions of the metropolitan labor force are facing increased separation of home from workplace.

In the initial section of this paper, I stated that the suburbanization of job opportunities has been particularly disadvantageous to minority groups who are residentially segregated in the central cities. To examine this issue, place-of-work data for Negroes and whites in 34 SMSAs were compared in 1960 and 1970. The sample includes all SMSAs which are longitudinally comparable by criteria previously described and which had comparable data on residences and workplaces of whites and Negroes in 1960 and 1970. Because the 1960 census provided place-of-work data for whites and nonwhites and the 1970 census for all workers and Negroes, we examined only SMSAs where Negroes constituted more than 90% of the nonwhite population.[14]

[14] Residence and workplace data for whites in 1970 were obtained by subtracting appropriate Negro data from the totals.

Table 8 provides comparative journey-to-work flows in the 34 SMSAs for Negroes and whites in 1960 and 1970. Not surprisingly, the data reveal that Negroes predominantly reside and work in the central cities. In 1960, 72.2% of the Negro labor force both lived and worked in the central cities compared with 46% of the white metropolitan labor force. In 1970, 64.6% of the Negro metropolitan labor force lived and worked in the central cities compared to less than one-third of the white metropolitan labor force.

The substantial drop during the 1960s of whites living and working in the central cities gives testimony to the massive centrifugal drift of residences and jobs occupied by whites. Even with expanding numbers and percentages of whites living in the suburbs and commuting to jobs in the central cities, total white employment in the 34 SMSA central cities dropped an average of 27,000 positions between 1960 and 1970.

Table 8 further reveals that the number and percentage of Negroes involved in all four types of nonlateral commuting streams increased between 1960 and 1970. Of particular note is the fact that, while the percentage of Negroes reverse commuting from central-city residence to suburban jobs increased substantially during the 1960s, the percentage of metropolitan Negroes living and working in the suburban rings actually declined from 1960 to 1970. It is apparent that housing opportunities for Negroes are falling far short of job opportunities in the suburbs.

Although some might argue that the lack of appropriate housing for Negroes near suburban employment is largely a class rather than a racial

TABLE 8

MEAN NUMBER AND PERCENTAGE DISTRIBUTION OF NEGRO AND WHITE EMPLOYEES BY PLACE OF RESIDENCE AND PLACE OF WORK, ADJUSTED FOR ANNEXATION, 34 SELECTED SMSAS, 1960 AND 1970

		NEGROES		WHITES	
LIVE	WORK	1960	1970	1960	1970
Central city	Central city	37,451 (72.2)	39,715 (64.6)	182,988 (46.0)	143,715 (32.7)
Central city	Suburban ring	3,316 (6.4)	7,342 (12.0)	15,219 (3.8)	24,413 (5.6)
Suburban ring	Central city	1,854 (3.6)	2,792 (4.5)	58,735 (14.8)	70,899 (16.1)
Suburban ring	Suburban ring	7,957 (15.3)	9,011 (14.7)	122,809 (30.9)	172,924 (39.3)
Suburban ring	Outside SMSA	453 (0.9)	877 (1.5)	12,787 (3.2)	20,652 (4.7)
Central city	Outside SMSA	830 (1.6)	1,701 (2.8)	5,072 (1.3)	7,132 (1.6)

NOTE.—Figures in parentheses are percentages.

issue, data presented in table 9 belie this position.[15] Regardless of occupational status, Negroes employed in the suburban rings disproportionately commute from the central cities. Overall, 49% of Negroes employed in the suburbs commute from the central city compared to only 13.7% of white suburban workers. Without question, these figures reflect the intense segregation of Negroes in the central cities and the corresponding predominantly white racial composition of the suburban rings. Nevertheless, the fact that such high proportions of Negro suburban workers in all occupational categories commute from the city attests to the growing logistical problems they are facing with the suburbanization of economic opportunity in metropolitan America.

COMMENT

In this paper I have examined the implications of metropolitan expansion since World War II for the occupational structure of central cities and suburban areas. My guiding hypothesis has been that the expansion process has deepened problems of unemployment, poverty, and debt service in the central cities by redistributing the bulk of urban resources beyond central-

TABLE 9

RELATIVE AMOUNT OF REVERSE COMMUTING FROM CENTRAL CITIES TO
SUBURBAN RINGS OF NEGRO AND WHITE WORKERS, BY
OCCUPATION FOR 84 SELECTED SMSAs, 1970

SUBURBAN RING	% SUBURBAN WORKERS COMMUTING FROM CENTRAL CITY		
OCCUPATION	Negroes	Whites	Total
Professional and technical	45.4	13.5	14.7
Managers and proprietors	41.6	12.3	12.9
Clerical workers	51.0	13.3	15.2
Sales workers....................	45.7	12.2	12.9
Craftsmen......................	54.4	15.5	17.7
Operatives	54.7	16.6	21.7
Laborers	47.7	14.9	21.2
Service workers..................	43.4	11.3	17.8
Farm workers	8.8	2.2	3.1
All occupations	49.0	13.7	16.7

[15] The results in table 9 refer to those SMSAs for which Negro place-of-work data by occupation were published in 1970 and where Negroes constitute more than 90% of the nonwhite population ($N = 84$).

city boundaries and by dispersing employment opportunities appropriate to inner-city poor.

Although any predictions about future structural changes in the metropolis are necessarily speculative, the trend appears well established. That is, we may expect increased suburbanization of most types of economic activity along with middle- and upper-income population. This will be matched with continued declines in central-city blue-collar jobs and their partial replacement by higher-skilled white-collar functions. At the same time, the resident population of many central cities will become increasingly dominated by minority groups, the aged, and other poor.

If the above trends continue, as is anticipated, unemployment and poverty in our central cities will obviously worsen. Furthermore, since most central cities are currently stretched to their fiscal limits in providing public-service jobs, little promise exists for additional expansion of this sector. In fact, many central cities are already reducing the number of employees on municipal payrolls. The only feasible solution at this time appears to be large and continuous infusions of state and federal funds for inner-city jobs. These funds, no doubt, will increasingly come (indirectly at least) from the wallets and portfolios of the new suburban masses.

APPENDIX

Methods of Adjusting SMSA Place-of-Work Data by Residence, Occupation, and Race for Annexation, 1960–70

Annexation tends to artificially inflate central-city employment growth and understate suburban-ring employment growth when longitudinal analyses are based on metropolitan place-of-work data. Employment totals for central cities and suburban rings in 1970 must, therefore, be adjusted for annexation occurring during the 1960–70 decade. The method of adjustment can be described in several steps.

1. An estimate of total "annexed employment" is made from published census figures of total annexed resident population. The assumption is made that suburban jobs within the SMSA are transferred to the central city by annexation in the same proportion that residents are transferred. The formula for estimating total annexed employment is TAE = TCE × (ANNEX/CCPOP), where TAE is total annexed employment, TCE is total central-city employment (obtained by summing employees who live in the city and work in the city with employees who live in the suburban ring and work in the city), ANNEX is the population residing in the area annexed by the central city from 1960 to 1970, and CCPOP is the central-city population in 1970.

The adjusted central-city and suburban-ring employment figures are obtained by subtracting total annexed employment from the reported 1970 total central-city employment and adding the same figure to the reported 1970 suburban-ring employment total.

2. To estimate the amount of annexed employment by occupational categories, consideration must be taken of the fact that not all occupations are likely to be annexed in equal numbers. Here, the best estimate of annexed employment by occupation is the proportion that each occupation constitutes of total central-city employment. For example, if professional and technical employees constitute 9% of a city's work force, then they are assumed to constitute the same proportion of total annexed employment. Annexed employment by occupation is calculated by simply multiplying total annexed city employment by each occupational category's proportion of total-city employment. Or, to take professional and technical workers as an example, the estimation formula is APTW = (TPTWCC/TCE) × TAE, where APTW is the estimated number of annexed professional and technical workers, TPTWCC is the total number of professional and technical employees working in the central city, and TCE and TAE are the same as above. The "adjustment" for professional and technical job annexation subtracts annexed professional and technical employment from the reported 1970 total for that occupational category in the central city and adds it to that occupational category in the ring. Similar adjustments are made for the remaining occupational categories.

Adjustments become more complex when correcting commuting patterns for annexation, because residences as well as jobs (workplaces) may be annexed. To adjust commuting data for possible residence and job annexation, the following basic assumptions are made: (a) central-city resident labor force is increased by annexation in the same proportion as the city's population is increased by annexation, and (b) central-city employment is increased by annexation in the same proportion as the city's population is increased by annexation.

To calculate the adjusted journey-to-work flows, we first correct for resident labor-force annexation and second for job (workplace) annexation. In the first step, the central-city resident labor force is decreased and the suburban-ring resident labor force is increased by the estimate of annexed central-city resident labor force. However, as in the case of occupational annexation, the estimated annexed resident labor force must be distributed among the three subcategories of reported place of work for central city and ring residents (i.e., the central city, the ring, and outside the SMSA). For example, the formula for allocating the annexed resident labor force to the subcategory "live in the city and work in the city" is ANRLFCC = (ECC/TLC) × TARLF, where ANRLFCC is the annexed resident labor force that lives in the city and works in the city, ECC is the reported number of employees who live in the city *and* work in the city, TLC is the total number of employees who live in the city regardless of place of work, TARLF is the total estimated annexed resident labor force computed by multiplying the total central-city resident labor force (TLC) by the ratio of annexed central-city population to total 1970 central-city population (ANNEX/CCPOP). Then, ANRLFCC is subtracted from the reported number of central-city residents who worked in the central city in 1970.

The other workplace allocations for city residents annexed are computed by substituting ECR (employees living in the city and·working in the ring) and ECO (employees living in the city and working outside the SMSA) for ECC in the above formula. These allocations are likewise subtracted from the appropriate place-of-work data reported for central-city residents. Next, the estimated total annexed resident labor force is *added* to the three suburban ring *resident* place-of-work subcategories in proportions equivalent to the reported 1970 distribution of place of work of suburban-ring residents. With these computations completed, the resident labor forces of the central city and suburban ring have been adjusted for *residence* annexation.

The second step involves further adjusting the residence–workplace commuting streams (ring–city, city–city, ring–ring, and city–ring) for job annexation. (The city–outside SMSA and ring–outside SMSA commuting streams have been corrected for residence annexation but are not affected by job annexation.) To make this adjustment, we first estimate total city employment that has been annexed by multiplying the number of all SMSA residents employed in the central city (TCE) by the ratio of annexed central-city population to total 1970 central-city population. The estimated total annexed city employment is then split into separate proportions of (*a*) annexed city employees who live in the city and (*b*) annexed city employees who live in the ring. The estimated total annexed city employment is, at the same time, distributed to ring employment in proportion to the reported residence distribution of ring employees. Finally, each estimate of annexed employment is either subtracted from the respective central-city employees commuting stream (city–city or ring–city) or added to the respective suburban employees commuting stream (either city–ring or ring–ring).

Considering again employees living in the central city and working in the central city, the complete equation, which adjusts for both residence and job (workplace) annexation, is as follows: $\text{ADRJCC} = \text{ADRCC} - (\text{ECC}/\text{TCE} \times [(\text{ANNEX}/\text{CCPOP}) \times \text{TCE}]$, where ADRJCC is the labor force living and working in the city adjusted for residence *and* job annexation; ADRCC is the labor force living and working in the city adjusted for residence annexation; and ECC, TCE, ANNEX, and CCPOP are the same as described above. The adjustment formula for those living in the ring and working in the city is the same, except that ADRCC and ECC are replaced by ADRRC and ERC representing, respectively, those living in the ring and working in the city adjusted for residence annexation and the reported number living in the ring and working in the city. For the residence–workplace commuting categories city–ring and ring–ring, the total estimated employment annexed must be *added* to each residence-adjusted category in proportion to the residence distribution of total-ring employment. Thus, if published place-of-work data indicate that 15% of ring employees commute from residences in the central city, then 15% of the estimated annexed jobs are added to that category.

The same two-step procedure may be extended to adjust commuting streams for annexation of employees of particular occupations or occupational categories, such as blue-collar or white-collar workers. This is done by applying the residence and workplace (job) adjustment formulas to place-of-work data subcategorized by residence and occupation. For example, the adjustment formula for residence annexation of white-collar workers living in the city and working in the city is $ADRWHTCC = WHTCC - (WHTCC/TLC) \times (ANNEX/CCPOP) \times TLC$, where $ADRWHTCC$ is white-collar workers living in the city and working in the city adjusted for residence annexation; $WHTCC$ is the reported number of white-collar workers living and working in the central city; and TLC, $ANNEX$, and $CCPOP$ are the same as described above.

In our final adjustments of commuting streams by occupational groupings, two sets of annexation adjustment were calculated: first, a two-step adjustment as described above correcting for both residence and job annexation, and second, an adjustment for job annexation only. When adjustments are computed for jobs only and commuting patterns are summed by work location, the workplace totals are equivalent to the city and ring totals presented in tables 5 and 6. The two-step adjustment procedure on which the residence-workplace results in table 7 are based does not yield equivalent totals to tables 5 and 6, although the results are very close. The differences may be attributed to rounding error and the fact that, in the two-step procedure, the second set of equations, adjusting for job annexation, contains a term that had been previously altered by the adjustment for residence annexation. It was believed, however, that the two-step procedure provides a more valid adjustment when comparing changes in intrametropolitan commuting streams that may have been altered by residence as well as job annexation.

NEGRO RESIDENCE–WORKPLACE ANNEXATION ADJUSTMENTS

Because Negroes constitute only a small percentage of the suburban resident population and suburban employment in many SMSAs, it is necessary to consider this when adjusting their residence and workplace data for possible annexation. To accomplish this, the total estimated resident labor force annexed as computed above is multiplied by the proportion of the SMSA Negro labor force *living* in the ring. Similarly, the total estimated number of jobs annexed is multiplied by the proportion of SMSA Negro labor force *working* in the ring. These two additional adjustments provide us with estimates of (*a*) the number of Negro residences annexed, and (*b*) the number of Negro workplaces annexed. The estimated annexed Negro residences and workplaces are then used in the two-step procedure described above for adjusting place-of-work data for both residence and job annexation.

REFERENCES

Armstrong, Regina B. 1972. *The Office Industry: Patterns of Growth and Location.* Cambridge, Mass.: M.I.T. Press.

Berry, Brian J. L., and Yehoshua S. Cohen. 1973. "Decentralization of Commerce and Industry: The Restructuring of Metropolitan America." Pp. 431–55 in *The Urbanization of the Suburbs,* edited by Louis Masotti and Jeffrey K. Hadden. Urban Affairs Annual Reviews, vol. 7. Beverly Hills, Calif.: Sage.

Carruth, Eleanor. 1969. "Manhattan's Office Building Binge." *Fortune* 80 (October): 114–25.

Chinitz, Benjamin, ed. 1964. *City and Suburb.* Englewood Cliffs, N.J.: Prentice-Hall.

Cowan, Peter, Daniel Fine, John Ireland, Clive Jordan, Dilys Mercer, and Angela Sears. 1969. *The Office: A Facet of Urban Growth.* New York: American Elsevier.

Downs, Anthony. 1973. *Opening Up the Suburbs: An Urban Strategy for America.* New Haven, Conn.: Yale University Press.

Friedlander, Stanley. 1972. *Unemployment in the Urban Core.* New York: Praeger.

Guest, Avery M. 1971. "Retesting the Burgess Zonal Hypothesis: The Location of White-Collar Workers." *American Journal of Sociology* 76 (May): 1094–1108.

Haggerty, Lee J. 1971. "Another Look at the Burgess Hypothesis: Time as an Important Variable." *American Journal of Sociology* 76 (May): 1084–93.

Harrison, Bennett. 1972. *Education, Training, and the Urban Ghetto.* Baltimore: Johns Hopkins University Press.

Hawley, Amos H., and Basil G. Zimmer. 1970. *The Metropolitan Community: Its People and Government.* Beverly Hills, Calif.: Sage.

Hosken, Fran P. 1973. *The Functions of Cities.* Cambridge, Mass.: Schenkman.

Kain, John F. 1968. "Housing Segregation, Negro Employment, and Metropolitan Decentralization." *Quarterly Journal of Economics* 82 (May): 175–97.

Kasarda, John D. 1972*a*. "The Impact of Suburban Population Growth on Central City Service Functions." *American Journal of Sociology* 77 (May): 1111–24.

———. 1972*b*. "The Theory of Ecological Expansion: An Empirical Test." *Social Forces* 51 (December): 165–75.

———. 1974. "The Centrifugal Drift of Metropolitan Population." Paper presented at the annual meeting of the Population Association of America, New York, April.

McQuade, Walter. 1973. "A Daring New Generation of Skyscrapers." *Fortune* 84 (February): 78–82.

Manners, Gerald. 1974. "The Office in the Metropolis: An Opportunity for Shaping Metropolitan America." *Economic Geography* 50 (April): 93–110.

Masotti, Louis H., and Jeffrey K. Hadden, eds. 1974. *Suburbia in Transition.* New York: New Viewpoints.

National Bureau of Standards. 1973. *Standard Metropolitan Statistical Areas.* Publication 8-3 (August 15). Washington, D.C.: Government Printing Office.

National Commission on Civil Disorders. 1968. *Report on U.S. Riots.* New York: Bantam.

National Committee against Discrimination in Housing. 1970. *Jobs and Housing.* New York: National Committee against Discrimination in Housing.

Pinkerton, James. 1969. "City-Suburban Residential Patterns by Social Class: A Review of the Literature." *Urban Affairs Quarterly* 4 (June): 499–519.

Schnore, Leo. 1972. *Class and Race in Cities and Suburbs.* Chicago: Markham.

Smith, Joel. 1970. "Another Look at Socioeconomic Status Distributions in Urbanized Areas." *Urban Affairs Quarterly* 5 (June): 423–53.

Thompson, Wilbur R. 1965. *A Preface to Urban Economics.* Baltimore: Johns Hopkins University Press.

U.S. News and World Report. 1974. 79 (September 30): 67.

Vernon, Raymond. 1960. *Metropolis 1985.* Cambridge, Mass.: Harvard University Press.

6   The Push Hypothesis: Minority Presence, Crime, and Urban Deconcentration

Thomas M. Guterbock
Memphis State University

Beginning early in this century, and particularly since World War II, a process of spatial redistribution of residences and workplaces has transformed the metropolitan areas of North America and Western Europe from core-oriented industrial cities into decentralized urban systems. The social scientists who have described this process—which they call "suburbanization," "urban sprawl," "dispersal," "decentralization," or "deconcentration"[1]—are agreed on many of its causes. Without technological advances such as motorized transport, super highways, and automation in industry, the deconcentration process would not have been possible. The "pull" of cheaper land, newer housing, lower densities, and more homogeneous neighborhoods in the suburbs gives impetus to the outward movement of people, commercial and industrial enterprises, and services. The host of factors that determine the spatial structure of the housing market, such as racial discrimination, tax structures, federal housing programs, and "a value system that idealizes the suburban way of life" (Sjoberg 1968, p. 456), interact to make the suburbs more attractive than the inner city for many people.

Does "pull" sufficiently explain the depopulation of the older areas of the metropolis that has occurred in recent decades? Some observers think not; they advance an additional explanation of deconcentration which may be called the *push hypothesis*. According to this view, urban population redistribution is substantially affected by changing social conditions in the central

Funds for computer time used in processing data for this study were provided by the Department of Sociology of the University of Chicago. Early stages of this research benefited greatly from the guidance of William L. Parish, Jr., Morris Janowitz, John D. Kasarda, and an anonymous referee of the *American Journal of Sociology* who made valuable comments on an earlier version of this paper. Thanks are also due to Carole S. Guterbock and Barry Schwartz for editorial assistance.

[1] It should be noted that "decentralization" and "deconcentration" are both also used to describe distinct kinds of redistribution of administrative control in organizations. For the present discussion of spatial redistribution of physical entities, I have followed Hawley's suggestion (1971, p. 161 n.), choosing "deconcentration" in preference to "decentralization." The term is not to be understood here in the special urban-geographic sense introduced by Berry, Simmons, and Tennant (1970, p. 293), who distinguish "deconcentration" (decline in extrapolated central density) from "decompaction" (reduction in density gradient). In this paper "concentration" denotes not only a large population within a given area but a pattern of spatial distribution in which density decreases with increasing distance from a central place.

city, conditions which white middle-class Americans perceive as threatening. Chief among these are the presence in large and increasing numbers of low-status minority group members and decreased personal safety. These two factors are closely associated with (but not always causally related to) such other frequently cited push factors as "poor schools" and "neighborhood deterioration." The push hypothesis assumes that the middle-class majority would locate quite differently were it not for minority presence and crime in the central city. It views deconcentration as a forced "flight to the suburbs" involving substantial social costs for those who "flee."

Grodzins ([1958] 1970, p. 493) enumerates some of these hypothetical costs: "the isolation of the dormitory suburbs, the large fraction of life demanded for commuting, and the social restriction of village living." He suggests that if the large concentrations of blacks were broken up and new amenities provided by massive government intervention, whites would readily return to the central cities to escape what he calls "the suburban sadness." The out-migration of whites from central cities in the 1960s exceeded all predictions. To explain this, Berry (1973) refers to "mounting racial tensions," "racial polarization," and "the mutually repulsive interactions of antagonistic social groups." He notes that the largest 1960–70 out-migration losses were for counties containing big cities that had large, growing black populations. Less explicit statements of the push hypothesis are also to be found in the literature on suburbanization, for example, Kasarda (1972, p. 1119): "The 'flight to the suburbs' has been greatest in those cities that have experienced the largest influx of nonwhite migrants in the past 25 years."

The racial tensions of the 1960s, the continued growth of black percentages in the central cities, and the tremendous rise in urban crime rates contribute to the plausibility of the push hypothesis. It has the weight of "common sense" behind it and allows suburbanization to be seen as an extension of the familiar process of racial "invasion" and succession in city neighborhoods. However, the notion of "white flight" has also been extensively criticized, particularly in the context of neighborhood change (see Molotch 1972). This paper presents data which challenge the push hypothesis in the larger, metropolitan context as well.

THE PROBLEM

The push hypothesis states that the movement of American urban populations from central city to suburb is partly caused by minority presence and crime in the central cities. In testing this thesis, we will ascertain whether Standard Metropolitan Statistical Areas (SMSAs) that had large or increasing black populations and high or rising crime rates in their central cities suburbanized more rapidly than other SMSAs in the 1950s and 1960s. If conditions of the central city do correlate with SMSA deconcentration rates, we must decide whether the former are cause or consequence of the latter. These tests require measures which permit comparison among SMSAs not only of deconcentration rates but of levels of concentration at successive points in time.

Simple Measures

The relationship between simple measures of deconcentration and increase in black population seems to support the push hypothesis. Figures 1 and 2 display such a relationship. In the majority of deconcentration studies, differences in rates of growth between central cities and their suburban rings are used to measure deconcentration. In these scattergrams we use the difference between the growth rate of the entire SMSA and that of the central city to avoid the exaggerated growth difference that results for cities where relatively few persons live outside the city line. The increase in number of central-city blacks between census years has been divided by the total central-city population at the start of the decade to avoid the exaggerated growth rate that might result if the initial black population were used as a base. For 39 monocentric SMSAs[2] the correlation of these variables is substantial and appears to be linear for both the 1950–60 and 1960–70 periods.

Before these correlations can be accepted in support of the push hypothesis, other possible explanations must be explored. First, the relationship may be spurious, resulting from the effect of prior variables not controlled here. The growth rate of the SMSA, for example, is positively related to both variables in the scattergrams. But given the measures used here, we cannot control for growth because the SMSA growth rate is related (artificially) to the city growth lag measure as well as (functionally) to deconcentration itself. Second, even if the relationship held up under adequate controls, its causal direction would still not be established. Perhaps black increase is the *result* of deconcentration rather than its cause. It might be argued that cities with high deconcentration rates have more inexpensive housing units available and consequently attract more low-income migrants, many of whom are black. We cannot choose among alternatives such as these by continuing to work with rough indicators of change. A new measure of deconcentration that is independent of the artificial effects of confounding variables is pre-

---

[2] The 39 cities are Akron, Baltimore, Birmingham, Bridgeport, Buffalo, Canton, Chattanooga, Chicago, Cincinnati, Cleveland, Denver, Detroit, Erie, Flint, Grand Rapids, Hartford, Kansas City, Knoxville, Nashville, New Bedford, New Haven, New Orleans, Peoria, Philadelphia, Portland, Reading, Richmond, Rochester, Saint Louis, Salt Lake City, South Bend, Spokane, Syracuse, Tacoma, Toledo, Trenton, Washington, D.C., Waterbury, and Worcester. These comprised the data base for earlier stages of this research. For the procedure by which these cities were selected, see Guterbock (1972, pp. 5–8).

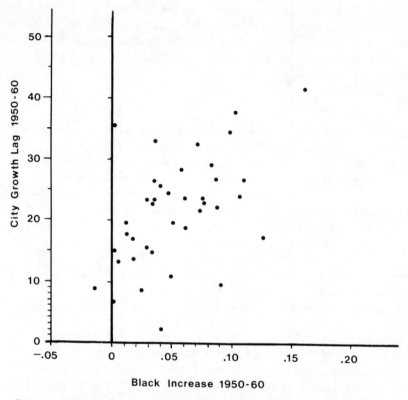

FIG. 1.—Difference between central-city growth rate and SMSA growth rate related to black increase as a proportion of 1950 central-city population, 39 cities, 1950–60; $r = .523$.

sented in this paper, along with a method of measuring concentration at a single point in time which permits the use of a path model for panel analysis that reveals the causal direction of observed relationships.

METHOD

Measuring Urban Concentration

If we accept the considerable evidence that "a single pattern of urban densities is repeated in a large number of very different cities" (Rees 1970, p. 276), it is possible to determine the degree of concentration of a city using U.S. census figures for SMSA population, SMSA land area, central-city population, and central-city land area. In most cities, population density tends to decline at an exponential rate with distance from the city's center,

$$D_x = ae^{-bx},$$

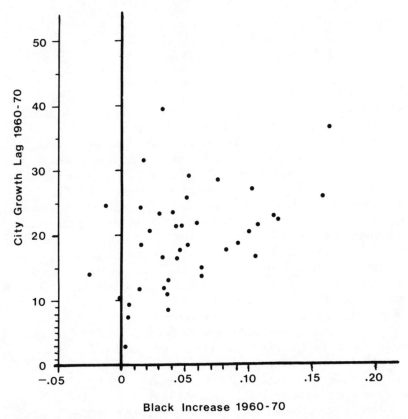

FIG. 2.—Difference between central-city growth rate and SMSA growth rate related to black increase as a proportion of 1960 central-city population, 39 cities, 1960–70; $r = .418$.

where D_x = population density at distance x from the city's center, a and b are positive parameters, and e is the base of the system of natural logarithms. The parameters a and b are different for different cities and change over time. The rate of decline of density with distance, b, is the density gradient. The smaller the density gradient, the less concentrated the city. The value of a is equal to the population density at the city's center, or, rather, the extrapolated central density which would obtain if the central area were used for residences and density increased exponentially to the city's center. Clark (1951) was the first to show that the density patterns of some large cities tended to conform to this equation and that their density gradients were declining over time. Muth (1961) and Berry, Simmons, and Tennant (1970) have further established the generality of the inverse exponential density pattern. Given the population and land area of a SMSA and its central city, we can calculate a and b if we assume that the city and SMSA boundaries approximate concentric circles or sectors of circles around the point of highest extrapolated density. The technique by which these parameters are estimated is detailed in Section 1 of the Appendix.

Selection of Cities

The method used here to measure concentration is valid only for cities which conform in shape to a rough circle or "pie slice" sector of a circle and in which the central city is surrounded in all available directions by a band of suburban settlement. It is not valid for cities where densely settled, aging areas close to the central business district are defined as lying outside the central city, as in the case of riverbank cities like Saint Louis or Hartford. I selected a data base by examining Census Bureau maps of 1950, 1960, and 1970 urbanized areas, starting with the 75 SMSAs which had a single central city whose 1950 population exceeded 100,000. A few cities were eliminated because of annexation which radically expanded the area of the central city so that little of the suburban ring as defined in the 1960 census was urban. Many cities were eliminated because their urban fringe was very discontinuous in 1950 or in 1960. Several others were dropped because their urban fringe included areas close to the city's core. A few other cities, such as New Orleans and San Francisco, had complex shapes determined by natural topography and could not be approximated by sectors of circles. This left 22 cities, for which sector sizes were estimated and density gradients and extrapolated central densities were calculated (table 1). This is a small data base and is not necessarily representative of all large American cities, so results reported here can only be generalized on a tentative basis pending further research.

The Dependent Variable: Deconcentration

If a city's degree of concentration can be meaningfully represented by any single quantity, the density gradient is that quantity. It would be inappropriate, however, simply to use the absolute or proportional change in density gradient as a measure of deconcentration. Can we expect an initially low density gradient to decline as much as an initially high gradient under the same influences? If technological and structural changes have made lower urban concentrations most efficient, are not the most concentrated cities those which must deconcentrate most rapidly? And is there not an inescapable link between population growth and deconcentration? To take these complexities into account, we shall measure deconcentration between time 1 and time 2 by calculating an "expected" time 2 density gradient for each city, based on some plausible assumptions about the deconcentration process, and comparing this with the observed time 2 density gradient.

In cities with an inverse exponential density pattern, changes in density gradient, extrapolated central density, and population size are interdependent.

TABLE 1

ESTIMATED PARAMETERS OF DENSITY FUNCTIONS, AND DECON SCORES

CITY AND SECTOR SIZE	BASED ON 1950 AREAS					BASED ON 1960 AREAS				
	b_{1950}	a_{1950}	b_{1960}	a_{1960}	1950–60 Decon	b_{1960}	a_{1960}	b_{1970}	a_{1970}	1960–70 Decon
Baltimore (300)	.453	52,556	.352	38,698	−.0243	.331	36,231	.283	30,154	−.0355
Boston (270)	.255	34,708	.213	26,884	−.0254	.214	26,965	.188	23,131	−.0405
Bridgeport (180)	.663	37,108	.520	28,736	−.0027	.443	22,256	.381	19,691	−.0325
Buffalo (180)	.356	44,012	.279	32,429	.0098	.279	32,429	.242	25,265	.0142
Canton (360)	.667	20,804	.558	16,913	−.0493	.558	16,913	.474	13,451	.0023
Chicago (180)	.196	67,328	.154	50,819	−.0259	.160	50,697	.134	40,501	−.0117
Cleveland (220)	.333	42,952	.238	28,199	.0581	.238	28,199	.185	19,763	.0670
Columbus (360)	.756	45,764	.546	32,659	−.0105	.436	21,162	.371	19,169	−.0675
Dayton (360)	.634	29,248	.456	20,662	.0139	.400	17,738	.329	14,218	−.0032
Denver (360)	.569	29,110	.388	20,438	.0173	.375	20,772	.273	14,593	.0594
Detroit (180)	.219	46,199	.156	29,924	.0736	.156	29,924	.127	23,120	.0216
Grand Rapids (360)	.761	26,560	.588	19,973	−.0121	.588	19,973	.479	15,065	.0237
Milwaukee (180)	.442	55,631	.320	37,317	.0433	.271	28,332	.235	23,414	−.0100
New Haven (240)	.703	31,762	.546	22,822	.0253	.544	22,759	.449	17,585	.0210
Pittsburgh (360)	.268	25,285	.231	20,620	−.0486	.231	20,620	.208	16,727	−.0138
Portland (360)	.394	17,378	.331	14,323	−.0282	.332	14,406	.275	12,167	−.0214
Richmond (360)	.711	26,415	.525	17,945	.0397	.525	17,945	.413	13,243	.0384
Rochester (360)	.694	37,378	.534	26,693	−.0031	.534	26,693	.412	19,541	.0312
Syracuse (360)	.776	32,804	.603	24,500	−.0195	.471	19,886	.398	16,056	−.0105
Washington, D.C. (360)	.415	40,141	.297	28,361	*	.297	28,361	.228	23,450	*
Flint (360)	.663	18,999	.571	19,439	†	.571	19,439	.475	16,108	†
Miami (180)	.362	20,621	.242	17,471	†	.242	17,471	.214	18,502	†

NOTE.—b = density gradient; a = extrapolated central density.

$$\text{Decon } 1950\text{–}60 = \{[2{,}230.41(1/a_{1950}) + .649998]/(a_{1960}/a_{1950})\}^{1/2} - 1$$

$$\text{Decon } 1960\text{–}70 = \{[1950.49(1/a_{1960}) + .742797]/(a_{1970}/a_{1960})\}^{1/2} - 1$$

*Excluded from data base because of extreme scores on minority presence measures.

†Excluded from data base because of extremely low deconcentration.

As population rises, either central density rises or the square of the density gradient declines. Even though all 22 cities gained population, the trend has been for central densities to decrease (table 1). Table 2 shows that population change is strongly correlated with density gradient change in both decades but less strongly related to change in central density and almost independent of it in the second decade. We will assume in this analysis that changes in central density are not dependent on the rate of population increase.

There are ample theoretical grounds for this assumption. In cities, population densities are linked directly to land values, because occupancy of expensive land is economically feasible only at high density. The value of land at the city's center is a function of the importance of the city center in the economic life of the urban region. As transportation and communication technologies have developed, modern cities have become less core oriented. Increased population size will hardly increase demand for central locations when the obsolescent land use pattern in the inner city already exceeds optimum density. When people and services pour into the modern metropolis, it expands outward rather than upward. (For more on the linkage of urban growth with declining gradients, see Berry and Horton [1970, pp. 297–302] and Hoover [1968].)

While an increase in population size may not increase the value of centrally located land, we can nevertheless expect densities to be higher in urban regions where natural obstacles reduce the amount of land available at any given distance from the center. We will assume that two similarly concentrated urban regions with equal populations and different sector sizes will have identical density gradients and central densities inversely proportional to their sector size. We eliminate the effect of sector size on the density function of each SMSA by multiplying its extrapolated central density as displayed in table 1 by its sector size (in degrees) and dividing by 360.

Given a SMSA's density gradient and central density (adjusted for sector

TABLE 2

ZERO-ORDER CORRELATIONS OF CHANGES IN POPULATION, DENSITY GRADIENT,
AND EXTRAPOLATED CENTRAL DENSITY, 19 CITIES

	1950–60			1960–70		
	$\hat{P}_s$	$\hat{b}$	$\hat{a}$	$\hat{P}_s$	$\hat{b}$	$\hat{a}$
$\hat{P}_s$	1.000	−.768	−.416	1.000	−.689	−.117
$\hat{b}$	...	1.000	.889	...	1.000	.761
$\hat{a}$	...	...	1.000	...	...	1.000

NOTE.—$\hat{P}_s$ = SMSA population change, $\hat{b}$ = density gradient change, and $\hat{a}$ = central density change.

size) at time 1, the "expected" time 2 density gradient is constructed under these assumptions: (1) population growth causes the density gradient to decline; (2) central densities decline independently of population growth; and (3) the greater the central density, the faster it decreases; specifically, central densities are tending downward toward an optimum which is identical for all cities in each decade, and the decline in central density is proportional to the difference between initial central density and this optimum.

We estimate from the data for each decade the optimum central density and the rate at which it tends to be approached. We can then calculate an expected time 2 density gradient for any SMSA on the basis of its time 1 density gradient, time 1 central density, and population growth. Our measure of deconcentration is the proportional difference between the observed and expected time 2 density gradient, which I call "Decon." Section 2 of the Appendix describes this measure in more detail and shows how it can be calculated from central density scores alone. These Decon scores have a straightforward interpretation: a 1950–60 score of .05 indicates that a city deconcentrated more than could be expected from its degree of concentration in 1950 and its population growth during 1950–60, and that the expected 1960 density gradient was 5% larger than the observed 1960 density gradient. A score of − .05 means less deconcentration than expected, with an expected 1960 gradient 5% smaller than observed.

Before calculating the optimum central densities and Decon scores, we eliminated three cities from the data base: Flint and Miami because their central densities increased rather than decreased and Washington because of its extremely high black population and rate of black increase. Inclusion of these cities would have meant that a few outlying values on the dependent and independent variables would have controlled the outcome of multiple regression analysis—in a direction opposite that predicted by the push hypothesis.

Annexation is controlled in these calculations, since the central densities used to calculate Decon scores for each decade were based on population and land area data for the SMSAs and central cities as defined at the outset of the decade.

Independent Variables

Log SMSA size was computed by the formula

$$\ln \left[\left(\frac{\text{SMSA population}}{1,000} \right) - 100 \right].$$

This logarithmic transformation smooths out the distribution of raw population scores, which would be badly skewed by the inclusion of a few very large SMSAs.

Standardized crime was based on an index used by Angell (1951) which

145

summarizes the number of crimes reported annually under the categories "murder and nonnegligent manslaughter," "robbery," and "burglary" for each city (crimes reported by U.S. Federal Bureau of Investigation [1950 –70]). This index was chosen because these three categories of crime most directly threaten the personal security of urban residents. The 1950 index was based on 1950 and 1951 reports, the 1960 index on 1959 and 1960, and the 1970 index on 1969 and 1970. Standard yearly frequencies per 100,000 population were established for each category of crime and each census year by combining the summary listings for cities of over 100,000. For each year, the standard burglary frequency was then divided by the frequency for each of the other two categories and the square root of the quotients was taken. Weights for homicides, robberies, and burglaries proportional to the square roots of their frequencies were thus obtained. In 1950 these weights were 8.06, 2.35, and 1.00; in 1960 they were 10.18, 2.46, and 1.00; and in 1970, they were 10.95, 1.98, and 1.00. The weighted sums of the three categories were divided by the population of the central city to yield the crime indices, for example,

$$1950 \text{ crime} = \frac{\begin{aligned}(8.06)(\text{murders 1950} + \text{murders 1951}) \\ + (2.35)(\text{robberies 1950} + \text{robberies 1951}) \\ + (\text{burglaries 1950} + \text{burglaries 1951})\end{aligned}}{[(2)(\text{city population 1950})]/1,000}.$$

As a final step, the crime scores for each census year were divided by their standard deviation. Standardization was necessary because the variance of the crime scores differed widely between census years, and standardized regression coefficients relating unstandardized crime scores to the dependent variable would not have been comparable for the two decades.

The unreliability of reported crime as a measure of real crime rates is well known. However, this crime index should reflect real differences in the degree of personal danger felt by residents of different cities at different times, if only because their perception of their own safety is based in part on publicly reported crime rates. In any case, no detailed data more accurate than reported crime statistics are available.

Positional crime change is simply the time 2 standardized crime score minus the time 1 score. The term "positional change" for the difference between successive standardized scores is that suggested by Duncan, Cuzzort, and Duncan (1961, p. 162).

Proportion black is the number of blacks living in the central city in each of the three census years divided by the total 1950 central-city population.

Black increase is the absolute change in black population between census years divided by the 1950 population. This measure is independent of changes in nonblack population and at the same time indicates the real impact of growing minority presence—not merely the number of white residents replaced by blacks but the symbolic importance of the city's black minority as a growing presence in the city.

RESULTS

Explaining Deconcentration

Table 3 is a zero-order correlation matrix for the variables. Table 4 gives the results of multiple regression analysis designed to test the push hypothesis for the two intercensal decades. In these regression equations we have controlled for log SMSA size, although omission of the size variable from any of these equations would have no important effect on the coefficients for the remaining predictors or the amount of variance explained. Equations (1), (2), (6), and (7) in table 4 use only the initial levels of minority presence and crime to predict deconcentration; the other six equations include changes in independent variables as predictors of deconcentration. These change scores are introduced as predictors to test the idea that deconcentration is a response not only to initially high levels of minority presence and crime but also to the push inherent in rapidly increasing levels.

The effects of proportion black and standardized crime shown in equations (1), (2), (6), and (7) in table 4 are small and statistically nonsignificant, but they *are* in the direction predicted by the push hypothesis. Proportion black seems to be the more important push factor in the first decade; crime seems more important in the second. But even if we give maximum credence to the coefficients calculated here (instead of dismissing them as probable results of error), proportion black and standardized crime account for less than 10% of the variance in deconcentration.

The only strong positive relationship that emerges in any of these equations is that between Decon and black increase for 1950–60; it contrasts sharply with the weak, negative relationship between the same variables for 1960–70. This is not a spurious result of the effects of urban growth: if growth were added to the prediction equation, the coefficient for black increase during 1950–60 would increase further. Does this mean that minority presence constituted a major push for urban deconcentration before 1960 but not after? This seems implausible; more likely, we are again confronting the problem of interpreting causal direction, and black increase in the 1950s should be seen as a concomitant or consequence of deconcentration rather than its cause. The causal direction of the small positive relationship for both decades between crime change and deconcentration should also be questioned. Only middle- and upper-income families can afford the move from the central city to better housing. Thus, the proportion of low-income persons in the central city increases with suburbanization, and rising crime rates are to be expected.

TABLE 3

Zero-Order Correlations of Variables, 19 Cities

	X_1	X_2	X_3	X_4	X_5	X_6	X_7	X_8	X_9	X_{10}	X_{11}	X_{12}	X_{13}	X_{14}	X_{15}	X_{16}	X_{17}	X_{18}	X_{19}	X_{20}
X_1	1.000	.563	.285	.394	.443	.588	.415	.163	.173	.378	-.024	.303	.040	.063	.068	.074	.056	.357	.368	.524
X_2		1.000	.100	.111	.081	.111	.081	.190	.181	.141	-.066	-.025	-.106	-.085	-.099	-.093	.164	.329	.025	.320
X_3			1.000	.976	.926	.653	.262	.420	.480	.541	.001	.158	.260	.275	.253	.256	-.312	-.204	-.285	-.227
X_4				1.000	.979	.803	.405	.372	.421	.569	-.006	.267	.263	.282	.262	.266	-.333	-.191	-.228	-.170
X_5					1.000	.867	.583	.327	.369	.592	-.007	.358	.265	.285	.270	.276	-.389	-.228	-.239	-.191
X_6						1.000	.688	.143	.150	.498	-.024	.491	.202	.227	.218	.221	-.303	-.106	-.012	.030
X_7							1.000	-.015	-.021	.387	-.008	.545	.141	.155	.163	.177	-.419	-.263	-.162	-.180
X_8								1.000	.881	.512	-.482	-.355	.123	.177	.149	.198	-.109	-.058	-.163	-.093
X_9									1.000	.694	-.010	-.252	.325	.371	.352	.393	-.068	-.010	-.151	-.086
X_{10}										1.000	.202	.522	.394	.419	.412	.432	-.021	.099	-.061	-.007
X_{11}											1.000	.282	.340	.314	.338	.307	.105	.105	.065	.036
X_{12}												1.000	.145	.124	.137	.116	.052	.144	.097	.092
X_{13}													1.000	.997	.992	.986	-.200	-.166	-.314	-.321
X_{14}														1.000	.996	.994	-.233	-.191	-.332	-.332
X_{15}															1.000	.997	-.251	-.206	-.327	-.331
X_{16}																1.000	-.274	-.226	-.344	-.347
X_{17}																	1.000	.952	.808	.814
X_{18}																		1.000	.863	.918
X_{19}																			1.000	.955
X_{20}																				1.000
Mean	0.0017	0.0017	0.0964	0.1596	0.2150	0.0631	0.0554	1.771	1.734	2.078	-0.0371	0.3434	6.408	6.657	6.705	6.850	0.0061	0.0072	0.0074	0.0083
SD	0.0346	0.0346	0.0818	0.1040	0.1170	0.0301	0.0260	0.8967	0.7855	0.8912	0.4252	0.6634	1.076	1.024	0.994	0.959	0.00080	0.00087	0.00089	0.00097

Key to Table.—X_1 = Decon 1950–60; X_2 = Decon 1960–70; X_3 = proportion black 1950; X_4 = proportion black 1960; X_5 = proportion black 1970; X_6 = black increase 1950–60; X_7 = black increase 1960–70; X_8 = standardized crime 1950; X_9 = standardized crime 1960–70; X_{10} = standardized crime 1960; X_{11} = positional crime change 1950–60; X_{12} = positional crime change 1960–70; X_{13} = log SMSA size 1950 (1950 boundaries); X_{14} = log SMSA size 1960 (1950 boundaries); X_{15} = log SMSA size 1960 (1960 boundaries); X_{16} = log SMSA size 1970 (1960 boundaries); X_{17} = square root of $1/a$ 1950 (1960 boundaries); X_{18} = square root of $1/a$ 1960 (1950 boundaries); X_{19} = square root of $1/a$ 1960 (1960 boundaries); and X_{20} = square root of $1/a$ 1970 (1960 boundaries).

TABLE 4

MULTIPLE REGRESSION RESULTS

DEPENDENT VARIABLE: DECON 1950–60

INDEPENDENT VARIABLE	Simple r	Eq. (1) β	F	Eq. (2) β	F	Eq. (3) β	F	Eq. (4) β	F	Eq. (5) β	F
X_3 = proportion black 1950	.285	.294	1.41	.272	0.95	−.159	0.33	…	…	−.309	0.89
X_6 = black increase 1950–60	.588	…	…	…	…	.704	6.70	…	…	.780	7.05
X_9 = standardized crime 1950	.163	…	…	.053	0.04	…	…	.201	0.42	.283	0.89
X_{11} = pos. crime change 1950–60	−.024	…	…	…	…	…	…	.077	0.06	.177	0.39
X_{13} = log SMSA size 1950	.040	−.037	0.02	−.038	0.02	−.061	0.08	−.011	0.00	−.133	0.29
Multiple R^2		.082		.085		.366		.031		.407	

DEPENDENT VARIABLE: DECON 1960–70

INDEPENDENT VARIABLE	Simple r	Eq. (6) β	F	Eq. (7) β	F	Eq. (8) β	F	Eq. (9) β	F	Eq. (10) β	F
X_4 = proportion black 1960	.111	.147	0.33	.071	0.06	.204	0.51	…	…	.094	0.08
X_7 = black increase 1960–70	−.081	…	…	…	…	−.145	0.28	…	…	−.146	0.19
X_9 = standardized crime 1960	.181	…	…	.221	0.59	…	…	.270	0.90	.238	0.48
X_{12} = pos. crime change 1960–70	−.025	…	…	…	…	…	…	.067	0.06	.113	0.11
X_{15} = log SMSA size 1960	−.099	−.126	0.24	−.187	0.47	−.120	0.21	−.194	0.49	−.191	0.42
Multiple R^2		.027		.064		.045		.064		.079	

NOTE.—$N = 19$; β = standardized regression coefficient; F = square of the ratio of the regression coefficient to its standard deviation.

Panel Analysis

To resolve the issue of causal direction in these relationships, we can make use of a path model for two-wave panel analysis (see Heise 1970). The model is appropriate because a city's density pattern cannot change instantaneously but is affected by push factors over a finite period—if it is affected by them at all. If a variable has a time-lagged effect on a city's degree of concentration, then we expect the effect of that variable measured at time 1 on the degree of concentration at time 2 to be greater than the effect of concentration at time 1 on the variable at time 2. To compare these effects, we compute path coefficients from all time 1 variables to each time 2 variable using standard multiple regression techniques. We can then compare the appropriate "cross-lagged" pair of path coefficients to identify the causal direction of the time-lagged relationship between any two variables.

In the two-wave path model, the time 1 level of concentration is one predictor of the time 2 level of concentration; other time 1 variables act to explain the residuals from this interperiod regression. We must select a measure of concentration for the panel analysis for which residuals from an interperiod linear regression are equivalent to the deconcentration scores we used in the above analysis of change scores. As shown in Section 3 of the Appendix, the reciprocal of the square root of central density meets this criterion. Therefore, in the panel analysis we will use $1/\sqrt{a}$ as our measure of a city's concentration: the higher the value, the less concentrated the city. A positive path from a time 1 variable to this measure indicates a deconcentrating effect.

The path model for panel analysis is based on the assumption "that there are no instantaneous effects in the system—that every cause-effect relationship exists across some finite time interval" (Heise 1970, p. 11). It would be hard to argue that the correlations of SMSA size with black percentage and crime rate, and the correlation between the latter two variables, are all the result of time-lagged causal relationships. It seemed advisable to adjust these variables to eliminate their instantaneous effects on each other before subjecting them to panel analysis under the path model. Instead of proportion black, we used the residuals from a linear prediction of proportion black from log SMSA size computed separately for each time period by simple least-squares regression. Instead of standardized crime, we used the residuals from a two-variable linear prediction of standardized crime from log SMSA size and proportion black computed separately for each time period by multiple regression. (However, if the correction for instantaneous effects is omitted and the uncorrected variables used, the results of the path analysis differ only slightly from those reported below.) The results of path model panel analysis of the four variables $1/\sqrt{a}$, log SMSA size, residual black proportion, and residual crime are presented in table 5 and the figures which accompany it. The figures are *not* complete path diagrams; they show only those pairs of crossed paths which are to be compared in assessing causal direction.

From figures A and B in table 5 we can see that central-city crime is not causing cities to deconcentrate, since the path coefficients from time 1 residual crime to time 2 concentration (.066, .052) are exceeded by the coefficients from time 1 concentration to time 2 crime (.137, .225). In both decades, there appears to be a time-lagged push effect of residual black proportion on concentration. Size has different effects in the two decades: it contributes slightly to deconcentration in the first decade and to increased concentration in the second decade.

In figures C and D of table 5 the path coefficients are recomputed with the residual crime variable eliminated from the model. They are almost identical to the corresponding coefficients of figures A and B. The push effect of residual proportion black was greater in the 1950s than in the 1960s, as shown by the greater difference between the cross-lagged path coefficients and by the higher coefficient for the path from time 1 minority presence to time 2 concentration in the earlier decade. However, the 1950 residual black proportion accounts for only 9.8% of the variance in 1960 concentration not accounted for by 1950 concentration and 1950 size; the corresponding percentage for the later decade is a mere 3.3%. We have again found a small and statistically nonsignificant effect in the direction predicted by the push hypothesis.

DISCUSSION

We have used a small data base in this paper because relatively few cities meet the assumptions of the method by which urban concentrations were determined. However, the outcome of this analysis is consistent with that which resulted when less refined methods were applied to a larger data base.[3] Whether density functions were calculated from SMSA or urbanized-area data, by the iterative procedure used here or by crude approximation, with or without corrections for sector size, and with outlier cases retained or eliminated, for 39 cities or fewer, no strong evidence to support the push hypothesis could be discovered.

Increases in central-city crime rates and in the size of central-city black populations are associated with metropolitan deconcentration rates if crude measures of urban concentration are used. But when deconcentration is ade-

---

[3] See Guterbock (1972) for an early report of results that seemed to support the push hypothesis. Later the computer data set used for that analysis was found to contain a fatal punching error. When the data were corrected, evidence for the push hypothesis all but disappeared and further refinements of the measures used failed to resurrect this evidence.

TABLE 5

Path Analysis Results

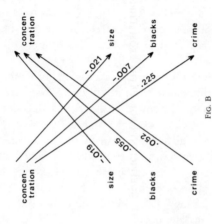

Fig. A

Fig. B

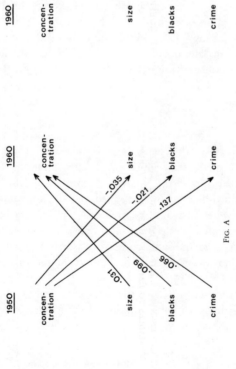

A. Coefficients for Paths from Four 1950 Variables to Each of Four 1960 Variables

From	X₁₈	X₁₄	X₄·₁₄	X₉·₁₄,₄
X_{17}	.985	-.035	-.021	.137
X_{13}	.031	.990	-.023	-.018
$X_{3·13}$	.099	.007	.969	.132
$X_{8·13,3}$	.066	.053	-.058	.854
	($R^2 = .917$)			

B. Coefficients for Paths from Four 1960 Variables to Each of Four 1970 Variables

From	X₂₀	X₁₆	X₅·₁₆	X₁₀·₁₆,₅
X_{19}	.956	-.021	-.007	.225
X_{15}	-.019	.991	-.008	.052
$X_{4·15}$	.055	.001	.977	.026
$X_{9·15,4}$	.052	.046	-.068	.600
	($R^2 = .917$)			

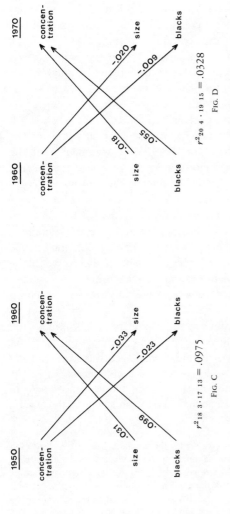

1950 | 1960

concentration · size · blacks

−.033 −.023 .099 .031

$r^2_{18\ 3\cdot 17\ 13} = .0975$

Fig. C

1960 | 1970

concentration · size · blacks

−.020 −.009 −.018 .055

$r^2_{20\ 4\cdot 19\ 15} = .0328$

Fig. D

C. Coefficients for Paths from Three 1950
Variables to Each of Three 1960 Variables

From	To X_{18}	X_{14}	$X_{4\cdot 14}$
X_{17}	.985	−.033	−.023
X_{13}	.031	.990	−.023
$X_{3\cdot 13}$	.099	.007	.968
$(R^2 = .917)$			

D. Coefficients for Paths from Three 1960
Variables to Each of Three 1970 Variables

From	To X_{20}	X_{16}	$X_{5\cdot 16}$
X_{19}	.957	−.020	−.009
X_{15}	−.018	.991	−.008
$X_{4\cdot 15}$	.055	.001	.977
$(R^2 = .914)$			

Note.—Variables are numbered as in table 3. A variable with dot subscript is the residual from the linear fit of the variable preceding the dot on the variable(s) following the dot; e.g., $X_{8\cdot 13\cdot 3}$ indicates (residual) standardized crime 1950 after log SMSA size 1950 and proportion black 1950 are controlled.

quately measured, variation in metropolitan size is controlled, and the causal direction of relationships between variables is established by path analysis, we find that crime rates rise as a *consequence* of metropolitan deconcentration and that the push effect of minority presence is small and statistically nonsignificant. We find nothing to indicate that racial tension caused more deconcentration in the 1960s than in the 1950s. On the contrary, what weak evidence there is indicates that the 1950s effect was stronger. We find that American cities deconcentrate at about the same rapid rate whether or not low-status minority group members are present in large numbers and whether or not the incidence of crime in the central city is high.

In fact, there does not seem to be much variation in the rate at which most SMSAs deconcentrate. If we control for metropolitan size and growth, we find that density gradients dropped 27.4% between 1950 and 1960, but deviations from this rapid rate of decline account for only 8.7% of the variance in 1960 gradients. The average amount of decline from 1960 to 1970 was 24.8%, with deviations from that rate accounting for only 9.3% of the variance in 1970 gradients.[4] Assume, for the sake of argument, that the statistically nonsignificant effect of minority presence on concentration suggested by the panel analysis results is real and not the chance result of error. The 1950 black proportion in the central city would then account for 9.8% of the variance in 1960 concentration that was not accounted for by 1950 concentration and 1950 size. But this would mean that the push hypothesis accounted for 9.8% of 8.7%, or less than 1%, of the intercity variation in 1960 density gradients. Its practical significance for 1970 gradients would be smaller still. Clearly, differences in the extent of suburbanization in urban areas are not the consequence of differences in push factors in the central cities.

We can now see that the "commonsense" notion of the "flight to the suburbs" is without foundation, just as the "panic selling" phenomenon becomes suspect when the realities of neighborhood succession are carefully analyzed. Our thinking about urban deconcentration would be advanced if we spoke of the *rush* to the suburbs rather than the flight, a movement in response to pull rather than push. In an affluent nation at mid-20th century,

---

[4] To arrive at these figures, we calculated in each decade the unstandardized partial regression coefficient of the time 2 density gradient on the time 1 density gradient with the log of time 1 SMSA size and the log of time 2 SMSA size controlled. This second-order partial slope subtracted from 1 yields the rate of decline in the gradient. The square of the corresponding second-order partial correlation coefficient was subtracted from 1 to yield the variance unexplained by the time 1 density gradient after size and growth were taken into account. The effect of size is to reduce further the amount of variation in the gradient decline. Note that these quantities were calculated for a group of 19 cities from which two cities had been deliberately excluded because they showed exceptionally little decline in density gradient as measured for this research.

the residential densities typical of the classic industrial city were simply obsolete.

The suburban subdivisions created to meet the new demand are not ideal places in which to live. Doubtless there are social costs incurred by those who migrate to dormitory communities. But it is a mistake to count these costs as part of the price Americans pay for their irrational racial hatreds and fears. In the press for less crowded and more modern quarters, certain population groups were denied access to the suburbs: the poor, the elderly, and members of conspicuous low-status minorities. The exclusion of blacks from most suburbs combined with the northward migration of southern black families to create massive concentrations of blacks in some central cities.

But we have seen that the rush to the suburbs also occurred in cities which received few black newcomers. The residents of the latter cities seem to be as willing to bear the costs of suburban life as those whose choice of residence is supposed to be governed by prejudice and fear. The suburbanization of whites coupled with the ghettoization of blacks exacerbates problems of inequality, discrimination, crime, and conflict, which we seem unable to solve. We pay a great price in America for our racial divisions. But deconcentration itself is not part of this price.

The implications go further. The push hypothesis, based on the notion that middle-class whites incur a social cost to gain separation from threatening conditions, is not solely a critique of American whites and the motives that govern their housing choices. It is easily transposed into an ugly kind of wishful thinking: "If only the blacks [or the Latins, or the criminals, or whatever] were not here, we would not have any urban problems." In abandoning the push hypothesis, we refresh our thinking by removing from our explanations of suburbanization the tendentious elements of blame.

APPENDIX

This Appendix provides the interested reader with details on several points in the text which are best described mathematically. We discuss first the calculation of the parameters of density functions from census data, then the Decon measure, and finally the selection of an appropriate concentration measure for panel analysis.

1. MEASURING CONCENTRATION

Imagine a metropolis whose population is distributed around a center according to the formula

$$D_x = ae^{-bx} , \tag{A1}$$

where, as in the text, D_x = population density at distance x from the city's center and a and b are positive parameters. If we plot the curve described by equation (A1) for positive values of x, we have an exponential curve whose slope is negative and decreases in absolute value. The curve reaches height a where $x = 0$ and approaches the x-axis asymptotically. If we rotate this curve about the line $x = 0$, we generate a three-dimensional, "cone-shaped" surface with concave sides that rises sharply from an infinite plane to a point at height a. This surface represents the density pattern of our imaginary city, and the height of the surface above any point on the plane represents the population density at that spot in the city. This is the model density pattern to which real cities conform to a large extent, despite the fact that real cities do not extend to infinite distance and usually have low residential densities at the very center where commercial land uses are concentrated.

In the model density pattern, the population contained within a radius r of the city's center is equal to the volume inside a cylinder of radius r and under the cone-shaped surface. Clark (1951) gives the formula for this population:

$$P_r = \int_0^r ae^{-bx}(2\pi x)\,dx = \frac{2\pi a}{b^2}\left[1 - (1 + br)e^{-br}\right].\qquad\text{(A2)}$$

The formula assumes that habitable land extends in all directions from the center. We can alter it to apply to cases where natural barriers restrict "sector size" to less than a full circle, leaving a habitable region shaped like a sliced pie,

$$P_r = \frac{ga}{b^2}\left[1 - (1 + br)e^{-br}\right],\qquad\text{(A3)}$$

where g is sector size in radians. Clark further points out that the indefinite integral of equation (A1) applied to the full circle or an appropriate sector of a circle gives the population within infinite distance, or the total population:

$$P_T = \frac{ga}{b^2}.\qquad\text{(A4)}$$

Suppose that the central city and SMSA of a metropolis approximate concentric circles (or sectors of circles) around the center. Let P_s, A_s, P_r, and A_r represent the populations and land areas of the SMSA and central city, respectively. First, calculate s and r, the average radii of SMSA and city:

$$s = \sqrt{\frac{A_s}{g}}, \qquad r = \sqrt{\frac{A_r}{g}}.\qquad\text{(A5)}$$

From formula (A3) we have

$$\frac{P_r}{P_s} = \frac{(ga/b^2)[1 - (1 + br)e^{-br}]}{(ga/b^2)[1 - (1 + bs)e^{-bs}]} = \frac{1 - (1 + br)e^{-br}}{1 - (1 + bs)e^{-bs}}.\qquad\text{(A6)}$$

This equation can be rewritten in simpler form if we define the new quantities $q = P_r/P_s$, $p = r/s$, and $z = bs$. Equation (A6) then becomes

$$q = \frac{1 - (1 + pz)e^{-pz}}{1 - (1 + z)e^{-z}}, \tag{A7}$$

which involves the ratio of central city and SMSA populations, the ratio of their average radii, and the unknown z.

We can use a numerical method to solve equation (A7) for z. Equation (A7) can be rewritten by straightforward algebraic manipulation as

$$z = \ln\left[\frac{(1 + pz)e^{(1-p)z} - q(z + 1)}{1 - q}\right]. \tag{A8}$$

This equation provides an algorithm by which the value of z can be determined for any q and p such that $0 < p < 1$, $0 < q < 1$, and $q > p^2$. An arbitrary positive starting value for z is selected, and the right side of equation (A8) is evaluated. This supplies a new value for z closer to the correct value which can again be plugged into the right side of equation (A8) to arrive at a still closer value, and so on in iterative fashion. Solution by this method is practical only with the aid of a programmable calculator or computer, but with enough iterations z can be evaluated to any desired degree of accuracy. Once we know z, we have $b = z/s$, and we can evaluate

$$a = \frac{(P_s)b^2}{g[1 - (1 + bs)e^{-bs}]}. \tag{A9}$$

Mills (1972, pp. 38–40) presents a slightly different method for calculating these parameters from SMSA and central-city population and area. His method deviates from that outlined above in that it assumes that zero density is reached at a distance equal to the SMSA radius. The effect of this assumption is that Mills's method will slightly overestimate density gradients.[5]

2. THE DECON MEASURE

We move now to a discussion of changes in concentration. Let a_t and a_{t+1} refer to the value of a at successive points in time, and let $\hat{a} = a_{t+1}/a_t$, $\hat{b} = b_{t+1}/b_t$, and $\hat{P}_T = P_{T_{t+1}}/P_{T_t}$. Then, from equation (A4),

$$\hat{P}_T = \frac{(ga_{t+1})/(b_{t+1})^2}{(ga_t)/(b_t)^2} = \frac{\hat{a}}{(\hat{b})^2} \tag{A10}$$

[5] I was not aware of Mills's work when I developed the materials in this section. The

Guterbock

and

$$\hat{b} = \sqrt{\hat{a}/\hat{P}_T} \, . \tag{A11}$$

We see that the decrease in b depends on the amount of decrease in a. We assume that a city with low initial central density (a_t) will not experience as great a proportional decrease in central density as a city with high a_t. That is,

$$E(\hat{a}) = F(a_t) \, , \tag{A12}$$

where $E(\hat{a})$ is the expected $\hat{a}$ and $F(a_t)$ is some function of a_t. Therefore, given the growth rate and initial central density of a city, we would expect deconcentration as reflected in the density gradient change to be

$$E(\hat{b}) = \sqrt{E(\hat{a})/\hat{P}_T} \, . \tag{A13}$$

To arrive at a formula for $E(\hat{a})$, we assume that the central densities of large American cities are tending downward toward an optimum central density, a_{opt}, that is identical for all cities during a given period. We assume that, on the average, the decline in a is proportional to the difference between a_t and the optimum for that decade. Then

$$E(a_{t+1}) = a_t - c(a_t - a_{\mathrm{opt}}) = (1 - c)a_t + c(a_{\mathrm{opt}}) \tag{A14}$$

and

$$E(\hat{a}) = \frac{E(a_{t+1})}{a_t} = c(a_{\mathrm{opt}}) \frac{1}{a_t} + (1 - c) \, , \tag{A15}$$

where c is some number between 0 and 1. The last equation shows that, under these assumptions, $E(\hat{a})$ is a linear function of $1/a_t$ whose slope and intercept in each decade can be estimated by regression of observed values of $\hat{a}$ on observed values of $1/a_t$. With $E(\hat{a})$ determined in this way, we can use equation (A13) to calculate an expected change in density gradient for any city on the basis of the initial central density and the rate of population growth. Our measure of deconcentration is the proportional difference between the observed and expected b_{t+1}:

$$\mathrm{Decon} = \frac{E(b_{t+1}) - b_{t+1}}{b_{t+1}} = \frac{b_t[E(\hat{b})] - b_{t+1}}{b_{t+1}} \, . \tag{A16}$$

---

re-parameterization of equation (A6) into equation (A7) was suggested by Henri Theil. David McFarland helped in the development of the numerical solution for equation (A7). David Morgan worked closely with me in the application of this solution and wrote computer programs which simplified the work.

Note, however, that from equations (A10) and (A13) we get

$$E(\hat{b}) = \sqrt{\frac{E(\hat{a})}{\hat{a}/\hat{b}^2}} = \hat{b}\sqrt{\frac{E(\hat{a})}{\hat{a}}} \; ; \tag{A17}$$

therefore,

$$E(b_{t+1}) = b_t[E(\hat{b})] = b_t(\hat{b})\sqrt{\frac{E(\hat{a})}{\hat{a}}} = b_{t+1}\sqrt{\frac{E(\hat{a})}{\hat{a}}} \tag{A18}$$

and

$$\mathrm{Decon} = \frac{b_{t+1}\sqrt{E(\hat{a})/\hat{a}} - b_{t+1}}{b_{t+1}} = \sqrt{\frac{E(\hat{a})}{\hat{a}}} - 1 . \tag{A19}$$

Although our strategy in measuring deconcentration has been to compare expected with observed time 2 density gradients, our assumptions about changes in density patterns have led us to a measure that actually compares expected and observed changes in central densities.

For 19 cities, regression of $\hat{a}$ on $1/a_t$ (with a corrected for sector size) yielded $c = .3500$, $a_{opt} = 6,372.5$ for 1950–60, and $c = .2572$, $a_{opt} = 3,695.5$ for 1960–70. These values were used in equations (A15) and (A19) to calculate the Decon values displayed in table 1.

3. CHOICE OF A MEASURE FOR PANEL ANALYSIS

A measure of concentration is needed for the panel analysis for which residuals from an interperiod linear regression are equivalent to the deconcentration scores used in the analysis of change data.

From equations (A15) and (A19) we see that

$$(\mathrm{Decon} + 1) = \sqrt{\frac{E(\hat{a})}{\hat{a}}} = \sqrt{\frac{j(1/a_t) + k}{a_{t+1}/a_t}} , \tag{A20}$$

where j and k are constants. Dividing both sides by $\sqrt{E(\hat{a})}$, we get

$$\frac{1}{\sqrt{j + ka_t}} (\mathrm{Decon} + 1) = \frac{1}{\sqrt{a_{t+1}}} . \tag{A21}$$

It is clear that $(\mathrm{Decon} + 1)$ is an error *coefficient* which represents the discrepancy between the observed inverse square root of a_{t+1} and a prediction of it from the inverse square root of a_t. Decon is thus closely related to the

159

error term r in a linear prediction equation for the inverse square root of a_{t+1}, which would have the form

$$\frac{1}{\sqrt{a_{t+1}}} = E\left(\frac{1}{\sqrt{a_{t+1}}}\right) + r = \left[v\sqrt{\frac{1}{a_t}} + w\right] + r, \qquad \text{(A22)}$$

where v and w are constants and r is an error term different for each case. For the data base used here, the correlation of Decon with r exceeds .99 in both decades studied. For purposes of correlation and regression, then, the residuals from linear regression of $\sqrt{1/a_{t+1}}$ on $\sqrt{1/a_t}$ are equivalent to Decon.

REFERENCES

Angell, Robert Cooley. 1951. "The Moral Integration of American Cities." *American Journal of Sociology* 57, no. 1, suppl. (July): 1–140.

Berry, Brian J. L. 1973. "Contemporary Urbanization Processes." Pp. 94–107 in *Geographical Perspectives on Urban Problems: A Symposium Organized by the Committee on Geography of the Division of Earth Sciences, September 20–21, 1971.* Washington, D.C.: National Academy of Sciences.

Berry, Brian J. L., and Frank E. Horton, eds. 1970. *Geographic Perspectives on Urban Systems.* Englewood Cliffs, N.J.: Prentice-Hall.

Berry, Brian J. L., James W. Simmons, and Robert J. Tennant. 1970. "Temporal and Cross-cultural Comparisons." Pp. 288–93 in *Geographic Perspectives on Urban Systems,* edited by Brian J. L. Berry and Frank E. Horton. Englewood Cliffs, N.J.: Prentice-Hall.

Clark, Colin. 1951. "Urban Population Densities." *Journal of the Royal Statistical Society* 114 (4): 490–96.

Duncan, Otis Dudley, Ray P. Cuzzort, and Beverly Duncan. 1961. *Statistical Geography: Problems in Analyzing Areal Data.* Glencoe, Ill.: Free Press.

Grodzins, Morton. (1958) 1970. "The Metropolitan Area as a Racial Problem." Pp. 479–501 in *Neighborhood, City, and Metropolis,* edited by David Popenoe and Robert Gutman. New York: Random House.

Guterbock, Thomas M. 1972. "Social Causation of Suburbanization in American Urban Areas." Mimeographed. Working Paper no. 200. Chicago: Center for Social Organization Studies.

Hawley, Amos H. 1971. *Urban Society: An Ecological Approach.* New York: Ronald.

Heise, David R. 1970. "Causal Inference from Panel Data." Pp. 3–27 in *Sociological Methodology 1970,* edited by Edgar F. Borgatta and George W. Bohrnstedt. San Francisco: Jossey-Bass.

Hoover, Edgar M. 1968. "The Evolving Form and Organization of the Metropolis." Pp. 237–84 in *Issues in Urban Economics,* edited by Harvey S. Perloff and Lowdon Wingo, Jr. Baltimore: Johns Hopkins University Press.

Kasarda, John D. 1972. "The Impact of Suburban Population Growth on Central City Service Functions." *American Journal of Sociology* 77 (May): 1111–24.

Mills, Edwin H. 1972. *Studies in the Structure of the Urban Economy.* Baltimore: Johns Hopkins University Press.

Molotch, Harvey L. 1972. *Managed Integration: Dilemmas of Doing Good in the City.* Berkeley: University of California Press.

Muth, Richard F. 1961. "The Spatial Structure of the Housing Market." *Papers and Proceedings of the Regional Science Association* 7:207–20.

Rees, Philip H. 1970. "The Axioms of Intra-urban Structure and Growth." Pp. 276–88 in *Geographic Perspectives on Urban Systems,* edited by Brian J. L. Berry and Frank E. Horton. Englewood Cliffs, N.J.: Prentice-Hall.

Sjoberg, Gideon. 1968. "City: The Modern City." Pp. 455–59 in *International Encyclopedia of the Social Sciences.* New York: Macmillan.

U.S. Federal Bureau of Investigation. Annually for 1950–70. *Uniform Crime Reports for the United States.* Washington, D.C.: Government Printing Office.

PART II

Institutional and Behavioral Ramifications

7   Suburbanization and Changing Political Structures

Basil G. Zimmer
Brown University

By the turn of the century the nation had been settled and the urban network largely established. The shift in population distribution since that time has been toward the city.[1] By 1920 a majority of the population lived in urban places. The United States had become an urban society. In the years to follow the urban population continued to increase more rapidly than the total population. The changing distribution of population has not only been in the direction of urban places but more particularly toward large urban centers.

In the early stages of urban development, with limited local transportation available, the population necessarily settled in rather compact units. As one author (Hawley 1971, pp. 88–89) has noted, " . . . the city of this period [the 19th century] was a pedestrian city; it was confined, therefore, to a radius of not more, and usually less, than three miles . . . houses were closely built on lots of twenty- to thirty-foot frontages. . . . space could not be squandered on yards and open spaces about each house." We find empirical support for this in a study of the population of Chicago in 1898, which reported that half of the 1.69 million inhabitants lived within a radial distance of 3.2 miles of the center of the city (Cressey 1938, p. 59). However, as short-distance transportation and communication improved and cities continued to increase in size, rapid growth took place on the periphery. A reversed pattern of population movement as well as communal organization was set in motion. The radius of daily interaction and the opportunities for increased contacts within the local community setting have grown as the barriers to communication and short-distance travel have decreased. The process of local expansion has been under way throughout the present century, involving a reconstitution of the old compact urban community on a new territorial basis and a different pattern of functional as well as spatial alignments (Hawley 1971, p. 145; McKenzie 1933, p. 81). In short, the compact urban center of the 19th century rapidly gave way to a much more wide-

---

[1] The movement pattern was largely at the expense of the rural farm areas in particular. With the persistent movement out of farm areas in excess of natural increase, the farm population decreased in absolute size.

spread type of community organization. The city gave way to the metropolitan community (Zimmer 1974).[2]

The increased scale of local community organization has been characterized thus:

> Local expansion created a new kind of urban center at the core of the enlarged and more highly integrated urban region. Instead of the dense, compact settlement unit laid down in the preceding century, there emerged a new, much more diffuse type of communal unit. Not only was the territorial scope of the sixty-minute radius increased to approximately twenty-five miles, the frequency and intensity of interactions within that expanded area were multiplied several-fold by the motor vehicle, the telephone, and other changes that facilitated communications. . . .
>
> Within the enlarged radius of daily communications, villages and open country settlements that had lived more or less aloof from the large center nearby were in a short space of time incorporated into an urban community. [Hawley 1971]

The increased scale of local community life is reflected in changes in the overall spatial patterning of the population.[3] This is evident when we focus on the changes in the territorial scope of daily activities which are reflected in the rate of growth and the changing distribution of population within metropolitan areas during the present century. Throughout the 70-year period, metropolitan area growth exceeded the growth rate of the total population. These data are shown in table 1. For each census period since 1900 the rate of growth of metropolitan areas exceeded the growth rate of central cities within metropolitan areas, while the growth rate of the areas outside of the central city exceeded that of the total metropolitan population. Thus, it is clearly evident that while there has been a continuous centripetal movement of population during the present century toward metropolitan areas, there has, at the same time, been a centrifugal drift of population within metropolitan areas. For each census period during the present century the

[2] Standard Metropolitan Statistical Areas (SMSAs) are operational concepts for the metropolitan community worked out by the U.S. Bureau of the Budget and used by the Census Bureau and other government agencies in reporting data. For a definition of SMSAs, see U.S. Bureau of the Budget (1967).

[3] One author has noted that "to achieve for a given population the same facility of circulation that the older concentrated cities had for pedestrian, horse-drawn, or even rail traffic, the modern city requires a land area many times greater. When movement and interchange were pedestrian and horse-drawn, an efficient area for a population of 200,000 might be about four square miles, for 200,000 people now, on a one or two persons per car basis (increasingly the normal pattern), the most efficient area might well be 100 square miles." The same author also noted that in 1850 Philadelphia had a population of 121,000, and an area of two square miles (Willbern 1964, p. 15).

areas outside of the central cities increased more rapidly than the population in the central cities. The differential growth rates have increased markedly in recent years.[4]

TABLE 1

CHANGE IN POPULATION IN UNITED STATES IN METROPOLITAN
AREAS AND NONMETROPOLITAN AREAS, 1900–1970
(%)

Selected Periods	Total Population	Metropolitan Areas (N)	Metropolitan Population	Central Cities	Outside Central Cities	Non-Metropolitan Areas
1900–1910	21.0	44	34.6	33.6	38.2	16.4
1910–20	14.9	58	26.9	25.2	32.0	9.6
1920–30	16.1	97	28.3	22.3	44.0	7.9
1930–40	7.2	140	8.1	5.1	15.1	6.5
1940–50	14.5	168	22.0	13.9	35.9	6.1
1950–60	18.5	212	26.3	10.7	48.6	7.1
1960–70	13.3	243	16.6	6.5	26.7	−4.0

SOURCES.—1900–1940, Thompson 1947; 1940–50, Hawley 1956, p. 2; 1950–60, U.S. Bureau of the Census 1961, p. xxvi; 1960–70; U.S. Bureau of the Census 1971, p. 143.

During the period 1950–60 the total population of the United States increased by approximately 28 million. Nearly 85% of the growth (23.6 million) was added to the 212 metropolitan areas. But of even more significance for the problem at hand is the fact that of the 23.6-million increase in population within metropolitan areas 18 million were added in the areas outside of central cities. This means that the suburban growth rate exceeded the central city growth rate by fivefold. During the 1960–70 period the outside areas increased more than four times the rate in the central cities. But these data understate what happened in metropolitan areas during both decades since most of the growth in central city population was due to the annexation of suburban territory. To illustrate, of the 5.6-million increase in central city population during the 1950 decade, 4.9 million had been added through annexation. Thus, of the 23.6-million increase in metropolitan area population during that decade, not 18 million but 22.9 million (97%) were added outside the boundaries of the central city at the beginning of the

[4] In the comparisons throughout the period, the same areas are used at both the beginning and end of the decade to avoid the inclusion of new territory. However, during each decade the number of metropolitan areas increased, caused either by natural growth or changes in definition. For example, in 1950 the metropolitan district was replaced by the Standard Metropolitan Statistical Area (SMSA) concept, which differed considerably in definition. For a discussion of change in definition, see Gist and Fava (1964), pp. 39–48.

period. Similarly, during the 1960 decade of the 3.9-million increase in central cities, 3.8 million or 98.7% were added through annexation. Thus, the centrifugal drift of population within metropolitan areas was even more marked in recent years than the Census Bureau reported. As shown in table 2, growth in the suburban areas would have been substantially higher if the suburbs had not lost population to the central cities through annexation (Zimmer 1974).

TABLE 2

RATE OF POPULATION GROWTH IN METROPOLITAN AREAS BY TYPE OF PLACE,
WITH AND WITHOUT ANNEXATION, 1950–60 AND 1960–70

	1950–60		1960–70	
	With Annexation	Without Annexation	With Annexation	Without Annexation
AREA	(212)	(212)	(243)	(243)
Total United States	18.5	18.5	13.3	13.3
Metropolitan areas	26.3	26.3	16.6	16.6
Central cities	10.8	1.5	6.5	0.1
Outside area	48.5	61.6	26.7	33.1

SOURCES.—1960–70, U.S. Bureau of the Census 1971*a*, p. 193; 1950–60, U.S. Bureau of the Census 1961, p. xxvi.
NOTE.—No. of areas shown in parentheses.

The more rapid growth of population in the suburban areas has changed the distribution of population within metropolitan areas. The consistent trend has been a decline in the proportion of the metropolitan area population living in central cities. For example, in 1910 three-fourths of the population lived in central cities, but this had decreased to only 45% by 1970. It is clearly evident that the population is becoming increasingly concentrated in metropolitan areas, and, at the same time and at an even more rapid rate, the population is becoming more widely distributed within the metropolitan community with a majority living in suburban areas.[5] The growth of metropolitan organization, which has greatly expanded the scope of daily life, has resulted from "the conquest of distance" as a barrier to community size.[6]

[5] Within metropolitan areas, many central cities have lost population in recent years. For example, of the 292 municipalities designated as central cities, 130 lost population during the 1960 decade. The aggregate population loss of these cities was 2.3 million (Lowry 1971, pp. 3–4).

[6] To limit the analysis to the SMSA may understate the amount of dispersion that has taken place. For example, "The Census Bureau defines the Indianapolis Metropolitan area as Marian County. This area increased in population by 24 percent between 1950 and 1960, a very substantial rate of growth. But the counties immediately to the north, east, south and west of

The decrease in travel time has been one of the major factors which has made the expansion of the urban unit possible (Foley 1974). In an analysis of changes in travel time in the Providence metropolitan area during the 10-year period 1955–65, it was reported that the distance one could travel with no increase in time had expanded substantially. And the amount of change increased as one moved further away from the central city. In the latter part of the period it was possible to travel approximately 15 miles further in 50 minutes than at the beginning. In 1955 it required 70 minutes to travel 40 miles from the center, but this was reduced to 50 minutes by 1965 (Zimmer 1974).[7]

The increased scope of daily activities or communal organization is partially reflected in the expansion of the urbanized portion of the metropolitan community. This unit of analysis markedly understates the expansion of local community life since it is limited to only the population that is densely settled in and around the core city.[8] The changes that have taken place from 1950 to 1970, even in this restricted area, are nonetheless instructive.

For the 155 urbanized areas identified in 1950, the central city population increased by 32% while the outlying areas increased by 160%. By 1970 only slightly more than half (52%) of the urbanized population lived in the central city area. During this period the urbanized territory increased from 12,800 to more than 30,000 square miles. Since land area expanded more rapidly than population there was a decrease in population density during the 20-year period (Zimmer 1974).

The increased scale of local community life is reflected in the expanded radial distance from the center to the outer boundary of the urbanized area, as shown in table 3. It is noted, however, that these data understate the distances involved in the urbanized area, since radial distance assumes equal development in all directions from the center whereas the actual settlement pattern is likely to be uneven in some directions and also more likely to

---

Marian County, not included in the census-defined metropolitan area, had growth rates of 40, 30, 67, and 65 percent respectively. The growth of these counties . . . is not considered in the statistics to be suburban growth, but the percentage growth has often been even greater than that of the suburban areas within the official metropolitan areas" (Willbern 1964, p. 18).

[7] It has been noted that it takes no longer to travel from the old city to the new suburbs today than it once took to cover the distance between the city's central business district and some of its residential areas (Abrams 1965).

[8] The urbanized area concept was first introduced in the 1950 census to provide a better separation of urban and rural population in the vicinity of the larger cities. An urbanized area contains at least one city of 50,000 inhabitants or more and includes the surrounding closely settled population. For a detailed description, see U.S. Bureau of the Census (1971), pp. xii–xiii.

extend along radial highways out from the center, thus resulting in a star-shaped rather than a circular pattern. Nonetheless, radial distance reflects the overall expansion that has taken place. While the widespread pattern of settlement is evident in all size classes, recent expansion tends to vary inversely by size of urbanized area. Radial distance at any given point in time, however, varies directly by size of urbanized population (Zimmer 1974).

TABLE 3

AVERAGE RADIAL DISTANCE OF URBANIZED AREA AND PERCENT
CHANGE, 1950–70, BY SIZE OF URBANIZED AREA

| | DISTANCE IN MILES | | | * PERCENT INCREASE |
SIZE OF AREA*	1950	1960	1970	1950–70
3 million or more	17.3	21.2	23.7	36.5
1–3 million	9.3	12.5	13.9	49.5
500,000–1 million	6.9	10.0	11.5	65.2
250,000–500,000	5.1	7.0	8.4	63.0
100,000–250,000	3.6	4.9	5.8	61.5
Under 100,000	2.6	3.6	4.0	52.7

*Based on 1950 population of urbanized areas.

THE POLITICAL STRUCTURE OF THE SUBURBAN RING

The growth of population and the marked changes in the distribution of population, as well as the changes in location of economic activities, reflect an increase in the scale of local community organization. It is important to note, for the problem at hand, that such changes occurred with little or no basic change in the overall political structure of metropolitan areas. Rather, this new widespread pattern of settlement has been largely superimposed on an existing system of local government and school systems which had been created during an earlier period when conditions of life were much different. As a consequence, school and municipal problems have reached acute forms in many metropolitan areas.[9] The segmentation of local governmental units

[9] The findings of a recent study by the Advisory Commission on Intergovernmental Relations of metropolitan fiscal disparities clearly substantiate the widespread belief that most of our major cities are now in desperate need, due to the rapid increase of "high-cost" citizens and the decrease in taxable resources. Cities are falling further behind their suburban neighbors with each passing year (Advisory Commission on Intergovernmental Relations 1967, 1970). On the average, the central city tax burden (taxes as a percentage of income) runs 30%–50% higher than that of the suburbs.

in metropolitan areas is extensive, as is shown in the discussion below, and the fragmentation of administrative units continues to increase at a rapid pace.

In one sense the changing distribution of population to the periphery areas of the community is a continuation of a long-term trend. American cities have always grown by adding population to the fringes of the previously built-up areas. And even the selective aspect of the outward-movement pattern is not of recent origin (Burgess 1923; Warner 1962). What makes this movement pattern essentially different is that the outward movement of population involves a movement across political boundaries that have remained largely unchanged. During an earlier period, particularly prior to the 1920s, the boundaries of the community tended to expand through annexation to accommodate the more widespread settlement pattern. But in more recent years annexation has become increasingly difficult and has lagged behind the territorial expansion of the settlement pattern. In more recent years, instead of the expansion of the central city area through annexation as had occurred historically, independent suburban governments sprang up or old governmental structures were remodeled to provide needed municipal services that formerly came only from city governments (Campbell and Dollenmayer 1974, p. 1).[10] As a consequence there has been a proliferation of local governmental units as suburban areas have attempted in many instances to replicate the government of the central city by incorporating the population living in close proximity. And where replication has not taken place alternative measures such as the establishment of special districts to provide selected urban-type services have been common (Zimmer 1974; Danielson 1971).

The proliferation of governmental units is evident from the data shown in table 4. The large number of administrative structures indicates the amount of fragmentation that has taken place within the metropolitan community. In 1962 there were more than 18,000 separate units of government, excluding 600 dependent school systems, in the 212 metropolitan areas. During the next 10 years more than 50 areas had increased in size of population so as to qualify as a metropolitan area, and by this time there were more than 22,000 separate governmental units, excluding 517 dependent school systems, in the 264 metropolitan areas. Most of the increase in number of governmental units in metropolitan areas during this period was due to the rapid increase in special district governments, but there was also a substantial

---

[10] These same authors point out that, while "annexation was alive and well in the 1960's in a few sections of the country, especially in the Southwest, it created a rash of new incorporations intended to prevent annexations by central cities" (Campbell and Dollenmayer 1974, p. 16).

increase in the number of municipalities in metropolitan areas. Some of this increase was due to the additional 50 areas attaining metropolitan status during the 10-year period, but most of the increase was due to separate incorporations. As noted previously, incorporation has frequently been used to protect areas from annexation to the central cities. However, it is also evident that there has been a marked decline (21%) in the number of school systems in metropolitan areas even though the number of areas increased by nearly one-fourth during the period.

The specific changes occurring in metropolitan areas become more evident when we focus on changes during specific time intervals for the same number of metropolitan areas. For each of the three time periods considered separately the same pattern of change is evident, but the amount of change is substantially less in more recent years. These data suggest that the fragmentation of governmental units may have largely stabilized by the time of the 1972 census of government. At least the rate of increase has declined. Since 1962 the total number of governmental units in metropolitan areas, when number of areas is held constant, declined. This decrease was due entirely to the decline in number of school systems, which decreased by nearly 20% during the 1957–62 period for the 212 metropolitan areas. During the next five years, for the 227 areas classified as metropolitan areas the number of school systems declined by more than 2,000, which is an additional decrease of nearly one-third. The decline continued during the next period also, but at a much lower rate. Throughout the 15-year period 1957–72 the number of school systems in metropolitan areas declined from 7,486 to 4,758 even though the number of metropolitan areas had increased from 212 to 264 during the period and the number of municipalities and townships increased markedly. The average number of independent school systems per metropolitan area declined during this period from 35 to 18.[11] In short, the number of school systems per metropolitan area had declined by nearly 50%. The significance of these changes will be explored more fully below.

Returning to the data shown in table 4, it is evident that the increase in counties from 311 in 1957 to 444 by 1972 was due entirely to the increase in number of metropolitan areas. While some of the increase in number of municipalities is also due to an increase in number of areas, a substantial part of the increase was due to separate incorporations, most of which occurred during the 1957–62 period. The increase in number of special districts for each of the periods covered in this analysis was substantial. Here, too, the most rapid increase occurred during the 1957–62 period when the number of special districts increased by approximately 45%. Special districts continued

---

[11] Dependent school districts are not counted as separate governmental units.

TABLE 4

NUMBER OF GOVERNMENTAL UNITS IN METROPOLITAN AREAS BY TYPE OF GOVERNMENT AND PERCENT CHANGE FOR SELECTED YEARS FOR CONSTANT AREAS

TYPE OF GOVERNMENTS	212 METROPOLITAN AREAS			227 METROPOLITAN AREAS			264 METROPOLITAN AREAS		
	1957	1962	Percent Change	1962	1967	Percent Change	1967	1972	Percent Change
School districts	7,486	6,004	−19.8	7,072	5,018	−29.0	5,421	4,758	−12.2
Other local governments	10,498	12,438	18.5	14,745	15,685	6.4	16,820	17,427	3.6
Counties	311	310	−0.3	407	404	−0.7	447	444	−0.7
Municipalities	3,844	4,144	7.8	4,903	4,977	1.5	5,319	5,467	2.8
Townships	2,607	2,573	−1.3	3,282	3,255	−0.8	3,485	3,462	−0.7
Special districts	3,736	5,411	44.8	6,153	7,049	14.6	7,569	8,054	6.4
Total	17,984*	18,442*	2.6	21,817*	20,703*	−5.1	22,241*	22,185*	−0.3

*Excludes dependent school systems.

to increase during the latter periods also but at a much lower rate. During the 15-year period there was a marked proliferation in the number of special districts, which more than doubled while the number of metropolitan areas increased by only 25%.

The fragmentation of governmental units varies substantially by size of metropolitan area. During the 10-year period 1962–72 the number of non-school-system governments increased from slightly less than 12,000 to nearly 17,000 units. These data are shown in table 5. The average number of units per metropolitan area increased from 56 to 64. Thus, while the number of such governmental units increased by 40% during the period, it is evident that during recent years most of this increase was due to the increase in number of metropolitan areas, since the average number of units increased by only 15%.

The average number of governmental units per metropolitan area increased in all size classes except one during the period. By 1972 the number of units ranged from a low of 14 per area in the smallest metropolitan areas to nearly 200 in the largest.[12] However, the average population per governmental unit also tends to vary directly by size of population. In the size classes below 500,000 there are approximately 5,000 or 6,000 people for each unit of government, but the average population per unit exceeds 12,000 in the largest metropolitan areas. Thus, while the smaller areas do support substantially fewer governmental units than the larger areas, they appear to be even more wasteful and more fragmented because of the small number of people in such areas to support each governmental unit.

What types of governmental units make up the fragmented structure of government in metropolitan areas? It is to this question that we now turn our attention, but only nonschool-system governments will be considered in the first part of our discussion. While municipal governments make up about one-third of the governmental units, such areas contain nearly three-fourths of the metropolitan area population.[13] However, the proportion of

---

[12] This ranges to as high as 1,172 local governments for the Chicago metropolitan area (U.S. Bureau of the Census 1972), 1:11.

[13] "For purposes of Census classification, a municipality is a political subdivision within which a municipal corporation has been established to provide general local government for a specific population concentration in a defined area. A municipality may be legally termed a city, village, borough (except in Alaska), or town (except in the New England States, New York, and Wisconsin). In Alaska, the term 'borough' corresponds to units classed as county governments and in New England, New York, and Wisconsin, the term 'town' relates to an area subdivision which (although it may be legally termed a municipal corporation and have a similar governmental organization) has no necessary relationship to a concentration of population and thus corresponds to townships in other states. The above concept of munici-palities corresponds generally to the 'incorporated places' that are recognized in Census Bu-reau reporting of population and housing statistics subject to an important qualification—the

TABLE 5

AVERAGE NUMBER OF GOVERNMENTAL UNITS AND AVERAGE POPULATION PER UNIT
FOR TOTAL GOVERNMENTAL UNITS AND NONSCHOOL-SYSTEM GOVERNMENTS
FOR SELECTED YEARS BY SIZE OF METROPOLITAN AREA

SIZE OF METROPOLITAN AREA	AREAS (N)	TOTAL GOVERNMENTAL UNITS			NONSCHOOL-SYSTEM GOVERNMENTS		
		Government Units (N)	$\bar{X}$ No. per Area	$\bar{X}$ Population per Unit	Government Units (N)	$\bar{X}$ No. per Area	$\bar{X}$ Population per Unit
				1962			
1 million or more	24	7,229	301.2	8,519	4,638	193.3	13,278
500,000–999,999	29	2,857	98.5	6,726	1,965	67.8	9,779
300,000–499,999	28	2,144	76.6	4,838	1,332	47.6	7,788
200,000–299,999	41	3,142	76.6	3,241	2,046	49.9	4,977
100,000–199,999	68	2,539	37.3	3,849	1,625	23.9	6,014
50,000–99,999	22	531	24.1	3,316	232	10.6	7,591
Total	212	18,442	87.0	6,121	11,838	55.8	9,536
				1972			
1 million or more	33	8,847	268.1	9,119	6,566	199.0	12,287
500,000–999,999	33	3,307	100.2	6,815	2,522	76.4	8,937
300,000–499,999	36	3,213	89.3	4,144	2,485	69.0	5,358
200,000–299,999	51	2,784	54.6	4,563	2,251	44.1	5,644
100,000–199,999	84	3,505	41.7	3,381	2,721	32.4	4,355
50,000–99,999	27	529	19.6	4,130	365	13.5	5,986
Total	264	22,185	84.0	6,458	16,910	64.1	8,472

population living in such areas has declined slightly over the past 10 years as the pattern of settlement has become more widespread. In 1962 municipal areas accounted for 75.2% of the metropolitan population, but this had declined to 72.3% by 1972. On the other hand, township areas increased their proportion of the total population from 19.5% to 20.9% during the same period. While none of these changes is sizable, the consistency of the trend is noteworthy since unincorporated township areas are more likely to be further from the central cities than municipalities.

As shown in table 6, a very large proportion of the municipal units within metropolitan areas have a population of less than 5,000. For each of the census periods covered about two out of three municipalities were below this size limit. Actually one-half of the units have a population of less than 2,500, and nearly one in three had a population of less than 1,000. What is strikingly clear from the data on population distribution is that only a very small proportion of the municipal population lives in a large number of small areas, but the proportion has increased slightly over the 10-year period from 4.7% in 1962 to 5.2% in 1972. During this same period the proportion of municipal population living in the core areas of 50,000 or more had declined from 74.7% in 1962 to 70.1% at the time of the last census. It is noteworthy that the large number of small municipality areas contains only a small proportion of the total metropolitan area population living in municipal areas. The marked difference between the distribution of municipalities and the distribution of population by size of municipality is to be noted since it clearly shows that the proliferation of separate incorporations of small populations within metropolitan areas has been brought about by a very small segment of the metropolitan population. In 1972 one-half of the municipalities had a population of less than 2,500, but these areas accounted for only 2.5% of the population living in municipalities within metropolitan areas.

When we examine the distribution of townships and the distribution of population by size of township, as shown in table 7, we continue to find that a large number of autonomous units contain only a small proportion of the metropolitan area population that lives in township areas. For example, for each census period one-fifth of the township areas had a population of less than 1,000, and the combined population living in such areas accounted for less than 2% of the population living in township areas. On the other hand, approximately one-half of the township population lived in areas with a population of 25,000 or more, but such areas accounted for only 7.5% of the

---

count of municipalities in this report excludes places which are reported as currently governmentally inactive" (ibid., 1:2).

TABLE 6

Number and Percent Distribution of Municipalities in Metropolitan Areas by Size of Municipality for Selected Years, 1962–72

Size of Municipality	1962 (212)		1967 (227)		1972 (264)	
	N	%	N	%	N	%
	Municipal Units					
50,000 or more	310	7.5	314	6.3	384	7.0
25,000–49,999	196	4.7	212	4.3	303	5.5
10,000–24,999	456	11.0	505	10.1	651	11.9
5,000–9,999	512	12.4	586	11.8	677	12.4
2,500–4,999	564	13.6	666	13.4	775	14.2
1,000–2,499	845	20.4	1,032	20.7	1,064	19.5
Less than 1,000	1,261	30.4	1,662	33.4	1,613	29.5
Total	4,144	100.0	4,977	100.0	5,467	100.0
	Population (Thousands) in Municipal Units					
50,000 or more	63,460	74.7	64,044	72.6	72,629	70.1
25,000–49,999	6,780	8.0	7,421	8.4	10,593	10.2
10,000–24,999	7,081	8.3	7,805	8.8	10,293	9.9
5,000–9,999	3,638	4.3	4,159	4.7	4,803	4.6
2,500–4,999	2,001	2.4	2,356	2.7	2,762	2.7
1,000–2,499	1,386	1.6	1,675	1.9	1,763	1.7
Less than 1,000	590	0.7	783	0.9	793	0.8
Total	84,936	100.0	88,243	100.0	103,636	100.0

Sources.—1962: U.S. Bureau of the Census 1964, p. 4; 1967: U.S. Bureau of the Census 1969, p. 20; 1972: U.S. Bureau of the Census 1973, p. 84.
Note.—No. of Metropolitan areas shown in parentheses.

townships in metropolitan areas. Thus here, too, we find that a large proportion of the township areas contain only a small proportion of the population. Again it is evident that the marked fragmentation of governmental units within metropolitan areas involves only a small minority of the metropolitan area population. In 1972 less than 7% of the township population and less than 3% of the municipal population lived in governmental areas of less than 2,500 population. Such areas, however, accounted for approximately half of the areas of each type. By way of contrast, only 7% of the municipalities had a population of 50,000 or more, but these areas accounted for 70% of the municipality population. And while less than 37% of the townships had a population of 50,000 or more, such areas contained one-third of the township population.

That the fragmentation of governmental units in metropolitan areas is made up disproportionately of very small jurisdictions is even more evident

TABLE 7

Number and Percent Distribution of Townships and Population of
Townships in Metropolitan Areas by Size of Township for
Selected Years, 1962–72

Size of Township	1962		1967		1972	
	N	%	N	%	N	%
	Townships					
50,000 or more ⎫			⎧ 71	2.2	92	2.7
25,000–49,999 ⎬ ...	514	20.0	⎨ 111	3.4	161	4.7
10,000–24,999 ⎭			⎩ 357	11.0	459	·13.3
5,000–9,999 ⎫			⎧ 437	13.4	472	13.6
2,500–4,999 ⎬ ...	1,531	59.5	⎨ 582	17.9	627	18.1
1,000–2,499 ⎭			⎩ 983	30.2	977	28.2
Less than 1,000	528	20.5	714	21.9	674	19.5
Total	2,573	100.0	3,255	100.0	3,462	100.0
	Population (Thousands)					
50,000 or more ⎫			⎧ 7,282	30.8	9,761	32.6
25,000–49,999 ⎬ ...	16,269	73.8	⎨ 3,767	15.9	5,478	18.3
10,000–24,999 ⎭			⎩ 5,426	22.9	7,113	23.8
5,000–9,999 ⎫			⎧ 3,093	13.1	3,329	11.1
2,500–4,999 ⎬ ...	5,476	24.9	⎨ 2,052	8.7	2,224	7.4
1,000–2,499 ⎭			⎩ 1,618	6.8	2,224	5.5
Less than 1,000	291	1.3	413	1.8	369	1.2
Total	22,036	100.0	23,651	100.0	29,905	100.0

Sources.—1962: U.S. Bureau of the Census 1964, p. 21; 1967: U.S. Bureau of the Census 1969, p. 19; 1972: U.S. Bureau of the Census 1973, p. 84.

from the data shown in table 8. The typical metropolitan area consists of 34 separate political jurisdictions, that is, municipalities or townships. Of this number 21 are municipalities and 13 are township areas. The typical metropolitan area, in addition to the large central city, has a suburban area which is made up of two jurisdictions with a population of 25,000–49,990, about nine areas between 5,000 and 24,999, and 22 areas of less than 5,000 population. It is of particular interest to note that the 10 municipalities and nearly seven townships with a population of less than 2,500, which on the average account for nearly half of the jurisdictions in each metropolitan area, contain approximately 3% of the total metropolitan population. Actually such units contain only slightly more than 6% of the population that is classified as suburban even though they account for 50% of the jurisdictions in suburban areas.

It is evident from the distribution of jurisdictions and of population that

TABLE 8

AVERAGE NUMBER AND PERCENT DISTRIBUTION OF MUNICIPALITIES AND
TOWNSHIPS AND POPULATION PER UNIT BY SIZE OF AREA, 1972

Size of Unit by Type	Units (N)	Average N per Area	Distribution (%)	Average Population per Unit	Distribution of Population (%)
			Municipalities		
50,000 or more	384	1.5	4.3	189,130	50.7
25,000–49,999	303	1.2	3.4	34,961	7.4
10,000–24,999	651	2.5	7.3	15,811	7.2
5,000–9,999	677	2.6	7.6	7,094	3.4
2,500–4,999	775	2.9	8.7	3,565	1.9
1,000–2,499	1,064	4.0	11.9	1,660	1.2
Less than 1,000	1,613	6.1	18.1	492	0.6
Total	5,467	20.7	61.3	18,956	72.3*
			Townships		
50,000 or more	92	0.4	1.0	106,097	6.8
25,000–49,999	161	0.6	1.8	34,026	3.8
10,000–24,999	459	1.7	5.1	15,496	5.0
5,000–9,999	472	1.8	5.3	7,075	2.3
2,500–4,999	627	2.4	7.0	3,546	1.6
1,000–2,499	977	3.7	10.9	1,670	1.1
Less than 1,000	674	2.6	7.6	547	0.3
Total	3,462	13.1	38.7	8,638	20.9*
Total metro-politan area ..	8,929	33.8	100.0	16,045	100.0

SOURCE.—U.S. Bureau of the Census 1973, p. 84, table 17.
*Does not add to 100.0 since 6.8% of the metropolitan area population lived outside such areas.

two out of every three residents in metropolitan areas live in jurisdictions with a population in excess of 25,000 while only a very small minority live in the large numbers of jurisdictions with less than 2,500 population. These data clearly show, as already noted, that a very high proportion of the fragmentation of government is attributed to the large number of small jurisdictions which contain a very small proportion of the metropolitan population. The average number of jurisdictions and the average population per unit, in each size class, are shown in table 8, along with the percentage distribution of units and of population within the metropolitan area by size classes. The number of municipalities and township units increases inversely by size class while the size and proportion of the metropolitan population vary in the opposite direction. To illustrate, while there is an average of six

179

municipalities in each metropolitan area with a population of less than 1,000, which accounts for nearly one-fifth of all jurisdictions within the metropolitan area, only slightly more than one-half of 1% of the metropolitan population lives in such areas.

Another aspect of the segmentation of governmental units in metropolitan areas is the growth of special districts. The creation of special districts is facilitated by state laws which usually do not provide for a popular referendum on the question of the creation of the district. Existing local governments continue to perform all of the regular functions with the exception of the one(s) assigned to the special districts (Zimmerman 1974). As is shown in table 9, special districts in metropolitan areas have increased from 5,411 in 1962 to 8,054 in 1972. Thus, during the 10-year period such units, most of which have independent property taxing powers, increased by approximately 50%. As noted previously, no other type of governmental unit increased at such a high rate during the period. However, the proportion has been on the decrease in recent years. More than nine out of every 10 special districts provide only a single function, but in recent years there has been a sizable increase in the number and proportion of special districts that perform more than one function. Yet, even as late as 1972 only 7% were classified as multifunction districts.

Special-district governments are becoming of increased importance as a method of resolving service problems in metropolitan areas. By 1972 they accounted for nearly half (46%) of the nonschool governmental units in metropolitan areas. Only a small proportion of the special districts are territorially coterminous with any other unit of government, but there has been a slight increase in recent years. By 1972 about one district out of five was coterminous with either a municipal or township area. With the exception of the 5% that were countywide in area served, all of the other special districts crossed over boundary lines of other governmental units. Two out of three special districts crossed either a municipal or township boundary or both. Special districts have been widely criticized because of their low political and fiscal visibility (Scott and Corzine 1971). It is in the special-district areas that have boundaries which are diffuse, overlapping, or unknown to the voter that voter turnout is least, since no definite and familiar geographical boundaries exist (Koepp 1962). One of the reasons given for voter apathy and lack of concern is that citizens are not informed about or interested in district activities. Also, sheer number of districts and the frequency of elections make impossible demands upon the voters' time and attention (Scott and Corzine 1971).[14] At any rate, special districts continue to perform

---

[14] These same authors state, "Special district elections [in the San Francisco Bay area] are scheduled according to statute. The election date varies, depending on the type of district. Fire protection districts, for example, hold their elections annually on the first Tuesday of April;

urban-type service functions for selected parts of the metropolitan area population.[15]

Since most special districts rely upon user charges, they are not restricted by constitutional and statutory tax limits. Thus revenue bonds, exempt from tax limits, can be issued without a popular referendum. It has been noted that special districts further fragment an already fractionated political system and make the government of the metropolis more complex. It is not unusual to have several special districts within a given metropolitan area, and each one may have different geographical boundaries. Consequently, the coordination of district and local government activities has at times been difficult and cumbersome. Critics have frequently charged that metropolitan special districts exceed their authority and that many are responsible to no one, since only a small minority of the governing bodies of these districts are popularly elected. The members of most governing bodies are appointed or hold office by virtue of other offices they hold (Zimmerman 1974). It is of more than passing interest to note that, while suburban residents resist areawide government because of their desire for local autonomy and their desire to be close to their government, they have nonetheless attempted to resolve their service problems by creating a unit of government in which they largely lose popular control over both the financing and the administration of selected service functions.

In addition to the segmentation of governmental units already considered is the large number of independent and dependent school systems that are superimposed on the governmental structure of metropolitan areas. While there has been a marked decline in the number of school systems in metro-

---

sanitary districts, biennially, on the second Tuesday in September in even numbered years; county water districts, biennially, on the fourth Tuesday in March every second year after the districts' formation; and public utility districts on the first Tuesday in May every second year after formation. The elections are seldom given wide publicity. . ." (Scott and Corzine 1971, p. 203).

[15] Another frequently used ad hoc approach to service problems is for local units to contract for a service either with another governmental unit or with private firms. Data on the extensiveness of such agreements are limited since they are not reported as governmental units. However, in a 1972 mail questionnaire study of some 5,900 areas of 2,500 population or over made under the sponsorship of the Advisory Commission on Intergovernmental Relations and the International City Management Association, it was found that 63% of the 2,375 municipalities (40%) who responded to the inquiry had entered into formal or informal agreements for the provision of services to their citizens by other governmental units or private firms. In general, larger units were more likely to enter such agreements than smaller ones. These agreements further complicate local government structure. These data suggest that fragmentation of the service function is even more extensive than shown by the U.S. Bureau of the Census (1973).

TABLE 9

SELECTED CHARACTERISTICS OF SPECIAL DISTRICTS FOR
SELECTED YEARS, 1962–72
(%)

Selected Characteristic	1962 (5,411)	1967 (7,049)	1972 (8,054)
Nonschool governments	43.6	44.9	46.2
With taxing powers	58.2	55.1	53.9
Single-function districts	96.7	96.0	93.0
Multifunction districts	3.3	4.0	7.0
		Area Served	
Coterminous with other units:			
Countywide	*	5.3	5.6
Citywide	*	9.9	11.0
Townshipwide	*	8.0	8.5
Total	*	23.2	25.1
Noncoterminous with other units:			
Multicounty	*	7.5	7.4
Other	*	69.3	67.5
Total	*	76.8	74.9

NOTE.—*N*'s shown in parentheses.
*Data not available.

politan areas, even though the number of such areas has increased, it is nonetheless noted that there were still about 20 school systems in each metropolitan area at the time of the last census of government in 1972. Significant changes have occurred in recent years, however, as shown in table 10. There has been a substantial decline in the number as well as the proportion of the school systems that are either nonoperating or provide for the elementary grades only. Nonoperating districts declined from 912 in 1962 to only 43 in 1972. While such districts accounted for 14% of the school systems in the earlier period, they had declined to less than 1% by 1972.[16] During the same period the proportion of systems providing for the elementary grades only decreased from approximately two-fifths to only one-fourth of the systems in metropolitan areas. On the other hand, there

[16] Nonoperating systems carry out their responsibility by providing transportation and paying tuition or reimbursement to other school systems for any public school students who live in their respective areas (U.S. Bureau of the Census 1973, 1:6).

TABLE 10

SELECTED CHARACTERISTICS OF SCHOOL SYSTEMS IN METROPOLITAN
AREAS FOR SELECTED YEARS, 1962–72

SELECTED CHARACTERISTICS	1962		1967		1972	
	N	%	N	%	N	%
Grades provided:						
Elementary only .	2,548	38.6	1,652	29.9	1,385	26.3
Secondary only ..	362	5.5	378	6.8	471	8.9
Both	2,782	42.1	3,249	58.8	3,376	64.0
Nonoperating ...	912	13.8	250	4.5	43	0.8
Total	6,604	100.0	5,529	100.0	5,275	100.0
			Area Served			
Coterminous with:						
County	74	1.1	142	2.7	186	3.5
City	834	12.6	599	10.8	564	10.7
Township	946	14.3	593	10.7	505	9.6
Total	1,854	28.1	1,334	24.1	1,255	23.8
Noncoterminous ...	4,750	71.9	4,195	75.9	4,020	76.2

SOURCES.—U.S. Bureau of the Census 1962, 1964, 1973.

was a sharp increase in the proportion of systems that provided both elementary and secondary grades. Such school systems increased from two-fifths to two-thirds during the 10-year period.

It is noted further that there was a decrease in the proportion of school districts that were coterminous with other local government areas. Systems that were coterminous with either city or township boundaries decreased from one in four in 1962 to one in five by 1972. The number of such districts declined from 1,780 to 1,069. No doubt these changes resulted from the enlargement of systems to extend beyond the boundary lines of such areas. Some of the change is reflected in the threefold increase in the proportion of districts that serve a countywide area. But even by 1972 such systems accounted for less than 4% of the school systems in metropolitan areas. A large majority of the school systems, that is, three out of four, are not coterminous with any other local government area. Most such districts are in suburban zones superimposed on the large number of small municipality and township areas, thus further fragmenting the governmental structure of such areas.

In recent years there has been a marked change in the size of school systems, measured by number of pupils enrolled in metropolitan areas.[17] As shown in table 11, while the total number of school systems in metropolitan areas declined by one-fifth during the 10-year period 1962–72, the number of systems with 1,200 or more pupils increased by nearly 40%. All other-sized districts declined during the period. The rate of decline, however, varied from 25% for the systems with enrollments between 300 and 1,200 to a high of 95% among the nonoperating systems. While only two-fifths of the systems had 1,200 or more enrollments in 1962, the proportion increased to slightly more than two-thirds by 1972. Thus, it is evident that a large number of the smaller districts were eliminated through district reorganization. This did not, however, have much of an impact on the proportion of pupils enrolled in the larger districts, since even in the earlier period only 5% of the total enrollments were in the 60% of the districts under 1,200 pupils.

The changes in number of school systems should be viewed with caution as there is a danger that these changes would suggest that substantial progress was being made in resolving the issue of fragmentation of the education function in metropolitan areas. Certainly the reduction of school systems from an average of 31 in 1962 to only 20 in 1972 represents a significant reduction in number of systems, but it does not reflect a resolution of the basic problem of a multiplicity of school systems within metropolitan areas. Quite the contrary, the changes that have taken place are due largely to the elimination through consolidation of only the very small systems which are likely in the outer fringes of the metropolitan area. Little progress has been made in reorganizing districts on a scale that would even approach the establishment of a metropolitan school system. Fragmentation remains high, particularly in the larger metropolitan areas. It seems that most of the decrease in school systems affected only a very small proportion of the pupils that had been in nonoperating or very small enrollment systems during the earlier period.

The changes that have taken place in school systems by size of metropolitan area are shown in table 12. While the total number of metropolitan areas increased by one-fifth, the number of school systems decreased by the same proportion. The average number of school systems per metropolitan area declined by nearly one-third, decreasing from 31 to 20 systems. The average number of school systems per metropolitan area varies directly by size of metropolitan area. The number ranged from 14 in the smallest to 108 in the largest metropolitan area in 1962. Ten years later, however, the range was from only six to 69 for the same sized classes. The relative decline in number

---

[17] The enrollment counted for each school system is intended to cover not only pupils enrolled from within its own area but also any nonresident pupils transferred in from other areas. On this basis, zero enrollment is reported for nonoperating school systems (U.S. Bureau of the Census 1973, 1:6).

TABLE 11

Number and Percent Distribution of School Systems and Enrollments in Metropolitan Areas by Size of Enrollments for Selected Years

Size of Enrollment	1962 (212)		1967 (227)		1972 (264)		Percent Change 1962–72
	N	%	N	%	N	%	
School Systems							
1,200 or more	2,556	38.7	3,112	56.3	3,563	67.6	39.4
300–1,199	1,410	21.4	1,218	22.0	1,065	20.2	−24.5
50–299	1,066	16.2	691	12.5	491	9.3	−53.9
1–49	660	10.0	258	4.6	113	2.2	−82.9
None	912	13.8	250	4.5	43	0.8	−95.3
Total	6,604	100.0	5,529	100.0	5,275	100.0	−20.1
Enrollments (Thousands)							
1,200 or more	21,296	94.9	27,503	96.6	32,349	97.5	51.9
300–1,199	968	4.3	855	3.0	758	2.3	−21.7
50–299	159	0.7	106	0.4	79	0.3	−50.3
1–49	16	0.1	7	…	3	…	−81.3
None	…	…	…	…	…	…	…
Total	22,440	100.0	28,472	100.0	33,189	100.0	47.9

SOURCES.—1962: U.S. Bureau of the Census 1964, p. 5; 1967: U.S. Bureau of the Census 1969, p. 10; 1972: U.S. Bureau of the Census 1973, p. 11.

NOTE.—Total SMSAs shown in parentheses.

of school systems was largest in the smaller metropolitan areas.

The increase in the proportion of larger and the decrease in the proportion of the smaller districts is worthy of note. While only half of the districts in the larger metropolitan areas in 1962 enrolled 1,200 or more pupils, this had increased to three-fourths by 1972. In the smallest metropolitan areas the increase in the larger systems was from 13% to 42% during the same period. Even larger changes are noted in the decline of the smaller systems, that is, those that enrolled fewer than 300 pupils or were nonoperating systems. In the largest metropolitan areas the decline was from 30% to 9%, and in the smallest areas the proportion decreased from 74% to 29% during the period. A comparable pattern of change is noted for each size class. The most marked decrease in the number of school systems occurred in the smaller metropolitan areas even though the number of such metropolitan areas increased more than the total number of metropolitan areas. These changes are shown in the bottom portion of table 12. Even though substantial changes have been under way, it is noted that there is still a large number of small school systems in metropolitan areas, ranging from nearly one in 10 in the larger metropolitan areas to more than one in four in the small metropolitan areas. While three out of four of the systems in the larger metropolitan areas have enrollments of 1,200 or more, in the smaller metropolitan areas only half or less of the systems are of this size—again suggesting that fragmentation of the education function continues to characterize the average metropolitan area.[18]

THE PROBLEM OF REORGANIZATION

When these structures are added to the larger number of municipalities, townships, and special districts in metropolitan areas, it becomes evident that such areas have made little progress in recent years in the resolution of the problem associated with the segmentation of governmental units in metropolitan areas. The proliferation of governmental units of all types tends to vary directly by size of metropolitan area. In short, as the population continues to spread out from the center in a more widespread pattern of settlement, the area becomes increasingly fragmented into a number of autonomous governmental units. Not only has there been a large number of municipalities incorporated within commuting distance of metropolitan centers,[19] but

---

[18] The marked disparity in resources for central city and suburban schools is also worthy of note. The educational expenditure gap in favor of the suburbs has widened substantially in recent years.

[19] About half of the municipalities in metropolitan areas have less than a single square mile of land area (National Commission on Urban Problems 1969, p. 7).

TABLE 12

PERCENT DISTRIBUTION OF SCHOOL SYSTEMS AND PERCENT CHANGE BY SIZE OF PUBLIC SCHOOL ENROLLMENTS BY SIZE OF METROPOLITAN AREA FOR SELECTED YEARS

SIZE OF ENROLLMENT	Total	SIZE OF METROPOLITAN AREA					
		1,000,000 or More	500,000–999,999	300,000–499,999	200,000–299,999	100,000–199,999	50,000–99,999
				1962			
Metropolitan areas (N)	212	24	29	28	41	68	22
Total %	100.0	100.0	100.0	100.0	100.0	100.0	100.0
School systems (N)	6,604	2,591	892	812	1,096	914	299
1,200 or more	38.7	49.2	48.4	32.8	25.7	28.7	13.0
300–1,199	21.4	21.2	22.2	24.4	18.2	24.8	13.0
50–299	16.2	12.1	16.1	18.4	17.5	22.2	21.4
1–49	10.0	4.4	6.3	9.5	17.6	15.7	25.4
None	13.8	13.1	7.0	14.9	21.0	8.6	27.1
Average N	31.1	108.0	30.8	29.0	26.7	13.4	13.6
				1972			
Metropolitan areas (N)	264	33	33	36	51	84	27
Total %	100.0	100.0	100.0	100.0	100.0	100.0	100.0
School systems (N)	5,275	2,281	785	728	533	784	164
1,200 or more	67.5	74.7	73.5	59.9	70.9	51.1	41.5
300–1,199	20.2	16.8	16.9	25.3	17.1	28.7	29.9
50–299	9.3	6.6	6.6	11.0	9.2	17.0	16.5
1–49	2.2	1.3	1.7	2.3	2.8	2.8	9.8
None	0.8	0.7	1.3	1.5	…	0.4	2.4
Average N	20.0	69.1	23.8	20.2	10.5	9.3	6.1
Percent change of:							
Metropolitan areas	12.5	37.5	13.8	12.9	24.4	23.5	22.7
School systems	-20.1	-12.0	-12.0	-10.3	-51.4	-14.2	-45.2

there has also been a marked growth in ad hoc special districts in attempts to meet the urban service needs of small areas independently of the center. It has been claimed that the pattern of metropolitan growth has divided among many governmental units what are actually indivisible problems (Gulick 1962, p. 24). Yet attempts to reorganize the structure of government in metropolitan areas have not been successful. Quite the contrary; the record of failures is extensive.

In the past quarter-century some 36 major metropolitan reorganizations, involving city-county consolidations, have been tried. Most of these attempts and all of the 10 successes occurred in the South. Major efforts in other regions of the country have all failed. It has been argued that the stronger role played by county government in the South may partly explain the region's willingness to consolidate cities with counties. Further, four of the 10 reorganizations occurred in Virginia, where unique annexation laws provide strong motivation for reorganization (Campbell and Dollenmayer 1974).[20] But even in Virginia, when consolidation has been attempted through referenda the proposed reorganization was likely to meet defeat. At any rate, five out of eight attempts between 1952 and 1972 were defeated by popular vote.[21]

If one examines the proposed large-scale reorganization attempts for selected 10-year intervals since the first attempt in 1949, as shown in table 13, it becomes evident that the failure rate has even increased in recent years. While the number of attempts is limited in each time interval, the failure rate increased from one-third in the 1949–58 period to more than 85% since 1969. But apparently the problems of fragmentation are such that the high failure rate has not caused reorganizers to stop trying. Marando (1973) reports that at that time there were more than 60 major reorganizations being considered in the United States. Most of these were city-county consolidations which involved a comprehensive change in local government structure in metropolitan areas.[22] But based on past experience prospects for such

[20] Referenda are not required. First-class cities can be separated from the county by judicial process (Bollens and Schmandt 1970, pp. 222–23; Bain 1966).

[21] It is of interest to note that two city-county consolidation attempts, that is, Richmond–Henrico County (1961) and Roanoke–Roanoke County (1967), were approved by popular vote but failed to pass because of the "double-majority requirement." Although the total combined city-county vote was in support of the proposal, 54% and 66%, respectively, a majority of the out-county voters did not approve of the reorganization; thus the proposal was defeated.

[22] City-county consolidation is frequently not as extensive as the concept implies since small municipalities within the county may be excluded from the proposed change and may continue to function as autonomous units after consolidation. Excluding the smaller municipalities appears to be a viable strategy for increasing voter support (Marando and Whitley 1972, p. 192). Special districts are another factor that has a negative effect on voter support for city-county consolidation (ibid., p. 192).

TABLE 13

ATTEMPTS TO REORGANIZE GOVERNMENT IN
METROPOLITAN AREA BY OUTCOME FOR
SELECTED YEARS, 1949–72*

Years of Vote	Attempts (N)	Successes (N)	Successes (%)
1949–58	6	4†	66.7
1959–68	16	4	25.0
1969–72	14	2	14.3
Total	36	10	27.7

*Based on data reported in Marando 1973.
†Two of these proposals passed with a 1% margin.

widespread change are not promising since, when given the opportunity, voters have generally rejected this form of government reorganization, as already noted (Marando and Whitley 1972). The major source of opposition to past proposals has come from noncentral city residents. Central city residents are much more likely to favor consolidation. In an analysis of the outcome of nine consolidation proposals for which data were available, it was found that the average proportion voting against such proposals was 72% in the county as compared with only 49% in the central city (Marando and Whitley 1972). It is evident that when separate majorities are needed such proposals are almost certain to meet failure. In each of the areas examined at least three-fifths or more of the county residents voted in opposition, but this ranged from a low of 61% in the Richmond, Virginia, metropolitan area to a high of 88% in the Charlotte, North Carolina, metropolitan area. By way of contrast, only 40% and 57% of the respective central city areas voted against the consolidation proposal. Thus even though there was overall support for reorganization in the Richmond area (54% of the total vote) the proposal was defeated because of the negative vote in the county, despite the fact that the latter residents made up only a minority of the population in the metropolitan area. The specific way the vote is counted varies among the states and can have a marked impact on the failure rate. For example, the Columbus–Muscogee County consolidation proposals would have failed if a double majority had been required, even though 95% of the residents lived within the central city and strongly supported the proposed change. Therefore, while out-county residents voted firmly against consolidation the proposal passed, because in that area the outcome required a "double-count" majority; that is, consolidation approval was based on both a city- and countywide voter approval.[23]

[23] This means that the votes of the city residents are counted twice—once in the city balloting

To focus only on the outcome of the vote on proposed consolidations is to understate the amount of opposition to change, since in a large number of metropolitan areas the resistance is so marked or the level of interest so low that no attempt has been made to present such a proposal to the voters. Even attempts to establish study commissions to consider reorganization have been defeated in more than one-fourth of the efforts (Campbell and Dollenmayer 1974). When these are added to the large number of areas where the need is apparent but no attempt has been undertaken and to the number of areas that have rejected a proposed change, it becomes evident that there is little grass-roots support for widespread reorganization of local government in metropolitan areas. Actually no attempt has been made during this century to reorganize the larger metropolitan areas, that is, those with a population of 1 million or more. And it is in those areas that the fragmentation of government is most extensive and most in need of reorganization, but it has been noted that a high degree of fragmentation increases the probability that a proposal for change will be rejected by popular vote (Marando 1973).

Resistance to change in governmental organizational structures is widespread in metropolitan areas even though many objective observers have argued that the old structures have become obsolete, wasteful, and inefficient as well as costly. We have already noted that, whereas the need for reorganization has usually been well documented, major efforts to establish an areawide government for the metropolitan area have been consistently rejected in popular referenda. In the following discussion attention is focused on attitudes toward change as reflected in sample survey data. In a large sample survey of residents and officials in central city and suburban areas, it was found that failure to support change rests not so much on apathy as on strong opposition in suburban areas to reorganization proposals. Available data indicate that, while central city officials and residents tend to support such programs, proposals for change usually fail due to lack of support, not only from residents of suburban areas but also from the officials of their governmental units (Zimmer and Hawley 1968).

In this study reorganization of school districts and of local government tended to be viewed as largely different dimensions of the same thing; however, resistance to change in local government was not as widespread as resistance to change in the organizational structure of school systems. While

---

and again in the countywide tabulations since city residents are also county residents (ibid.). A double majority would have required majority support from both the central-city and the out-county residents. If a majority of the residents in either area voted against the proposal, it would be rejected. The double-majority requirement is generally fatal to reorganization proposals.

support for areawide reorganization was favored by less than a majority of the residents, there were large central city–suburban differences.[24] Focusing first on schools, it was found that when residents were asked how they would vote on a proposal to set up a single school system which would combine the city and the suburban districts support for change came disproportionately from central city residents, but in none of the areas did a majority favor such a change. While there was widespread opposition expressed by suburban residents the proportion favoring change varied by size of metropolitan area. Size of area, however, was not important for the city resident; that is, the same amount of support for change was found in each population size class. But in none of the areas did a clear-cut majority of the city residents support change. However, it is perhaps even more important to note that in none of the areas did more than approximately one-third of the residents report that they would vote against such a proposal. A sizable proportion, ranging from 10% to 15%, had not yet decided how they would respond to such a proposed change, but in each size class there was more support than opposition to such a proposal among central city residents. The responses in the suburban areas were markedly different, for here the opposition was clearly evident. The proportion who would vote for such a change ranged from a low of only 22% in the large-area suburbs to a high of 36% in the small areas. By way of contrast, about 45% of the city residents in each size class favored such a change. On the other hand, while opposition to such a proposal was expressed by nearly 70% of the large-area suburban residents, the proportion declined consistently by size of area. In the small-area suburbs, only half of the residents expressed opposition, whereas only slightly more than one-third of the central city residents shared this view. These data suggest that attitudes toward change are such that there is little likelihood that a metropolitan areawide school system could be established, with the possible exception of the small metropolitan areas where opposition is less marked, but even here such a proposal would pass only if the proposed change required a single-majority vote for the whole area. The type of vote usually required, however, is a double majority.[25]

[24] In each of the areas included in the study, the community was divided into a number of independent school districts and local governmental units which varied widely in respect to size as well as resources available. Consequently the quality of the programs and services provided varied substantially between central city and suburban areas and among suburban areas.

[25] "In most states the procedures for reorganization of school districts have been cumbersome and difficult to set in motion. With few exceptions a favorable majority vote has been required in each of the districts in the proposed new district—that provision alone has always been sufficient to restrain reorganization progress to a snail's pace" (Fitzwater 1957, p. 7).

Much less opposition was expressed concerning reorganization when the suburban residents were asked how they would vote on a proposal to set up a single school district with neighboring suburban districts only. This proved to be a much more attractive alternative. In none of the areas did a clear-cut majority report that they would vote in opposition. But even for this proposal there was more opposition than support, except in the small-area suburbs where 43% favored the proposal as compared with 35% who reported that they would vote against it. There was a high proportion of residents in all areas who were undecided. At any rate, a proposal for the reorganization of school systems would have a much better chance to win majority support from the suburban residents if the change involved only suburban systems. However, when the proposed change combined the central city and suburban systems into a single areawide system, resistance increased to a level where the opposition was substantial. It is noteworthy also that a majority of the suburban residents had already decided that they would vote against such a proposal. By way of contrast, not only were suburban residents less likely to oppose a change that excluded the city, but a larger proportion had not yet decided how they would vote on a proposal that would involve only other suburban systems. Thus, the latter issue remained open, or at least a majority had not already decided to vote in opposition.

School officials tended to hold quite different views on reorganization of school districts on an areawide basis than the residents they represented. The extent of difference is summarized for large and small metropolitan areas in table 14 for selected proposals. While central city school officials tended to favor a single school system for the whole metropolitan area, there was widespread opposition among suburban officials. And the opposition was particularly marked in the large metropolitan areas. Three out of four city officials in the large metropolitan areas favored change compared with only one in 10 among the suburban officials. In the city there was much more support for change among officials than among the residents, whereas suburban officials were less likely to favor change than the residents in their area. Officials in small-area suburbs were more than three times as likely to support an areawide system as officials in large-area suburbs. Among suburban residents the amount of support was also much higher in the smaller areas, but in none of the suburban areas was support sufficient to successfully pass such a proposal.

Support for the present autonomous system was found to decline substantially, however, when the condition for maintaining it involved an increase in local taxes. The amount of support declined among officials and residents alike, but even under these conditions a clear majority of the suburban school officials continued to favor the present system. While only a minority of the residents shared this view, support was much higher in the large than in the small areas.

TABLE 14

ATTITUDES OF OFFICIALS AND RESIDENTS REGARDING SELECTED
ISSUES BY SIZE OF METROPOLITAN AREA
(%)

	SIZE OF METROPOLITAN AREA			
	Large		Small	
SELECTED ISSUES AND TYPE OF RESPONDENT	City	Suburbs	City	Suburbs
1. Favor single district for area:				
School officials	73.3	10.0	68.8	34.4
Residents	46.5	22.0	44.4	35.8
2. Opposed to single district for area:				
School officials	26.7	88.3	25.0	63.9
Residents	36.3	68.9	37.5	49.8
3. Think people in own area would be opposed to single district:				
School officials	40.0	98.3	37.5	67.2
Residents	35.0	68.9	42.2	54.5
4. Prefer present district with higher taxes:				
School officials	26.7	71.7	6.3	55.7
Residents	23.1	47.9	22.5	28.7
5. Prefer single district with lower taxes:				
School officials	73.3	21.7	93.8	37.7
Residents	62.1	41.0	63.5	57.3

SOURCE.—Zimmer and Hawley 1968 (1 and 2, table 10.8; 3, table 10.9; 4 and 5, table 10.11).

A clear majority of residents in all areas except the large-area suburbs would support a single district if it meant lower taxes. Support for such a proposal even in the large-area suburbs increased to more than 40%, which is nearly double the proportion who reported that they would vote for reorganization when the tax dimension was not included. Further, it was noted that support for a single district was substantially higher, even among suburban school officials, if the change was accompanied by a tax decrease. However, it was found that only a very small minority of the officials or the residents expected that change would actually result in lower taxes. It was much more common for both to expect a tax increase. And the people sharing such a view were the ones who expressed the most opposition to the reorganization of schools on an areawide basis.[26]

It is quite evident that central city officials and, to a lesser extent, resi-

---

[26] For an extensive discussion of the factors associated with resistance to change, see Zimmer and Hawley (1968).

dents tended to favor the reorganization of school systems within the metropolitan community context, whereas opposition was widespread among both suburban officials and the people in their area. The prospects for change on an areawide basis are not promising. Quite the contrary; the available data suggest almost certain defeat for such a proposal, particularly in the large metropolitan areas. However, reorganization of suburban systems only may find sufficient support to bring about such a change. But even this change would likely not be approved in the large-area suburbs.

Let us turn now to an examination of the findings reported on attitudes toward change in the structure of local governmental units in metropolitan areas (Hawley and Zimmer 1970). Attention here will first be focused on whether or not residents would ever vote for an areawide government and their first choice as to the governmental mechanisms that should be used to resolve local urban service problems. Also the approach most opposed will be examined.

The survey data available, as summarized in table 15, suggest that an areawide government would likely also find support among central city residents. While the amount of support varies inversely by size of metropolitan area, approximately one-half of the residents in all city areas reported that they would vote in favor of a single government for the whole area right now if given the opportunity. Another 10% or so reported that, while they would not support such a change at this time, they would do so at a later date. Thus, in the long run, at least a substantial proportion of the central city residents in all size classes would support a metropolitan area government.[27]

On the other hand, resistance to change among suburban residents tended to be extensive, particularly in the large metropolitan areas where less than one in five would have supported reorganization at the time of the survey. However, even in these areas support increased to nearly one-third for some later date. Apparently such people saw the need for change, but they wanted to postpone it as long as possible. Nonetheless, close to a majority of the

---

[27] It may be, however, that the black vote will become increasingly important in efforts to reorganize metropolitan area government. Recently, blacks have become more critical of such proposals since many black leaders see this new governmental form as another ruse to dilute black political power just when the blacks are beginning to attain significant political influence in a number of central city areas as they become a larger proportion of the total city population. It has been noted that the black vote in Cleveland changed from a majority in favor of change to a majority against it as the black population grew to the point where there was a possibility that they could capture city hall (Campbell and Dollenmayer 1974). One can only speculate how the suburbanization of blacks would affect this view. However, it is likely to be several decades before the blacks will be of sufficient numbers to have any significant political influence in the suburban areas except in small municipal enclaves.

TABLE 15

How Residents Would Vote on Proposal for Single Government for Area by Size of Area and Place of Residence

Size of Area	For, Now		For, Later		Never Vote For		Don't Know and No Answer	
	City	Suburbs	City	Suburbs	City	Suburbs	City	Suburbs
Large	47.8	18.2	57.2	30.7	19.5	47.5	23.3	21.8
Medium	49.9	30.4	60.6	44.0	15.8	30.8	23.6	25.5
Small	53.7	37.8	61.9	48.6	18.0	35.8	20.1	15.7

Source.—Hawley and Zimmer 1970, adapted from table 54.

residents in the large-area suburbs reported that they would never vote for a single government for the whole area. In the small-area suburbs, however, approximately half of the residents reported that they would eventually support an areawide government proposal. It is noteworthy also that here, too, nearly one in five did not know how they would vote on such a proposal.

At any rate, at the time of the survey a proposal for an areawide government would likely be approved by central city residents but would meet with almost certain defeat in the suburban areas regardless of size. Here again it is noted that how the vote is counted would materially affect the outcome of such a proposal. A double-majority vote requirement would likely result in defeat, whereas under a single vote (a double-count majority) the prospects for success would improve substantially. But in most areas, both central city and suburban area approval is necessary for such a proposal to pass successfully. And as noted above, when actual referenda were undertaken it was usually the out-county residents that defeated the proposals. This is what would be expected according to the survey findings reviewed here.

But quite apart from an areawide government, various other alternatives are available. These were examined in the same study. When residents, given a list of possible alternatives, were asked to state their first preference and the approach most opposed in resolving the problem of providing urban services in their areas, it was found that city and suburban residents differed rather markedly in their responses, as did their officials.[28]

The most prevalent first choice in all subareas was to maintain the status quo in governmental organization, leaving each local unit solely responsible for its public or urban services. However, much more support for this was found among suburban area residents than among those in the central city, and the amount of support declined from a distinct majority (63%) in the large-area suburbs to a substantial minority (39%) in the small-area suburbs. The latter differed only slightly from the amount of support found for the status quo among city residents where approximately one out of three preferred not to change the present fragmented system.[29] The preference for

---

[28] Each respondent was asked to consider six different procedures and to indicate his first choice and the procedure to which he was most opposed. The six procedures presented in the interview are: (1) consolidate the governments in the suburban zone with that of the central; (2) annex the densely settled suburban territory to the central city; (3) the central city should sell services to the surrounding suburban governments; (4) special assessment districts to provide particular services should be created in the suburban zone; (5) suburban governments should combine to solve their service problems independently of the central city; and (6) things should remain as they are, with each local government providing its own urban services.

[29] Residents who wished to preserve the status quo, whether they resided in central cities or suburban areas, viewed their respective governments and the officials who managed them as

some kind of overall merger, that is, consolidation or annexation, varied around 40% in the central cities. In the suburbs the proportion who preferred to solve their problems by joining in a single government increased as the size of area declined, but reached a maximum of only 30% in the smallest areas. Less than one-half this proportion favored such a change in the large-area suburbs.

However, in both areas officials expressed more extreme views than the residents. Widespread support for a unified government for the area was expressed by central city officials where more than seven out of 10 shared this view compared with approximately four out of 10 residents. But suburban officials expressed very little support for a single government. Quite the contrary; of all of the possible alternatives offered, this was the one that was most opposed by suburban officials in all size classes, as shown in table 16. The frequency of opposition in each size class was higher among officials than among residents, but even among the latter it tended to be a majority opinion. In other words, there was widespread opposition to a single government for the area among both officials and residents in suburban areas. While the amount of opposition declined substantially by size of area, it never fell below 50%. No other response showed such a high amount of agreement, particularly among suburban officials. By way of comparison, less than one-fifth of the central city officials and less than two-fifths of the residents reported that they would be more opposed to a single government than to any of the other proposals.

The first-choice preference of suburban officials was to resolve their service problems independently from the city. In their opinion either the suburban areas should jointly provide such services or each area should attempt to do so separately as an autonomous unit. Suburban residents tended to express similar preferences, but the degree of consensus declined by size of area. In some respects these views appear to be inconsistent with their evaluation of services in the suburbs since a substantial majority of the residents, as well as officials, in all sizes and types of places held the opinion that suburban services were inadequate. And a sizable proportion of the residents (33%–42%) as well as suburban officials (32%–47%) reported the view that the multiplicity of government in the metropolitan area was wasteful. Yet they expressed strong support for the status quo. From the point of view of reform it would appear that rationality may not be an effective weapon against defeat among the suburban voters.

relatively superior to those of the opposite zone. That is, they believed their governments to be less burdensome both economically and administratively and less subject to influence from special interest groups. They contended also that their officials were more approachable and more interested in the problems of their neighborhoods (Hawley and Zimmer 1970, p. 113).

TABLE 16

OFFICIALS AND RESIDENTS MOST OPPOSED TO CONSOLIDATION
OR ANNEXATION AS SOLUTION TO SERVICE PROBLEMS BY
SIZE OF AREA AND PLACE OF RESIDENCE
(%)

Type of Respondent and Area	Large	Medium	Small
Central city:			
Officials	19	16	15
Residents	38	38	24
Suburban area:			
Officials	87	76	76
Residents	73	55	50

SOURCE.—Hawley and Zimmer 1970, adapted from tables 50 and 59.

It is of more than incidental interest to note the very small proportion of residents in all zones and size classes that preferred to solve their service problems by establishing special districts. In none of the areas was this viewed as a first-choice solution by more than 8% of the residents. The highest proportion was found in the small-area suburbs, where the need for urban-type service is most evident, since the service facilities in these areas were found to be very limited in scope. Yet, in actual practice this has been the most rapidly growing type of governmental approach to service problems in metropolitan areas in recent years, as shown earlier in our discussions.[30]

In response to the open-ended question, "In your opinion what changes, if any, should be made in the way local government is handled in metropolitan areas in the United States?" more than 80% of the officials, in suburbs as well as in central cities, believed that some kind of change was necessary. Central city officials tended to concentrate on the need for a general governmental reorganization, whereas suburban officials tended to deal largely with

[30] The question of balancing service costs is an unsolved problem in areas serviced by special districts. Cities can weigh the costs of their different services against one another. They cannot afford to let the cost of the service throw the whole city budget out of line, leading to neglect of other city functions. Special districts, however, are concerned only with specific functions without regard for resources available for other functions. Consequently there is likely to be little or no coordination or communication among the local government agencies servicing the same area, and this fragmented government can be expensive (Scott and Corzine 1971, p. 213).

modifications and improvements in local governments as presently constituted. Clearly, suburban officials recognized the deficiencies of local government, but they did not believe that the remedy must be so extreme as governmental consolidation (Hawley and Zimmer 1970, p. 136). The recognition of needed changes and the willingness to accept modifications, but not overall consolidation, likely account for the proliferation of special districts. They provide a mechanism for providing services without loss of local autonomy and without threat to official positions and do not endanger local control of land use and zoning which can be effectively used to encourage or discourage certain types of development.

DISCUSSION

In short, the jurisdiction over the suburban areas is shared by a miscellany of governmental units—cities, villages, counties, townships, and school districts—most of which are ill-adapted to the provision of services. The large number of autonomous governmental units and their arbitrary boundaries and overlapping jurisdictions complicate and more often than not defeat concerted efforts to effect the governmental changes necessary for the development of satisfactory solutions to local as well as areawide problems (Zimmer and Hawley 1956).

Observers of the scene have often commented on the administrative inefficiency and consequent economic waste inherent in such government disunity (Gulick 1962, chap. 1; Fiser 1962, pp. 1–11). Nonetheless, widespread opposition to the reorganization of governments in metropolitan areas continues to persist, and the problems become more serious with the passing of time and the continued growth of population. It seems doubtful that effective areawide solutions will be forthcoming as long as the controlling vote rests with the suburban population. There are, however, a number of potential changes in view that could have a substantial impact on local government. For example, one can only speculate as to what is likely to happen in the future if the courts rule that the property tax, which results in wide variations in fiscal support among school systems, is unconstitutional as a source of support for education since it denies equal educational opportunity to all children. Recent court decisions have already ruled that the quality of public education in a school district must not be determined by the wealth of the child's parents and their neighbors (Danielson 1972, p. 168; Campbell and Dollenmayer 1974, p. 50). Such a ruling would have a marked impact on the disparities found among school districts within metropolitan areas. But it may also have implications much broader in scope than the disparities between central city and suburban areas or among suburban areas, since if the principle of equality is accepted it is only a matter of time before the differentials among states will be challenged. And eventually it would seem logical to expect that the principle would be further extended to include the "right" of all citizens to enjoy the same level of a range of community-provided services regardless of local resources. While the final decision of the courts is yet to be made, the direction of the courts seems inevitable, and the ramifications are potentially extensive.

Other evidence of potential change is found in the federal government's efforts to encourage areawide planning agencies through the Model Cities Act (Demonstration Cities and Metropolitan Development Act of 1966)[31] and the programs to encourage the establishment of councils of governments on a voluntary basis. In the future these types of programs are likely to have economic sanctions attached to grant programs,[32] and this in turn is likely to have a long-run impact on the organization of local governments in suburban areas.[33] However, in the short run at least, fragmentation, and to a lesser extent the proliferation of local governmental units, is likely to continue to be one of the major obstacles to the effective resolution of areawide urban service problems. From all the data at hand suburban residents would be expected to continue to resist proposals that threaten their local autonomy, and, more particularly, suburban officials will continue to defend the status quo for in so doing they also defend their official positions. The prospects for an areawide reorganization of the multiplicity of governmental units in metropolitan areas do not appear to be promising. At least, not in the near future. In the meantime, however, the available evidence is quite

[31] This act requires that local applications for federal aid be reviewed by an areawide body to insure consistency with metropolitan plans and priorities.

[32] Such efforts to date have not been successful. For example, plans developed in HUD to use water and sewer grants to promote low-cost housing were ruled out in December 1970 because of the president's belief "that forced integration of the suburbs is not in the national interest" (Danielson 1972, p. 171). An additional counterforce may be the increase in the number of congressmen in the House of Representatives who have a suburban constituency. From 1950 to 1970 the major characteristic of the reapportionment of the nation's congressional representation was a sharp increase in the number of congressmen coming from the suburban areas of major metropolitan areas (Lehne 1972). The one man, one vote principle worked to the advantage of the suburbs since these are the areas of greatest population growth. Also, revenue sharing may further encourage the fragmentation of governments since it will add to the resources of autonomous units (U.S. Department of the Treasury 1974).

[33] It is of interest to note that the United States Civil Rights Commission has recently called for a federal law requiring states that receive community-development funds to establish metropolitan agencies that could govern housing development throughout an entire metropolitan area. Any local laws and regulations which impeded that plan could be overridden by the metropolitan agencies—that would include zoning laws, building codes, and minimum square footage requirements.

convincing that the meaning of local vicinage, particularly within the metropolitan context, has lost much of its original significance when transportation and communication facilities were more limited and the scale of local community life more circumscribed. In other words, even though the social significance of proximity has declined, the fragmented administrative structures of small-area local governments in the metropolitan community continue to persist in their earlier form.

REFERENCES

Abrams, C. 1965. "The City at Bay." Pp. 3–18 in *The City Is the Frontier*. New York: Harper & Row.
Advisory Commission on Intergovernmental Relations. 1967. *Metropolitan Fiscal Disparities*. Washington, D.C.: Government Printing Office.
————. 1970. *Metropolitan Disparities: A Second Reading*. Information Bulletin no. 70-1. Washington, D.C.: Government Printing Office.
Bain, C. W. 1966. *Annexation in Virginia*. Charlottesville: University of Virginia Press.
Bollens, J. C., and H. J. Schmandt. 1970. *The Metropolis: Its People, Politics, and Economic Life*. 2d ed. New York: Harper & Row.
Burgess, E. W. 1923. "The Growth of the City: An Introduction to a Research Project." *Proceedings of the American Sociological Society* 18:85–97.
Campbell, A. K., and J. A. Dollenmayer. 1974. "Governance in a Metropolitan Society." Pp. 379–430 in *Metropolitan America: Papers on the State of Knowledge*, edited by V. Rock and A. Hawley. Washington, D.C.: National Academy of Sciences.
Cressey, P. F. 1938. "Population Succession in Chicago: 1898–1930." *American Journal of Sociology* 44 (July): 59–69.
Danielson, M. N. 1971. "Suburbia and the Politics of Accommodation." Pp. 191–95 in *Metropolitan Politics: A Reader*, edited by M. N. Danielson. Boston: Little, Brown.
————. 1972. "Differentiation, Segregation, and Political Fragmentation in an American Metropolis." Pp. 143–76 in *Governance and Population: The Governmental Implications of Population Change*, edited by A. E. Keir Nash. Commission on Population Growth and the American Future, Research Reports, vol. 4. Washington, D.C.: Government Printing Office.
Fiser, W. S. 1962. *Mastery of the Metropolis*. Englewood Cliffs, N.J.: Prentice-Hall.
Fitzwater, C. O. 1957. *School District Reorganization: Policies and Procedures*. Washington, D.C.: Government Printing Office.
Foley, D. 1974. "Accessibility for Residents in the Metropolitan Environment." Pp. 161–209 in *Metropolitan America: Papers on the State of Knowledge*, edited by V. Rock and A. Hawley. Washington, D.C.: National Academy of Sciences.
Gist, N. P., and S. F. Fava. 1964. *Urban Society*. 5th ed. New York: Crowell.
Gulick, L. 1962. *The Metropolitan Problem and American Ideas*. New York: Knopf.
Hawley, A. H. 1956. *The Changing Shape of Metropolitan America: Deconcentration since 1920*. Glencoe, Ill.: Free Press.
————. 1971. *Urban Society: An Ecological Approach*. New York: Ronald.
Hawley, A. H., and B. G. Zimmer. 1970. *The Metropolitan Community: Its People and Government*. Beverly Hills, Calif.: Sage.
Koepp, D. 1962. "Nonpartisan Elections in the San Francisco Bay Area." *Public Affairs Report* 3 (August): 3.
Lehne, R. 1972. "Population Change and Congressional Representation." Pp. 83–98 in *Gover-*

nance and Population: The Governmental Implications of Population Change, edited by A. E. Keir Nash. Commission on Population Growth and the American Future, Research Reports, vol. 4. Washington, D.C.: Government Printing Office.

Lowry, I. S. 1971. *Housing Assistance for Low-Income Families: A Fresh Approach.* Document 4645. New York: RAND.

McKenzie, R. D. 1933. *The Metropolitan Community.* New York: McGraw-Hill.

Marando, V. L. 1973. *Local Government Reorganization: An Overview.* Washington, D.C.: Government Printing Office.

Marando, V. L., and C. R. Whitley. 1972. "City-County Consolidation: An Overview of Voter Response." *Urban Affairs Quarterly* 7 (December): 181–203.

National Commission on Urban Problems. 1969. *Building the American City.* New York: Praeger.

Scott, S., and J. Corzine. 1971. "Special Districts in the San Francisco Bay Area." Pp. 201–14 in *Metropolitan Politics: A Reader*, edited by M. N. Danielson. Boston: Little, Brown.

Thompson, W. S. 1947. *The Growth of Metropolitan Districts: 1900–1940.* Washington, D.C.: Government Printing Office.

U.S. Bureau of the Budget. 1967. *Standard Metropolitan Statistical Areas.* Washington, D.C.: Government Printing Office.

U.S. Bureau of the Census. 1961. *Census of Population: 1960. Number of Inhabitants, United States Summary.* Final Report PC(1)-1A. Washington, D.C.: Government Printing Office.

———. 1964. *Census of Government: 1962. Local Government in Metropolitan Areas.* Vol. 5. Washington, D.C.: Government Printing Office.

———. 1969. *Census of Government: 1967. Local Government in Metropolitan Areas.* Vol. 5. Washington, D.C.: Government Printing Office.

———. 1971. *Census of Population: 1970. Number of Inhabitants, United States Summary.* Final Report PC(1)-A1. Washington, D.C.: Government Printing Office.

———. 1973. *Census of Government: 1972. Governmental Organization.* Vol. 1. Washington, D.C.: Government Printing Office.

U.S. Department of the Treasury. 1974. *Getting Involved: Your Guide to General Revenue Sharing.* Washington, D.C.: Government Printing Office.

Warner, S. B., Jr. 1962. *Streetcar Suburbs: The Process of Growth in Boston, 1870–1900.* Cambridge, Mass.: Harvard University Press.

Willbern, Y. 1964. *The Withering Away of the City.* University: University of Alabama Press.

Zimmer, B. G. 1974. "The Urban Centrifugal Drift." Pp. 15–90 in *Metropolitan America: Papers on the State of Knowledge*, edited by V. Rock and A. Hawley. Washington, D. C.: National Academy of Sciences.

Zimmer, B. G., and A. H. Hawley. 1956. "Approaches to the Solution of Fringe Problems: Preferences of Residents in the Flint Metropolitan Area." *Public Administration Review* 16 (Fall): 258–68.

———. 1968. *Metropolitan Area Schools: Resistance to District Reorganization.* Beverly Hills, Calif.: Sage.

Zimmerman, J. F. 1974. "The Patchwork Approach: Adaptive Responses to Increasing Urbanization." Pp. 465–509 in *Metropolitan America: Papers on the State of Knowledge*, edited by V. Rock and A. Hawley. Washington, D. C.: National Academy of Sciences.

8 Suburban Political Behavior: A Matter of Trust

Ann Lennarson Greer and Scott Greer
University of Wisconsin—Milwaukee

Most suburban areas and people are structured as municipal corporations of one grade or another. In Robert Wood's phrase, they are defined legally as "Republics in Miniature." It is hard to decide which aphorism fits best—are they examples of "the trivial act and the tremendous consequence," or of "the tremendous act and the trivial consequence"? The classic phrase of T. S. Eliot probably applies to most democratic politics; the vote is seldom critical to the voter, but aggregated votes determine policy. In the same fashion, the day-to-day decisions of suburban councils and zoning boards are individually lightweight; collectively they prevent effective metropolitan government and therefore area-wide planning. On the other hand, it is clear that all the elaborate structure of popular democracy results in a government which is noncompetitive, often inactive, and unaccountable to the views of the people. This occurs because, paradoxically, the elected councils are so selfless that they "couldn't care less" about remaining in office (Prewitt 1970, p. 7). A trivial republic is a republic in miniature within contemporary large-scale society.

Thus in one sense suburban political behavior is unimportant. So little happens; that which does is usually the consequence of private aggrandizement in the market sphere. Yet a great deal does *not* happen because of existing structures, supported by current political behavior. Scott and Nathan (1969, p. 311) quote John Gardner: " 'The times cry out for swift institutional change to avert disaster, but our institutions resist change with grim stubbornness. And as they resist change they come under attack by critics whose anger and impatience lead them to totally destructive ends.' " The egalitarianism of the suburban governments, their rigidity, and their general rejection of political brokerage systems give them considerable importance in a rapidly changing society.

Our approach will be one which emphasizes levels of government and political contention, moving from the more general to the more local. We will consider suburban political behavior from the perspective of national politics, at the metropolitan-area level where suburbs live with central cities,

We wish to thank Bennett Berger, Jeffrey Pressman, and J. John Palen for their helpful comments on this paper.

and within the municipality. In each case we will look at the major research themes and political issues.

SUBURBS AND THE FEDERAL POLITY

A 15-year housing moratorium, due to the Depression and World War II, and a suppressed birth rate, due to the same historical events, both climaxed and reversed in the late 1940s and 1950s. The boom in housing and the boom in babies coincided: both took place in the underbuilt, outlying properties of the metropolis. They rapidly created a new zone of standardized housing, stretching for miles around the older centers of settlement. These were the mass-produced suburbs, sometimes known as the "mass society" suburbs (for they did appear, from outside, remarkably homogeneous). A rich mythology developed for them, even as they were a-borning.

The major myth was that suburbs were simultaneously *the* future of the United States and irrevocably Republican and conservative in political behavior. This mythic prediction was based on (1) extrapolation, for suburbs had tended to vote Republican in past presidential elections, and (2) poor sampling, for the suburbs studied had been either unusual or aggregated in an undiscriminating fashion (Wirt et al. 1972, pp. 51–56). Thus we have the prediction of a coming Republican majority, and all that goes with that. It is important to remember that these notions were voiced during the Eisenhower years, years of spectacular Republican victories in the presidential elections. So a small and unusual sample of elections (1952 and 1956) and an unusual sample of suburban votes were combined to reach the propositions: (1) America is becoming suburban, (2) suburban residents vote Republican, and (3) America is becoming Republican.

The truth seems to be that American voters liked Ike in both the central city and suburbs. Their variation in Republican vote for the president remained exactly the same, but the mean shifted toward Eisenhower (Wirt et al. 1972, chap. 6). Furthermore, there is little indication from the voting for lesser officials of *any* shift toward the Republican party. Indeed, if we turn our attention to a longer sample of time, it is quite likely that, as the center of gravity of metropolitan America becomes suburban, the suburbs become more Democratic.

Earlier explanations of the supposed trend relied on two notions. First, those who moved from the city were assumed to be selected Republicans; second, those who moved were thought to be converted to Republicanism by the preexisting communities of the homogeneous suburban areas. The trouble was that this notion ignored the changing nature of suburbia. As those settled areas outside the center city became a majority of the metropolitan population, as an electorate they became working class to middle class, tending toward the Democratic party in their national preferences.

In short, the search for the national political destiny in the political behavior of suburban residents turned out to be a wild goose chase. Suburban residents in national elections behave about the same as they would have had they lived in the central city. (It is hard now to imagine why this should *not* have been the case.) The key variables seem to be socioeconomic status, ethnicity (including religion), and life style (including stage in the life cycle.)

It seems to us that the fears and values of intellectuals and social scientists were reflected in their interpretation of the ecological dispersion that followed World War II. It was feared that the weakening relative power of the older central city would end national brokerage politics and the representation of minorities. Suburbia in fact and the suburbia of the mind were identified; both were seen as threats to a competitive politics.

We have seen, however, that there is no uniformity among suburbs in their national political behavior. There is no national suburban coalition, no policy by and for the suburbs. In the federal Congress, party affiliation consistently overrides the urban-suburban distinction in voting. Thus when we talk of a "national suburban policy" we are referring to a policy *for* the suburbs, initiated through the Congress and the administration. The latter, as Frederick M. Wirt and his colleagues point out, have great difficulty in acting on the generally accepted fact that suburbs are highly differentiated. Some are very poor, suburban ghettos indeed; some include the richest municipal corporations in the country. It is difficult to craft a program for such diverse populations and their problems, however the latter are defined (Wirt et al. 1972, chap. 13). (The same is true of central cities, a fact usually ignored in the "crisis of our cities" literature *and* in legislation.) We must remember that many suburbs do not need federal funds; many have no hopes of receiving such funds though they could certainly use them: witness the estimate of 800,000 suburban poor in the New York metropolitan area. And many suburbanites do not believe in federal intervention in their municipality.

SUBURBS AND CENTRAL CITY: "THE METROPOLITAN PROBLEM"

At the same time that the mythic view of suburbia as a vast teaching machine in the service of the Republican party emerged, a more general view of the metropolis gained currency. This view, in brief, saw the problems of our urban areas as essentially problems of government structure. In this view, the suburbs were barriers to the solutions of area-wide problems and should probably be politically integrated within a metropolitan-area government.

It is worthwhile to look at the political behavior, the contention for control, involved. We will discuss briefly the nature of our triple-schizoid local polity, its causes and consequences. Then we will consider the politics of efforts to create a polity for the metropolis as a whole, or "metropolitics."

The three dimensions of our political shizophrenia are the conflicts between public and private control, national and local control, and general versus special functional control. The battle line wavers over time, but there is always conflict between these antinomies. To spell out the reasons in detail is beyond the purpose of this essay. For now let us say that in the settlement of the United States the surplus of new land and the scarcity of government, under a constitution which implies that government tends toward tyranny, produced a continual Wild West (though sometimes it was located Down East, Far North, or Deep South). The general presumption was that a person had a right to do what he wanted to with any land he owned, that any settlement was free to incorporate and govern itself.

As a result, the United States became one of the biggest uncontrolled real estate developments in history. It is instructive to compare the Canadian and the U.S. management of westward expansion. In Canada the forces of law and order outpaced the movement of population and enterprise; Canada had no wild west, for the Canadian Royal Mounted Police got there first. In the United States, within an ineffectual system of territorial government, one constituted his own police force, or at least banded together with others having similar interests in the *posse vigilante*. The right to private exploitation without concern for social consequences is a deeply implanted norm (Stegner 1962).

Then we must remember that the federal government was the result of compromise; political formulae were as critical here as in the history of all crafted states. Thus the compromise over slavery and the compromise over "states' rights," which produced a Senate where the rule of "one vote to one voter" is violated. In short, jealousy of local control over local affairs, rationalized perhaps by Jefferson's notions that the localities represent in some fashion the "voice of the people," served to maintain a continuing jousting for control between the state as a whole and its various political subdivisions (Greer 1965, p. 119).

As a result, during the period of rapid increase in scale, America's cities grew with *local* control and very little of it. The market in land and labor largely determined growth patterns. The city remained a political unit as long as the newly settled frontiers on its outskirts were clearly dependent on the center for such facilities as sewerage, water, and transport. When various technological changes made the growing edge less dependent, peripheral areas ceased to incorporate with the center. The causes are various and many, but once the peripheral areas decided to go it alone, incorporation was the safest way to avoid annexation to the center city. State law, geared to a small-town and agrarian society, usually facilitated incorporation and made annexation very difficult. The lasting power of an invisible political boundary is nowhere more apparent than in our metropolitan areas, where, as in Newark, as much as 80% of the population may live outside the central city. The resulting municipal units are in theory creatures of the states. They are not mentioned in the federal Constitution and have only powers explicitly granted from the state's charters. However, in fact they have developed a presumed "home rule" and, performing a wide range of services, have come to be defined as *general* government. (The archetype of the city-state dies hard.) They become symbolic centers for many citizens, and governmental entitivity is confused with social community.

This governmental bifurcation of the metropolis, into a large central city and a gaggle of suburban municipalities, has a number of consequences. Briefly, it makes many needed public functions such as planning, ethnic integration in work, education, and residence, transportation, and the like difficult—failing an unprecedented degree of cooperation among dozens, or hundreds, of municipal governments. The obvious need for coordination, in turn, produces new governmental units with a few functions, or even one major one. The primal special-district governments were the school districts; such governments have since been created for just about every function served at the local level for local interests (Bollens 1957).

And between general and special-district government there are intellectual and pragmatic conflicts. Defined as "above politics," special-district governments such as the New York Port Authority have the best of both worlds. They may make huge profits (as the Port Authority has done), reinvest these without responsibility to either the citizens they serve or the municipalities in their franchise, yet take acclaim for efficiency and economy because they are "nonpolitical." Whoever can pursue his political aims with an aura of being above politics is a strong contender in the American political arena.

The result of these norms, applied during a period of rapid urbanization, was a metropolitan governmental pattern some people found dismaying in theory and practice. Considering the metropolis as an interdependent social structure, these "metropoliticians" believed it should be governed from a single center. Generally consisting of ambitious officials, young intellectual lawyers, idealists, publicists, political scientists, metropolitan daily newspapermen, and the League of Women Voters, the metropoliticians set out to make "metropolitan government" an issue.

Their task was difficult, for the issue is very complex and requires a concern for long-run policy that is not common among the voters. Bringing it off is unlikely despite the misleading ease with which such a campaign can begin: through petition and referendum. While it is somewhat of an overstatement, the conclusion of Scott and Nathan that the referendum is both undesirable and unnecessary seems much more useful than the contrary (1970, p. 321).

An intensive before-and-after study of the referendum for the Metropolitan District Plan in Saint Louis documents such a proposition. It was overwhelmingly defeated by two to one in the central city and three to one in the suburbs. About the voters: "Though they talked, and some learned, they did not really know much about the issue of the election. Only a minority of the voters could have been correctly informed on any aspect of the District Plan, among either electorate. Nevertheless, they defeated it overwhelmingly. However, if few knew the facts, many could give good points in the plan—vague as they were—and only a few volunteered their own arguments against it. This was complemented by a general friendliness to the notion of future efforts at metropolitan integration" (Greer 1963, p. 163). As for those who led the campaigns for and against the plan: ". . . the voters hardly knew who they were. They didn't recognize the face, and if they did they didn't know which side the leader was on or why he was there" (Greer 1963, p. 191). It is significant that the only two leaders who were correctly identified by their position on the plan in the *suburban sample* were the two highest officials in the government of the *city* of Saint Louis—the mayor (by 33% of the sample) and the president of the Board of Aldermen (by 18%). The mayor was con, the aldermen pro.

Traditional political parties do not take part in such referenda; the issues tend to be very divisive within each party. This leaves the mass media with their spotlights on the already prominent. Endorsement, in such a case, more nearly resembles the celebrity's endorsement of a charitable organization than the organizational commitment of powerful leaders in powerful groups.

Indeed, the existing structure of government in those metropolitan areas where politics is for privilege and self provides a ready-made machine for opposing change: the incumbents. Given little personal advantage and the probability of losses, they are not apt to use their position for the metropolitan cause. Further, such campaigns have been typically nonpartisan, engaging no organized party. But the voters, confused and doubtful, are incapable of moving without leadership. Under these circumstances, there is a strong argument that such change should come from the state level; after all, these suburbs and cities are creatures of the state, not independent political entities. Investigating the reasons why conservative Indianapolis created a metropolitan-area government ("Unigov"), P. Myers found the following explanation: "Unigov's supporters have several answers: a fortuitous combination of political factors, hard work, *shrewdness in pushing through Unigov without a referendum*—thus avoiding the risk of 'narrow-minded suburban and rural opposition' which has torpedoed similar moves elsewhere" (quoted in Scott and Nathan 1970, p. 323; italics added). It should be noted, however, that in both Cleveland and Saint Louis the *central* city rejected the merger plan.

Those in the central city who profited from brokerage politics (including blacks in increasing numbers) saw no reason to submerge their electorates in a larger metropolitan government where they would be outnumbered. In both suburbs and city the basic conservatism of the voters tended to produce a "no" vote when they were confronted with such complex issues.

INTERNAL POLITICS: POLITICAL STYLES

At the level of the locality, suburbs have been associated in the literature with participatory democracy and with reform government. Suburbanization, as Robert Wood has shown, was thought of as a return to participatory citizen government. Small size itself seemed one necessary component. As Wood describes the ideology: "Small towns offer certain indigenous qualities which . . . create a milieu in which the American aims of equality, and liberty are best secured. . . . Whether found in the small town of other centuries or in the modern suburb, propinquity, interdependence, common beliefs and backgrounds, and some measure of leisure time are thought to encourage political activity which almost guarantees effective democratic government" (1958, p. 266).

A second component which was claimed to be necessary in returning government to citizens was to "take politics out of government" through reform of city charters. Proponents of reform urged that city charters be drawn so as to discourage the professional politician and encourage "the best man for the job." The job was supposed to seek the candidate; thus political jobs and political parties were stripped of tangible rewards and political powers. Nominating powers passed from political parties to nonpartisan citizen groups. "At-large" elections were urged in place of ward representation. Spoils and patronage were to be replaced by competitive bidding and civil service employment. Responsibility for day-to-day city business passed from the full-time political head to the professional manager.

The reform movement represented an upper-middle-class reaction against the big city machines of the Eastern cities. It coincided with rapid suburbanization and influenced the choice of governmental form which the newly incorporated municipalities adopted. It should be noted that the reform movement also coincided with the growth of large Western cities and influenced their choice of governmental form as well.

Social science studies in various ways supported the assumptions regarding suburban participation. Many researchers found that the familistic residents of outer areas did participate more in local affairs than typical central-city dwellers (Greer 1962b; Greer and Orleans 1962; Bell and Force 1956; Orbell and Uno 1972; Kasarda and Janowitz 1974; Zikmund and Smith 1969) Working-class suburbanites compared with inner-city workers seemed especially influenced toward increased participation in and knowledgeability about community affairs (Greer and Orleans 1962; Orbell and Uno 1972).

Observers differed as to whether this increased participation enhanced democratic government. Some (Wood 1958, esp. pp. 283, 293; Greer 1962a; Danielson 1971) argued that suburban incorporation removed citizens from meaningful political choice and that participation in the smaller unit was often a sham. Others (Zikmund and Smith 1969, p. 450) argued that the preservation of small local units is necessary for maintaining the tradition of citizen participation in government. These authors suggested that other arrangements, such as federation, should be employed to resolve metropolitan fragmentation.

The reform movement also found support in the social science literature. Banfield and Wilson (1963) argued that there were two types of people who demanded two types of government. According to these authors, the working-class immigrants of the big cities were "private-regarding." That is, they identified with their ethnic group, their families, their neighborhood, and their ward. Conversely, old Americans, the heirs of western and northern European culture, identified with the community as a whole and were more "public-regarding."

It therefore followed that cities with many of the first type of person (uneducated, working class, ethnic) developed political machines to act as brokers among the groups. Communities populated with the latter type of person (better-educated, higher-social-rank WASPs) adopted reform or, as it was called, "good government." While this theory has not held up well under examination (Henessey 1970; Hawkins and Prather 1969, 1971), it supported the idea that the public-regarding suburban-bound could leave the political brokers behind and enjoy public-interest government in suburban municipalities.

The value premises involved in the Banfield and Wilson theory and in reform government in general have been attacked by numerous scholars, who charge that both approaches equate the public interest with the interests of the upper middle class. Observers have argued further that governments designed to further the public interest *suppress* minority viewpoints (Vidich and Bensman 1958; Wood 1958).

LOCAL ELECTORATES IN THE SUBURBS

Recent studies have shed some additional light on the character of democratic participation in local areas. Prewitt and Eulau (1971) collected election and interview data in 80 San Francisco Bay Area cities. Each city had a reformed structure: elected officials were nonsalaried, nonpartisan, and elected at large.

Prewitt (1970) reports that the office of councilman in these reformed cities attracted candidates who reported no political ambitions He concludes that "when political office confers no status, then the motive for seeking office is not political ambition, but, for instance, civic duty." Councilmen so selected reported they did not feel responsible to voters but acted according to their own image of the public good, or what Prewitt calls *"bourgeois oblige."* The voters did little to increase accountability: electoral participation was low and incumbents were rarely removed from office.

Yet, within the Bay Area communities studied, there were interesting variations. Crossing participation in elections with the rate at which incumbents were evicted from office, Prewitt and Eulau (1971, p. 300) derive four types of electorates (see table 1).

TABLE 1

FOUR TYPES OF ELECTORAL CONTEXT PRODUCED BY
COMBINATION OF VOTER TURNOUT AND EVICTION

	VOTER TURNOUT	
FREQUENCY OF EVICTION	Relatively Low	Relatively High
Relatively low	Permissive	Supportive
Relatively high	Discriminative	Volatile

SOURCE.—Prewitt and Eulau 1971, p. 300.

They argue that volatile and discriminating electorates are those which vote on the basis of issues and hold politicians accountable. In their view, the volatile electorate displays both participation and eviction and thereby approximates the ideal model of participatory democracy as they see it—that is, many contending groups have a chance to gain office (1971, p. 314).

Tabulating Prewitt and Eulau's published data differently, we discover a social class correlate to the electoral behavior they present: richer electorates are low in participation and dissent (permissive); poorer electorates are high in participation and dissent (volatile) (table 2).

Interestingly this same pattern was found by Minar (1968) in his study of elections in 48 suburban school districts.[1] To explain this pattern, Minar hypothesized that the reform model works best in those districts where

---

[1] Minar's study, very similar to Prewitt and Eulau's, is concerned with at-large election of nonsalaried, nonpartisan officials. The methodology is essentially the same, although Minar used a less demanding measure of dissent: votes cast for losing candidates, rather than eviction from office.

TABLE 2

COMPARISON OF HIGH- AND LOW-RANK COMMUNITIES
WITH RESPECT TO PARTICIPATION AND DISSENT
IN LOCAL ELECTIONS IN BAY AREA CITIES

	COMMUNITY SOCIAL RANK	
	High Status (N = 40)	Low Status (N = 40)
Participation:		
High	12	29
Low	28	11
Eviction:		
High	14	26
Low	26	14

SOURCE.—Reorganization of data in Prewitt and Eulau (1971, p. 306, table 1).

conflict management attitudes and skills are prevalent in the community. These attitudes and skills, he suggests, are related to professional managerial occupations and high level of education.

Minar argues that "high status low-conflict districts are likely to lean more heavily on technical authority, to hire expertise, retain it for long periods of time and grant it decision-making latitude" (1968, p. 259). Voters in low-status, high-conflict districts are less familiar with delegation, the role of expertise, and the division of labor. They are less apt to develop and use mechanisms of conflict control (such as the caucus). Conflicts over day-to-day issues become rancorous, and officials are held accountable at the polls.

Minar disagrees with Prewitt and Eulau that a permissive electorate does not discriminate. He found a positive, if slight, correlation between high rank and turnout at referenda. The voters seemed to be turning out to mandate the administration, since the correlation with dissent was again negative.

This picture of participation is confirmed by the research of one of the present authors in a study of mayoral politics in a medium-sized city where a variety of constituencies existed (Greer 1974). The middle-income "issue voters" who lived on the outskirts of the city participated and dissented more often than did high-rank voters. Yet the mayor characterized them as "cheese and cracker millionaires," by which he meant that they lacked what he considered to be a workable perspective. They had rejected brokerage politics but had not acquired a perspective which encompassed the complexities of formal organization, finance, or city development. The result was an exaggerated notion of what tax dollars would buy and a lack of sympathy with government. All of this resulted in turmoil and an aldermanic turnover greater than in other areas of the city, but very little change in policies. The vote was over issues, but the issues stayed the same: garbage pickup, water in the basement, mosquito abatement (Greer 1974, pp. 58–66).

High- and low-rank suburbs are likely to have reform structures. Yet only the high-rank electorates have the managerial skills and attitudes which make the reform alternative effective. Lower-status suburbs end up with neither professional politics nor professional management.

Robert Dahl has suggested that middle-class children are socialized to distrust power and those who wield it (Dahl 1960, p. 37). Bennett Berger (personal communication) has commented that this distrust of power is limited to overt political power and does not extend to economic power. From this perspective, reform government resembles the governance of corporations, with the citizen's power resembling that of the stockholder.

In thinking about local democracy, we are interested in another of the electoral contexts defined by Prewitt and Eulau, the supportive context (high participation, low eviction). They pay little attention to it, judging that it consists of undiscriminating voters. It seems to us, however, that it is necessary to explain this relatively enthusiastic politics, especially since it is the only one of the four electoral contexts which shows no relationship to social class.

LEADERSHIP AND ELECTORATES

We propose that a supportive context indicates the presence of aggressive political leadership. Effective leadership heads off conflict, encourages identification, and orchestrates integration. It may turn a permissive electorate into a supportive electorate, as occurred in the mayoral study cited (Greer 1974). It is capable of and inclined to recruit from the larger community, since it seeks new adherents (Prewitt and Eulau 1971, pp. 312–13); thus democratic input may be creative as well as obstructive. Continuity is likely to be sufficient for the aggregation of power and the professionalization of elected officials. Secure in power, officials may bargain effectively on behalf of the community in dealings with other units of government or with economic interests.

The circumstances under which political leadership emerges in suburban government remain unspecified, although several authors have speculated about its absence. We have already alluded to the literature which sees the reform structure itself as mitigating against the emergence of committed leaders (Prewitt 1970; Downes 1971). Other authors see a more fundamental problem.

It is commonplace to believe that the triviality of suburban politics accounts for or allows the antipolitical bias of reform governments. Thomas

M. Scott argues that suburban government is too small and too segmental to do more than supply services efficiently (Scott 1973, p. 235). Minar states:

In the classic democratic view, value is ascribed to high participation and real choice among alternatives. From this standpoint, the system in which choice is "managed" and public conflict thus avoided can scarcely be regarded with favor. . . . On the other hand, it can be argued that the local . . . system is simply not an appropriate site or level for public conflict. Such a position may rest on arguments about the need for technical decision . . . , about the overriding need to maintain consensus and organic solidarity in the local community, or about the greater effectiveness of democratic choice as it operates at more general levels of government. . . . [1968, p. 262]

The corollary argument is expressed by Wood, who states that the active politics absent in suburban municipalities arise necessarily in large cities in order to accommodate their social complexity. The precarious balance of forces never allows leaders to ignore conflict (Wood 1958, p. 293). In partial support of this argument, James W. Clarke reports data which suggest that more functionally autonomous communities may choose more aggressive government. He found that more autonomous cities were more likely than less autonomous cities to consider changing from the decentralized commission form of government to a form which would give government more power. He attributes this to the greater stress placed on these governments (Clarke 1969, pp. 1176–78).

Suburbs provide us with an important laboratory for examining the relationship between complexity or autonomy and political aggressiveness, since, as Masotti and Hadden say, they are becoming "urbanized." Many of the suburbs which have been relatively homogeneous are facing distinctively "urban" problems. They are developing complex economic bases and diverse populations (Masotti and Hadden 1973).

Other authors argue that *politics* will not necessarily become more central, even when units are larger or problems more visible. Jeffrey Pressman (1972) has written about government in Oakland, California, a city with a population of over 350,000, 35% of which is black. Its unemployment rate is twice the national average. In spite of its diversity of people and problems, Oakland's governmental form is the reform model popular on the West Coast. Oakland has a council-manager government and at-large, nonpartisan elections. It pays a salary to the manager which is more than five times as large as the mayor's.

Significantly, it is not only Oakland's governmental form but its politics as well which resembles the suburban model. Pressman reports that two-thirds of the city council members of 1969 had originally been appointed rather than elected. These appointed officials survived with ease. In 16 years no appointed alderman who sought subsequent election had been defeated in the ensuing race (Pressman 1972, p. 516). This pattern of volunteer government is more extreme than the norm described by Prewitt and Eulau.

Pressman's description of the mayor's career is instructive with respect to both the system of government and the personalities it recruits: "Mayor Reading finds himself facing a fundamental dilemma: He is a political leader who does not like politics. . . . Recognizing that differences of opinion do exist in public life Mayor Reading tries to deal with them by using what might be called the 'big round table' method. He believes that if people could just get together on a personal level, around a table, and talk over their differences, then everything could be settled" (p. 519).

Mayor Reading was occupied as a tamale manufacturer when he was asked to fill a position on the Oakland City Council. "Reading was reluctant at first, but he felt that his advocacy of civic involvement meant that he should take the responsibility" (p. 517). He was subsequently elected by the council to fill out an unexpired mayoral term. He did not want to run for reelection but decided to do so after "a look at the alternative candidates. . . . Civic responsibility . . . (overcame) personal predilection" (p. 519). In this context of limited structural power and personal rejection of it by public officials, Oakland's aggressive manager took over.

Politics such as those in Oakland raise questions about politics in municipalities in general and about the characteristics which have been assumed to distinguish suburban governments. Pressman's research suggests that communities do not necessarily develop an active politics as their populations become clearly diverse and their problems great. By what logic, then, do we assume that homogeneity or a lack of significant issues account for the predominance of "managed" suburbs? Should all decisions be raised to the higher levels of state or nation?[2] Or are the very conditions for legitimacy in an antipolitical society sufficient to prevent effective government of any sort?

POLITICAL TRUST

Lack of political trust seems to be at the heart of the problem. Citizens do not trust politicians; elected officials disavow any political connection. Under these circumstances, we feel that it is necessary to look into the nature of political trust and to examine the ways in which it is created.

While previous students of suburban politics have documented a startling absence of trust, they have also recorded differences in the support consti-

---

[2] Becquart's (1974) analysis of the centralized French system suggests that central administration itself may create distrust of, and hostility toward, politics.

tuencies accord their leaders. Support seems, in part at least, a function of social class experience. We speculate that three types of trust may be distinguished and related to such variables as education and occupation. The first, we hypothesize, is most comon among least advantaged constituents (as well as in peasant communities and political machines). It is characterized by an emphasis on primary relationships: "Trust in a primary relationship refers to the kind of trust . . . which is associated with solidarity—with *Gemeinschaft* society, with family and with friendship. In such relationships, the social unit is central. Within the group, there is recognized membership, personal status, and individual significance" (Greer 1974, p. 142). Within such a group, it is felt that the leader could not have an interest in deceiving the group. Trust is therefore diffuse. Politicians have great latitude.

Middle-class voters, we propose, tend toward trust in "value representation." It is "awarded to a person who is felt to represent important values. One trusts persons who are 'like' oneself (or what one values) to act on one's behalf" (Greer 1974, p. 162). This is a very specific form of trust which may be withdrawn if it is not carried out (often this means if the opposed condominium is built in the neighborhood). Where value trust prevails, we expect the electorate to be volatile. Because trust is specific and focused, it leaves politicians with very little latitude. It makes the elected official accountable but allows him little room for compromise or overall strategy. Indirectly, managers and technicians increase their power.

"Trust in role adequacy" is the delegative approach of professionals to professionals. "It is conferred on a political official who, it is believed, has achieved or is achieving what can be rationally expected or required of him in a given position. The trust assumes an understanding of the capabilities and the restraints of a particular office . . ." (Greer 1974, p. 174). It requires that those conferring it understand, in broad perspective, the institutional characteristics of the position. Trust of this sort implies periodic review of performance and "businesslike" relations.

Insofar as suburban communities have failed to recreate the conditions under which the first type of trust flourishes and have failed to achieve the large-scale perspective associated with the last, they will increasingly operate with the second. In our view this will result in cynicism and volatility. Both will increase with community heterogeneity. Political leadership will be difficult to achieve.

There remains, of course, the supportive electorate in suburbia. Very little has been said about the ways in which political leaders appeal to constituencies which vary along dimensions such as trust. Significantly, Prewitt and Eulau did not find the supportive electoral context to be predicted by social class. It depends, we believe, on the development of political leadership which has enough ingenuity to convert the model-railroad politics of the suburbs into real railroads, to use politics to bridge the schism and create a basis for public policy. What are the styles of politicians who successfully elicit the support of local electorates? Social scientists have paid relatively little attention to political leadership, leaving the subject to journalists and novelists.[3]

THE SOCIOLOGY OF POLITICS VERSUS POLITICAL SOCIOLOGY

The modish study of local politics in terms of inputs and outputs tends to ignore the political process which transforms one into the other.[4] Thus sociologists appear in the same posture as the good-government reformers who denied the relevance of political choice and sought governmental forms which eliminated it (or hid it from view). Our review of the literature on suburban politics has highlighted for us the unpopularity among scholars of the concepts indicated by both "suburban" and "politics." Each is a curious omission, since one designates the geographic life space in which most Americans find themselves, and the other, the potential for communities of human beings to create futures. Taken alone, the attention to background variables and output variables which has characterized the study of local politics seems more a convenience of scientists than a strategy serving science. We feel the time has come for sociologists to focus on the modes of political action which characterize contemporary America. It is naive to operate as if, in leaving the big city machines behind, we have left politics also. We are simply very uninformed about the politics in today's suburbs.

Giovanni Sartori has spoken eloquently of the need for social scientists to study the dynamic character of politics:

> The power of power is growing at a tremendous pace, both with reference to the manipulative and coercive capability of state power and at the other extreme with reference to the explosive potentialities of state power vacuums. Now the greater the range of politics the smaller the role of "objective factors." All our *objective certainties* are increasingly exposed to *political uncertainty*. If so, it is an extraordinary paradox that the social sciences should be ever more prompted to explain politics by going *beyond* politics, by developing a fetishism for an "invisible hand." [More appropriate is] the opposite assumption: that sociologists should catch up with the hazardous uncertainties of politics. [Sartori 1969, pp. 93–94]

[3] Paige remarks on the lack of interest political scientists have, until recently, shown in political leadership. He notes that, between 1906 and 1963, only 17 of the 2,614 articles which appeared in the *American Political Science Review* contained any reference to leadership. Only one referred to "politician" and only one to "mayor" (Paige 1972, p. 5).

[4] For a collection of articles reviewing the community-politics literature and highlighting the need to complement existing research with study of political variables, see Downes (1971).

In short, most sociologists tend to think of politics as *reflecting* social structure; in Sartori's terms, it is more appropriate to think of political process as interpreting and channeling social structure. Upon the quality of the work of politicians depend the comity and the polity.

REFERENCES

Banfield, Edward, and James Q. Wilson. 1963. *City Politics.* Cambridge, Mass.: Harvard University Press and M.I.T. Press.

Becquart, Jeannette. 1974. "Political Inheritance and Apolitism: Some Paradoxes of Local Power in France." Paper presented at the annual meeting of the Midwest Sociological Society, Omaha, April.

Bell, Wendell, and Maryanne T. Force. 1956. "Urban Participation Types and Participation in Formal Associations." *American Sociological Review* 21 (February): 25–34.

Bollens, John C. 1957. *Special District Government in the United States.* Berkeley: University of California Press.

Clarke, James W. 1969. "Environment, Process, and Policy: A Reconsideration." *American Political Science Review* 63 (December): 1172–82.

Dahl, Robert. 1960. "The Analysis of Influence in Local Communities." Pp. 25–42 in *Social Sciences and Community Action,* edited by Charles R. Adrian. East Lansing, Mich.: Institute for Community Development.

Danielson, Michael N. 1971. *Metropolitan Politics.* Boston: Little, Brown.

Downes, Bryan T., ed. 1971. *Cities and Suburbs.* Belmont, Calif.: Duxbury.

Greer, Ann Lennarson. 1974. *The Mayor's Mandate: Municipal Statecraft and Political Trust.* Cambridge, Mass.: Schenkman.

Greer, Scott. 1962a. *Governing the Metropolis.* New York: Wiley.

———. 1962b. "The Social Structure and Political Process of Suburbia: An Empirical Test." *Rural Sociology* 27 (December): 438–59.

———. 1963. *Metropolitics.* New York: Wiley.

———. 1965. *Urban Renewal and American Cities.* Indianapolis: Bobbs-Merrill.

Greer, Scott, and Peter Orleans. 1962. "The Mass Society and the Parapolitical Structure." *American Sociological Review* 27 (October): 643–46.

Hawkins, Brett W., and James E. Prather. 1969. "Measuring Private Regardingness." Paper presented at the annual meeting of the Southern Political Science Association, Miami, November.

———. 1971. "Measuring Components of the Ethos Theory: A First Step." *Journal of Politics* 33 (August), pp. 642–58.

Hennessey, Timothy M. 1970. "Theory and Concept Formation in Comparative Urban Research." *Midwest Journal of Political Science* 14 (November): 537–64.

Kasarda, John D., and Morris Janowitz. 1974. "Community Attachment in Mass Society." *American Sociological Review* 39 (June): 328–39.

Masotti, Louis H., and Jeffrey K. Hadden, eds. 1973. *The Urbanization of the Suburbs.* Urban Affairs Annual Reviews, vol. 7. Beverly Hills, Calif.: Sage.

Minar, David W. 1968. "The Community Basis of Conflict in School System Politics." Pp. 246–63 in *The New Urbanization,* edited by Scott Greer et al. New York: St. Martin's.

Orbell, John M., and Toro Uno. 1972. "A Theory of Neighborhood Problem Solving." *American Political Science Review* 66 (June): 471–89.

Paige, Glenn D., ed. 1972. *Political Leadership.* New York: Collier & Macmillan.

Pressman, Jeffrey. 1972. "Preconditions of Mayoral Leadership." *American Political Science Review* 66 (June): 511–24.

Prewitt, Kenneth. 1970. "Political Ambitions, Volunteerism, and Electoral Accountability." *American Political Science Review* 64 (March): 5–17.

Prewitt, Kenneth, and Heinz Eulau. 1971. "Social Bias in Leadership Selection, Political Recruitment and Electoral Context." *Journal of Politics* 33 (May): 293–315.

Sartori, Giovanni. 1969. "From the Sociology of Politics to Political Sociology." Pp. 65–100 in *Politics and the Social Sciences*, edited by Seymour M. Lipset. New York: Oxford University Press.

Scott, Stanley, and Harriet Nathan. 1970. "Public Referenda: A Critical Reappraisal." *Urban Affairs Quarterly* 5 (March): 311–27.

Scott, Thomas M. 1973. "Suburban Governmental Structures." Pp. 213–38 in *The Urbanization of the Suburbs*, edited by Louis H. Masotti and Jeffrey K. Hadden. Urban Affairs Annual Reviews, vol. 7. Beverly Hills, Calif.: Sage.

Stegner, Wallace. 1962. *Wolf Willow*. New York: Viking.

Vidich, Arthur, and Joseph Bensman. 1958. *Small Town in Mass Society*. Princeton, N.J.: Princeton University Press.

Wirt, Frederick M., Benjamin Walter, Francine F. Rabinovitz, and Deborah R. Hensler. 1972. *On the City's Rim: Politics and Policy in Suburbia*. Lexington, Mass.: Heath.

Wood, Robert C. 1958. *Suburbia: Its People and Their Politics*. Boston: Houghton Mifflin.

Zikmund, Joseph, II, and Robert Smith. 1969. "Political Participation in an Upper Middle Class Suburb." *Urban Affairs Quarterly* 4 (June): 443–58.

9 Attitudes toward Integration: The Role of Status in Community Response to Racial Change

Brian J. L. Berry
University of Chicago

Carole A. Goodwin
Illinois Institute of Technology

Robert W. Lake
Rutgers—The State University

Katherine B. Smith
Department of Development and Planning, City of Chicago

Racial relationships are changing in metropolitan America. While a tide of residential resegregation continues to roll across the central city as departing whites are replaced by blacks and other minorities, it does so with a new velocity, eliciting a mixture of responses from residents of "threatened" neighborhoods. Meanwhile, many experiments in integration maintenance are being conducted in suburbia while, simultaneously, new forms of black containment are emerging.

While the scale and substance of racial relationships are changing, the resulting residential patterns in American cities and suburbs continue to reflect a basic underlying white reluctance to share residential space with blacks. Recent changes in racial relationships therefore seem to involve the search for new methods of achieving old objectives. It is with the interplay between the changing forms of white response and the continuity in underlying rationale that this paper is concerned.

We begin with summaries of six case studies in the Chicago region, both to dispel some myths about what is happening in metropolitan housing markets and to provide an indication of the variety of experiences. Both inner-city and suburban cases are described, placing the range of responses in a regional context. This macro-level analysis focuses on organizational response as an indication of the role of neighborhood associations—schools, real estate dealers, banks, etc.—in determining white behavior in changing neighborhoods. Then, a micro-level analysis focuses on the factors—identi-

Financial support from the National Science Foundation under the provisions of grant no. GS-28588 is gratefully acknowledged.

ty, status, reference group orientation, and the meaning of residential proximity—which provide an underlying continuity fundamental to racial relationships in American cities.

THE PROBLEM

The Chicago case studies reported here and a variety of studies published
elsewhere document the widespread negative white response to the arrival of
blacks in a broad spectrum of urban and suburban neighborhoods with
widely divergent populations and varying conditions of black entry (Fishman 1961; Henderson 1964; Kerckhoff 1957; Mayer 1960; Molotch 1969;
Tillman 1961a; Winder 1951; Wolf 1965). While the process varies in
intensity and scale, residential desegregation leads to white avoidance and
abandonment, racial transition, and resegregation.

The components of this process have been well documented. A dwelling
once occupied by a black family rarely reverts to white occupancy (Taeuber
and Taeuber 1965, p. 112), and whites tend to avoid purchasing a home
adjacent to a black household (Rapkin and Grigsby 1960, pp. 29–30). When
an "integrated neighborhood" was defined as one attracting *both* blacks and
whites, a national survey found a median black population of only 3% in
such neighborhoods (Bradburn, Sudman, and Gockel 1970, p. 30). This
finding not only calls into question much of the survey's subsequent analysis
of "integrated neighborhoods" but also, and more important, graphically
portrays the result of myriad white decisions to shun residential integration
on other than a token basis.

Our macro-level analysis of six Chicago-area communities identifies the
broad range of white organizational responses—violence, steering, managed
integration, resignation—to racial integration. *Across the range of white responses, however, is the general conclusion that at each income level and regardless of
socioeconomic characteristics, a concentration of black families is perceived negatively
by whites.* This is true regardless of the fact that, to afford the housing,
incoming blacks must be equal in achieved socioeconomic status to their
white neighbors. Why does it matter to a white community—urban or
suburban—if incoming residents are black rather than white? How does the
symbolism of race determine the definition of a black residential concentration as undesirable for whites? Finally, given this attitudinal common denominator, is it possible to identify those characteristics of communities which
explain the variation in intensity and method of response?

In order to seek explanation of the processes manifest at the macro scale
of community and region, our analysis looks at individual and group responses manifest at the micro level of face-to-face confrontation of blacks
and whites as homeowners and neighbors. This analysis focuses on status

consciousness as a basic explanatory factor. As a vital intervening variable coloring the individual's perception of his residential environment, the fear of status deprivation exerts a fundamental influence on the pace and intensity of the racial change process. Several basic attitudinal dimensions related to status consciousness can be identified, and it is hypothesized that behavioral variations among communities are associated with variation along these basic attitudinal dimensions. Our discussion in this section ranges over three general areas: (1) the basic relationship between status and space in general, (2) the somewhat more specific status implications of residential proximity, and (3) the status-related dimensions along which communities can be differentiated and which determine the manner and extent to which the basic underlying regularities implied by (1) and (2) impact on white behavior.

The focus on status in the study of racial change is not new. Gans, for instance, discussing population homogeneity and heterogeneity, suggests that racial integration (as opposed to transition and resegregation) is possible ". . . provided, however, the whites are not beset by status fears. Indeed," Gans concludes, "the major barrier to effective integration is fear of status deprivation" (1967, p. 174). Simply to state the case, however, is clearly not sufficient for an understanding of the process. While status fears are widespread among the population and status consciousness is a fundamental dimension of the racial change process, a search of the literature reveals the absence of an explicit statement outlining the relationship between the social dynamics of status and the spatial process of residential transition. How does the neighborhood environment, including the racial characteristics of one's neighbors, affect an individual's social status? Conversely, how does status concern influence the individual's perception of and response to his residential environment? How do individuals (and groups) vary in the extent to which their status fears are translated to the local spatial context? What determines, in short, whether whites *are* in fact "beset by status fears" or how these fears become manifest?

The following summary of the Chicago experience suggests the scale and essential parameters of the racial change process; our concern is to demonstrate the subtleties in the range of white responses to racial integration. At this exploratory stage in our analysis, the discussion provides no firm conclusions; rather, our aim is to stimulate further research into the relationship between status-related social processes and the spatially manifested processes of racial residential distribution.

THE CHICAGO EXPERIENCE

Between 1960 and 1970, 481,553 new housing units were built in the Chicago metropolitan area, 129,496 in the central city and 352,057 in the six-county suburban region. Chicago's suburban population growth of 941,000 was the greatest in the nation in the decade, yet the number of households in the metropolitan area increased by only 263,609—168,971 white and 94,638 black—so that the ratio of new housing units to new families was 1.8:1.0. The result was a growing housing surplus that enabled a massive chain of successive housing moves to take place, culminating in abandonment in the oldest inner-city neighborhoods. Homes vacated by occupants of the new units were purchased or rented by other families seeking better housing, and so on in echelon—the surplus filtering simultaneously down the scale of housing values and inward from the suburbs to the core of the city. One consequence was that downward pressure was exerted on the prices of older housing units, and discriminatory pricing of identical units—blacks paying more than whites—was eliminated. Not only did a substantial improvement result in the housing condition of Chicago's central-city minorities—for example, over 128,000 units were transferred from white to black occupancy (these, plus 33,000 new units in the central city occupied by blacks, exceeded the growth in black families in the central city in the decade by a ratio of 2.0:1.0, which compares with 1.75:1.0 for the white community)—but 63,000 of the worst units in the city could be demolished at the same time that thousands of additional undesirable units were being abandoned. The Chicago region thus provides a classic example of filtering mechanisms at work, because *surpluses* rather than deficits characterized Chicago's housing market in the 1960s, an important and frequently unrecognized fact.

However, this dramatic improvement in housing access still took place within the context of a dual housing market. In the decade, 352,057 new suburban housing units were constructed. But in spite of this, in the entire six-county metropolitan area, only 4,188 out of 233,845 new homes and 3,712 out of 111,290 new apartments were obtained by blacks, while an additional 3,208 black families purchased homes previously owned by whites, and 3,153 black families moved into apartments previously rented by whites. Thus, in contrast to the net increase of 287,000 white families in suburban Chicago, only 13,261 new black families were able to obtain residences in the rest of the six-county area. Some 12,168 of these new black families moved into or adjacent to the traditional ghettos of the crescent of industrial satellite communities ringing the metropolis (Waukegan, Elgin, Aurora, Joliet, Harvey, and Chicago Heights) or into those suburbs with long-standing black enclaves such as Evanston and Wheaton. The increase in black families elsewhere in suburbia was only 1,093, bringing the total from 1,217 to 2,310.

But even these numbers are illusory. Of this increase, 20% was in two communities, Park Forest and Oak Park (which together absorbed an additional 976 black families in the next four years, 1970–74). Only 569 of the remaining 2,084 black families lived in suburbs with over 2,500 residents in

1970; the remaining 1,515 families lived in smaller places or in isolated rural backwaters that have had black populations for many years. In 1970, 68 of 148 suburbs with populations of more than 2,500 had no black families in residence, 54 had a token four or less, 15 had between five and nine, nine had 10–24, and only two had more than 50. There are so few blacks in suburban DuPage County that they have formed their own organization, the Black Suburbanites Club, to provide a social outlet and a basis for mutual aid amid white indifference or enmity. Thus, the civil rights advocates and fair housing groups who, coordinated by the Leadership Council for Metropolitan Open Communities, concluded in their monitoring efforts that only 411 black families were able to find homes in otherwise white suburbs in metropolitan Chicago in the years 1959–68—180 of these in Park Forest—were not far short of the mark. These 411 in the entire period 1959–68 should be compared with the 976 these same groups estimate to have moved into Park Forest and Oak Park alone in the years 1970–74, years in which the developing new town of Park Forest South became 20% black. We will have more to say about this numeric change, for the question it raises is whether Park Forest and Oak Park represent integration breakthroughs or simply the beginnings of ghetto extension into suburbia.

Contrast the picture of suburban constraints with that of the central city. There was a net decline of 41,500 white homeowners and 76,900 white renters in the central city in the 1960–70 decade. Net increases in the central-city black population consisted of 37,669 new homeowners (more than doubling black home ownership in the decade) and 43,708 new renters.

The complex dynamics of white-to-black filtering that maintained racially segregated living in the city were as follows: some 128,829 units were transferred from white to black occupancy, allowing net increases over new construction of 28,008 in black home ownership and 20,267 in black rental of good-quality apartments. In total, the new housing inventory available to black families increased by 81,377 units, in spite of the fact that 63,000 units were demolished in the decade within the area of the 1960 ghetto. Finally, there was a net increase by 1970 of 17,554 units vacant in the expanded black residential area of 1970, many of these the precursors to abandonment.

What these figures show is important. As white families withdrew to the suburbs, black families gained access to large numbers of good-quality housing units in previously white areas. There, population increased and school enrollments escalated as black child-rearing families replaced whites at later stages in the life cycle. In turn, the traditional South and West Side ghettos were depopulated. The population in the 1960 area of ghetto declined 19% in 1960–70, and the communities in which population declines in the decade were greatest were also the communities with the greatest amounts of abandoned housing. Increasing the pressures on substandard private-market housing that would otherwise have to be occupied by the welfare poor, 13,250 of

19,000 units of public housing built in the decade were located within the 1960 ghetto. Also manifesting the changed market conditions, Chicago's overall vacancy rate increased from 3.7% to 4.6%, with the rate exceeding 6% within the 1960 ghetto area.

White Reactions at the Frontiers of Racial Change: Six Cases

These numbers suggest several important conclusions. The stock of housing available to blacks increased rapidly after 1960, enabling them to upgrade their housing conditions and also causing numbers of less desirable units in the worst central-city neighborhoods to drop out of the market. At the same time, the dual housing market has continued to restrict access of blacks to the total housing supply, and particularly to that of suburbia. On the one hand, filtering processes appear to have been working well (that is, except for the financially afflicted—the elderly poor, the welfare poor, the sick and infirm poor—who, if they do not or cannot occupy public housing, are unable to participate in normal housing market channels on any basis and are thus left the dregs unwanted by any market participant). Yet, on the other hand, subdivision of the housing supply into racially segregated submarkets is as profound as it ever was. The question is, Why?

As suggested earlier, we believe that the reasons are to be found in the social psychology of white-black residential proximity. For whites influenced by status consciousness, there is an aversion to sharing residential space with blacks. To explicate this aversion, we next offer six case studies of white responses to the arrival and expansion of black populations in the Chicago region, and then attempt to draw together the general principles that may be involved. Emphasis in the case studies is on the extent and direction of *organized* response as a generalized expression of community sentiment. Three of the case studies relate to heavily ethnic central-city communities: West Englewood, in which Francis X. Lawlor, a Catholic priest and Chicago alderman, has organized a defensive network of block clubs; Garfield Ridge, where the community organization recently joined a coalition of 19 Northwest and South Side groups in charging that black public housing tenants threatened their communities with "social pollution"; and South Shore, in which Molotch (1972) documented the failure of "managed integration." The other three cases are in the suburbs of Evanston, Oak Park, and Park Forest, trying by a variety of individual and collective strategies to attain the sometimes conflicting objectives of containing black increase while maintaining viable open communities.

West Englewood: Father Lawlor's Defensive Network

West Englewood sits astride the watershed between Chicago's Southwest Side blue-collar ethnic refuges and the growth of black residential areas westward from the main South Side axis of ghetto expansion. For many years, a racial boundary line had been recognized along Ashland Avenue within the community, but this boundary came under increasing pressure as the black percentage in the area increased between 1960 and 1970. Finally, racial confrontation came to the fore as the Ashland line was breached north of Sixty-seventh Street, and blacks moved westward into neighborhoods heavily populated by Catholics of Polish, Irish, and Italian origins.

The public schools have been leading elements in this community change. Overcrowding in black schools east of Ashland Avenue was "solved" by the Chicago Board of Education by changing attendance area boundaries and assigning black students to adjacent schools.

The result was growing racial conflict in the schools, compounded by blockbusting and panic peddling. Plans for location of dispersed public housing units in the area have been strongly opposed by West Englewood's white population, who fear it would bring low-income blacks into the area and precipitate even greater racial change. Fear of crime, declining city services and the growth of "problem" businesses, such as taverns, have all played a part in the community's reactions.

Of the white community organizations which arose in response to imminent racial change, three predominated. One, the South Lynne Community Council (SLCC), had existed since 1957 as a liberal-oriented neighborhood improvement association. It expanded its activities in the 1960s to include a free rent referral service and a center for rumor clearance. In 1963 the SLCC supported open housing, espousing "balanced integration" as preferable to inundation by blacks. The SLCC's housing policy was to encourage white residents to remain along racial borderlines, aggressively recruit new white families to move in, and assist black families in locating in predominantly white areas west of the racial border. It vigorously fought panic peddlers, to little avail, and monitored property maintenance. The SLCC battled for quality schools and pressured the Chicago Board of Education and the state for more financial support for education. The organization tried to welcome blacks into the community and prevent racial violence, but, as one observer commented, it was "so successful that there are few whites left now to welcome new blacks." The SLCC is now largely black and concerned with posttransition problems.

The South West Associated Block Clubs (SWABC) is the most interesting organization operating in West Englewood because of its leader, Roman Catholic priest Francis Xavier Lawlor. Father Lawlor formed the first block clubs in 1967 in defiance of the Catholic archdiocese's integration policies and, as a result, has been forbidden to perform his priestly functions. However, his charismatic personality has been crucial in organizing many Englewood residents. Signs in windows announce "Jesus Loves Father Lawlor." Elected as an independent in 1971, Father Lawlor is alderman of the Fifteenth Ward.

While SWABC is overtly a home improvement association, its implicit objective is to "hold the line at Ashland Avenue." While Father Lawlor maintains he is not a racist, SWABC's policy has been to exclude blacks from West Englewood until certain preconditions have been met. Primarily these are the rectifying of what he believes to be inherent "socioeconomic, cultural" differences between blacks and whites. He characterizes the black community as essentially riddled with crime, lacking respect for either persons or property, and completely "unprepared" for home ownership. Until the black community solves "its own problems," Father Lawlor suggests buffer zones and quotas for each block.

To organize white fringe neighborhoods, Father Lawlor has focused on three issues: crime, schools, and real estate practices. To offer protection against crime, the block clubs instituted nightly mobile patrols, and they regularly demand increased police protection.

SWABC considers the Chicago Board of Education's integration policy its major enemy and has resorted to picketing to prevent its realization. "The Board of Education is the biggest block-buster in Chicago," Father Lawlor has been quoted as saying.

Other enemies of stable housing according to SWABC are panic-peddling brokers, the federal government, Chicago politicians, and large developers. Hundreds of signs bearing the message, "We are going TO STAY—down with FHA," could be seen in windows of homes west of Ashland Avenue in 1971. The city government is viewed by SWABC with even greater suspicion than the federal government. Says Father Lawlor:

> The powers-that-be have decided that the part of the city that counts is the lakefront, and they are determined to save it. The big realtors, the downtown politicians, the business community . . . are united in this situation. To them the part of Chicago that matters is the high rises of Lake Shore Drive, the high income districts in and around the Loop, and the string of institutions on the south side running from Michael Reese Hospital to the University of Chicago. The rest of the city? Let that go to the swiftest and the strongest, be he black or blue-collar white. [*Chicago Journalism Review* (February 1973)]

One objective of SWABC has been to promote solidarity in the face of solicitations by real estate agents. As vacancies occur, SWABC has tried to fill them with "persons of the same cultural, social, and economic background as our own community," which has meant trying to prevent the sale or rental of properties to blacks.

The third organization operating in West Englewood is the Murray Park Civic Association (MPCA). Subsumed by SWABC, it includes some of Father Lawlor's strongest supporters and encompasses an area whose inhabitants are chiefly of Italian descent. Murray Park takes a wild-west approach to black encroachment: it has a history of racial violence. In 1971 four homes into which black families were moving were burned down. The year before, shots were fired and bricks thrown through the windows of a home owned by blacks in an all-white block. Earlier a storefront church was bombed on Easter Sunday, and there were three days of rioting around a house when it was rumored that blacks were planning to move in. Summed up the president of MPCA: "When you hear of an incident in this community of a garage being burned or a house being bombed, it's not because the people in this community are doing it for kicks. We're letting everyone know we mean business" (*Southtown Economist* [September 5, 1971]).

Early black penetration of the Ashland Avenue dividing line was made into South Lynne, where less resistance was encountered than from Sixty-seventh to Eighty-seventh Streets, the stronghold of SWABC and MPCA. The SWABC's success in "holding the line" since 1967 is largely due to the organizing ability of Father Lawlor, the vigilance of the block clubs, and the violent resistance to black move-ins in Murray Park. However, the prospect for West Englewood is one of erosion of the remaining white community and its replacement by blacks. As the percentage of black students in the schools continues to rise, whites move away or enroll their children in parochial schools. The critical question is when the situation is seen by the residents of any block as too serious to fight any longer. When that perception becomes widespread, the block not only undergoes racial transition, but undergoes it very rapidly—more rapidly than in other communities where turnover does not involve white flight but is contained within the "normal" turnover of the market.

Garfield Ridge: Establishment of a Defensive Boundary

The establishment of a defensive boundary in West Englewood may typify blue-collar response, for the same pattern has been repeated in many other central-city communities. One such is Garfield Ridge, a working-class community of single-family homes located on the western edge of the city of Chicago. Small frame and brick homes are fronted by carefully tended lawns arranged along tree-lined streets, giving the community a suburban look. The ethnic composition is predominantly Polish, Italian, and other Eastern European: 90%–95% of the residents are Catholic.

The community differs from other areas experiencing racial change because it is a relatively new community located far from the central ghetto. Blacks came in 1951 with construction of the Chicago Housing Authority's LeClaire Courts public housing project. While they were in the minority for the first five years, half of the 615 families were black by 1956, and LeClaire has been more than 90% black since 1964.

In 1968, black families began moving out and buying homes in the blocks directly south of the Courts. As they did, the total black population of the community increased dramatically. Between 1960 and 1970, while the white population increased by 4.3%, the black population increased by 32.9%. Garfield Ridge thus was drawn into the confrontation between whites and blacks over housing, and today exhibits the full range of problems associated with racial change: the fabric of daily life is influenced by the presence of racial conflict. Whites now have established a barrier between white and black residential areas at Forty-seventh Street; most of the homes to the north of this dividing line have been purchased by black families and the area has been abandoned by the white community. In 1970, the ward boundary was redrawn at Forty-seventh Street, removing the area north of Forty-seventh Street from the Twenty-third Ward, to which it is contiguous, and annexing it to the Twelfth Ward, from which it is separated by extensive railroad yards and industrial facilities. School attendance boundaries have been redrawn along Forty-seventh Street to further the de facto segregation.

Located adjacent to the black residential area north of the Forty-seventh Street barrier, residents of the area known as Vittum Park feel themselves to be the most threatened. "The community is like a tinder box . . . a bomb about to explode," said a resident. At meetings of the Vittum Park Civic League, emotions run high, and several have ended in disorder when residents disagreed over policy or methods. Homes which come up for sale in Vittum Park are listed with the Civic League and are not advertised through normal real estate channels. White respondents outside Vittum Park estimate that up to 100 homes there are available for sale in the course of normal turnover, but suggest that the Civic League is unable to find buyers.

Although white residents in the rest of the community feel less threatened, racial tensions are high. Continued controversy over scattered-site public housing has kept the issue in the forefront of attention:

> These liberals come on with these beautiful programs that are to integrate us. . . . How are you going to integrate when they just inundate us. . . . Their kids got better bikes than we got. Why? They come across 47th Street and steal them. [*Chicago Sun-Times* (June 6, 1973)]

> I want the privilege of living in an all-white neighborhood. [*Southwest News-Herald* (June 8, 1972)]

> We don't want no other form of people to come and burn our houses and take away our families and tear them up. . . . I don't want no neighbor throwing no garbage and barbecuing no beef out in the yard. [*Chicago Daily Defender* (June 7, 1972)]

The white residents of Garfield Ridge are vehemently concerned with protecting neighborhood status. They feel that they have "made it," that Garfield Ridge is a community that satisfies their status aspirations, at least for the present. The competition between races in Garfield Ridge is clearly defined in terms of territory. Because of the absolute refusal of whites to share residential space with blacks, white residents continue to leave Garfield

Ridge in step with the continuing arrival of black families. Even a small infusion of black families on an all-white block results in the rapid evacuation of the area by whites. Thus, while the eventual transition of the community depends on the rate of growth of the black population, it is clear that only a small increase in the number of blacks is sufficient to place the entire area within the boundaries of the black housing market. The vehemence of white opposition ironically serves to speed transition in Garfield Ridge.

South Shore: The Failure of Managed Integration

South Shore, a community of 90,000 residents, lies 10 miles south of Chicago's Loop and has been undergoing racial change since the early 1960s. In 1960, South Shore was a solidly middle-class residential community inhabited by a relatively well-educated white population. There were indications, however, that South Shore was no longer a choice area for white middle-class residence. It possessed, according to Harvey Molotch (1972), many of the traits of an area likely to undergo racial change.

By the mid-1950s, it was apparent to some South Shore residents that black in-migration was a distinct possibility in the near future, as the ghetto approached from the north and west. In 1954, a priest, a minister, and a rabbi decided to use the South Shore Ministerial Association as the basis for a more extensive community organization, from which the South Shore Commission emerged.

The organization's principal concern was how to contain ghetto expansion. Initially a split existed between the exclusionists, who wanted to prevent black entry and ensure that South Shore remain white, and the integrationists, who believed that the middle-class character of the community could be maintained by controlling the balance between white and black residents. By 1966, the integrationist viewpoint prevailed, but a growing proportion of South Shore's northwesternmost population was already black, as the tide of ghetto expansion moved in from adjacent Woodlawn.

Although the South Shore Commission described itself as a democratic, grass-roots organization, its middle-class character was always apparent. Low-income and blue-collar people were not represented in the leadership. Blacks were represented on the Commission Board and Executive Committee only after 1963, but remained underrepresented through 1967. They did not play a major role in commission activities until after 1969.

The goal of the South Shore Commission throughout the 1960s was to make South Shore a community in which white middle-class individuals and families would choose to live. The strategy had two basic parts: (1) to create neighborhood and community conditions felt to be desirable to whites, and (2) to facilitate white move-ins by recruiting white, middle-class residents through actual intervention in the real estate market.

231

The first strategy involved tactics aimed at crime prevention and the improvement of education, housing, and other community amenities. The commission responded to a dramatic increase in serious crime between 1964 and 1966 by instituting citizen-manned radio patrols and pressuring police and courts for more arrests and convictions. The South Shore School-Community Plan was developed to give South Shore priority over other school districts in new educational facilities and programs, including authorization for a second high school (even though other southeast Chicago schools were significantly more crowded than South Shore High), "educational saturation centers," a program for high school computer science training, creation of an evening junior college, and establishment of reading clinics and remedial classes. The South Shore Commission also served as a watchdog over building maintenance and code enforcement.

The most important phase of the housing market intervention strategy was the Tenant Referral Service. Using listings provided by local landlords and rental agents, the commission took applications for apartments and referred applicants to vacancies. Referrals were made with the object of moving whites into integrated buildings; in other words, "reverse steering" was practiced. On the other hand, the commission did not want to refer blacks to a mixed building if white tenants could be found, and it was also reluctant to refer blacks to buildings which were all white. An attempt was made to increase the number of white applicants by advertising in local newspapers serving the nearby Hyde Park community where the University of Chicago is located. Similar efforts to reach black prospects were not made. In fact, the commission hoped to discourage black occupancy by cooperating with the Leadership Council for Metropolitan Open Communities, Chicago's major fair-housing group, in the operation of a neighborhood Fair Housing Center, which attempted to make black home seekers aware of housing opportunities in all-white communities elsewhere in the metropolitan Chicago area. This center operated with little success from 1967 until it was terminated in 1969.

The Tenant Referral Service served a total of 750 applicants, 675 of whom did locate in South Shore; 200 of the 675 were black. The TRS became a major force in the local real estate industry. Landlords and agents were asked to hold units vacant until white renters could be found, and those who did not cooperate could be excluded from TRS or given the least desirable prospects. However, as more blacks came to the community, white demand sagged and black demand grew. While TRS may have helped the market operate more efficiently by unifying listings, it could not significantly affect the pattern of transition. By 1970, 57% of South Shore's population was black, and by 1974, 80%, and the goal of the South Shore Commission had changed to the maintenance of South Shore as a stable middle-class *black* community.

Evanston: A Traditional Ghetto Expands

Evanston, one of Chicago's oldest suburban towns, lies 13 miles north of the Loop in the luxurious North Shore. The community's early growth was linked to the commuter railroads and to Northwestern University, founded by the Methodist Episcopal Church in 1851. During the 1860s, Northwestern sold land at low prices to attract new residents. Purchasers were warned the land would revert back to the university if the owner permitted "intoxicating drink to be manufactured, sold or given away on the premises," or allowed "any gambling to be carried on." Evanston became the national headquarters of the Women's Christian Temperance Union, and, until 1972, no liquor was sold within the city limits. Many churches settled in the community and are still dominant in its landscape. Termed by its residents, at various times, the "City of Gracious Living" and the "Athens of the Middle West," Evanston always has projected an aura of intense respectability.

The first blacks settled in Evanston in the 1800s and were trades- and craftsmen. After World War I, the opportunity for blacks in domestic service swelled the size of the black population. Evanston's total 1970 population was 79,808, of whom 12,861 (16%) were black. While some blacks live in predominantly white neighborhoods, and one area apparently has been stably and substantially mixed for over a decade, Evanston, on the whole, has been composed of two divided but coexisting communities. Throughout its history, white Evanston largely ignored black Evanston, reacting to it only in periods of real or fancied crisis.

Natural boundaries have maintained Evanston's social and ethnic distinctions on a geographic basis. Blacks, foreign born, and Jews have been concentrated in a roughly triangular area on the southeast side of Evanston, which covers approximately one-half of the city's land area and is separated from the affluent lake front and northwest Evanston neighborhoods by the Chicago Sanitary District's North Shore Channel and the Chicago and Northwestern Railroad tracks. In 1900, the northern tip of this triangle formed the nucleus of Evanston's black ghetto, which has expanded southward since. More recently, the core of a second ghetto has developed along the eastern edge of the triangle.

Thus, in 1970, there were two vectors of black expansion in Evanston, south and southeast from the old black community and northwest from the newly forming ghetto. Both of these areas exhibited signs of the classic transition pattern, with blocks of high black occupancy rates flanked by blocks of rather abruptly decreasing percentages of blacks. This drop in black population in "fringe" blocks, however, was not as sharp as is typical in transitional neighborhoods in Chicago. Together with the presence of a few blacks scattered in white, nontransitional neighborhoods and the existence of one long-standing integrated neighborhood, this fact may account for the apparent perception on the part of some white residents that true integration rather than transition is taking place. This perception, however, is not shared by whites living in the neighborhoods close to the black residential areas.

In addition to the threat of continued ghetto expansion, Evanston has been confronted with declining white demand relative to black demand in the suburb as a whole. Between 1960 and 1970, the white population decreased as the black population grew. The aging of the housing stock and the increasing dependence of the city on residential property tax revenues as nearby shopping centers cut into Evanston's share of the North Shore retail dollar jeopardized the city's attractiveness to whites, while for blacks it still represented an opportunity for a desirable, middle-class suburban life style, with good schools and the other amenities which that implies.

Further aggravating the situation was evidence of racial steering on the part of North Shore real estate brokers. In July 1972, after nine months of investigation of real estate practices in Evanston and other North Shore suburbs, the Evanston Human Relations Commission released findings which showed discrimination taking much the same form as it had for a half-century or more. One broker checked a buyer's choice of listings to make sure they were not located in a "Jewish, colored, or student area." Most sales people assumed that the critical factor in the buyer's choice would be the racial or religious composition of the neighborhood. In general, whites were steered to houses in north and lakeshore Evanston or out of Evanston entirely, while blacks and Jews were shown houses in the triangle.

The threat perceived by white residents stemming from the expansion of Evanston's ghetto and the potential decline of white demand for housing in Evanston has been complicated over the past decade by increasingly vocal dissatisfaction and demands for social equality emanating from its black community. The black-white struggle has been played out most dramatically in the schools.

In 1966, Evanston's elementary schools were voluntarily desegregated through a combined strategy of redistricting and busing of black pupils. As controversial as school integration was, it appeared to have majority support of both white and black citizens. The real conflict arose around the new superintendent, Dr. Gregory Coffin, who had been hired specifically for his record on integration to implement the school integration plan. Friction developed between Dr. Coffin and the school board, which the board alleged was due to Coffin's failure to cooperate with and, in fact, his deliberate deception of the school board. However, to his supporters, who included the majority of Evanston's blacks, Dr. Coffin had become the symbol of a promise finally kept. When the school board voted in June 1969 to fire Dr. Coffin, Evanston was torn apart: the real meaning of the battle went far beyond the mere issue of schools, raising the issues of power and representation in Evanston's social and political life generally. The Coffin controversy blew the lid off the long-standing splits between liberal and conservative, black and white, "old Evanston" and "new Evanston."

In 1973, after six years of desegregated education, at least two serious problems remained. One was the old and unresolved issue of black representation and participation. The other involved the reciprocal relationship of school racial composition and neighborhood transition. In 1973, the school system was still substantially integrated, but the district was faced with state-imposed necessity of further redistricting as the black enrollment of one school approached 50%. Continuing neighborhood transition will mean that redistricting or other strategies for maintaining school integration must be an ongoing process, and continued redistricting, in turn, has the effect of speeding white flight. A May 1972 report by the U.S. Civil Rights Commission concluded that Evanston's school integration program had been a success, but said of the decline of white enrollment: "Some . . . may be attributable to such factors as birth rates, but several school officials view the decline as white flight from newly desegregated districts" (*Evanston Review* [February 1, 1973]).

Racial conflict has become an increasingly open problem in the high school as well, where, despite an extremely high black dropout rate, almost one-fourth of the student population is black. Yet a relatively low level of organizational response to racial change is noticeable. In 1963, the West End Neighbors Organization, serving the area just south of the ghetto, formed "as a result of occupancy changes." The group held discussions among residents, pressured real estate brokers and the *Evanston Review* to refrain from listing housing on a racial basis, and proposed an ordinance for nondiscriminatory advertising of housing. By 1970 its efforts had failed, for the neighborhood was then largely black. Other neighborhood organizations followed with similar tactics, but while there was a proliferation of groups involved with the issue of racial change on a local neighborhood basis, their efforts were fragmented and appear in most cases to have amounted to too little, too late. Nothing even resembling a concerted, community-wide attack on the problem of neighborhood transition existed until 1973, when some local activists united in an informal coalition to put pressure on the real estate industry to end racial steering. No program for stabilization has yet come from the city government, from Evanston's central institutions, or from the grass-roots level. Yet, meanwhile, block-by-block expansion of the ghetto continues in the triangle.

Oak Park: Reverse Steering and Quota Systems

A more affirmative response has come in another old Chicago suburb, Oak Park, which, despite its size (62,506 in 1970) and location (bordering Chicago, nine miles west of the Loop), has maintained the ambience of a respectable and quietly affluent suburban town. Solidly built up in the 1920s, its increasingly heterogeneous population and the rapid development of Chicago's western suburban fringe contributed to Oak Park's decline from the ranks of the elite. However its residents remained assured of a high quality of life in the community, a quality sustained by such things as its symphony orchestra, repertory theater, and an ample lecture schedule. Schools and public services are reputedly good, transportation to the Loop via rapid transit and an expressway is excellent, and the housing stock, despite its age, is sound.

From the viewpoint of its residents, Oak Park's main liability is that it is separated only by Austin Boulevard from Chicago's large, expanding West Side black ghetto. By the summer of 1973, Oak Park had over 1,000 black residents (up from 132 in 1970), who tended to be concentrated in neighborhoods closest to the Chicago ghetto. Only one block was over 50% black, however, and nearly 40% of the black population lived in areas further removed from the ghetto.

As in most white suburbs, blacks found it nearly impossible to buy or rent homes in Oak Park until the mid-1960s. A very few had obtained homes through white "straw buyers." However, a strong fair-housing group, the Oak Park–River Forest Citizens' Committee for Human Rights had emerged in the early 1960s, and it succeeded in 1968 in persuading the village board of trustees to pass a fair-housing ordinance. The law, which was considered a strong one, seemed to be effective in controlling brokers' practices. Most apartments, however, still excluded blacks. In the two years between the passage of the fair-housing law and the 1970 census, the black population of Oak Park rose only negligibly, in spite of the considerable efforts by the Citizens' Committee to attract black residents.

However, Oak Parkers generally did not welcome black neighbors, and the fair-housing law brought angry protests. Black families who did move into Oak Park suffered harassment and ostracism but no serious physical attacks. Overt violence was not Oak Park's style, and in this the village was sharply contrasted with its neighbor to the south, Cicero. Blue-collar ethnic Cicero also adjoins the Chicago ghetto, and some blacks who have unwittingly ventured across its corporate limits have been beaten or shot. The contrast between Oak Park and its neighbor, together with the fact that "liberals" dominated the village's political process, gave Oak Park an "open" reputation.

Oak Park residents feel that the openness of their community makes it the most likely target for expansion of the ghetto, and the possibility that large sections of Oak Park will turn entirely black is perceived as a great threat. Furthermore, the liberal ideology of Oak Park's political leaders has posed the moral and practical dilemma of how to maintain an open, nondiscriminatory housing market without white flight.

The solution was thought to be a strategy of "dispersal," that is, encouraging blacks to move into parts of Oak Park in a pattern that would minimize black concentration. Beginning in 1961, real estate brokers were asked to refer black clients to a "counseling program," the objective of which was to discourage blacks from buying in the southeast side of Oak Park abutting the Chicago ghetto, where blacks were tending to cluster. It was also intended as a means of monitoring real estate practices. The flaw in the plan, of course, was its completely voluntary nature.

The Oak Park Housing Center, a private no-fee housing referral service, opened in May 1972, with the goal of maintaining and promoting integration by attracting new white residents to the village. The Housing Center's advertising was directly aimed at a young, liberal target population, and in its first year of operation about 85% of its clients were white. The Housing Center engaged in "reverse steering." White clients were encouraged to locate in the southeast sector of Oak Park, while blacks were not shown listings in this "sensitive" area. The Housing Center had no formal connection with the village government, but the two worked in close cooperation, and the Housing Center activities were supported informally by village officials. The Housing Center thus represented the first instance since the passage of the fair-housing law in which the village establishment explicitly condoned some form of discrimination in the sale and rental of housing.

In April 1973, the village board passed a policy resolution calling for the maintenance of stable "dispersed integration." The board had come to see serious limitations on the effectiveness of voluntary plans for dispersed black residency. While the village authorities had condoned discrimination by the Housing Center, they did not officially sanction it until November 1973, when the "exempt location" clause of the fair-housing ordinance was applied for the first time. This provision, written into the 1968 fair-housing ordinance, allowed the village government to exempt areas from prosecution if it was determined that serious attempts at integration were being made and that their success might be jeopardized by strict enforcement of the fair-housing ordinance. The board granted exemption to one block and one apartment building, both over 50% black, when petitions signed by over half the white and black residents were presented. This action by the board did not prevent black move-ins; it merely permitted racial discrimination in the two exempt locations. Soon after the Board's action, however, another move which would legally prevent black move-ins to certain areas was receiving serious consideration.

In December 1973, an amendment to the fair-housing ordinance putting into operation a quota system was proposed by a trustee and referred to the Community Relations Commission. If enacted into law, this quota provision would hold the black population of a still unspecified area of the village to 30%. Public hearings turned up much opposition to the new quota plan, though it is probable that a majority of residents, most of whom do not attend such hearings, would support it. The quota was finally tabled, and apparently killed, primarily as a result of the extremely adverse publicity the plan received from the metropolitan news media. In May 1974, the village board began discussion of a multifaceted, but quota-less, integration maintenance program. However, selective discrimination has already replaced non-discrimination as official policy.

Park Forest: A Program of Fair Housing Maintenance

Park Forest, the setting for William Whyte's *The Organization Man*, gained nation-wide fame as one of the first "planned" communities in the Chicago area, and is now taking the most affirmative steps toward integration maintenance. Developed in the late 1940s, Park Forest won the 1953 "All America City" award given by the National Municipal League and *Look* magazine. The 4.5-square-mile village is located in the southernmost part of Cook County, 30 miles from Chicago's Loop. Anticipated industrial development in the village did not occur, and Park Forest has remained a dormitory suburb of Chicago. The 1970 census showed that Park Forest had a total population of 30,638, 694 (2.3%) of whom were black; later surveys showed that by 1973 black population had risen to 7%, scattered throughout the village.

Early integration efforts were begun by Park Forest residents acting independently of any organization. Whites bought houses in the village and transferred them to blacks contacted through fair-housing groups and black churches in Chicago. The sole criterion was economic: if an individual could afford housing in Park Forest, he could move into it. The first black move-in occurred in 1959, but "managed" integration proceeded slowly, for in 1965 the village reported only 18 black families living in single-family homes and 19 in rental units. However, a great deal of effort was necessary to absorb peacefully even this limited number of blacks. As each move-in occurred, the village government and the Commission on Human Relations circulated memoranda to Park Forest clergy, rabbinate, and real estate brokers giving information about the family and the location of the property. It was hoped that brokers would concentrate on selling surrounding houses to whites to avoid clustering. (This was done until 1968 when federal civil rights laws made such tactics illegal.) When a difficult move-in was anticipated, members of the Human Relations Commission visited the neighbors involved. Nevertheless, there were black/white confrontations: epithets were hurled, a cross was burned near a home owned by a black, a fence facing a black family's house was painted black on one side and white on the other. One successful occupancy was described as "moved in today; no cakes and no problems."

The community remained stable during the 1960s and continued to attract white families. In 1969 the *Park Forest Star* noted that " . . . the village is now home to an estimated 160 Negro families, making it the most integrated of Chicago's predominantly white suburbs. . . . In January, 1968, the village adopted an open housing ordinance deemed to be among the strongest in the state." As Park Forest tried to maintain an open-door policy, outside factors came into play that were to threaten its future as an integrated community, however. Adjacent to Park Forest and included within its School District 163 lies a section of suburban Chicago Heights whose proximity has had profound implications for Park Forest. Beacon Hill–Forest Heights is an area of over 500 homes, 87% of which are black occupied. The land on which Beacon Hill–Forest Heights is built was once owned by the developers of Park Forest, American Community Builders, and was intended for development as an industrial park. In 1952, when Park Forest consolidated its four school districts into one, this area was included in the annexation in the hope that future industry would augment the district's tax base. In 1959, when it became apparent that no industrial development was likely to occur, the land was transferred to Andover Development Corporation and rezoned and platted for about 550 houses. In 1960 Andover Development began building in Beacon Hill but sold out in 1962 to United States Steel Homes Division. By 1963, 270 homes in the $17,000–$18,000 price range had been constructed. Although all of the original purchasers were white, some of the houses were abandoned and placed on FHA foreclosure lists, and several were purchased by black families.

In 1970, Kaufman and Broad, the nation's largest home building company, began to develop the land in Forest Heights to the east of Beacon Hill. By 1971 some 270 low-cost poorly constructed houses had been built (subsequently, the company's representatives were convicted of a variety of federal offenses in connection with this and other low-cost housing developments in the Chicago region). The FHA allotted the Forest Heights' development 255 Section 235 mortgages—about 95% of the total development. Thus homes could be bought for as little as $200 down and $135 a month by persons eligible under HUD criteria. Although advertised as an integrated development, the majority of the homes were sold to blacks. The marketing was done on a racial basis; the bulk of Kaufman and Broad's advertising was placed in the black media. By 1972, Forest Heights was 99% black, while adjacent Beacon Hill's black population rose to 87%. In short, Beacon Hill–Forest Heights blossomed into a suburban mini-ghetto.

Between the end of the 1970 and the beginning of the 1971 school year, the Beacon Hill grammar school, built originally for 350 students, changed from 25% to 90% black, while its enrollment soared to 700. Black enrollment in Blackhawk and Westwood Junior High Schools increased from almost zero in 1969 to 15% in 1971, and these two schools were the first to experience racial conflict. More serious racial disturbances occurred at Rich Central High School in Olympia Fields where Beacon Hill–Forest Heights students are assigned after completing junior high in Park Forest; 250 Beacon Hill–Forest Heights' students, many from families receiving welfare, were mixed in with classmates from a community which has a median income of $30,000 a year.

The situation in the area's junior high schools and high school provoked a strong response from Park Foresters but not as heated as that called forth by the decision to desegregate the District 163 elementary schools. In 1970 none of Park Forest's 11 elementary schools fulfilled the racial guidelines of 80% white/20% black stipulated by State Superintendent of Education Michael Bakalis. While Beacon Hill School was almost totally black, the other schools averaged 7% black. In April 1972 the Board of Education adopted a voluntary magnet school plan whereby Beacon Hill School would have become the district's laboratory school, which students would have voluntarily requested to attend. Mandatory grade reorganization was accepted as the backup plan. The magnet school failed to attract sufficient volunteers, and the grade reorganization plan had to be implemented. In September 1972 about 1,500 of 4,600 students in Park Forest were bused from their neighborhoods. Busing has been carried out in an orderly fashion, but the attitude of many Park Foresters has been ambivalent.

The greatest amount of criticism concerning busing has come from residents of the Eastgate area of Park Forest, the area closest to Beacon Hill–Forest Heights. The majority of children assigned to Beacon Hill School are from this area, which has the least expensive housing in Park Forest. Real estate brokers had told residents the value of their property would decline because of the school assignments. Many whites wanted to sell their houses, real estate firms began steering whites away, and several black families moved into one section of Eastgate. At this point, the Eastgate Residents Association (ERA), organized in 1968 to protest a proposed highway and since restructured to encourage home maintenance and beautification of Eastgate, met with village officials and local real estate interests. A representative of ERA stated:

> In recent months there has been a new turnover of houses, and many new families have moved here. . .in this instance we do not feel that "clustering" is in our best interest. With the housing market so short of low-income housing, and our homes being the lowest priced in Park Forest, we are particularly vulnerable at this time to become another racially dominated area such as Beacon Hill–Forest Heights. The fact that our village practices "open housing" and surrounds villages who apparently do not do their share makes us more vulnerable than ever. [*Park Forest Star* (May 11, 1972)]

A study conducted in 1972 by ERA revealed that residents of Eastgate were disappointed with the school situation and busing program. According to the survey, if things do not change for the better, many may move from Park Forest.

Paralleling the Eastgate residents' concerns, other Park Foresters began to feel threatened by the influx of blacks. Since Beacon Hill–Forest Heights has no stores, its residents shop primarily in Park Forest. Blacks thus became highly visible in the community, and some whites began to shun Norwood Plaza shopping center, a small complex situated closest to Beacon Hill–Forest Heights, because they felt it had begun to take on a "ghetto-like" look. In cooperation with the Human Relations Commission, the village felt it necessary in 1971 to establish a rumor-control telephone service to alleviate tense conditions. Some of the occupants in the inexpensive cooperative units south of the Eastgate area became apprehensive as move-outs occurred; they also felt very vulnerable to black inundation. The 1970 census figures show that 10 courts were, at that time, from 4% to 19% black.

While the Beacon Hill–Forest Heights situation and the busing of schoolchildren created dilemmas for Park Forest, another, perhaps graver, threat to the community began to surface. Because Park Forest had been well publicized as an integrated community and many of the suburbs around it are known to be highly resistant to black immigration, increasing numbers of blacks began to seek homes within its confines. At an April 1973 meeting at the Village Hall, one real estate man remarked, "We are getting more and more blacks—almost more than whites—in the offices."

This particular meeting had been initiated by some residents of the Lincolnwood area of Park Forest, where the highest-priced homes are located, to protest the "clustering" of blacks on certain streets in their area. One resident said: "There is a difference between integrated housing and clustering. No one has objections to colored," while another remarked: "I once approved the rate of integration here, but it is getting reckless now. . . .Park Forest is a soft touch for colored. . . .The community has made a big mistake in publicizing integration so we have been attracting more than our share of what we are trying to get away from." It was suggested that the village should provide by ordinance a definition for resegregation and make it illegal for real estate firms to sell property to blacks within a geographic distance as spelled out by village code, also that the village should supply real estate firms with minority residents' addresses. However, two days after the meeting the village attorney rejected both suggestions as violations of both the state and federal Constitutions.

Park Forest confirmed its position as an equal-opportunity community by passing into law on November 26, 1973 a package of "integration maintenance" ordinances calling for:

1. Prohibition of "steering" prospective home buyers into or out of neighborhoods on the basis of religious or racial composition.
2. The establishment of a Fair Housing Review Board, a quasi-judicial body with the powers of subpoena to revoke brokers' licenses, and to refer complaints to court.
3. Reorganization of the Human Relations Commission establishing for it an advocacy role and granting it subpoena powers.
4. Authority of the Village Manager to take administrative action on housing discrimination complaints before referring them to any other bodies.
5. Prohibition of "redlining" by lending firms.

These ordinances back up the efforts of the village government to eliminate discrimination. It has been characteristic of the village's official response, since the first fair-housing ordinance was passed in 1968, that the emphasis has been on enforcing the constitutional right of minorities to housing of their choice, while stopping short of attempts to "manage" integration by direct intervention in the locational choices of individuals, despite considerable external and internal pressures to do so. Suggestions that there be legal restrictions on "clustering" or pressure on real estate brokers to actively discourage it have been rejected. A proposed "exempt location" provision in the new set of ordinances, which would have permitted "steering" for the purposes of maintaining racial balance in certain areas, created a furor among black residents and a controversy among whites, and it was dropped from consideration. Nor have village officials been persuaded by popular sentiment and the exhortations of real estate people to maintain a lower profile with regard to open housing. Commented one broker on the ordinances, "I wish they would be more quiet and wouldn't make so much noise." On the contrary, the Human Relations Commission chairman felt that ". . . the revision of the current ordinances moves our village into the ranks of municipalities that have the most forward-looking and workable structure for dealing with today's very real problems." For Park Forest officials (as implied by their use of the term "integration maintenance" for their new laws) the assumption seems to be that integration can occur naturally in a housing market which is free from racial bias. If fair housing brings with it some perils, the solution is more fair housing.

Contrasting Attitudes: "No-CHA" versus the Regional Housing Coalition

The attitudes represented by these case studies are summarized in two broad-scale organizational responses to the region-wide pressure for racial integration. The actions of a coalition of locality-based Northwest and Southwest Side central-city white community organizations are contrasted with the program of a regional coalition of suburban fair-housing groups.

No-CHA.—In the early years of the nation's public housing program, the

Chicago Housing Authority (CHA) sought to build public housing scattered throughout Chicago. The City Council, in the belief that most prospective public housing tenants were black, proposed, however, to restrict such housing to ghetto areas. Since each alderman had a veto over site selection in his ward, CHA had to go along with the City Council if any public housing was to be constructed. Chicago's public housing was constructed and rented on a racially segregated basis.

As a result, the CHA administered regular (family), elderly, and Section 23 (leasing) public housing to keep blacks out of white areas. Regular public housing was located in ghetto neighborhoods to minimize the number of blacks displaced by slum clearance, and, in turn, the related programs were located in all-white neighborhoods. In the four housing projects in white neighborhoods, quotas kept the number of black tenants at zero or a minimal level. In projects for the elderly, tenant assignment policies ensured that white elderly occupied most of the housing in white neighborhoods. Only in racially changing areas were "integrated" projects—that is, those with a second racial group of more than 10%—to be found, and these projects and areas ultimately became all black. Leased housing was treated in the same fashion. Tenant selection was delegated to landlords by the CHA, giving them the right to refuse tenants because of "undesirability." Landlords were allowed to select tenants who were not on CHA's almost all-black waiting list. In sum, the white elderly were placed in public housing in white areas, while blacks were located in ghetto projects (Lazin 1973).

Throughout the 1960s federal civil rights laws and regulations were valueless in producing any changes. While HUD was aware that the CHA was violating HUD regulations covering racial discrimination, it opted to serve rather than regulate the local constituency. Finally, in August 1966, fair-housing interests filed suit in U.S. District Court accusing the CHA of discrimination against blacks (*Gautreaux* v. *CHA*). Judge Richard B. Austin, in February 1969, found the CHA guilty as charged and issued an order designed to promote integration by construction of public housing in all-white areas. As a result of CHA's refusal to abide by the court's directive and HUD's refusal to enforce compliance, all public housing construction in Chicago ceased during the 1969–74 period.

It was only under continuing pressure from Judge Austin that CHA finally announced plans in 1973 for a program of scattered-site public housing in the white Northwest and Southwest Sides of the city. Residents of the white neighborhoods were aghast, for another element in their web of territorial defense was threatened. The attitudes that lay behind the ward politicians' earlier vetoes of public housing surfaced in an attempt by a consortium of 19 Northwest and Southwest Side white community organizations (including two from Garfield Ridge) to use the National Environmental Policy Act of 1969 to prevent the Chicago Housing Authority from acting in accordance with Judge Austin's ruling. The argument of the Nucleus of Chicago Homeowners Association (No-CHA) was

> As a statistical whole, low-income families of the kind that reside in housing provided by the Chicago Housing Authority possess certain social class characteristics which will and have been inimical and harmful to the legitimate interests of the plaintiffs.

> Regardless of the cause, be it family conditioning, genetics, or environmental conditions beyond their control, members of low-income families of the kind that reside in housing provided by the Chicago Housing Authority possess, as a statistical whole, the following characteristics:

(a) As compared to the social class characteristics of the plaintiffs, such low-income family members possess a higher propensity toward criminal behavior and acts of physical violence than do the social classes of the plaintiffs.

(b) As compared to the social class characteristics of the plaintiffs, such low-income family members possess a disregard for physical and aesthetic maintenance of real and personal property which is in direct contrast to the high level of care with which the plaintiffs' social classes treat their property.

(c) As compared to the social class characteristics of the plaintiffs, such low-income family members possess a lower commitment to hard work for future-oriented goals with little or no immediate reward than do the social classes of the plaintiffs.

> By placing low-rent housing populated by persons with the social characteristics of low-income families described above in residential areas populated by persons with social class characteristics of the plaintiffs, defendant CHA will increase the hazards of criminal acts, physical violence and aesthetic and economic decline in the neighborhoods in the immediate vicinity of the sites. The increase in these hazards resulting from CHA's siting actions will have a direct adverse impact upon the physical safety of those plaintiffs residing in close proximity to the sites, as well as a direct adverse effect upon the aesthetic and economic quality of their lives.

U.S. District Court Judge Julius J. Hoffman ruled on November 26, 1973 that "it must be noted that although human beings may be polluters, they are not themselves pollution." Assistant U.S. Attorney Michael H. Berman added, "Public housing residents are not untouchables and the judge rightly accepts this view." However, the suit indicated clearly enough that Chicago's Northwest and Southwest Side communities do not!

The Regional Housing Coalition.—Meanwhile, in the suburbs and in metropolitan-wide civil rights organizations, two sets of interests have come together in a Regional Housing Coalition designed to promote "fair shares" of "low-income" (= minority) housing throughout the six-county area. On the one hand, there is the general desire to ensure civil rights, equity of treatment, and access to housing under conditions of accelerated decentralization of employment from the central city. On the other hand, there is the feeling that unless a regional solution to low-income minority housing is found, the more liberal communities like Park Forest and Oak Park will be beggared by their recalcitrant neighbors.

The Regional Housing Coalition (RHC), a partnership consisting of the Leadership Council for Metropolitan Open Communities,[1] the Northeastern Illinois Planning Commision, a steering committee of suburban mayors and village presidents, and business, religious, and civic organizations, announced its "Interim Plan for Balanced Distribution of Housing Opportunities for Northeastern Illinois" on October 1, 1973. The plan points up the immediate need for 167,600 housing units for people of low and moderate income throughout the six-county metropolitan area.

While housing for minorities is nowhere mentioned in the RHC proposal, its intention was to provide housing for blacks and other minorities in suburbs other than those few to which most suburban-bound blacks were migrating. It represented the convergence of interests of the Leadership Council, which was committed to fair housing in the metropolitan area, and such suburbs as Oak Park and Park Forest, which also were committed to fair housing and active integration efforts that now seemed destined to fail if the surrounding areas would not accept their "fair share" of the responsibility of providing housing for minority groups. Thus the RHC plan was motivated simultaneously by ideology and self-interest. It appealed to those whose ultimate goal was increasing the number and proportion of blacks living in the suburbs, that is, the Leadership Council and local fair-housing groups; at the same time it appealed to those whose concern was limiting the numbers of blacks moving into their own area, that is, Oak Park and Park Forest.

Clearly, if the RHC plan were expressly formulated as a plan for integrating the suburban area, the opposition would be far greater than the support. Therefore, it also was designed to appeal to yet a third set of interests, that is, the need to provide a labor supply for the growing industrial and com-

[1] The Leadership Council was formed in the wake of open housing demonstrations by a civil rights coalition led by the late Dr. Martin Luther King in 1966. Leaders of Chicago's government, business community, real estate corporations, trade unions, religious organizations, and civil rights groups met to explore new ways to break down racial barriers in the real estate market throughout metropolitan Chicago. Currently the council is engaged in a broad spectrum of programs to this end. During the past four years its legal-action program, using the Civil Rights Act of 1968, filed 250 + cases, with an 85% success record. Through its affiliate, the Metropolitan Housing Development Corporation, it had developed, marketed, and made plans to initiate two low- and moderate-income suburban developments, and made plans to initiate two more. Its third strategy is one of affirmative marketing to overcome the past system of discrimination and to reach minority home seekers with a positive invitation to consider the total city and suburban housing market.

mercial base of the suburban area. Yet, even phrased as a plan to encourage economic as opposed to racial integration, the RHC plan faced formidable resistance from suburban whites, as evidenced in their failure to date to support low-income housing. In 1972, only 3,000 of the metropolitan area's 44,000 public housing units were located in the suburbs, and many of these units were housing for the (white) elderly. Whatever the motivations of its backers, the RHC strategy of dispersal and "fair share," developed in response to continued racial and economic segregation, stands in sharp contrast to the containment strategy pursued by No-CHA.

MICRO ANALYSIS: SEEKING COMMON DENOMINATORS

There has thus been a broad range of white responses to racial integration, from violence in West Englewood to the erection of defensive barriers in Garfield Ridge, minimal organizational response in Evanston, reverse steering and "managed integration" in South Shore and Oak Park, and an avowed commitment to unrestricted open housing in Park Forest. *Across this range of white responses is the general conclusion that, regardless of socioeconomic characteristics, a concentration of black families is perceived negatively by whites.* Why does it matter to communities like these that their new residents are black rather than white? How does the symbolism of race determine the definition of a black residential concentration as undesirable for whites? In order to seek explanation of processes manifest at the macro scale of community and region, it is necessary to focus on individual response at the micro level of face-to-face confrontation of blacks and whites as homeowners and neighbors. The status consciousness of white residents is viewed as a basic factor underlying their perception and evaluation of racial change.

Status is defined in the Weberian sense of the "social estimation of honor" (Eisenstadt 1968, p. 177) and, as such, is clearly distinguished from the concept of "class." Status consciousness is "the degree to which status considerations are important to the individual, the extent to which he is concerned about his own relative status or to which status factors tend to color his interaction with others" (Blalock 1959, p. 243). The concept thus represents an *attitude* that one's status should be maintained and protected; this attitude is made manifest through explicit expedients designed to maintain social distance between individuals of unlike status.

It is with these definitions in mind that we argue that the desire for status protection underlies white behavior in racially changing neighborhoods and that this desire is usually manifested as avoidance behavior based on status consciousness. Our focus is on the social and cultural mechanisms which prompt an individual's latent status consciousness to become manifest. This takes place within the context of the residential structure of the city, which we view as a spatially arrayed stratification system. City residents (individuals) and city neighborhoods (areas) are seen as being ranked in congruent hierarchical systems, with the mechanisms of social status serving to relate the "vertical" structure of social stratification to the "horizontal" structure of urban residential areas ranked by "exclusiveness" and "desirability." A reciprocal relationship thus is seen between an individual's residential location and his position (status) in the social stratification system, and residential mobility is viewed as a sifting process whereby like-statused individuals tend to cluster in distinguishable subareas of the city.

This notion of a direct relationship between the city's residential structure and its status hierarchy is a venerable ecological principle that stems from the observation, first noted by Robert Park ([1926] 1967, p. 61), that social mobility is often reflected in residential mobility: the upwardly mobile improve their "residential status" to keep pace with improvements in their social status. Individuals tend to choose a residential location which, within the constraints imposed by available resources, satisfies their desire for symbolic expression of their self-conceived status.

In contrast to the emphasis placed on locational shifts associated with improved status, however, less attention has been paid to the corollary process by which individuals, having selected a residential location, strive to protect their status. Two processes ultimately account for the socio-spatial structure of the city: (1) the tendency toward mobility and change and (2) the tendency toward stability and resistance to change. Racial transition encompasses both, with the friction between arriving blacks and resisting whites attributable to differential perspectives of the environment. Upwardly mobile blacks view the contested area as compatible with both their housing needs and their self-conception of status. The resident white population, having in some earlier period identified the area as congruent to their status needs, tend to oppose changes perceived as leading to status deterioration.

These interactions must be understood from the perspective of the American cultural context in which "black" carries the imputation of status inferiority, and a black or integrated neighborhood is considered low status (Hughes 1945; Abrams 1955). In an insightful discussion of the social and psychological factors involved, Fishman notes: "After all is said and done, an interracial . . .neighborhood is a step-up for most Negroes. Any white who is appreciably concerned for his status in the larger white world . . .may conclude that for him such a community is a step down" (1961, p. 46). And a similar point has been made by Mayer: "Our culture has developed in a direction where persons who view themselves as related to the dominant cultural norms cannot 'afford' to live in a bi-racial neighborhood. This means most people, including those who are not prejudiced individuals, as we now measure prejudice" (1957, p. 4). Despite their general veracity, these statements must be examined in detail. Careful questioning would suggest that numerous factors intervene in the relationship between the individual's social and cultural environment and his attitudes toward and perceptions of the residential environment during the course of racial change. Which "dominant cultural norms" come into play? How are individuals "related" to these norms, and where and how large—from a few blocks to the scale of an international fraternity—is the "larger white world"? How do individuals and groups vary in their perceptions of a neighborhood as being "bi-racial"? In the attempt to deal with these questions, the discussion which follows is organized into two major sections.

First, attention is focused on the social and cultural milieu which imbues the socio-spatial setting with meaning. It is argued that *the status implications of residential proximity depend on the cultural definitions of the social and spatial symbols manifested in the sharing of residential space.*

Second, emphasis is placed on the specific cultural environment in which the individual lives and the particular social group(s) of which he is—or aspires to become—a member. The overall cultural setting outlined above defines the "dominant cultural norms" and the "larger white world" to which Mayer and Fishman refer. Within this general framework, *the immediate social group provides positive and negative reinforcement for the individual's attitudes toward status. These attitudes influence his attitudes toward the residential environment, which in turn influence perception of and response to racial change.*

Status as an Organizing Principle

In 1926, Harvey Zorbaugh noted the central role played by the quest for status in American urban life: "Now, in the intimate economic relationships in which all people are in the city everyone is, in a sense, in competition with everyone else. It is an impersonal competition—the individual does not know his competitors. It is a competition for other values in addition to those represented by money. One of the forms it takes is competition for position in the community" ([1926] 1961, pp. 46–47). And Charles Abrams remarked some 30 years later: "The suburb and the quest for status are shaping the American personality of the future as the frontier once shaped the American personality of the past" (1955, p. 140). Zorbaugh's concept of "position in the community" reflects the significance of status as an element of the individual's definition of self in society. In turn, individuals sharing a designated status constitute *status groups*, which are characterized by "communal action" arising from the "feeling of the actors that they belong together." Membership in a particular status group aspired to or achieved has the behavioral implication that ". . . status honor is normally expressed by the fact that above all else a specific *style of life* can be expected from all those who wish to belong to the circle" (Eisenstadt 1968, p. 178). Hence, status groups are characterized by (1) an externally derived and perceived measure of "honor" within a ranked hierarchy of status groups, (2) an internally shared sense of belonging to the group, and (3) symbolic expression of status-group membership through a characteristic life style. The significance of status as an organizing principle in American life thus derives from the importance of status as an element of self-identity. Status expresses the individual's sense of his position in the city's ranked social hierarchy, recognition of this position by others in the social system, and sharing of the position with other members of the same status group. Finally, it includes an important element of what Park termed "self-consciousness": "the fear. . . that we shall not be able to live up to our conception of ourselves, and particularly, that we shall not be able to live up to the conception which we should like other persons to have of us." This is the impelling force underlying the very literal "struggle for status" in which every individual finds himself" (Park [1926] 1967, p. 68).

"Measures of Honor": Spatial Proximity and Social Distance

Status rankings are operationalized in society through the imposition of social distance (Park [1926] 1967, p. 68; Beshers 1962, p. 50). In turn, there are complex interrelationships between social distance and physical proximity that depend on the cultural definition of the situation. Normally, propinquity engenders social interaction, but the social distance between individuals can control the quantity and quality of their social interaction. Thus, Tillman writes that in race relations "physical proximity is the issue only insofar as the 'presumption of equality' is superimposed upon it" (1961*b*, p. 334). Examples abound: the close physical proximity allowed a Negro servant (Frazier 1935) or the residential proximity allowed an on-premises black janitor (Abrams 1955), to cite only two instances in which proximity was not a threat because social distance maintained status differences. Indeed, the Jim Crow restrictions imposed on blacks in the South regarding the use of public accomodations were designed largely to prohibit the symbolic assumption of equal status rather than to prohibit the use of the specific facility per se: "It is not the sitting next to a Negro at a table or washing at the next basin that is repulsive to a white, but the fact that this implies equal status. Historically, the most intimate relationships have been approved between black and white so long as status of white superiority versus Negro inferiority has been clear" (Clark 1965, p. 11). Social distance, *symbolically* imposed through uniforms, separate facilities, etc., thus can maintain status differences despite physical proximity. On the other hand, as van den Berghe (1960) has shown, complete spatial segregation will be imposed in those instances where "etiquette"—the recognition of social distance symbols—breaks down as a means of maintaining status differences. Examples of situations in which physical separation is used to enforce social distance include cities, migrant port-of-entry areas, which segregate individuals who might not be cognizant of local social distance symbols, and areas undergoing marked social change, such as southern cities in which residential segregation has been increasing in recent years.

The extent to which physical separation is required to maintain social distance between individuals (or groups) of unlike status depends on the ability of the dominant higher-status group or individual to manipulate symbols which determine the cultural definition of the situation. Tensions become severe when the relevant symbols contradict the dominant group's claim of higher status. The equal-status connotations of residential proximity then assume special importance for the maintenance of social status. An insightful explanation of the social-psychological mechanisms involved is offered by Tillman:

> In the United States, the majority group has sought to compartmentalize by gradually and grudgingly giving and imputing equality to minority peoples in the fields of education and employment. The granting of equality of opportunity in these fields, indeed, did not require the majority group to impute equality to the total or whole personalities of minority group members. Fair housing will make it impossible for this condition of compartmentalized equality and inequality to continue. Fair housing will require the majority group to view minority people as whole and complete personalities. [1961–62, p. 32]

That residential segregation tends to persist long after the barriers have come down in schools and workplaces has often been noted (Bauer 1951, p. 250; Rosen and Rosen 1962, p. 67). Westie (1952) measured social distance between blacks and whites by occupation, using four different dimensions of social distance: residential distance; "position" distance (related to white respondents' willingness to have blacks in positions of power or prestige in the community); interpersonal-physical distance; and interpersonal social distance. He concluded that as black occupational status improves, whites are more willing to decrease position distance and interpersonal-social distance, while maintaining interpersonal-physical distance and residential distance regardless of the occupational status of blacks.

The most important implication of the above is the notion of a special significance of the home and neighborhood environment and the individual's personal space in maintaining social distance between individuals of unlike status, and a lesser significance of spatial separation in other contexts of daily contact. Physical proximity and residential proximity communicate an imputation of status equality to third-party observers, regardless of the feelings or intentions of the participants that the presumption of inequality is always maintained and communicated to others. In social contexts, boundaries between status groups can be maintained and even allowed to fluctuate within limits through social conventions of posture, facial expression, condescension, language, etc. In impersonal physical contexts, however—those of interpersonal physical distance and residential distance—individuals tend to lose the ability to manipulate symbols and thus determine the definition of the social situation. Instead, inanimate symbols of equality—the home and neighborhood, or the adjacent seat on the bus—become manifest and dominate the definition of the situation. In these cases, then, status-conscious whites must resort to spatial separation of *all* blacks regardless of occupation, in order to prevent what would be interpreted as equal-status contact by third-party observers.

Status and Neighborhood Identification

Having examined the cultural roots of residential segregation—the way in which physical space becomes imbued with symbolic status meanings—we now turn to some of the psychological aspects of the issue, that is, the individual's perception of an identification with the local residential area as representing a status group.

The individual's sense of membership in the residentially based status group derives from his perception of and identification with the neighborhood. Perception of the local residential environment comprises two complementary perceptual scales: macro-scale perception provides the individual with an image of how his residential area fits into the city-wide hierarchy of neighborhoods ranked in terms of status; micro-scale perception focuses on the residential area itself as home, turf, or territory and relates to the individual's personal identification with and use of the local neighborhood. The confluence of these two perceptual streams produces the individual's cognitive image of the internal structure of his residential area and its place within the city.

Micro-scale perception provides the individual with a cognitive and evaluative image of his local residential environment, including the extent to which the area constitutes an element of his personal identity. Oak Park's residents' attempts to maintain a viable community in the face of racial change are at least in part impelled by a sense of possessiveness for its tree-lined ambience and unique architectural heritage. The importance of the individual's personal identification with his house and neighborhood has been alluded to by numerous writers. As Rainwater (1966, p. 24) points out, "The house acquires a sacred character from its complex intertwining with the self and from the symbolic character it has as a representation of the family," and he adds that this conception of the house is "readily generalized to the area around it, to the neighborhood." Webber writes, "The physical place becomes an extension of one's ego" (1964, p. 63). The individual's personal identification with his local neighborhood environment, engendered through the mechanisms of his micro-scale perceptions, thus contributes to his sense of belonging to the neighborhood.

The macro-scale level of neighborhood perception derives from what Suttles has referred to as the "foreign relations" of neighborhoods: "Residential groups gain their identity by their most apparent differences from one another. . . .Residential identities, then, are imbedded in a contrastive structure in which each neighborhood is known primarily as a counterpart to some of the others, and relative differences are probably more important than any single and widely shared social characteristic" (1972, p. 51). Relative differences between residential areas give each area an identity and a "place" in the city's residential hierarchy. Thus, the working-class white residents of Chicago's Northwest and Southwest Side communities violently oppose integration of the local high schools, not because of their concern for the quality of education per se but because they fear that integration and a possible drop in the quality of education will reflect poorly on their community's image in the rest of the metropolitan area. Because of the linkages between the city's residential structure and its social structure, an address carries firm connotations of the individual's position in the city's status hierarchy. The sense of social position is shared with one's neighbors by simple virtue of residential propinquity; on the scale of the metropolitan area, residents of a neighborhood are "all in it together."

While the two perceptual dimensions contribute independently to the individual's sense of membership in the residential status group, they also interact in complex ways. Gans's description of the mechanisms by which micro-scale perceptions contribute to a macro-scale sense of place in suburban Levittown deserves to be quoted at length:

> The feelings about the black neighbors, friends, and favorite organizations were sometimes translated into a more general identification with Levittown as the best possible place to live, and some people took pride in a winning football team or an organizational achievement that lent distinction to Levittown. These feelings were neither intense nor of long duration; they were generated less by intrinsic qualities of the community than by the desire to put Levittown "on the map" in the unending competition with other communities. "The map" was usually Burlington County, but when L.Y.S.A. [Levittown Youth Sports Association] asked the Township Committee to finance a local team to play in the county baseball league, it pointed out that this league was regularly scouted by the majors, so that a $1,000 municipal subsidy might one day enable a Levittowner to represent the community in the American or National League. Even the name change that transformed Levittown to Willingboro was justified largely by the negative headlines about the town in the Philadelphia area press, and reflected less a concern about the community than the belief that the name created a community image (and a *persona* for its residents) which they wanted the outside world to respect. [Gans 1967, pp. 144–45]

The individual's experience of the residential area on the micro scale contributes to a concern for the neighborhood's status on the macro-scale level of the metropolitan community. On the one hand, satisfaction at the micro level leads to a desire to protect (or even boost) the neighborhood's macro-level image; on the other hand, concern for the macro-level image of the community leads to a desire to protect against harmful change at the micro level. The culmination of the individual's perception of his residential area along both dimensions is a sense of membership or belonging in the neighborhood.

Identification with the neighborhood as a status group has direct and obvious consequences for white response to the arrival of blacks. Since blacks are viewed as detrimental to neighborhood status, their arrival upsets the harmony between the white resident's cognitive image of the neighborhood and his status claims based on self-image. The more congruent these images, the greater the likelihood that white residents will oppose black entry. With the continued presence of blacks in the neighborhood and consequent confirmation of the discrepancy in neighborhood status, satisfaction with the residential environment decreases and the likelihood that whites will begin to move out increases.

The earlier discussion of equal-status connotations of residential proximity stressed the inability of residents to manipulate environmental symbols in order to indicate status differences to third-party observers. Residents can manipulate the symbols of home and neighborhood to augment their own status or that of the neighborhood; they can do little, however, to prevent others, whom they might consider of lower status, from manipulating residential status symbols in the same way and thereby claiming status equality. Further, status-conscious individuals can do little to directly manipulate the home and neighborhood symbols of others perceived as lower status to advertise the status differences to third-party observers. Aside from the obvious terror tactics involved, it is possible that at least part of the motivations for the defacing of homes of unwanted "low-status" neighbors derives from the (conscious or subconscious) desire to prevent a family perceived as low status from claiming equal status through the symbol of the home, and to indicate graphically to others that the "intruders" are not of equal status. Thus, white residents of Chicago's Garfield Ridge community tolerated the presence of a large black population while it was confined to the nearby LeClaire Courts public housing project; the stigma of residence in public housing is so pervasive that it would be clear to all that any black person in the area was a public housing tenant and thereby not of equal status with white residents of the neighborhood. White opposition became intense, however, as soon as blacks purchased homes in the neighborhood and thus claimed equal status with whites on the basis of the immutable symbolism of equal property ownership. The difficulty in manipulating the status symbolism involved in residential proximity suggests that the greater the visibility of the black families in a neighborhood, the greater the likelihood that status-conscious whites will move out in an attempt to avoid inclusion in the status group that is in conflict with their self-perception of status. Thus, as Wolf (1963) cogently argues, white opposition to the initial arrival of one or a few black families is based on the fear of a future inundation of blacks which would give the area the image of a "black neighborhood."

There is a presumption in the foregoing of a preference for neighborhood homogeneity. This similarity of life style within residentially proximate groups derives from the spatial distribution of housing types and the widespread preference held by most residents for similar neighbors. But neighborhood homogeneity is clearly a relative concept: there is no doubt that "homogeneous" neighborhoods contain a population with an often broad range of occupations, educational backgrounds, and even class affiliations. When viewed in terms of the city-wide or metropolitan population pool from which residents of a given neighborhood are drawn, however, it is clearly demonstrable that residents of the neighborhood are more similar to each other than to other people in other neighborhoods. Such population homogeneity in residential areas connotes a compatability of values concerning the use of the residential environment (see, e.g., Gans 1967, pp. 165–74).

Concern for having the "right kind of neighbors" is of major importance in the decision making relative to residential mobility. First, the social composition of a neighborhood is a prime consideration in choosing a home. Wolf and Lebeaux conclude that "the physical standards of an area seem to play a minor role in the residential decision of white households, at least in comparison with the importance of the social characteristics of the area's population. There are, of course, a number of largely Negro-occupied areas in many cities which present an excellent appearance. However, this was not sufficient to maintain the racial mixtures which such areas did possess at one time in the past" (1967, pp. 101–2). And Abrams has noted: "It is no longer the type of house but the type of neighborhood which reflects social standing. . . .Fine looking homes in Chicago may be still as fine looking but are considered blighted when Negroes or other minorities live in the neighborhood" (1955, p. 139). Because of limitations in both the individual's resources and the supply of appropriate housing, the decision maker must, of course, "trade-off desirable properties on a less important criterion for desirable properties of a more important element" (Moore 1972, p. 14). A national survey by Butler et al. indicated the prominence of the social characteristics of the neighborhood over such major factors as the desirability of the house itself and the accessibility of the neighborhood (Butler, Sabagh, and Van Arsdol 1964, p. 14). From similar data, Stegman (1969) found that, when offered a choice between a dwelling in an accessible but less desirable neighborhood and an equal-priced dwelling in a more desirable but less accessible neighborhood, 83% of the suburban sample and 61% of the city sample of recent movers chose the latter neighborhood.

Neighborhood "attractiveness" is clearly associated with the type of social relationships desired in the neighborhood. Status aspirations seem to supersede all or most other considerations in residential mobility inasmuch as alternatives for housing are only considered within those neighborhoods which are consistent with the individual's or family's conception of its own status. While this conception often reflects a commitment to upward mobility, in general residents tend to choose neighbors at a roughly similar level of status (Gans 1967, p. 414–15). The Levittowners studied by Gans were not seeking higher status through home and neighborhood but were nonetheless highly status conscious—fearful, Gans explains, of their "self-image." What Gans refers to as "fears about self-image" derived from the desire for status protection or maintenance. While residents were not necessarily seeking higher status (otherwise they would presumably have moved to a higher-status area), their concern was most often with *maintenance* of their present status and the integrity of the residentially based status group.

Maintenance of residential homogeneity over time may be problematical in light of the extremely high rate of intraurban mobility characteristic of urban areas. Twenty percent of the population changes residence from one year to the next, and two-thirds of all moves are within the same metropolitan area (Simmons 1970, p. 395). Concern for homogeneity requires residents to continually monitor the characteristics of new arrivals in the neighborhood. White residents of Chicago's Southwest Side, for example, opposed a municipal ordinance banning "For Sale" signs on homes because, despite the usual fear that a blossoming of such signs engenders a rash of panic sales, residents felt they could better monitor the characteristics of new homeowners with the aid of signs identifying those homes available for sale (*South West News Herald* [October 19, 1971]).

The persistence of residential homogeneity is, however, simplified by the general stability of the pattern of population distribution in the city. Thus, Simmons notes that "perhaps the most remarkable aspect of intra-urban mobility is the stability of the spatial structure of social characteristics despite high rates of mobility throughout the city" (1970, p. 409). In general, continuity over time in the characteristics and the price of housing in an area tends to attract an incoming population similar to the outgoing population in respect to income and other socioeconomic characteristics (Duncan and Duncan 1957; Taeuber and Taeuber 1965), and this is true whatever the color of the newcomers.

Despite this general similarity of characteristics between incoming blacks and resident whites, however, racial differences clearly suffice to dispel a perception of neighborhood homogeneity in changing areas. In-migration of blacks differs from the more general process of residential mobility in that the incoming population is *perceived* as substantially different by the resident white population. The perception of a critical difference in the incoming black population stems from the imputation of low status as a result of the "master status-determining trait" of skin color. While the arrival of an equal-status white family is viewed with equanimity and possibly even ignored, arrival of a black family is noted as a substantial change in the residential environment. In four study areas in Philadelphia, Rossi reports that incoming families were only perceived as "different" when they were also perceived as of lower status than the families they were replacing (1955, p. 53). Thus, the imputation of status inferiority to blacks results in a perception of black in-migrants as different and a threat to neighborhood homogeneity; the perception of a lack of residential homogeneity in turn influences white attitudes toward the neighborhood, engenders opposition to the arrival of blacks, decreases satisfaction with the area, increases the desire to move out, and produces an attitude on the part of other residents of the city that the neighborhood is inadequate for felt status needs and therefore no longer to be considered a desirable place to move to. Thus, the sentiment voiced by an outspoken Garfield Ridge resident that he didn't "want no neighbor throwing no garbage and barbecuing no beef out in the back" stemmed from the frequently expressed fear of the neighborhood going "downhill" and reflecting badly on remaining residents. The often-noted tendency for white residents to redefine the boundaries of their neighborhood to exclude areas which have 'gone black" reflects the perhaps subconscious realization of shared group membership among residentially proximate individuals (see, e.g., Hunter 1971; Molotch 1972). The same process is likely at work in the attempts by residents of West Englewood and Garfield Ridge to impose defensive barriers along particular thoroughfares and to block, by force if necessary, minorities from crossing that barrier.

In fact, shared opposition to the intrusion of low-status groups may be the strongest communal bond in an otherwise unorganized locality. Thus, Tillman, reporting on a study of integration in nine suburban communities in Minneapolis, concludes that "many inhabitants viewed homogeneity based on color as one of the important mechanisms of community cohesion" (1961b, p. 333). And similarly, Reginald Isaacs notes in his criticism of the traditional "neighborhood concept" in urban planning that "in many residential areas, the only real basis for solidarity is the fear of Negro infiltration" (1948b, p. 216); "the fear of minority group infiltration is substituted for a common denominator of neighborhood consciousness" (1948a, p. 19).

The Role of Status in Variations in Response to Racial Change

Residentially proximate groups fulfill Weber's characterization of communities as capable of "communal action" derived from the feeling that members "belong together." Within any given residential area, however, significant variation is likely to exist in the extent to which the common bond of shared status-group membership is acknowledged. While, on the one hand, perception of status threat influences attitudes toward the neighborhood, on the other hand a unique constellation of past experiences and future expectations provides each individual with a unique set of attitudes that may lead one individual to perceive a status threat where another perceives none, or to strive to attain membership in a residential status group that another individual is striving to repudiate. It is again necessary, however, to specify that explanation of such variations need not be sought in the internal psychological states of the individuals involved. Individuals tend not to make outlandish status claims; their expectations are related to the perceived experiences and situations of individuals of similar status. A particular set of past experiences, sense of present status, and aspirations for the future determine the individual's selection of reference groups. Thus, Merton notes the systematic nature of reference group selection: "Presumably, there will be distinct shifts in reference [groups and] individuals and role models as people move through sequences of statuses during their life cycles. This would again imply that much of such selection is not idiosyncratic but is patterned by structurally determined and statistically frequent career sequences, actual, anticipated or desired" (1968, p. 357). The individual derives his status claims from within this patterned framework; on the basis of these claims, he relates to a set of membership and nonmembership groups which he evaluates either positively or negatively, and these reference groups, in turn, provide positive or negative reinforcement for the individual's status claims. A status claim is clearly a claim for membership in a particular status group. If a member of this status group, the individual strives to maintain membership; if claimed status is represented by a nonmembership group, the individual strives to repudiate membership in his present group and attain membership in the sought-for status group. Membership groups seen as detrimental to status claims are repudiated; nonmembership groups seen as detrimental to status claims are avoided; membership groups seen as supportive of status claims are maintained; and nonmembership groups seen as supportive of status claims function as status goals which the individual strives to attain.

The discussion thus far has dealt with the neighborhood as a status group with which the individual is identified by virtue of his residential address, and with which the individual identifies in defining his place in society. In both senses, the neighborhood operates as a reference group, and the individual evaluates membership in his neighborhood-based status group in the same terms as he does other reference groups. Membership in the neighborhood-qua-reference group is weighed against membership in all other neighborhood-based reference groups known to the individual in the present, remembered from the past, or aspired toward in the future.

In evaluating his environment, the individual, rather than operating *in vacuo*, refers to a set of reference groups to establish both a normative set of

257

Berry, Goodwin, Lake, and Smith

values and guidelines and a comparative framework against which evaluation can be made. The individual's attitude toward membership in the neighborhood group is derived from how well it contributes to his status claims: to what extent there exists a "harmony of consensus" between the individual's status claims and the status image of the neighborhood environment.

Evaluation of the neighborhood-qua-reference group is accomplished by means of a subjectively determined utility threshold, defined by Wolpert as "a weighted composite of a set of yardsticks for achievement. . . .The threshold functions as an evaluative mechanism for distinguishing, in a binary sense, between success and failure, or between positive or negative net utilities" (1965, pp. 161–62). The utility threshold is thus seen as an attitudinal boundary: evaluated as above the threshold, the neighborhood environment supports the individual's status claims and is viewed as a positive reference group, membership in which the individual strives to maintain; evaluated as below the threshold, the neighborhood environment detracts from the individual's status claim and is viewed as a negative reference group, membership in which the individual seeks to repudiate.

In examining the mechanisms by which the individual relates to the neighborhood as a reference group, it is possible to identify several key factors related to status which seem to influence both the determination of the threshold of utility and the individual's evaluation of the neighborhood's utility. By influencing the relationship between the individual and the neighborhood environment, each of these attitudinal dimensions also influences the individual's perception of racial change as a process which alters the residential environment. The three factors, which will be considered in turn, include reliance on the residential environment for status, orientation to the residential neighborhood, and attachment to the neighborhood.

For example, individuals and groups vary in the extent to which they rely on the symbolism of the neighborhood environment to substantiate their status claims. Evidence indicates that the upwardly and downwardly mobile, sensing the insecurity of uncertain status group membership, rely more heavily on the neighborhood environment as a source of status than do the nonmobile. Similarly, individuals facing incongruence in their status-determining traits tend to rely on the neighborhood as a visual symbol of status group membership.

An example of the significance of neighborhood status in substantiating status claims, and the consequent influence of this relationship on the perceived meaning of residential integration, is provided in a study of white response to integration in suburban Levittown, Pennsylvania. Bressler (1960) reports that arrival of the first black family was met with mass demonstrations, highly vocal and prolonged opposition, and considerable community polarization. The most vocal opponents were those who, upwardly mobile and with a strong sense of status incongruence, relied heavily on the physical

258

symbolism of the residential environment to substantiate claims to middle-class status. As Bressler notes:

> A skilled or semi-skilled laborer employed by the United States Steel Company, Kaiser Metal Products, or other local enterprises might well sense the disparity between his relative economic affluence and his modest occupational prestige. One method of resolving this ambiguity consists of *borrowing prestige from his community* which if it is to serve this purpose satisfactorily must then represent a pure distillate of middle-class lifestyles.
>
> The working class addiction to the coy middle-class symbolism so prevalent in Levittown, its "Sweetbriar Lanes" and "cook-outs," its "patios" and enthusiastic agronomy, is to an appreciable extent a simultaneous exercise in self-persuasion and ritualistic affirmation whose purpose it is to demonstrate that *life patterns in the community, and not the job, constitute the only valid basis for class assignment.* [Bressler 1960, p. 133; emphasis added]

To the opponents of integration, the neighborhood was well above the utility threshhold as long as it continued to support claims of membership in the middle-class reference group. Arrival of blacks was interpreted as lowering the utility of the neighborhood by changing the image. For individuals who rely on the status symbolism of their environment as a source of status—at whatever level in the status hierarchy—the arrival of blacks is clearly perceived as a status threat.

Related to the dependence on the residential environment as a source of status is the broader question of the individual's orientation to the local neighborhood as a normative reference group to which the individual turns in establishing a set of values and standards. This orientation has often been described in terms of a scale continuum from localism to cosmopolitanism. Localites are generally said to be lower status, less mobile, and to seek their social contacts from among relatives, friends, and associates within the local community. As a result of this orientation, localites tend to express the greatest concern for "desirable neighbors" (Gans 1967), and they are most likely to vocally oppose black entry into the neighborhood. Cosmopolites, in contrast, have a less restricted range in which they establish social contacts, carry out daily activities, and derive a set of values; cosmopolites thus tend to relate to reference groups outside the local community, as in the liaison between suburban fair housing groups in Chicago's Regional Housing Coalition. Bressler reports that supporters of integration in Levittown, Pennsylvania were ". . . cosmopolitans, persons who refused to define the situation primarily and exclusively in terms of its impact on the tight little island of suburbia" (1960, p. 137). Much the same can be said of integrationists in Park Forest and Oak Park.

In a case study which provides an interesting contrast to the situation described by Bressler, Gans (1967) reports that integration in Levittown,

New Jersey, occurred relatively uneventfully. While residents of the New Jersey community were not necessarily supportive of integration, their concern was to avoid visible demonstrations against new black families, fearing that such demonstrations would reflect poorly on the community. Gans reports that ". . . as it turned out, Levittowners favored peace and order even more than segregation. . . . Many knew that racial conflict might well begin to reduce Levittown's prestige, and even those who opposed integration often said it was preferrable to a riot" (1967, p. 375). The racial conflict in the Pennsylvania community, which occurred prior to integration in the New Jersey Levittown, was described by the New Jersey residents as a ". . . stone-throwing riot, giving the older Levittown a worldwide reputation as a riot-torn community and placing a blot on its escutcheon which the residents of the newest one wanted desperately to avoid" (Gans 1967, p. 382).

While the local orientation of opponents in Pennsylvania and the cosmopolitan orientation of supporters in New Jersey had different outcomes in terms of influencing white response to the arrival of blacks, both responses are to be explained in terms of residents' concern for status. Opponents in Levittown, Pennsylvania, were responding to localized reference groups which stressed the importance of the physical image of the neighborhood and visible characteristics of their neighbors. The cosmopolitan orientation of supporters of integration led them to respond to reinforcements provided by reference groups located outside the community; what reached these groups was not the physical image of the neighborhood, which requires visible contact to be evaluated, but rather the press- and media-related public image which is transmitted to friends and associates outside the community. Oriented to reference groups outside the local area, attitudes toward integration on the part of the cosmopolitans in Levittown were prompted by a concern that the community not get a "bad press." A similar variation in orientation is seen as the primary factor differentiating the 19 local community organizations comprising No-CHA from the regional entities represented in the Regional Housing Coalition in Chicago.

CONCLUSIONS

The foregoing thus provides a framework for the interpretation of white response to racial change. The locally oriented individual who is upwardly mobile or who is uncertain about his status and feels his neighborhood environment contributes to his status claims will be most likely to oppose the entry of blacks into the neighborhood. His sense of status consciousness will be acute, and he will be most concerned with the status implications of sharing his residential space with blacks.

The greater the individual's *attachment* to the neighborhood, the greater the likelihood that he will seek to organize in response to the entry of blacks. *Orientation* to the neighborhood suggests the value system which will be brought to bear in determining the objectives of the organization. Thus, locally oriented individuals with a high sense of attachment to the local area are likely to organize to oppose black entry and keep blacks out of the neighborhood, as in Chicago's ethnic neighborhoods; cosmopolitan individuals attached to the neighborhood are likely to organize to encourage peaceful integration while maintaining neighborhood stability, as in Oak Park; cosmopolitan individuals with little sense of attachment, oriented away from the local neighborhood, find it easier simply to move away, as happened in South Shore when neighborhood stability could not be maintained.

The Chicago cases thus illustrate the whole range of responses to racial invasion. It has often been taken for granted that, as ghetto encroachment threatens, the whites in adjacent neighborhoods either resist vigorously, rapidly abandon the area, or both, with flight following temporary resistance. But such exclusionary tactics generally are used only by the blue-collar ethnic communities bounding ghetto areas. As these neighborhoods were among the first to feel the pressure of black expansion, their characteristic responses sometimes have been assumed to be the dominant form. However, with the continuing enlargement of Chicago's ghettos and the parallel expansion of suburban minighettos, the threat has been felt in the formerly safe refuges of higher-status inhabitants. The experience of these communities has indicated that the traditional "fight and run" pattern is not necessarily typical. Only when such communities as South Shore or the suburbs of Evanston, Oak Park, and Park Forest became threatened, did the range and variety of responses begin to emerge. It is thus our conclusion that the differences in status among communities are the basic determinant of the range of response.

This conclusion provides interesting insights into a report to HUD by the National Academy of Sciences (1972), entitled *Freedom of Choice in Housing*, as a framework for evaluating prospects for racial integration in housing and formulating national housing policy. The Academy concluded, "For both blacks and whites, the quality and convenience of housing and neighborhood services take precedence over racial prejudice in housing decisions." However our studies contradict this, since whites are abandoning "convenient" neighborhoods with good-quality housing, that is, South Shore and Garfield Ridge.

The Academy report also concluded that "there is no ratio of blacks to whites that is known to ensure success in racial mixing." It would seem that predictions and perceptions are more important than numbers: South Shore changed racial composition gradually; transition in Evanston, with a 16% black population, proceeded very slowly; but Garfield Ridge and other communities have turned over rapidly. Oak Parkers became panicky at the thought that large sections of their village might become all black when its black population was only 2%. More important than the black/white residential ratio are the schools. When overcrowding in black schools necessitates changing attendance area boundaries and assigning black students to adjacent schools, white tensions rise. As total enrollments and black student populations increase, white families will transfer their children to parochial schools or move (South Shore, West Englewood). Busing to achieve racial guidelines of 80% white/20% black (Evanston, Park Forest) also causes some white outmigration, while attracting only those white families actively seeking an integrated setting for the education of their children.

Another NAS conclusion was that "to be successful, a marketing strategy should emphasize the positive racial attitudes that do exist and should take into account the variations in these attitudes. . . .Attitude changes are effected where the physical and social conditions encourage and support behavioral changes." However this is just the point: the variations exist, but the physical and social conditions, the larger structure, prevents successful integration even in areas where residents are most favorable. The constraint of attitudes and responses at the No-CHA end of the scale patently obviates the success of responses emanating from the Park Forest end of the scale. Thus, the Chicago area studies confirm the NAS finding that "there is no evidence that socioeconomic mixing is feasible. The trend in the movements of urban population is toward increasing separation of socioeconomic categories. The tendency is manifested among blacks as well as among whites," thus casting serious doubts on the Regional Housing Coalition's ability to scatter "fair share" low-income housing throughout the six-county area. As to racial mixing, the Academy concluded: "It is unlikely that a policy of racial mixing can be consistently applied in metropolitan areas in which there are two or more autonomous governments. For any one locality to act in the total social interest is for it to put itself in a position to be beggared by others who do not accept similar responsibility voluntarily." Thus communities such as Oak Park and Park Forest which espouse "integration maintenance" policies will find themselves alone in the struggle as their reluctant neighbors maintain the status-quo closed-door policy.

Summed up, the Academy's report described sets of attitudinal and institutional constraints which perpetuate housing segregation and limit the efficacy of strategies aimed at integration. In this paper we have used the experience of the Chicago metropolitan area to explicate such patterns and constraints. The conclusion that must be drawn is that substantial residential integration by race is unlikely to emerge either in central city or in suburb in years to come; segregation will continue to be a fundamental feature of the American scene as long as race remains a "master status-determining trait."

REFERENCES

Abrams, Charles. 1955. *Forbidden Neighbors.* New York: Harper & Bros.
Bauer, Catherine. 1951. "Social Questions in Housing and Community Planning." *Journal of Social Issues* 7 (1): 1–34.
Beshers, James A. 1962. *Urban Social Structure.* Glencoe, Ill.: Free Press.
Blalock, Hubert M. 1959. "Status Consciousness: A Dimensional Analysis." *Social Forces* 37, no. 3 (March): 243–48.
Bradburn, Norman M., Seymour Sudman, and Galen L. Gockel. 1970. *Racial Integration in American Neighborhoods: A Comparative Study.* NORC Report no. 111-B. Chicago: National Opinion Research Center.
Bressler, Marvin. 1960. "The Myers Case: An Instance of Successful Racial Invasion." *Social Problems* 8 (March): 126–42.
Butler, Edgar W., George Sabagh, and Maurice D. Van Arsdol. 1964. "Demographic and Social Psychological Factors in Residential Mobility." *Sociology and Social Research* 48, no. 2 (January): 139–54.
Clark, Kenneth. 1965. *Dark Ghetto: Dilemmas of Social Power.* New York: Harper & Row.
Duncan, Otis Dudley, and Beverly Duncan. 1957. *The Negro Population of Chicago: A Study of Residential Succession.* Chicago: University of Chicago Press.
Eisenstadt, S. N., ed. 1968. *Max Weber on Charisma and Institution Building.* Chicago: University of Chicago Press.
Fishman, Joshua A. 1961. "Some Social and Psychological Determinants of Intergroup Relations in Changing Neighborhoods: An Introduction to the Bridgeview Study." *Social Forces* 40, no. 1 (October): 42–52.
Frazier, E. Franklin. 1935. "The Status of the Negro in the American Social Order." *Journal of Negro Education* 4, no. 3 (July): 293–307.
Gans, Herbert J. 1967. *The Levittowners: Ways of Life and Politics in a New Suburban Community.* New York: Random House.
Henderson, George. 1964. "Twelfth Street: An Analysis of a Changed Neighborhood." *Phylon* 25, no. 1 (Spring): 91–96.
Hughes, Everett C. 1945. "Dilemmas and Contradictions of Status." *American Journal of Sociology* 50, no. 5 (March): 353–59.
Hunter, Albert. 1971. "Symbolic Communities: A Study of Chicago's Local Communities." Paper presented at the Metropolitan Forum, Center for Urban Studies Conference on Social and Structural Change for the Chicago Metropolitan Area, Chicago, 1971.
Isaacs, Reginald. 1948a. "The Neighborhood Theory, an Analysis of Its Adequacy." *Journal of American Institute of Planners* 14, no. 2 (Spring): 15–23.
———. 1948b. "The Neighborhood Unit as an Instrument for Segregation." *Journal of Housing* 5, nos. 7, 8 (July, August): 177–80, 215–19.
Kerckhoff, Richard. 1957. "A Study of Racially Changing Neighborhoods." *Merrill-Palmer Quarterly* 4, no. 1 (Fall): 15–49.
Lazin, Frederick Aaron. 1973. "The Failure of Federal Enforcement of Civil Rights Regulations in Public Housing, 1963–1971: The Co-optation of a Federal Agency by Its Local Constituency." *Policy Sciences* 42 (2): 263–73.
Mayer, Albert J. 1957. "Race and Private Housing: A Social Problem and a Challenge to Understanding Human Behavior." *Journal of Social Issues* 13 (4): 263–73.
———. 1960. "Russell Woods: Change without Conflict: A Case Study of Neighborhood Racial Transition in Detroit." Pp. 198–220 in *Studies in Housing and Minority Groups*, edited by Nathan Glazer and Davis McEntire. Berkeley: University of California Press.
Merton, Robert K. 1968. *Social Theory and Social Structure.* 3d ed. New York: Free Press.
Molotch, Harvey. 1969. "Racial Change in a Stable Community." *American Journal of Sociology*

Berry, Goodwin, Lake, and Smith

75, no. 2 (September): 226–38.

————. 1972. *Managed Integration: Dilemmas of Doing Good in the City.* Berkeley: University of California Press.

Moore, Eric G. 1972. *Residential Mobility in the City.* Commission on College Geography Resource Paper no. 13. Washington, D.C.: Association of American Geographers.

National Academy of Sciences. 1972. *Freedom of Choice in Housing: Opportunities and Constraints.* Report of the Social Science Panel. Washington, D.C.: National Academy of Sciences.

Park, Robert E. (1926) 1967. "The Urban Community as a Spatial Pattern and a Moral Order." Pp. 55–68 in *Robert Park on Social Control and Collective Behavior,* edited by Ralph H. Turner. Chicago: University of Chicago Press.

Rainwater, Lee. 1966. "Fear and the House-as-Haven in the Lower Class." *Journal of American Institute of Planners* 32, no. 1 (January): 23–31.

Rapkin, Chester, and William G. Grigsby. 1960. *The Demand for Housing in Racially Mixed Areas.* Berkeley: University of California Press.

Rosen, Harry and David Rosen. 1962. *But Not Next Door.* New York: Obolensky.

Rossi, Peter H. 1955. *Why Families Move.* Glencoe, Ill: Free Press.

Simmons, James W. 1970. "Changing Residence in the City: A Review of Intra-urban Mobility." Pp. 395–413 in *Geographic Perspectives on Urban Systems,* edited by Brian J. L. Berry and Frank E. Horton. Englewood Cliffs, N.J.: Prentice-Hall.

Stegman, Michael A. 1969. "Accessibility Models and Residential Location." *Journal of American Institute of Planners* 35, no. 1 (January): 22–29.

Suttles, Gerald D. 1972. *The Social Construction of Communities.* Chicago: University of Chicago Press.

Taeuber, Karl E., and Alma F. Taeuber. 1965. *Negroes in Cities: Residential Segregation and Neighborhood Change.* Chicago: Aldine.

Tillman, James A. 1961a. "Morningtown, U.S.A.—a Composite Case History of Neighborhood Change." *Journal of Intergroup Relations* 2 (Spring): 156–66.

————. 1961b. "The Quest for Identity and Status: Facets of the Desegregation Process in the Upper Midwest." *Phylon* 22, no. 4 (Winter): 395–413.

————. 1961–62. "Rationalization, Residential Mobility, and Social Change." *Journal of Intergroup Relations* 3, no. 1 (Winter): 28–37.

van den Berghe, Pierre L. 1960. "Distance Mechanisms of Stratification." *Sociology and Social Research* 44 (January): 155–64.

Webber, Melvin. 1964. "Culture, Territoriality and the Elastic Mile." *Papers and Proceedings of the Regional Science Association* 13:59–69.

Westie, Frank. 1952. "Negro-White Status Differentials and Social Distance," *American Sociological Review* 17, no. 5 (October): 550–58.

Winder, Alvin. 1951. "Residential Invasion and Racial Antagonism in Chicago." *Phylon* 12, no. 3 (Fall): 239–41.

Wolf, Eleanor. 1963. "The Tipping Point in Racially Changing Neighborhoods." *Journal of American Institute of Planners* 29 (3): 217–22.

————. 1965. "The Baxter Area: A New Trend in Neighborhood Change?" *Phylon* 26, no. 4 (Winter): 344–54.

Wolf, Eleanor, and Charles N. Lebeaux. 1967. "Class and Race in the Changing City: Searching for New Approaches to Old Problems." In *Urban Research and Policy Planning,* edited by Leo F. Schnore and Henry Fagin. Urban Affairs Annual Reviews, vol. 1. Beverly Hills, Calif.: Sage.

Wolpert, Julian. 1965. "Behavioral Aspects of the Decision to Migrate." *Papers and Proceedings of the Regional Science Association* 15:159–69.

Zorbaugh, Harvey W. (1926) 1961. "The Natural Areas of the City." Pp. 45–49 in *Studies in Human Ecology,* edited by George A. Theodorson. New York: Harper & Bros.

10   Religion in Suburban America

William M. Newman
University of Connecticut

The study of suburbs represents one of the more bizarre chapters in the recent history of the social sciences. In less than two decades we have gone from viewing suburbs as a dramatic departure in American living to depicting them as little more than relocated urbanism (Masotti and Hadden 1973). We have moved from a passionate indictment of a middle-class monotonous melting pot (Whyte 1956) to a growing appreciation of the diversity both within and between suburban communities. Like various other areas of inquiry in the social sciences, the sociology of the suburbs created too many generalizations based upon too few empirical studies.

My purpose here is to consider the relationship between suburbanization and one particular sphere of social life, religion. These are the themes I shall stress. First, the available data are neither comprehensive nor conclusive. Most of our information about religion in the suburbs has been obtained as a by-product of community studies or through secondary analysis of data collected for other purposes. In 1925 H. Paul Douglass, in his pioneering work *The Suburban Trend*, lamented the absence of any detailed study of suburban churches (p. 205). Almost half a century later his characterization of our knowledge is still applicable. There has not yet been a single large-scale research project aimed at a scrutiny of religion in America's suburbs.

Second, like the general literature on suburbs, writing on suburban religion often has been more journalistic than scientific, more a reflection of impressions and value judgments than extensive empirical research. Accordingly, any attempt to understand the nature of religion in suburbia must distinguish between actual research findings and the interpretive themes these findings have been made to serve.

Third, our popular mythology about suburbia has had a considerable "spillover" effect upon our understanding of specific institutions in the suburbs, especially religion. Just as sociologists initially viewed everything about suburbs as new and distinctive, sociologists of religion have tended to interpret research findings on religion in the suburbs as evidence of new trends. I shall neither argue that suburban religion consists of a unique departure from the past nor that it is simply a continuation of previous patterns of religiosity. The truth lies somewhere between these two views. There have been changes. Many of them appear to be developments of trends first observed in urban America. Others are more appropriately characterized as trends in American religion rather than suburban religion. As Riesman observed in the late 1950s: "The very fact that suburbs have become . . . so characteristic a feature of the American landscape creates problems in separating what is due to suburban life and what to American developments in general" (1958, p. 776). With regard to religion, I shall argue that these trends are more general than suburban.

Finally, I wish to suggest that, until very recently, the most important area for research has been largely overlooked. I refer here to the interplay between religion and other major status variables—regionalism, ethnicity, race, class, and occupation—in American community life. The connections between these variables in both the individual's "identity kit" (Goffman 1959) and in the suburban social structure should be a major concern of sociological research.

THE RELIGIOUS REVIVAL REEXAMINED

The normative functions of religion in American community life—moral education, value reinforcement, and social control—have been a consistent theme of community studies from "Middletown" to "Yankee City," from "Elmtown" to "Levittown." It is therefore not surprising that churches, temples, synagogues, and cathedrals were among the first institutional structures to dot the suburban landscape. While suburban growth in the United States dates back to the period before the Civil War, it was not until the early 1920s that suburbs became the locus of large-scale residential development. During the early 1920s, H. Paul Douglass observed that the number of churches relative to population size was greater in the suburbs than in the cities (1925, p. 207). In this context, the suburbanization (or what Gibson Winter has called the "suburban captivity" [1961]) of American religion in the post–World War II period represents the continuation of an earlier trend.

The important question is whether this trend—first observed in the early 1920s and especially pronounced in the mid-1950s—constituted a religious revival, as Herberg (1955) and others have contended, or simply the culmination of a process of transplantation. The popular mythology, of course, is that the 1950s produced a return to religion in suburbia and that this religious revival reflected certain characteristics (frequently maligned) of suburban living (Rowland 1956).

One means of answering this question is to examine church attendance statistics. Several different community studies offer such data, but the composite findings that emerge from them are ambiguous. A California study by Greer and Kube (1959) shows increased levels of church attendance as one moves farther from the city. Yet, as Carlos (1970) has noted, since this study focused upon blue-collar suburbanites, it is questionable whether one can derive inferences about general population characteristics from it.

In contrast, Zimmer and Hawley (1959) found that church attendance decreases as one moves from the city to "fringe" areas. While it is not clear that their operational category "fringe areas" can be equated with "suburbs," a more recent study by Tallman and Morgner (1970) supports their findings that church attendance rates are higher for urban than suburban residents. Finally, Gans in *The Levittowners* reports that for 60% of his respondents the move to suburbia did not entail a change in church or synagogue attendance (1967, p. 264). Moreover, the patterns of change he did encounter were different between Protestants, Catholics, and Jews, men and women, and former urbanites and nonurbanites.

Ironically, while there is little agreement in the findings of these several studies, there appears to be a high degree of consensus over what they mean. Mueller (1966), Whyte (1956), Winter (1961), Carlos (1970), and even Gans (1967) contend that increased levels of church attendance in suburbia are a reflection of public solidarity, a consequence of home ownership and small-community life (Marshall 1973, p. 133). However, in my view church attendance statistics tell us relatively little about suburban as opposed to urban religiosity and even less about the alleged religious revival in the suburbs.

If one examines church membership rather than attendance statistics, there is at least one study that begins to overcome these problems. As Nash (1968) has shown, the impressive increases in church membership statistics that accompanied the suburban migration during the 1950s were little more than a reflection of the increased number of families with school-aged children in the United States. Nash's comparison of National Council of Churches membership data[1] with United States census data on families with children under age 18 reveals parallel rises and falls in these two indices. In simple terms, the suburban return to religion resulted from the very forces that produced the suburban migration itself. In the case of religion, the postwar "baby boom," coupled with the traditional desire of American parents to provide a religious education for their children, was the outstanding factor. As the number of school-aged children in the general population declined so did the alleged religious revival.

Given the ambiguities of these studies of church attendance and the revealing church membership patterns provided by Nash it is indeed tenuous to argue that suburban Americans are any more prone to religiosity than

---

[1] While sociologists have traditionally challenged the absolute value of these statistics, Nash only examines relative changes in them. They therefore provide appropriate data for testing his hypothesis.

their urban counterparts. The view that there was a religious revival and that the revival was intrinsically tied to suburbanism should probably be discarded along with the general "suburban myth" (Donaldson 1969). This does not mean that there have not been changes in American religion that have paralleled the suburban transition. The most clearly discernible changes have been in the functions of religious institutions.

RELIGIOUS INSTITUTIONS

The most important change in institutional religious life in the suburbs has been the acquisition of a host of social service, as opposed to explicitly religious, functions. Again, Douglass had already observed this trend in the early 1920s: "The outstanding peculiarity of the suburban church is, however, its great number of subsidiary organizations. In other words, the general tendency of the suburb to a multiplicity of minor organizations has attacked the church also" (1925, p. 207).

More recent studies of suburban religious institutions document the continuation of this trend for Protestant (Winter 1961), Catholic (Greeley 1959), and Jewish (Gans 1951, 1958; Gordon 1959) congregations alike. While it is frequently argued that these institutional patterns represent phases of cultural accommodation or assimilation for the immigrant Catholic and Jewish groups, the trend is ubiquitous. Its effects have been felt as strongly, if not more so, within Protestant denominations as among Jewish and Catholic organizations.

Regardless of how one evaluates this trend (and it is clear that sociologists and theologians alike have criticized suburban congregations for it) these patterns follow a long-acknowledged sociological axiom. The fewer the number of social institutions in any social system, the greater the number of functions each of them is likely to have. Given the emergence of new communities in which few of the accustomed institutions existed, religious institutions became the sponsors of everything from Girl Scouts and dancing clubs to bingo.

The growth of a social service emphasis in the program of local religious institutions has had important consequences for the occupational roles of the clergy. The role-conflict dilemmas that were first observed in relation to urban Protestant churches (Blizzard 1956) became even more acute in suburban religious institutions, both Christian and Jewish. The traditional practitioner roles—priest, preacher, and teacher—have been overshadowed by the emergent roles of administrator, organizer, and pastoral counselor (Glock and Stark 1965, pp. 144–50; Sklare 1955, pp. 174–80; Newman 1971). With the rapid growth of subsidiary clubs and groups within religious institutions, religious zeal and oratory skill have become almost secondary prerequisites for a successful career as a religious professional. The churches have had to produce their own version of the "organization man" (Fichter 1973). He is a religious leader possessing a B.D. or its equivalent, a rudimentary knowledge of how social organizations work, and hopefully an M.A. in psychological counseling. Today, success in the ministry means appointment to a large suburban parish—one that can boast of a new building, has an ability to meet its obligations to denominational fund-raising drives with ease, and has a multiperson professional staff, so that younger men can do the kinds of work that the "pastoral director" (Niebuhr, Williams, and Gustafson 1957) was neither trained to do nor wants to do. Studies of ex-clergymen have shown quite clearly that dropouts from the parish ministry do not undergo a loss or crisis of faith. They simply find the role performances demanded of them to be personally unrewarding. Much of their time is spent on purely organizational duties (Jud, Mills, and Burch 1970).

The move to suburbia, then, has meant not a diminished role for religious institutions but increased roles for them. While this transition has brought problems with it—clergy dissatisfaction with changing role demands, financial strains resulting from the building of new suburban edifices, and the task of disposing of now-abandoned urban properties—religious institutions are "alive and well" in America's suburbs.

As Shippey (1964) has observed, an immense amount of criticism has been directed toward suburban religious institutions for the predominance of these nonreligious functions. In spite of the absence of evidence to support such claims, religious leaders themselves have complained of a crisis of faith among suburban parishioners (Leinberger 1955; Rowland 1956). These criticisms must be understood as a blend of the popular "suburban myth" and some traditional theological griping. The suburban church member is depicted as being a conformist—an object-oriented person, seeking in a church or synagogue not spiritual uplift but leisure-time social activity. Implicit in these stereotypes is the assumption that things were somehow different in the city. I know of no empirical study that documents these implied differences.

Perhaps the one critic within the Protestant fold to be taken seriously is Gibson Winter. In his widely read treatise *The Suburban Captivity of the Churches* (1961) he warns that the most regrettable consequence of the suburbanization of American mainstream religion will be the abandonment of a religious witness in and mission to the inner city. Winter is at least correct in observing that the flight to the suburbs has also been a flight from trapped urban populations, urban social problems, and commitments to both. As Fichter (1966) has observed, most churches would rather move than integrate. Yet, even Winter assumes that urban religious institutions were providing an effective mission prior to their move to suburbia. To the contrary, the most dramatic experiments in social and religious outreach—

such as the famed East Harlem Protestant Parish—have occurred outside the framework of local religious congregations. During the 1960s both the civil rights and antiwar movements within the churches were primarily supported by denominational and interdenominational agencies, not local churches. Research has consistently shown that local religious organizations are more likely to comfort their member-clients than to involve them in significant challenges to the prevailing social order. Moreover, the major source of political and social activism in local religious organizations is the clergy not the laity (Glock, Ringer, and Babbie 1967; Hadden 1970; Campbell and Fukuyama 1970). Thus, while Winter and others are correct in arguing that the flight of religious institutions to the safe social-class and racial boundaries of the suburbs is also a flight from social responsibility, this is not unique to suburban religion. Suburbanization has simply made some forms of social irresponsibility easier for religious institutions.

Suburbanization has been a two-sided coin for religious institutions in the United States. On the one hand, it has brought increased organizational health and additional social functions. It must be cautioned though, that these changes have had little to do with anything inherently suburban. Rather, the very forces that have shaped American society in the past half-century and that created the suburban migration—a shortened work week, the automobile, increased leisure time, and material affluence—are the underlying factors affecting institutional religion in the suburbs. On the other hand, suburbanization has been accompanied by certain internal strains for religious institutions and has made social escapism somewhat easier for them.

INDIVIDUAL RELIGIOSITY IN SUBURBIA

Any assessment of the impact of suburbanization upon individual religious thought and conduct is beset by the same problems that impede the analysis of religious institutions—the absence of comparative, longitudinal data. As Demerath (1968) has suggested, this problem is endemic to the sociology of religion regardless of which particular aspect of the subject one wishes to examine. It is precisely for this reason that he has entered a persuasive argument for the inclusion of items on religion in the United States census. In the past decade, sociologists of religion have expended so much effort distinguishing the various dimensions of individual religiosity that relatively little attention has been given to the demographic factors that underlie them (Dittes 1969; King and Hunt 1972). With the exception of the early studies of H. Paul Douglass and the Institute for Social and Religious Research, few studies in the sociology of religion, and certainly none of the major ones (i.e., Lenski 1961; Glock and Stark 1965, 1966; Glock, Ringer, and Babbie 1967; Stark and Glock 1970), explore urban-rural-suburban differences.

Moreover, none of the national polling agencies that routinely ask questions about religion employs a reliable measure of suburban residence.

One study by Nash and Berger (1962, 1963) does focus upon both suburbanism and individual religiosity. Their findings are entirely consistent with those gleaned from several earlier studies of suburban communities (Whyte 1956; Gans 1951, 1958; Seeley, Sim, and Loosley 1956). Echoing the literature on the centrality of the family in the suburban life-style (Mowrer 1958), Nash and Berger report that most suburbanites join religious institutions primarily out of a desire to provide a religious education for their children. Most suburbanites do not join religious organizations because of a rebirth of religious faith, and most studies of church members generally show that fewer than half of those who join actually attend religious services regularly. Among Jews the attendance figures are even worse. Several researchers report that even the traditional "High Holyday" attendance by Jews is openly acknowledged by many to be more of a social than a religious ritual (Glassar 1970; Simon 1962).

It must, of course, be asked whether these findings are in any way unique to suburbia. A cross-denominational study of urban church members sponsored by the National Council of Churches in 1957 shows that "for the sake of my children" was one of several prominent reasons individuals gave for joining a church.[2] These data, problematic as they may be from a methodological standpoint, at least suggest that the relationship between the child-centeredness of the American family and individuals' motivations for involvement in organized religion is not uniquely suburban. However, several recent studies suggest that a more complex assortment of variables must be examined before this question can be adequately answered. For instance, Carlos (1970) finds that among Catholics in Montreal residence outside the central city is positively associated with attendance at Mass but negatively associated with devotional practices. In other words, place of residence may affect different aspects of religious belief and practice differently. Another recent study by Fischer (1975) shows that rates of church attendance are highest for suburbanites having children in the home and living in large Standard Metropolitan Statistical Areas (SMSAs). This group is distinct from other suburbanites as well as urbanites with or without children in the home. Both Fischer's and Carlos's studies suggest that one must examine not simply urban-suburban differences but different aspects of religion, sizes and types of suburbs, and, of course, family composition. Obviously, firm conclusions about these relationships require additional research.

The large number of studies of American Jewish community life conduct-

---

[2] I refer here to the "Effective City Church Study" and to frequency distributions shown in National Council of Churches of Christ (1960), p. 13. Other parts of these data are the basis of Demerath's 1965 analysis in *Social Class in American Protestantism.*

ed in the 1950s and 1960s represents an even more important source of information about religion and familialism. Almost every discussion of this subject I have read leans heavily upon Gans's studies of the suburb Park Forest (1951, 1958). However, as Sanua (1964) points out, there are innumerable studies of Jews in American cities and small towns. These studies provide the same themes as those offered by Gans. Simply stated, both the child-centeredness of the family and the importance of a religious education for children represent Jewish adaptation to an American middle-class lifestyle. It is important to stress here that these studies depict these patterns among Jews not as suburban but as middle-class American. Viewed in this context, claims that Berger and Nash as well as Gans have made about familialism and religion seem far from uniquely suburban. If, on the basis of these studies of American Jews, even the most modest inferences can be made about Protestants and Catholics, it is clear that all of the writing about familialism and religion in suburbia seems dramatic only because of the absence of comparative data. Where comparative data do exist, as is the case for American Jews, familialism and religion seem to operate in the same way in suburbs, cities, and small towns.

To state the case even differently, studies of religion, and especially individual involvement in organized religion in the suburbs, tell us what all other community studies have consistently shown: Religion is subjectively understood by Americans to provide an important ingredient in the moral education of the child and hence an important ingredient in the moral ethos of community life. It is this theme that unites Yankee City and Levittown, Middletown and Park Forest. It is not a suburban, but an American middle-class, theme.

These comments imply at least a modicum of agreement with the "civil religion" hypothesis of Bellah (1967), Herberg (1955), and others. These writers contend that denominational differences in the United States are of little consequence in the face of a generalized "common core" of civic and religious doctrine. While it may well be true that the belief that religion is a good thing is a prevalent quasi-theological tenet in the United States, this does not mean that subgroup religious differences are insignificant. It is precisely this question that is only now beginning to gain the attention of sociologists of religion. If it is correct to assume that the emerging shape of American society will be most clearly discernible in the suburbs, then a scrutiny of the interplay between religion, region, ethnicity, race, class, and occupation has significance well beyond the sociology of either the suburbs or religion.

SOCIORELIGIOUS COMMUNALISM

The interrelationships between religion and other major social-status variables in the United States have been the subject of immense theoretical vacillation. The "classic" statement, of course, is H. Richard Niebuhr's *The Social Sources of Denominationalism* (1929). In spite of Niebuhr's own commitment to the then-emerging ecumenical movement, and his hope that denominational differences within the Christian community could be eliminated, he provided a powerful demonstration of the ethnic, regional, racial, and social-class significance of denominationalism in the United States. As much as he regretted to admit it, Niebuhr saw that these social differences were even more important than apparent theological differences between the various denominational subgroups.

Unfortunately, most of the major treatises on this subject written during the 1950s and 1960s either implicitly or explicitly reject Niebuhr's insights. For instance, while Niebuhr attempted to expose the intrinsic relationship between religious denominationalism and ethnic pluralism, Herberg (1955) and Marty (1958) argue that religion has renewed social significance because of the death of ethnic pluralism. This, of course, was the core of Herberg's understanding of the alleged religious revival. Given his assumption of the disappearance of ethnic pluralism, religion becomes a new form of social belonging and social identity—a form that in Herberg's view is devoid of meaningful content. This is the essence of his critique of the suburban sameness of the religious revival.

These same themes are echoed in Glazer and Moynihan's widely read *Beyond the Melting Pot* (1963). They, too, contend that ethnicity—one of the key factors that Niebuhr argued sustained denominational differences—is defunct and imply that within another decade or so both religious and racial differences in the United States will recede as factors of intergroup differentiation. The most extreme presentation of this view is Robert Lee's work *The Social Sources of Church Unity* (1960). Lee argues that the ecumenical movement is but one index of an emerging social homogenization in the United States in which region, class, ethnicity, race, and theology will all be sublimated. In this context Bellah's "civil religion" thesis seems to be only the logical extension of themes that have been with us for almost two decades. Bellah would minimize the significance of social pluralism in America and religion's place in that pluralism, given his perception of an overriding constellation of religiocivic cultural values.

As I have tried to indicate elsewhere (Newman 1973), it is no accident that this avenue of theoretical interpretation emerged from within a dominant paradigm of a consensus theory of American society. The "suburban myth" was itself but another expression of the belief that American society was developing a nonpluralistic social structure, characterized by the unitive symbols of a mass culture. Given this framework, it is not surprising that sociologists of religion stopped investigating the interrelationships between the variables from which the social web of a pluralistic society was knit.

Ironically, on the very eve of the triumph of the consensus theory and assimilationist ideology that dominated our understanding of suburbia, its religious revival, the demise of ethnic pluralism, and indeed American society in general, at least one sociologist of religion warned of the fallacy of these sociological myths. Writing in 1961, J. Milton Yinger observed: "It is well to recognize that ethnic religions are sharing in the 'return to religion' that has affected the whole society" (p. 94). Yinger's view that the suburban religious revival entailed not a denial but a reaffirmation of traditional subgroup differences would gain acceptance only after the community studies of Dobriner (1963) and the later works of Gans (1962, 1967), the Supreme Court controversies of the 1960s over the role of religion in our public life, and the ethnic revivals of the 1970s.

There were at least two themes in the research of the 1960s that should have led us to question both the myth of the suburban melting pot and the myth of the sameness of suburban religion. First, in his landmark study *The Religious Factor* (1961), Lenski concluded that both associationalism and communalism are basic forms of religiosity in the United States. The sociology of religion after Lenski, most importantly the work of Glock and his associates, continued to study the nature of associational religion; so much so that various observers complained that the sociology of religion had become a sociology of the churches (Berger and Luckmann 1963). But few turned to Lenski's theme of the centrality of communal religion and especially to the other variables that intersect with religious communalism. Second, as I have already suggested, the larger significance of the numerous studies of American Jews were entirely overlooked. We appear to have assumed all those stereotypes about Jews being different and "clannish." Yet the Jewish community studies, even the earliest ones by Gans, clearly showed the reinstitutionalization of ethnoreligious communalism in suburbia. As Gans so forcefully demonstrated in his studies of Park Forest, the formation of distinctive Jewish adult social groups (B'nai B'rith and a chapter of the National Council of Jewish Women) occurred quickly, but the formation of an explicitly religious institution was a slower and, for several reasons, more controversial process.

Within the past several years we have begun to see the emergence of research that points to the endurance of a social pluralism in which religion and religious differences play a central role. For instance, both Abramson (1971, 1973) and Nelsen and Allen (1974) present data that dispel the myth of a monolithic Catholic community in the United States. These studies show that different ethnic groups practice Catholicism differently, and that these patterns are also affected differently by generation, intermarriage, and other variables. Similarly, Schuman's (1971) replication and reanalysis of Lenski's work points to both inter-Protestant differences and to the effects of occupational differences not examined in Lenski's original study. Studies by Hill (1966) and Nelsen, Madron, and Stewart (1973) show important relationships between religious ideology and regionalism; and a recent study by Grupp and Newman (1973) points to the enduring importance of religious differences in relation to regionalism, social class, and political ideology. Unfortunately none of these studies, all of which demonstrate both a complex pluralism and the central role of religion in that pluralism, examine urban-rural-suburban differences. It is simply my view that all of these studies depict a society that is far different from the image of an assimilated society characterized by a simple common-core religion and the retreat of traditional life-style differences that flow from occupational, class, ethnic, and regional diversity. As the community studies of Dobriner (1963), Berger (1960), and Gans (1962) only began to show, suburbia has not produced a monolith. It remains for the kinds of research findings I have referred to here to be placed in the context of our concern with the meaning of a suburban society.

In the final analysis Bressler seems to have been correct: "People bring to the suburbs the material, intellectual, spiritual and political furniture of their previous residences. The special fact of living between an urban and rural locale does not produce anything uniform, monolithic, distinctive or distinguishable" (1968, p. 98).

There can be little question that some of the furniture has been rearranged, some of it reupholstered. But I reject the hypothesis variously expressed by Bellah (1967), Berger (1967), Fenn (1972), and numerous others that we have entered an age characterized by the death of subgroup communalism and the emergence of an unprecedented religious privatism. The problem is that in the last several decades more research, especially within the sociology of religion, has focused upon the latter than the former. The persistence of ethnoreligious communalism and theological privatism need not be mutually exclusive. It can only be hoped that the decade of the 1970s will produce a renewed awareness of America's pluralism and the role of religion in that pluralism, especially in the suburbs.

REFERENCES

Abramson, Harold J. 1971. "Inter-ethnic Marriage among Catholic Americans and Changes in Religious Behavior." *Sociological Analysis* 32 (Spring): 31–44.
———. 1973. *Ethnic Diversity in Catholic America.* New York: Wiley.
Bellah, Robert N. 1967. "Civil Religion in America." *Daedalus* 96 (Winter): 1–21.
Berger, Bennett M. 1960. *Working-Class Suburb.* Berkeley: University of California Press.
Berger, Peter L. 1967. *The Sacred Canopy.* Garden City, N.Y.: Doubleday.
Berger, Peter L., and Thomas Luckmann. 1963. "Sociology of Religion and Sociology of Knowledge." *Sociology and Social Research* 47 (July): 417–27.
Blizzard, Samuel. 1956. "Role Conflicts of the Urban Parish Minister." *City Church* 7:13–15.

Bressler, Marvin. 1968. "To Suburbia with Love." *Public Interest* 10 (Winter): 97–103.

Campbell, Thomas, and Yoshio Fukuyama. 1970. *The Fragmented Laymen.* Philadelphia: Pilgrim.

Carlos, Serge. 1970. "Religious Participation and the Urban-Suburban Continuum." *American Journal of Sociology* 75 (March): 742–59.

Demerath, N. J., III. 1965. *Social Class in American Protestantism.* Chicago: Rand-McNally.

———. 1968. "Trends and Anti-Trends in Religious Change." Pp. 349–445 in *Indicators of Social Change,* edited by Eleanor Sheldon and Wilbert Moore. New York: Russell Sage Foundation.

Dittes, James. 1969. "Psychology of Religion." Pp. 602–59 in *Handbook of Social Psychology,* edited by Gardner Lindzey and E. Aronson. Vol. 5. Reading, Mass.: Addison-Wesley.

Dobriner, William M. 1963. *Class in Suburbia.* Englewood Cliffs, N.J.: Prentice-Hall.

Donaldson, Scott. 1969. *The Suburban Myth.* New York: Columbia University Press.

Douglass, H. Paul. 1925. *The Suburban Trend.* New York: Century.

Fenn, Richard K. 1972. "Toward a New Sociology of Religion." *Journal for the Scientific Study of Religion* 11 (March): 16–32.

Fichter, Joseph. 1966. "American Religion and the Negro." *Daedalus* 95 (Fall): 401–22.

———. 1973. *Organization Man in the Church.* Cambridge, Mass.: Schenkman.

Fischer, Claude S. 1975. "The Effect of Urban Life on Traditional Values." *Social Forces* 53 (March): 420–32.

Gans, Herbert J. 1951. "Park Forest: Birth of a Jewish Community." *Commentary* 11 (April): 330–39.

———. 1958. "The Origin and Growth of a Jewish Community in the Suburbs: A Study of the Jews of Park Forest." Pp. 205–48 in *The Jews,* eidted by Marshall Sklare. New York: Free Press.

———. 1962. *The Urban Villagers.* New York: Free Press.

———. 1967. *The Levittowners: Ways of Life and Politics in a New Suburban Community.* New York: Random House.

Glassar, Terry. 1970. "Jewburbia: A Portable Community." *New Society* 16 (October): 630–31.

Glazer, Nathan, and Daniel P. Moynihan. 1963. *Beyond the Melting Pot.* Cambridge, Mass.: M.I.T. Press.

Glock, Charles Y., Benjamin Ringer, and Earl Babbie. 1967. *To Comfort and to Challenge: The Dilemma of the Contemporary Church.* Berkeley: University of California Press.

Glock, Charles Y., and Rodney Stark. 1965. *Religion and Society in Tension.* Chicago: Rand-McNally.

———. 1966. *Christian Beliefs and Anti-Semitism.* New York: Harper & Row.

Goffman, Erving. 1959. *The Presentation of Self in Everyday Life.* Garden City, N.Y.: Doubleday.

Gordon, Albert I. 1959. *Jews in Suburbia.* Boston: Beacon.

Greeley, Andrew M. 1959. *The Church and the Suburbs.* New York: Sheed & Ward.

Greer, Scott, and E. Kube. 1959. "Urbanism and Social Structure: A Los Angeles Community Study." Pp. 93–112 in *Community Structure and Analysis,* edited by Marvin Susman. New York: Crowell.

Grupp, Fred W., Jr., and William M. Newman. 1973. "Political Ideology and Religious Preference: The John Birch Society and the Americans for Democratic Action." *Journal for the Scientific Study of Religion* 12 (September): 401–31.

Hadden, Jeffrey K. 1970. *The Gathering Storm in the Churches.* Garden City, N.Y.: Doubleday.

Herberg, Will. 1955. *Protestant-Catholic-Jew.* Garden City, N.Y.: Doubleday.

Hill, Samuel S. 1966. *Southern Churches in Crisis.* New York: Holt, Rinehart & Winston.

Jud, Gerald, Edgar Mills, and Genevieve Burch. 1970. *Ex-Pastors.* Philadelphia: Pilgrim.

King, Morton, and Richard Hunt. 1972. *Measuring Religious Dimensions.* Dallas: Southern Methodist University Press.

Lee, Robert. 1960. *The Social Sources of Church Unity.* Nashville, Tenn.: Abingdon.

Leinberger, Hugo. 1955. "The Church in the 'New Suburb.'" *Religious Education* 50 (January–February): 11–14.

Lenski, Gerhard. 1961. *The Religious Factor.* Garden City, N.Y.: Doubleday.

Marshall, Harvey. 1973. "Suburban Life Styles: A Contribution to the Debate." Pp. 123–48 in *The Urbanization of the Suburbs,* edited by Louis H. Masotti and Jeffrey K. Hadden. Urban Affairs Annual Reviews, vol. 7. Beverly Hills, Calif.: Sage.

Marty, Martin. 1958. *The New Shape of American Religion.* New York: Harper & Row.

Masotti, Louis H., and Jeffrey K. Hadden, eds. 1973. *The Urbanization of the Suburbs.* Urban Affairs Annual Reviews, vol. 7. Beverly Hills, Calif.: Sage.

Mowrer, Ernest R. 1958. "The Family in Suburbia." Pp. 147–64 in *The Suburban Community,* edited by William M. Dobriner. New York: Putnam's.

Mueller, Samuel A. 1966. "Changes in Social Status of Lutheranism in Ninety Chicago Suburbs." *Sociological Analysis* 27 (Fall): 375–408.

Nash, Dennison. 1968. "And a Little Child Shall Lead Them: A Test of an Hypothesis That Children Were the Source of the American 'Religious Revival.'" *Journal for the Scientific Study of Religion* 7 (Fall): 238–40.

Nash, Dennison, and Peter L. Berger. 1962. "The Child, the Family, and the 'Religious Revival' in Suburbia." *Journal for the Scientific Study of Religion* 2 (October): 85–93.

———. 1963. "Church Commitment in the American Suburb: An Analysis of the Decision to Join." *Archives de sociologie des religions* 13 (July): 105–20.

National Council of Churches of ·Christ. 1960. "Denominational and Interdenominational Responses to Church Membership Questionnaire." Mimeographed. New York: National Council of Churches Bureau of Survey and Research.

Nelsen, Hart, and H. David Allen. 1974. "Ethnicity, Americanization and Religious Attendance." *American Journal of Sociology* 79 (January): 906–22.

Nelsen, Hart, Thomas Madron, and Karen Stewart. 1973. "Image of God and Religious Ideology and Involvement: A Partial Test of Hill's Southern Culture–Religion Hypothesis." *Review of Religious Research* 15 (Fall): 37–43.

Newman, William M. 1971. "Role Conflict in the Ministry and the Role of the Seminary." *Sociological Analysis* 32 (Winter): 238–48.

———. 1973. *American Pluralism.* New York: Harper & Row.

Niebuhr, H. Richard. 1929. *The Social Sources of Denominationalism.* New York: Holt, Rinehart & Winston.

Niebuhr, H. Richard, D. D. Williams, and James M. Gustafson. 1957. *The Advancement of Theological Education.* New York: Harper & Bros.

Riesman, David. 1958. "The Suburban Sadness." Pp. 375–408 in *The Suburban Community,* edited by William M. Dobriner. New York: Putnam's.

Rowland, Stanley, Jr. 1956. "Suburbia Buys Religion." *Nation* 182 (June): 78–80.

Sanua, Victor D. 1964. "Patterns of Jewish Identification with the Jewish Community in the U.S.A." *Jewish Journal of Sociology* 6 (December): 190–212.

Schuman, Howard. 1971. "The Religious Factor in Detroit: Review, Replication and Reanalysis." *American Sociological Review* 36 (February): 30–48.

Seeley, John R., R. A. Sim, and E. W. Loosley. 1956. *Crestwood Heights.* New York: Wiley.

Shippey, Frederick A. 1964. *Protestantism in Suburban Life.* Nashville, Tenn.: Abingdon.

Simon, Edwin. 1962. "Suburbia: Its Effects on the American Jewish Teenager." *Journal of Educational Sociology* 36 (November): 124–33.

Sklare, Marshall. 1955. *Conservative Judaism.* Glencoe, Ill.: Free Press.

Stark, Rodney, and Charles Y. Glock. 1970. *American Piety.* Vol. 1. Berkeley: University of California Press.

Tallman, I., and R. Morgner. 1970. "Life-Style Differences among Urban and Suburban Blue-Collar Families." *Social Forces* 48 (March): 334–48.

Whyte, William H., Jr. 1956. *The Organization Man.* New York: Simon & Schuster.

Winter, Gibson. 1961. *The Suburban Captivity of the Churches.* Garden City, N.Y.: Doubleday.

Yinger, J. Milton. 1961. *Sociology Looks at Religion.* New York: Macmillan.

Zimmer, B., and Amos Hawley. 1959. "Suburbanization and Church Participation." *Social Forces* 37 (May): 348–54.

11   Suburbs, Networks, and Attitudes

Claude S. Fischer and Robert Max Jackson
University of California, Berkeley

Opinion on the social psychological nature of suburban life has undergone, as do many sociological topics, a historical cycle. At the turn of the century, residence on the urban fringe was proclaimed invigorating and ennobling (Donaldson 1969; Tarr 1973). At mid-century, it was decried as the breeding ground of the mass society (Riesman 1958; Whyte 1956). Today, general opinion hovers at a midpoint: the suburb is seen as essentially neutral, having no independent effect on small-group life or personality. Gans (1967, p. 228) best summarizes the contemporary point of view: ". . . when one looks at similar populations in city and suburb, their ways of life are remarkably alike. . . . The crucial difference between cities and suburbs, then is that they are often home for different kinds of people."

This paper will examine the accuracy of Gans's statement, with particular regard to one aspect of "ways of life": the degree to which individuals' social circles and interests are concentrated in their immediate residential localities. In the course of the ensuing discussion, we shall refer to five specific models relating suburbanism to this "localism":

I. *Nonecological theories,* of which there are three, deny any independent causal effect of suburbanism per se on behavior or attitudes.

1. The *simple null model* states that there are no city-suburban differences.

2. Gans's position may be termed an *individual traits model:* behavioral differences between city and suburb are accounted for by the personal characteristics of their residents.

3. The *contextual effects model* suggests that the composition of the populations resident in each locale affect individuals so as to generate differences above and beyond those created by personal traits (e.g., as in climates of opinion). Here, also, it is not suburbanism but the concentration in suburbs of certain population types which produces differences.

II. *Ecological theories* posit an independent causal effect due to place of residence.[1]

Support for this research was provided by the Institute of Urban and Regional Development, Berkeley, and by NIMH grant 1-RO3-MH25406-01 to the senior author. We thank Elihu Gerson, Lynne Jones, Paul Burstein and Charles Tilly for helpful comments.

[1] There is a type of ecological effect which is quite important but shall not concern us here: the facilitation of purposive changes. If, for example, suburbia permits home ownership or contact with nature, and if these are desired goals, we can expect appropriate behavior and

4. The *metropolitanism model* argues that residence at the urban fringe encourages metropolitan-wide activity and interest, thereby reducing the individual's relative involvement in his or her locality (cf. Webber 1968).

5. We shall devote some space to explicating what might be termed a *distance-cost model:* the ecological features of suburbs, especially distance from population concentrations, influence individual attitudes and shape social networks in the direction of greater localism.[2]

Deciding what suburbs do is not unrelated to deciding what suburbs are. They are metropolitan localities[3] distinguished by certain ecological features. These features commonly include distance from city center, residential land use, recency of development, low housing density, and political autonomy. Most other suggested criteria, such as commuting, homogeneity, and familism, are either derivative from these (cf. Dobriner 1963, chap. 1; Fine, Glenn, and Monts 1971) or do not explicitly capture what is usually meant by "suburb." There exists as yet no consensus on nor rule for judging the relative importance of these related dimensions.

Rather than attempt to resolve such confusions in definitions and meanings, we have chosen to examine the consequences of a few "suburban" dimensions. We will be most concerned with distance from the center of population, which we consider to be the principle dimension.[4]

---

contentment to result. These are the sorts of changes Gans (1967) and Michelson (1973*a*, 1973*b*) report. They are real and significant consequences. However, this paper is meant to enter into the debate over the determinative effects of urban structure (Wirth 1938; Fischer 1972). Are there constraints and latent influences which result from suburbanism and shape interactions and attitudes?

[2] These models are, of course, not exhaustive. For instance, the political nature of suburbs may also have consequences in this regard.

[3] This definition places suburbs within the class of urban subareas. An alternative perspective puts suburbs in the genus "small town," specifically as small towns near cities. The latter definition is to some degree valid, for suburbs and small towns, relative to central cities, share the characteristic of low access to population concentration ("population potential" [Stewart 1948; Carrothers 1956]). But fundamentally, suburbs are differentiated and specialized subareas of a metropolis.

[4] More specifically, the arguments for basing a definition of suburbia on distance from the metropolitan center include the following. (1) There may be variations in the typical American usage of the term "suburb," with regard to traits such as residentiality, but the term is never applied to inner-city districts. In that sense, distance is a necessary (though perhaps insufficient) criterion. (2) Historically, the term originally referred to communities outside the walls of medieval cities (e.g., *faubourg* [cf. Hawley 1971, p. 48]), a spatial definition. (3) Cross-culturally, the interrelationships among density, distance, residentiality, etc., that characterize American suburbs do not hold so firmly. The only global commonality appears to be distance. (4) Distance partly determines the other variables, for example, availability of open land and new, low-density housing (Guest 1972; see Evans 1973).

NETWORK AND ATTITUDINAL CONSEQUENCES

In this section, we shall consider the independent effects on primary groups and individual personalities which residence at varying distances from the city center may have. Then, we shall enlarge our analysis by considering people's anticipations of and adjustments to such effects.[5]

"Social worlds" are constructed of each individual's personal associations or networks. These relationships can be categorized in various ways by content (kinship, work, ethnicity, etc.) and by structure (intimacy, frequency, primacy, etc.). The initiations, durations, and qualities of different network links are variously affected by many contingencies. One we shall consider here is the time-distance cost of face-to-face interaction. The degree to which this circumstance influences networks probably varies greatly (perhaps it is trivial for professional relationships, e.g.) but it should significantly affect ' relationships of diffuse sociable interaction and personal intimacy, best epitomized as "friendship."

Sociability and friendship ties emerge largely out of other networks (co-workers, kin, neighbors, etc.). Of the many factors which determine the networks from which these close associates are drawn, we focus on three: (1) the number of people in each network, (2) the degree to which the members are suitable in personality and are rewarding to the individual, and (3) the costs of face-to-face interaction. How do the ecological dimensions of suburbia affect these relationships of sociability and friendship?

Distance affects indirectly the costs of interaction. Distance means little except insofar as it is translated into access. We are interested here in access from an individual's home to the homes and gathering places of people who are his real and potential associates.[6] Let us assume, for purposes of argu-

---

[5] Three critical assumptions guide this analysis: (1) the direct social effects of population concentration result from the achievement of critical masses within distinctive subcultures (Fischer 1975a); (2) personality, attitudes, and behavior are to a great extent determined by the content and structure of individuals' personal social networks; and (3) people choose network associates and continue interaction with them as a positive function of commonalities and as a negative function of the cost to the interaction; of particular concern here is distance time. This last assumption posits that the selection and maintenance of social relationships can be described by a model of "economic" rationality and that a major consideration in the implicit calculation of a relationship's "profitability" is the distance separating the individuals from face-to-face contact, in terms both of the direct costs of travel and of the opportunity costs of the travel time (see Thibaut and Kelley 1959, pp. 39–42; Roistacher 1974). Deductions from these assumptions have found some empirical support: people travel farther for more intimate associates (Stutz 1973); friendships maintained over long distances involves more similar friends than do those maintained over shorter distances (Athanasiou and Yoshioka 1973; Thibaut and Kelley 1959, pp. 41–42); and contact between friends is shaped by time-budget constraints (Verbrugge 1973).

[6] The problem of access is more complex than this simplification implies. The relationships among distance, access, and cost are probably not linear. Further, individual perceptions of

ment, an ideal-type metropolis circular in shape with density declining from the center. The farther from the center an individual is, the greater the average distance to other persons in the metropolitan area and the fewer the persons accessible within any given distance. Within a particular radius, suburbanites, relative to urbanites, reach less populated areas (of lower density) and more open space. (The effects of highways and subnuclei will be discussed later.) The average cost of interaction summated over the metropolis thus increases with an individual's distance from the center.[7]

A hypothesis about suburban social networks can be derived from this higher average distance cost of interaction borne by suburbanites. This hypothesis (the essence of model 5) assumes the reward-cost model of friendship choice described above. It also initially assumes, for ease of presentation, that all individual and areal variables other than distance from the center of population are held constant between city and suburb.[8]

The prediction is that the personal networks of suburban residents will tend to be more "localized" than those of city dwellers. That is, suburbanites' close associates and social activities will be located closer to their homes, relatively more frequently within the immediate vicinity.

The argument is that, by the nature of the distant location of suburbs, the cost to a suburbanite in time and money for initiating and maintaining associations across the metropolitan area is greater than the cost to a center-city resident. If the suburban and the city persons do not otherwise differ, then the former face a higher price than do the latter for seeing an "average" individual in the metropolitan area. The consequences of this higher "price" can be the expending of more time and money by the suburbanite (i.e., paying a higher price by traveling farther) and/or the favoring of closer associates over farther ones by the suburbanite, even if these might be less rewarding (i.e., buying a cheaper, closer "good"). Both probably occur. Our concern here is particularly with the latter consequence, for it implies that suburbanites' personal networks will be more localized than those of city residents. Put simply, suburbanites are too far from people other than their neighbors.

Additional ecological features presumed to characterize suburbs reinforce this localization: homogeneity, single-family homes, political autonomy, and residential land use.

---

access costs, which will determine travel behavior, are also not linear functions of distance. We recognize these problems, but the crude model we employ here should suffice for present purposes.

[7] This analysis of city-suburb differences in the capacity to aggregate people parallels one of urban-rural differences (Fischer 1975a): rural areas are unable to concentrate sufficient numbers of persons of certain types so as to maintain services or viable minority subcultures.

[8] Part of this *ceteris paribus* assumption is that the terms of trade—the quality of friendship versus the distance cost—are the same for city and suburb residents.

We do not intend to exaggerate the effect of home location on networks. People maintain relationships based on other spatial considerations (e.g., workplace) and on nonspatial ones (e.g., kinship). However, this model contends that residence has some effects, particularly, we argue, for certain subpopulations.

Further consequences can be derived: that suburbanites maintain associations of lower compatibility[9] and maintain more redundant ties (i.e., making double use of their associates [cf. Tilly 1974]) and that suburbanites will be less likely to aggregate sufficient numbers of like-minded persons to support viable minority subcultures and special services (Fischer 1975a; Riesman 1958).

A contrary argument to all this can be presented, one based on city-suburb differences in density rather than differences in distance. A resident of the dense urban center will have a greater number of potential associates within a given radius than will a resident on the sparse periphery. The suburbanite must go farther from home to find a satisfactory level of association. Conse-quently, it is the city dweller who will have the more localized social network.[10] This analysis is consistent with the metropolitanism model listed above (model 4) and serves as a counterhypothesis to the one just argued.

At this point, we introduce the problem of feedback. People both antici-pate and adapt to the sorts of consequences just described (cf. Michelson, Belgue, and Stewart 1973). The prediction of the distance-cost model must therefore be reconsidered.

A positive feedback process may exist which amplifies city-suburban dif-ferences. It has been suggested that it is precisely those persons who desire localism who move to suburbia (Bell 1958; Fava 1958). However, while such cases do exist, their number is minimal. Surveys of residential movers rarely discover such considerations stated as "push" factors, and in only a minority of cases are they stated as significant "pull" factors (Abu-Lughod and Foley 1960; Butler et al. 1968; Gans 1967; Hawley and Zimmer 1971; Lansing and Hedricks 1967; Lansing and Mueller 1964; Michelson et al. 1973; Rossi 1956; Simmons 1968). Neither is there evidence for "subliminal" or "uncon-scious" sociability seeking in the suburban move (Baldassare and Fischer 1975). Far more important are concerns for space, housing, and neighbor-hood quality. A mirror process—moving to cities to avoid neighbors—may

[9] The assumption which this prediction makes—that people accept less compatible friend-ships if they are less costly to maintain—is supported by a study of a housing development which found that respondents' distant friends (within the development) were more similar to themselves than were those nearby (Athanasiou and Yoshioka 1973).

[10] One difference between this model and the distance-cost one is that it assumes a "satisfic-ing" procedure: people accumulate "satisfactory" friendships up to some number. The dis-tance-cost model assumes "maximizing": people attempt to obtain the best friendship "re-turn" for their "investment."

also exist in a few cases. But, in general, self-selection based on preferences for localism contributes only in a minor way to city-suburb differences.

More critical are negative feedback processes operating to mitigate if not nullify the effects of distance. At the individual level, three can be mentioned. (1) Self-selection minimizes the costs of access to metropolitan people and places. People will avoid stretching their real or potential networks beyond tolerable distances. What is "tolerable" varies, both by individuals' means of transport and by their willingness to do without, and the result may be a spatial distribution in which the personal consequences of accessibility are equalized.[11] (2) People encourage their most cherished associates to move with them, in chain-migration fashion, creating suburban enclaves and also equalizing the effects of distance. (3) People will expend the additional costs necessary to maintain a constant radius of interaction, for example, by purchasing a second car (Clark 1966, p. 119) or tolerating longer trips. This, too, equalizes the effects of distance.

At the social level, purposive and incidental adjustments to suburban dispersal, especially of the affluent, are made. Peripheral and radial highways cut transit time sharply.[12] Subnuclei emerge; businesses bring jobs and services to where the people are (Zimmer 1974; Kasarda 1976; see Hawley 1971). All this equalizes access gradients.

That these adaptive processes are plainly visible demonstrates the pressures of distance. However, their existence also implies that, when viewed at a single point in time, the city-suburb differences we have suggested will be virtually erased. This can serve as a null hypothesis (model 1): individual and systemic adjustments to dispersion nullify potential consequences of suburbanization.

Yet we may still expect the hypothesized network consequences to be evident, at least in residual form, because of inefficiencies and lags in the adaptive mechanisms. Also, particular subpopulations should evidence the differences more sharply than others: (1) those persons who did not anticipate the consequences or, anticipating, welcomed them and (2) those who, through necessity or taste, traded off those consequences for other benefits, such as space. In regard to these two criteria, Michelson's (1973*b*) before and

---

[11] Thus, surveys of residential mobility show movers to have consciously traded off housing values against access. Those for whom the latter means most opted for the center city. About the others, Clark (1966, p. 140) writes: "the break of social ties of the past represented a price paid for suburban residence."

[12] The consequences of highway construction may be so great as to provide suburbanites with quicker access to downtown than center-city residents have (Stegman 1969). For our purposes, travel time to downtown may not be quite so critical as travel time to the other side of town; according to 1950s data, most vehicles entering the CBD were just passing through (Cole 1972, pp. 66–67).

after interviews with movers in the Toronto area are informative. The city-to-suburb movers characteristically ignored or discounted the locational factor in their decisions and anticipations; yet it became an increasingly acute source of dissatisfaction for them (Michelson 1973*b*, pp. 41–42). (3) A third population which would exhibit the effects of distance is composed of those who lack the means to overcome the access problem. Public-housing residents are a dramatic example[13] and carless housewives are another.

There is another population which should be affected in a more complex manner. Those who have a narrow choice for potential associates—subcultural minorities—can less easily substitute a nearer, cheaper "good" for a distant one. Therefore, they are likely to pay the higher "price" for travel and should least exhibit the effects of distance, except under two conditions: (1) if they cannot pay the price and instead are isolated (2) or if they have gathered into suburban enclaves.

With these qualifications and conditions, the predicted suburban effects on social networks should still be observed, even if they are greatly muted.

From these network differences, we can also predict attitudinal effects: more attention and attachment to the locality by suburbanites; more local consensus and "climate of opinion"; and less subcultural consciousness and less of the unconventionality which results from the influence of minority subcultures. Note the predictions which are not being made: that these differences will be dramatically large and that these ecological variables produce changes in personality (Baldassare and Fischer 1975).

This analysis serves to explicate model 5 of city-suburb differences: that the peripheral physical location of suburbanites encourages a social and psychological focus on the local area. This model is contrasted with one which predicts opposite effects of location (model 4) and is tested against simpler, nonecological models: that there are no city-suburb differences (model 1), that any such differences can be accounted for by the personal characteristics of the residents (model 2), and that they can be accounted for by personal characteristics plus contextual effects (model 3).

THE RESEARCH LITERATURE

A large number of studies show that neighboring and other localized activities increase with distance from city center.[14] A few of these studies control

---

[13] The material, social, and psychological costs to low-income residents resulting from the placement of public housing in inaccessible suburban locations have been noted in such metropolises as London (Young and Willmott 1957), San Francisco (Cooper 1972), and Rio de Janeiro (Perlman 1975).

[14] These include Berger (1960), Bradburn et al. (1970), Fava (1958), Fischer (1973, p. 320), Gans (1967), Greer (1967), Greer and Kube ([1959] 1972), Hawley and Zimmer (1971), Lopata (1972), who also, contrary to the generalization, reports that city housewives more

for individual-level covariates, and their findings imply that this correlation is due to suburbanism per se (Lopata 1972, p. 279; Fava 1958; Tomeh 1964; Tallman and Morgner 1970). Notably, Michelson (1973*b*) reports that people who moved to the suburbs increased their involvement with neighbors (or were isolated) and that those who moved downtown maintained or increased their interactions with friends and relatives.

The next issue is, then, to which suburban dimension should the differences in local activities be attributed: single-family housing (Dobriner 1963; Gans 1967; Laumann 1966, p. 72; vs. Kasarda and Janowitz 1974), purposeful self-selection (Donaldson 1969; Fava 1956; Bell 1958), homogeneity (Donaldson 1969; Gans 1967), recency (Marshall 1973; Greer 1967, p. 251), or still uncontrolled individual variables (Marshall 1973)? While all of these factors probably contribute to the urban-suburban differences, they seem less adequate than distance cost (model 5) for explaining two common interaction effects.

First, a number of studies suggest that suburban residence has greater effects on women than on men. There are larger differences between city and suburban women in the extent of local involvement; women are more likely to be displeased with suburban residence; and they frequently must sacrifice employment opportunities as a consequence of moving to the suburbs (see Berger 1960; Clark 1966; Young and Willmott 1957; Gans 1967; Tallman 1969; Abu-Lughod and Foley 1960, p. 186; Gillespie 1971; Jones 1974; Michelson 1973*b*, pp. 38 ff.). Less mobile and more committed to the home, women suffer the stress of distance. Gans concludes: "If there is malaise in Levittown, it is female but not suburban" (1967, p. 226). We feel it is female *and* suburban. A further consequence of this locational problem is the substitution by women of neighbors in place of friends and relatives.

Second, also as model 5 predicts, suburban residence has a greater impact on people who have specialized social needs and restricted mobility. Adoles-

---

frequently stated that their couple friends were recruited from neighbors but questions those results, McGahan (1973), Michelson (1973*b*), Roberts (1973), Smith, Form, and Stone (1954), Sutcliffe and Crabbe (1963), Tallman and Morgner (1970), Tallman (1969), and Tomeh (1964). Researchers have also compared average time or distance to social contacts, but the results are ambiguous. Stegman (1969) shows that city residents spend more time traveling to "best friends" than do suburbanites, indicating that the latter are more localized (see also Forrest 1974). However, other studies have found that suburbanites travel farther for social contacts than do city dwellers (von Rosenbladt 1972; Reimer and McNamara 1957). As in these studies, Hawley and Zimmer (1971) found that suburbanites tend to range greater distances for a variety of activities and, thus, were seemingly more cosmopolitan. But, when they controlled for place of previous residence (city versus suburb), the differences essentially washed out. This last point is relevant to all of the studies: since suburbanites are often likely to have moved from the city, they are also often likely to carry with them metropolis-wide ties—a suppressor effect on the differences in localism. Over time, however, longer-distance contacts drop off in favor of nearer ones (Clark 1966, pp. 157–59).

cents, single persons, the elderly, ethnic minorities, and culturally sophisticated housewives who find themselves in suburbs are more isolated than are
their neighbors or than are their kind in cities (Gans 1967; Tomeh 1964;
Carp 1975; Bourg 1975; Abu-Lughod and Foley 1960, p. 186).[15]

Both of these patterns of findings are most adequately explained by
distance and its depressive effects on population potential. Michelson's
(1973b) study reveals this problem sharply, leading him to recommend policies to alleviate suburban "vulnerability," "isolation," "boredom," and lack
of extraresidential activities, which are partly relieved currently by intensified neighboring.

The research which can be brought to bear on other hypotheses derived
from the distance-cost model is too fragmentary to be conclusive. We do
note, with regard to the predicted inability of dispersed populations to aggregate critical masses sufficient to support services, that the 'absence of facilities is a chronic suburban complaint (Warner 1969, p. 158; Clark 1966;
Hawley and Zimmer 1971; Michelson 1973b; von Rosenbladt 1972) and
that, in conjunction with their low numbers, minority subcultural groups
suffer most (Gans 1967).

The attitudinal predictions—more orientation to the locality, stronger
local "climates," less "unconventionality"—also suffer from a dearth of
evidence. Certain features of suburbia may operate to suppress concern for
the local community: jobs in other places (Martin 1958; Verba and Nie
1972, table 13:2), short length of residence (Kasarda and Janowitz 1974),
and the competing importance and notoriety of a huge center city (Fischer
1975b).

Yet, if local social ties lead to local psychological investment (Kasarda
and Janowitz 1974; Cox 1969; in contrast, Cornelius 1973), and if our earlier
hypotheses are valid, then suburbanites should be more interested and involved in their localities than are city residents. Shreds of evidence can be
found on these points. Suburban residents are more satisfied with their
communities than are city residents (Marans and Rodgers 1974; Greer 1967),
which may, of course, simply reflect objective quality. They are more likely
to read local papers (Greer 1967), to resist metropolitan government (Greer
1963), and to enjoy consensual local politics (Prewitt and Eulau 1967; Black
1974). Finally, while not generally more prejudiced than city residents, white
suburbanites are particularly resistant to open housing (Wirt et al. 1972;
Campbell 1971).[16]

---

[15] To quote Gans once again: "the smallness and homegeneity of the population made it
difficult for the culturally and socially deviant to find companions. Levittown benefitted the
majority but punished a minority with exclusion, what Whyte called the 'misery of the
deviate'" (Gans 1967, p. 239).

[16] Other data are more ambiguous. Wirt et al. (1972) report no association between suburbs
and local attachment, but their analysis is questionable. Kasarda and Janowitz (1974) find

Fischer and Jackson

In summary, except with regard to neighboring, we have few substantial comparative studies on city and suburban localism. What research exists suggests that there are differences which may not be fully accounted for by city-suburb differences in population composition. Some evidence implies that distance, in spite of self-selection and adaptation to it, accounts for these residual effects. In terms of the theories presented earlier, the simple null model (model 1) is best rejected and the metropolitanism model (model 4) seems contrary to the facts. We suggest that the distance-cost model (model 5) better accounts for the data than does either an individual traits (model 2) or a contextual effects (model 3) model, but the research conducted to date is not conclusive.[17]

The next two sections of this paper present secondary analyses of two social surveys which contain items relevant to the topic of suburbs and social networks. As secondary analyses, dependent on samples, procedures, and questions designed for other purposes, they cannot be definitive but only suggestive. We present them as additional data to be used in evaluating the alternative models of suburban life.

STUDY 1: NORC

The first survey we examined was conducted by the National Opinion Research Center (NORC) and reported by Bradburn, Sudman, and Gockel (1970; this includes sampling information and the entire questionnaire). The sampling procedure was somewhat unusual: NORC canvassed the United States in search of racially integrated neighborhoods (those open to blacks) and matched this set with control sets of white- and black-segregated neighborhoods. Within neighborhoods, households were sampled, yielding a male:female respondent ratio of approximately 1:3. For this paper, we used only white, nonsouthern, urban respondents ($N = 2,386$).[18]

In this space, we can consider only a few of the variables discussed or

little effect of density on community attachment in a British sample. Local political involvement is an unsure indicator of attachment, because suburban politics are generally ignored in metropolitan media. For example, though more educated, suburbanites are less likely to know the names of their officials (Hawley and Zimmer 1971; cf. also Verba and Nie 1972, chap. 13). Even so, Greer and Orleans (1962) indicate in a Saint Louis study that suburban politics is more likely to be localistic, urban involvement to be "cosmopolitan."

[17] Michelson's (1973a, 1973b) longitudinal study of movers appears to provide the strongest empirical data yet available, largely because of its quasi-experimental nature. Its results point toward the distance-cost model.

[18] We thank NORC for its permission to use the survey, E. M. and M. S. Gerson for their aid in obtaining it, and Ann Stueve and Lynne Jones for assistance in the analysis.

alluded to at the outset. We report, from both surveys, on items indicating (1) the extent of neighboring and attachment to neighbors, (2) the degree of localization of individuals' ties, and (3) interest and attitudinal involvement in the locality. Generally, our procedure was threefold, (1) to examine urban-suburban differences, (2) to attempt to assess the independent, additive effects of suburban residence, and (3) to examine the data for the sorts of specifications discussed above. This analysis was designed to reveal, where possible, whether there were correlations with suburbanism (testing model 1); if so, whether they were fully accounted for by individual traits (model 2) and/or contextual traits (model 3); if not fully accounted for, whether the remaining effect of suburbanism inclined individuals away from (model 4) or toward (model 5) the locality.

City-Suburban Differences

Table 1 presents a sample of items from the NORC survey showing the familiar pattern of city-suburb differences in local involvement. It should be noted that "suburb" is defined in this survey by the political boundary of the central city. As an operationalization of the concept, "suburban" employed in the theoretical discussion is only a rough approximation. The measurement error which is involved probably operates to weaken the results. Nevertheless, and although the differences are not large, suburbanites are shown to be more neighborly and more interested in their neighborhood than are city residents.[19]

Independent Effects

These results suggest that model 1 is inadequate: city and suburb do differ. Model 2 predicts that the differences can be accounted for by controlling for such traits as age, ethnicity, class, and so on. The remaining models predict that these controls will be insufficient. To test the predictions, we subjected the associations to very high order partialing in multiple-regression analyses. Three dependent variables were used: a "neighboring" scale composed of the three neighboring items in table 1; the question asking whether most friends lived in the neighborhood; and the question asking whether family members had attended a neighborhood meeting with neighbors. These variables were regressed on 5 individual traits and five variables indexing the neighborhood context, as well as on the city-suburb dichotomy. The reader should note that

---

[19] Another item on the NORC survey replicates the reported findings about services in the suburbs. Suburbanites (22%) were more likely to complain about neighborhood services than were city persons (15%) ($\chi^2 = 34.85$, 1 df, $P < .001$, $\gamma = .28$, $N = 2,373$).

TABLE 1

RESPONSES TO LOCALISM ITEMS, BY PLACE OF RESIDENCE (NORC)*

	City	Suburb†
Neighboring:		
In general, how often do neighbors get together socially?		
% often, sometimes	39	46
(N)	(951)	(1,257)
	$\chi^2 = 10.55, P < .005, \gamma = .14$	
Has anyone in your family in the past few months had an informal chat together in their home or your home with members of families who live in this neighborhood?		
% yes	60	73
(N)	(1,056)	(1,322)
	$\chi^2 = 43.22, P < .001, \gamma = .28$	
... had dinner or a party together at their home or your home ...?		
% yes	29	37
(N)	(1,056)	(1,320)
	$\chi^2 = 19.78, P < .001, \gamma = .20$	
Localization of ties:		
Do most of your friends live in the neighborhood, or do most of them live farther away?		
% most, some in neighborhood	33	36
(N)	(1,052)	(1,322)
	$\chi^2 = 3.29, P < .10, \gamma = .08$	
Interest in neighborhood:		
How about your family? Are they very much interested, somewhat interested, or not at all interested in neighborhood problems?		
% very	37	47
(N)	(1,029)	(1,300)
	$\chi^2 = 23.00, P < .001, \gamma = .20$	
Has anyone in your family in the past few months attended the meeting of a neighborhood organization or group together with members of families who live in this neighborhood?		
% yes	16	25
(N)	(1,056)	(1,320)
	$\chi^2 = 25.59, P < .001, \gamma = .26$	
If, for any reason, you had to move from here to some other neighborhood, would you be very unhappy, a little unhappy, or would you be happy to move—or wouldn't it make any difference?		
% very, somewhat unhappy	52	57
(N)	(1,040)	(1,315)
	$\chi^2 = 5.61, P < .025, \gamma = .10$	

*Subsample included only white, nonsouthern urban respondents.
†Census definition.

TABLE 2

Regression of Localism Items on Individual, Contextual, and Suburban
Variables (NORC, $N \approx 2,000$)[a]

| | | PARTIAL CORRELATIONS CONTROLLING FOR: | | |
| | | | And | |
	Zero-Order r	Individual Traits	Contextual Traits	Final Equation β
Neighboring scale:				
Contextual variables	...	.079*	...	...
City/suburb	.118**	.064**	.049*	.052*
(Total R^2)	...	(.098)	(.103)	(.105)
Localization of ties:				
Contextual variables	...	.097*	...	...
City/suburb	.034	.040	.046*	.051*
(Total R^2)	...	(.034)	(.043)	(.045)
Interest: attend neighborhood meetings:				
Contextual variables	...	.079*	...	...
City/suburb	.105**	.053*	.054*	.058*
(Total R^2)	...	(.078)	(.084)	(.087)

[a]Variable definitions are: (1) *dependent variables:* "neighboring scale," composed of the three neighboring items
listed in table 1; "localization of ties" and "attend meetings" are single items listed in table 1; (2) *individual traits:* age, sex,
education, occupational status of household head, family income, ethnicity (dummy), religion (two dummy variables),
degree of child dependency, years in the neighborhood, house vs. apartment, estimated number of cars in household,
whether woman of house works; (3) *contextual variables:* degree of racial integration, respondent's estimate of proportion of
neighborhood which is same religion as he or she, neighborhood variability in religion, education, and income (calculated by
NORC); (4) *suburbanism:* central city vs. suburb (census definition).
*$P < .05$.
**$P < .01$.

we used a long, conservative list of individual traits, including two—apartment versus house and car ownership—which might be more liberally interpreted as consequences of suburban residence itself. The contextual measures
reflect racial, religious, and social class composition (see footnotes to table 2
for details). Table 2 presents a summary of the results.

The first column provides the zero-order correlation between suburban
residence and each localism measure; the second provides the fifteenth-order
partial correlations for both the contextual variables (a multiple partial correlation) and city-suburban residence; and the third provides the suburban
partial correlation after controlling for the five contextual variables. The last
column indicates the partial standardized regression coefficient for suburb in
the final, 21-variable equation.

The statistics in table 2 indicate that no factor explained very much of the
variance in the dependent items; individual traits explained by far the highest proportion (the house-apartment distinction is critical); there remained

statistically significant but quite small effects of context and of suburb after individual controls; and there was a similarly small effect of suburbanism after controls for neighborhood context. In sum, the effects predicted by both the contextual model and the distance-cost model were, with regard to the sample as a whole, real but small.

However, this finding was partly anticipated in our discussion of the homeostatic processes which operate to nullify the effects of distance. Anticipations and adjustments to the unanticipated permit most people to maintain their desired styles of behavior. Therefore, we turned our attention to an examination of suburban effects within subgroups.

Specifications

It was expected that social class would interact with suburbanism, but the nature of that interaction was not expected. We found that the higher the educational level of the respondent, the greater the city-suburb differences. Among those with less than a high school diploma, suburban effects were nonexistent or contradictory; among the college-educated, they were quite strong. For example, among the former, the city-suburb dummy variable correlated .024 with reporting that most friends were in the neighborhood; among the latter, the correlation was .189. This result was suprising in that persons of higher social class should presumably be freer of locational constraints and thus be less affected by suburbanism.

One explanation of these results[20] is that self-selection can operate more effectively among the better-off than among those of lower status. That is, because of their greater freedom of choice, the well-to-do can reside in locations more consonant with their needs (e.g., raising children) and desires (e.g., owning a single-family home). This self-selection makes more likely a spurious association between place and behavior (spurious because it is due to background needs and desires) than is the case among those with less choice (see Evans 1973). There is some evidence to support this explanation. The associations between suburbanism and having young children, a single-family home, a nonworking wife, and a racially and economically homogeneous neighborhood all increased with respondents' education.[21] The consequence of statistically controlling for these background variables (by regres-

---

[20] Suggested by Kathleen Gerson.

[21] The correlations between suburban residence and these variables are, for those with less than a high school diploma and for those with a college diploma, respectively: having young children (.072, .219), living in a house (.271, .439), being or having a nonworking wife (−.055, .217), living in a white neighborhood (.114, .314), and living in an economically homogeneous neighborhood (.056, .256).

sions run within educational levels) was to eliminate the suburbanism ×
education interaction, leaving small suburban localism effects at each level
of education.[22]

The effects of distance on social networks should, according to the distance-cost model, be greatest for those with the fewest alternative bases of
association which might permit them (at least partly) to transcend constraints of distance. Kinship and workplace ties provide such alternatives.
Presumably, the smaller the extent of individuals' involvement in these sorts
of networks, the more they will be subject to ecological forces. There is
support for this argument in the data.

Table 3 presents the results of regression analyses similar to those reported in table 2 but run within subgroups. The zero-order and the final partial
correlations[23] of city-suburban residence with the localism items are displayed.

On each localism item, the respondents who were not much involved
with their relatives evidenced greater city-suburb differences than did those
who were. When 15 individual and five contextual traits were controlled,
this pattern was weakened but persisted, particularly in regard to neighborhood concentration of friends.

Similarly, when female respondents who worked or males whose wives
worked were contrasted with respondents in families with a housewife, it
was the latter who displayed suburban effects before and after controls,
particularly in neighboring. Thus, the fewer the nonresidential bases of
association available to an individual, the greater the influence of ecological
factors, specifically of suburbanism, in encouraging localism.

Our theoretical argument also generates the expectation that individuals
most "rooted" to their residences should most evidence city-suburb effects.
We find, in table 3, that house dwellers tended to be more "localized" by
suburban residence than were apartment dwellers. And the elderly were more
affected by suburbanism than was the rest of the population (data not
shown). An anomaly arose, however, when we considered the effect of
having children. As indicated in table 3, it was those respondents *without*
young children who consistently showed higher associations between subur-

---

[22] Another unexpected interaction which we discovered was suburbanism × sex. Contrary to
published research, males showed more city-suburb differences than did females, particularly
on the question regarding the proportion of friends reported to be living in the neighborhood
($r = .24$ for males, .01 for females). This was not due to the difference between workers and
housewives, because the sex interaction appeared for both employed and nonemployed respondents. We have not as yet pursued this finding.

[23] The unstandardized regression coefficients were examined and exhibit the same patterns as
the partial correlation coefficients.

TABLE 3

ZERO-ORDER AND PARTIAL ASSOCIATIONS OF LOCALISM ITEMS WITH SUBURBANISM WITHIN LEVELS OF SPECIFYING VARIABLES (NORC)[a]

SPECIFICATIONS	NEIGHBORING SCALE		LOCALIZATION OF TIES		ATTEND MEETINGS	
	r	Partial[b]	r	Partial	r	Partial
Sees kin frequently[c]	.091**	.040	−.012	.010	.083**	.060
Does not	.150**	.068	.085**	.084**	.128**	.050
Woman works	.042	.004	.028	.032	.016	.004
Does not	.162**	.077*	.027	.047	.148**	.082**
Apartment	.051	.060	−.032	−.020	−.039	.005
House	.130**	.027	.031	.072**	.102**	.060*
Has child under 12	.090**	.029	−.022	.006	.078*	.035
Does not	.105**	.063*	.063*	.080**	.100**	.070*

[a] Dependent variables are defined in footnotes to table 2.
[b] The variables used as controls are also listed in the notes to table 2. The specifying variable was of course excluded in those regressions.
[c] "Frequently" was defined as seeing any of the following sets of relatives once a week or more: parents, parents-in-law, siblings, siblings-in-law.
*P < .05.
**P < .01

banism and localism. One explanation which has some empirical support for this unanticipated interaction is that young children are such a "localizing" influence that all families, city and suburban, become neighborly. It is only among those with less responsibility that the delocalizing effect of city residence is possible. (Thus, among city dwellers, having young children discriminated those who neighbored highly from those who did not [partial $\beta = .126$, $P = .015$]; among suburban dwellers, it did not discriminate [partial $\beta = .064$, N.S.]. A similar difference appeared in the second survey we analyzed.)

In sum, results from analysis of the NORC survey indicate that suburbanites are more "localized" than city residents, largely because of individual differences, partly because of contextual differences, and slightly because of differences in ecological locations. The latter effect is especially evident within particular subgroups.

STUDY 2: DAS

The second survey we analyzed was the Detroit Area Study (DAS) of 1965–66, directed by Howard Schuman and Edward Laumann.[24] A number of reports on these data have been published, the most complete being Laumann's (1973), which includes the questionnaire and full sampling information. The survey was a multistage probability sample of dwelling units in the Detroit SMSA. Respondents were white males age 21–64, native- or Canadian-born, who were members of primary families. Actual interviews numbered 985, which were weighted to obtain an N of 1,013. To this data set we added information about respondents' census tracts, including statistics on distance and access.[25]

The advantage of this survey for our purposes is that it focused in detail on the male friendships of the respondents. Each was asked to name "the three men who are your closest friends and whom you see most often. They can be relatives or non-relatives."[26] Later questions asked the respondents to describe the social characteristics of their friends and the qualities of their relationships. The disadvantages of this survey for our purpose are the

[24] We wish to thank Professors Schuman and Laumann and the DAS for permission to use the data and for graciously answering our frequent queries.

[25] Ann Stueve was instrumental in collecting the census material and helping prepare this data set.

[26] A problem exists in these data as a result of the investigators' desire to analyze separately each respondent's closest brother and brother-in-law. "Best friends" who fit these categories were dropped from and replaced in the "three best friends" list. These friends would be best considered as "three best male friends other than closest brother and brother-in-law."

limited number of localism items and the restriction of the sample to a particularly mobile sector of the population: white males of labor force age.

Table 4 presents, first, the lone item in the DAS survey on neighboring. The association between suburbanism and reported involvement with neighbors was in the usual direction, but the differences were small.

Among the questions asked about friends was whether "any of the men live in this neighborhood—say, within 10 minutes of here—or do they live somewhere else in the Detroit area, or outside of the area?" Table 4 presents in different forms the cross-tabulation of friends' locations by respondents' locations. The general results support the hypothesis that friendships are more localized in the suburbs. In addition, there are indications that distance is the key to the pattern. When we categorized friends by whether or not they were seen "regularly where you work—that is, at least once or twice a week," we discovered that it was only among friends *not* seen at work that the suburban localization pattern appeared. It is presumably the nonwork friends for whom distance to an individual's home is critical. The final item, on the frequency with which respondents "get together" with their friends, provides similar evidence, though again via small differences, that the effect of suburbanism on social interaction operates through distance. Suburban residence was unrelated to frequency of contact with neighborhood friends but seems to have slightly retarded seeing friends who resided elsewhere in the Detroit area. Though the associations were not very strong in support of the distance-cost model, they do refute one of the alternative models of suburbia (model 4)—that suburbanites are metropolitan and cosmopolitan, while city residents are "urban villagers."[27]

Multiple Regression

By merging data on respondents' census tracts with the survey, we were able to examine the relative impact on the localism items of various contextual variables (as measured six years earlier) and various ecological ones. The best

[27] Three comments are in order: (1) Friendship ties are but one sort of relationship. Though these, we argue, are the ones most susceptible to distance effects, it is interesting to note comparable though nonsignificant trends for kin ties. The appropriate percentages of brother in the neighborhood are 35, 38, and 42; of brothers-in-law, 26, 32, and 34. (2) Neighborhood was defined as a 10-minute radius by the interviewers. One explanation of the findings might be that suburbanites can encompass more population in 10 minutes than can city dwellers. This is unlikely both because of differential housing density (correlated across respondents with zone at −.66) and because it is probable that relatively few respondents lacked automobiles. Though the number of cars was not asked, the sample is composed of white males of labor force age in a city with one of the highest car-to-household ratios in the nation. (3) Finally, there is no relationship between suburbanism and total number of friends ($r = -.012$).

TABLE 4

RESPONSES TO LOCALISM ITEMS, BY PLACE OF RESIDENCE (DAS)*

	Detroit†	Inner Suburbs	Outer Suburbs
Neighboring:			
Which of the following would best describe the relations you have with your several nearest neighbors?			
% often visit in home	7	15	14
% frequently chat in yard, street	41	36	39
% occasionally chat	36	36	35
% hardly know neighbors	16	13	13
(N of respondents)	(350)	(309)	(344)
		$\chi^2 = 11.92, P = .06, \gamma = .08$	
Localization of ties:			
Residence of three best male friends:‡			
% neighborhood	37	45	46
% elsewhere in SMSA	47	42	45
% outside SMSA	16	13	9
(N of friends)	(1,030)	(897)	(1,001)
		$\Sigma\chi^2 = 34.53, 12$ df, $P < .005, \bar{\gamma} = .13$§	
Including only friends in SMSA . . . :			
% neighborhood	44	51	50
(N of friends)	(865)	(781)	(909)
		$\Sigma\chi^2 = 13.24, 6$ df, $P < .05, \bar{\gamma} = .09$	
And seen at work:			
% neighborhood	34	36	37
(N of friends)	(259)	(238)	(290)
		$\Sigma\chi^2 = 3.15, 6$ df, $P < .50, \bar{\gamma} = -.05$	
And not seen at work:			
% neighborhood	48	58	57
(N of friends)	(606)	(543)	(619)
		$\Sigma\chi^2 = 14.79, 6$ df, $P < .05, \gamma = .12$	
Number of best friends in neighborhoods:‖			
% none	36	29	25
% one	32	28	35
% two, three	32	43	41
(N of respondents)	(348)	(303)	(341)
		$\chi^2 = 16.38, P < .01, \gamma = .14$	
All in all, how often do you usually get together with best friend (outside of work)?			
Of friends in neighborhood:			
% once a week plus	59	56	57
(N of friends)	(375)	(401)	(458)
		$\Sigma\chi^2 = 5.53, 6$ df, $P < .50, \bar{\gamma} = -.02$	
Of friends elsewhere in Detroit SMSA:			
% once a week plus	38	35	31
(N of friends)	(485)	(379)	(448)
		$\Sigma\chi^2 = 10.79, 6$ df, $P < .10, \bar{\gamma} = -.11$	

*Includes only white males 21–64 born in North America and members of primary families.
†"Detroit" includes two municipalities surrounded entirely by the city. "Inner suburbs" are contiguous to Detroit; "outer suburbs" do not share a border with Detroit. Rural areas of the Detroit SMSA were not sampled.
‡Specific question is quoted in text.
§Statistics represent summated χ^2 and averaged (weighted) γ's across separate tables run for each of three friends (categorized by order listed).
‖ This table excludes respondents with fewer than two best friends.

predictors among the contextual variables were the median income of families and unrelated individuals and the proportion of the population under 18—presumably indicative of the child-rearing stage in the life cycle. (Efforts to use homogeneity measures have not yet borne fruitful results.) In developing ecological measures, we sought to include all the variables suggested in the literature as distinctive of suburbs (recency of housing development, recency of arrival of the resident population, housing-unit density, and room density) as well as distance-access variables (concentric zone, distance from the Detroit central business district [CBD], distance from the nearest commercial subnuclei, and distance from the nearest major highway). Many of these variables were, of course, highly correlated. Of them, a three-variable set—zone, distance to CBD, and distance to subnuclei—seemed both to work best and to capture best the locational variable which defines suburbanism in the distance-cost model.[28]

Table 5 presents some of the results obtained in the multiple-regression analysis. (The equations employed here were simplified from larger models.) The degree to which respondents reported interacting with their neighbors was correlated with contextual variables and with suburbanism. These associations were not explained by individual traits but instead largely by the income level of the tract. In fact, that contextual variable was a better predictor than any individual trait variable, including age, number of children, and years in the neighborhood. (Gates, Stevens, and Wellman [1973] report that in their Toronto survey neighborhood social status affected the neighboring of males but not females.)

The second item, proportion of best friends (excluding those seen regularly at work) who live in the neighborhood, was also related to contextual and suburban variables. Again, the associations were not spuriously due to individual traits. Both tract income and tract youthfulness were positively related to localized friendships. The ecological variables also added a statistically significant amount to the explained variance, but the nature of their association was complex. The significant and opposite β's for zone and distance seem to indicate a complex function reflecting partly the discontinuous effect of zonal differences shown in table 4 (the shift at the Detroit city line) and a gradual tapering off of localization as distance became very large.

The third item, frequency of "getting together" with best friends, showed a persisting and statistically significant effect of distance from the CBD. The farther from the center of Detroit a respondent lived, the less frequent-

---

[28] An exception to this statement is housing-unit density, a variable which correlated slightly more highly with neighboring than did distance to the CBD. These two ecological variables correlated with each other, however, at $-.67$, making them somewhat redundant. In any case, it does appear that housing-unit density independently reduces reports of neighboring though not of other social activities (Baldassare 1975).

TABLE 5

REGRESSION OF LOCALISM ITEMS ON INDIVIDUAL, CONTEXTUAL, AND
ECOLOGICAL VARIABLES (DAS, $N \approx 900$)[a]

| | | PARTIAL CORRELATIONS CONTROLLING FOR: | | |
	Zero-Order r	Individual Traits	And Contextual Traits	Final Partial β's
Knowing neighbors:				
Contextual variables, 1960:				
Tract income	.167**	.158**	. . .	.152**
Tract youth	.089**	.088*	. . .	.049
Ecological variables:				
Zone	.088**	.088*	−.005	−.010
Miles to CBD	.119**	.116**	.005	.007
Miles to subnuclei	.038	.044	.019	.018
(Total R^2)	. . .	(.049)	(.075)	(.075)
% friends in neighborhood:				
Contextual variables, 1960:				
Tract income	.038	.073*	. . .	.083
Tract youth	.095**	.110**	. . .	.106*
Ecological variables:				
Zone	.097**	.108**	.037	.145*
Miles to CBD	.039	.061	−.044	−.183*
Miles to subnuclei	.036	.030	.016	.044
(Total R^2)	. . .	(.059)	(.072)	(.081)
Frequency of "get together":				
Contextual variables, 1960:				
Tract income	−.083*	−.036	. . .	.016
Tract youth	.000	.030	. . .	.112*
Ecological variables:				
Zone	−.039	−.016	−.033	.068
Miles to CBD	−.088**	−.055	−.087**	−.217**
Miles to subnuclei	.055	.060	.065*	.097**
(Total R^2)	. . .	(.085)	(.088)	(.104)

[a]Variable definitions are: (1) *dependent variables:* "knowing neighbors" = how much respondent interacts with neighbors, four-point scale, low to high; "% friends in neighborhood" = proportion of "best friends" other than those seen regularly at work who live in the neighborhood; "frequency of 'get together' " = sum of six-point response scale for each "best friend" on frequency with which respondent "gets together" with him, only for those who report three "best friends"; (2) *individual trait variables:* age, number of children at home, whether wife probably works (had to be constructed from indirect indices), occupational prestige, ethnoreligiosity (six dummy variables), and years in neighborhood; (3) *contextual variables:* median income of tract and proportion of tract population under 18 as of 1960; (4) *ecological variables:* urban zone (inner Detroit, outer Detroit, inner suburbs, outer suburbs); distance in half-miles to CBD; distance to nearest of five subnuclei: CBDs of Detroit, Dearborn, Warren, Pontiac, Royal Oak.
*P < .05.
**P < .01.

ly he reported seeing his best friends. (Controlling for the number of friends who lived in the neighborhood added 8% to the explained variance but did not otherwise alter the results.)

The results from the DAS survey lead us to attribute suburban neighboring to the affluence of suburban neighborhoods. But the localization of friendship ties is, to a small extent, a result of suburban location itself.

Specifications

The suburbanism $\times$ education interaction found in the NORC survey was marginally replicated here. What is of greater interest is that, in this data set, the social class context of the neighborhood seemed to explain the slight interaction. When the median income of the respondent's tract was controlled, the interaction was largely canceled. The final partial correlations of suburbanism with the dependent variables, controlling for individual and contextual variables, suggest the following conclusions. (1) Neighboring was encouraged by suburban residence among those who did not complete high school (partial r with zone was .137, $P < .05$) but slightly discouraged among those with at least some college education (partial r was $-.076$). (2) Localization of friends was affected by ecological factors among the less educated but showed a complex pattern (largely negative; the partial r with distance was $-.078$). The college-educated, however, evidenced a simple, small effect of localization of friends (partial r with zone was .084). (3) The frequency of "getting together" was most depressed by suburbanism among the middle group, those who completed high school (partial r with zone was $-.122$, $P < .01$; with distance, $-.226$, $P < .01$). In both the NORC and the DAS data, therefore, the unexpected interaction with education, in which the more educated appeared more affected by suburbanism, seems explainable by self-selection and contextual effects. For these Detroit males, it was the more educated whose local involvement was most influenced by the affluence of their neighbors.

Examination of the DAS data for theoretically relevant specifications was difficult because of both the nature of the sample and the selection of questions asked.[29] Nevertheless, some findings should be noted. As the results presented in table 4 indicate, when interpersonal associations based elsewhere than the home were controlled (i.e., excluding from the analysis friends who were seen at work), the effect of suburbanism was increased. Results in the table also indicate the effect of distance in the contrast between frequency of contact with neighborhood friends and frequency of contact with friends elsewhere in the Detroit area. It was the latter contact which was more affected by suburbanism.

We examined the data for other interactions, running the full regression model displayed in table 5 within levels of specifying variables. The results were by no means clear-cut, but it appears that suburbanism did have its

---

[29] For example, 90% of the respondents lived in single-family homes. And the questionnaire did not directly ask whether respondent's wife worked.

greatest effects among those with the least ability to overcome distance. For the older respondents (here, 55–64, $N = 151$), distance from the CBD had a uniformly negative effect, slightly reducing neighboring (partial $r = -.061$), reducing the proportion of friends in the neighborhood (partial $r = -.205$, $P < .05$), and reducing. frequency of contact (partial $r = -.204$, $P < .05$). This appears to indicate the syndrome of suburban isolation. (That is, relatively speaking, they neither saw extralocal friends nor neighbored to compensate; cf. Carp 1975; Bourg 1975.) Another vulnerable group, those living in low-income tracts (of less than $5,500 median income, $N \approx 100$), also showed major effects of suburbanism: residents of such neighborhoods in outlying zones reported more concentration of best friends (partial r with zone $= .199$, $P < .05$) and a lower frequency of contact (partial r with distance $= -.214$, $P < .05$). This pattern of results seems to indicate both the loss resulting from, and the coping mechanisms for, suburban residence.

The DAS survey provides findings that are hardly dramatic. But, as with the NORC data, the pattern of effects, if not their size, implies that suburban context and suburban location contribute to a localization of social networks.

DISCUSSION

The data analyses presented in the last two sections are not meant to be definitive tests of the models of suburbanism we discussed earlier. The analyses could not be conclusive, based as they were on samples and questions designed for other purposes. Rather, they represent additional bits of research to be placed in the balance with others when the empirical value of those alternative theories is weighed.

One pervasive discovery in the present data was that the effects and differences attributable to suburban residence, whether zero order or highly partialed, whether statistically significant or not, tended to be relatively small. This was not always the case—for instance, among the Detroit men over 55, distance from the CBD contributed over one-fourth of the explained variance in frequency of seeing best friends, more than any other individual or contextual variable—but was usually so. At first glance, one is tempted to dismiss ecological variables in general and suburbanism in particular as having real (i.e., nonrandom) effects but ones of no important consequence. We present here a few considerations to check that temptation.

There are various causes of small effects in addition to the possibility that they accurately reflect empirical reality. The independent variables may be poorly indexed (e.g., the city-suburb dichotomy in the NORC data) or the dependent variables insufficiently developed (e.g., the lone neighboring item in the DAS). Also, the use of a gross distinction rather than finer ones sacrifices explanatory power (e.g., using "suburb" instead of types of suburbs). All this considered, it is still probably the case that contextual variables—whether ecological or of population traits—in general produce small effects when those effects are measured in terms of the amount of interindividual variation in behavior they account for and when they are compared with the variation accounted for by individual traits. It is this standard, one by which contextual and ecological variables are often discounted, which we shall address.

1. The determination of substantive importance depends, of course, on the questions asked. If that question seeks the set of variables which most efficiently explains individual differences, then those factors which produce relatively small effects should be dismissed. If, however, the question seeks the consequences of specific independent variables, as is the case here, then the fact that other indicators are better predictors is of little relevance.

2. It is hardly surprising that individual differences in behavior are more effectively explained by individual differences in personally intimate and long-standing characteristics—age, sex, race, ethnicity, education, number of children, etc.—than they are by global environmental variables. In a sense, such individual and contextual variables form two separate and noncomparable classes; to judge one by the other seems inappropriate.

3. Another distinction between these classes of variables, individual versus contextual, has implications for assessing practical significance. One criterion of the importance of a variable is its malleability. Ascribed characteristics such as sex and ethnicity may predict behavior quite well but be difficult to alter. Even achieved statuses such as income level may be extremely difficult for an individual to change (at least upwardly). However, certain ecological variables, such as neighborhood type or city versus suburb, though of relatively low explanatory power, may be of relatively high malleability for individuals and/or societies.

4. Contextual variables also have the property of affecting aggregated rather than dispersed individuals. While it may be that the average suburban individual is "localized" only to a minute degree by his or her ecological location, the suburban community as a whole is composed of a group of such individuals. The cumulation of small individual effects in one place can have larger consequences at the aggregate level, for example, in the election of representatives hostile to metropolitan government. This phenomenon is the other side of the "ecological fallacy" coin. While ecological correlations can underestimate individual variability, individual correlations can underestimate aggregate differences.

5. Most importantly, contextual variables of the sort treated here call forth anticipatory and adaptive homeostatic processes which operate to negate, or at least obscure, simple determinative consequences of those envi-

ronmental factors. For example, it is partly because people anticipate neighborhood contextual effects that they seek localities populated by persons similar to themselves. And it is in part because suburban residence is inconvenient for reaching people and places that efforts are made to extend roads or build commuter railways. These processes operate well for most persons and communities (at least in this society) because they have sufficient freedom of choice to fulfill their expectations and sufficient resources to adjust to the unexpected. The mitigation of simple determinative effects by such homeostatic processes means that one observes the consequences of contextual variables mostly in indirect fashion. The distance cost of suburbanization is revealed not so much by the loss of customers for center-city business and their consequent bankruptcy as by the enterprises' moves to the suburbs (e.g., shopping malls and sports complexes), not so much by the isolation of housewives as by the purchase of a second car.

Most ecological factors, as well as most contextual ones, are important far less as causal "forces" impinging on individual behavior than as contingencies for the choices individuals make (based on preferences "caused" by individual traits). Given general freedom of choice, the ecological factors will be manifested directly only in marginal ways and cases. It is these sorts of marginal manifestations which our data revealed.

These comments are not designed to reinterpret small city-suburb differences into large ones but, rather, to suggest a perspective for evaluating them. Suburban effects, by and large, are quite small. If one would seek to encourage neighboring, for example, increasing suburbanization would be highly inefficient (it would be more effective to increase family income). Nevertheless, according to our data and to previous research, suburban effects are real, particularly for certain groups.

Suburbanites tend to be more involved in their localities and with their neighbors than are city residents. When not involved locally, they are more isolated than city residents. This is particularly so for persons who have restricted social circles, limited mobility, and/or specialized needs. This difference between city and suburb, no matter what the explanation for it is, has consequences for communities as wholes, moving them in a localized, neighborly direction.

The difference between city and suburb is explained greatly by self-selection. (Here, we refer to model 2, the individual traits model.) People with certain characteristics—education, affluence, a housewife, home ownership, children to rear—show up in the suburbs; these are characteristics which encourage local involvement. We saw that neighboring as a consequence of self-selection is particularly evident among those with the greatest freedom of choice.

In addition, the city-suburb difference is due to contextual effects which result from such self-selection (model 3). Because suburbs congregate populations of certain types, individual suburbanites are influenced in the directions characteristic of those types. One direction is localism. So, for example, the affluence of a neighborhood encourages individual neighboring as strongly as do most individual traits.

Finally, the very nature of the suburb as an outlying subarea of the metropolis contributes, at least marginally and for at least some groups, to localized social ties and interests (model 5).

These effects are, we repeat, small. Particular individuals are not likely to change dramatically if they move from city to suburb (though they are likely to change noticeably, according to Michelson's [1973b] research). Other variables, some more easily controlled than others, are of far more consequence to people. However, we should not allow small individual differences to mislead us about potentially significant community effects. As American society continues to suburbanize, a larger proportion of its population shifts from a city to suburban location and social context. Slight as the effects might be on each person, the balance moves increasingly, for better or for worse, from urban ways of life to suburban ones. That changing balance produces, for example, structural changes which make it easier to become a suburbanite and more difficult to remain in the center—highway construction, dispersal of jobs and businesses, decline of cheap mass transit, and so on.

Greer ([1962] 1972, p. 63) has observed that "the culture of the suburb is remarkably similar to that of the country towns in an earlier America." In neighboring and localism, as well as in other ways, small towns and suburbs are alike. In that sense, the increasing suburbanization of America may mean, in part, the deurbanization of America.

REFERENCES

Abu-Lughod, J., and M. M. Foley. 1960. "The Consumer Votes by Moving" and "Consumer Preferences: The City versus the Suburb." Pp. 134–214 in *Choices and Housing Constraints,* edited by N. N. Foote, J. Abu-Lughod, M. M. Foley, and L. Winnick. New York: McGraw-Hill.

Athanasiou, R., and G. A. Yoshioka. 1973. "The Spatial Character of Friendship Formation." *Environment and Behavior* 5 (March): 43–66.

Baldassare, M. 1975. "The Effects of Density on Social Behavior and Attitudes." *American Behavioral Scientist* 18 (July–August): 815–25.

Baldassare, M., and C. S. Fischer. 1975. "Suburban Life: Powerlessness and Need for Affiliation." *Urban Affairs Quarterly* 10 (March): 314–26.

Bell, W. 1958. "Social Choice, Life Styles, and Suburban Residence." Pp. 225–47 in *The Suburban Community,* edited by W. M. Dobriner. New York: Putnam's.

Berger, B. M. 1960. *Working-Class Suburb.* Berkeley: University of California Press.

Black, G. S. 1974. "Conflict in the Community: A Theory of the Effects of Community Size." *American Political Science Review* 68 (September): 1245–61.

Bourg, C. J. 1975. "Elderly in a Southern Metropolitan Area." *Gerontologist* 15 (February): 15–22.

Bradburn, N. M., S. Sudman, and G. L. Gockel. 1970. *Racial Integration in American Neighborhoods: A Comparative Study.* NORC Report no. 111-B. Chicago: National Opinion Research Center.

Butler, E. W., et al. 1968. *Moving Behavior and Residential Choice: A National Survey.* Chapel Hill, N.C.: Center for Urban and Regional Studies.

Campbell, A. 1971. *White Attitudes toward Black People.* Ann Arbor, Mich.: Institute for Social Research.

Carp, F. M. 1975. "Life-Style and Location within the City." *Gerontologist* 15 (February): 27–33.

Carrothers, G. A. P. 1956. "An Historical Review of the Gravity and Potential Concepts of Human Interaction." *Journal of American Institute of Planners* 22 (Spring): 94–102.

Clark, S. D. 1966. *The Suburban Society.* Toronto: University of Toronto Press.

Cole, L. M. 1972. "Suburban Mobility: Present Trends and Future Transportation Requirements." Pp. 65–72 in *The End of Innocence: A Suburban Reader,* edited by C. M. Haar. Glenview, Ill.: Scott Foresman.

Cooper, C. C. 1972 "Resident Dissatisfaction in Multi-Family Housing." Pp. 119–45 in *Behavior, Design, and Policy Aspects,* edited by W. M. Smith. Green Bay: University of Wisconsin Press.

Cornelius, W. A. 1973. *Political Learning among the Migrant Poor: The Impact of Residential Context.* Sage Professional Paper in Comparative Politics 01-037. Beverly Hills, Calif.: Sage.

Cox, K. 1969. "The Spatial Structure of Information Flow and Partisan Attitudes." Pp. 157–86 in *Social Ecology,* edited by M. Dogan and S. Rokkan. Cambridge, Mass.: M.I.T. Press.

Dobriner, W. M. 1963. *Class in Suburbia.* Englewood Cliffs, N.J.: Prentice-Hall.

Donaldson, S. 1969. *The Suburban Myth.* New York: Columbia University Press.

Evans, A. W. 1973. *The Economics of Residential Location.* London: Macmillan.

Fava, S. F. 1958. "Contrasts in Neighboring: New York City and a Suburban County." Pp. 122–30 in *The Suburban Community,* edited by W. M. Dobriner. New York: Putnam's.

Fine, J., N. D. Glenn, and J. K. Monts. 1971. "The Residential Segregation of Occupational Groups in Central Cities and Suburbs." *Demography* 8 (February): 91–101.

Fischer, C. S. 1972. "'Urbanism as a Way of Life': A Review and an Agenda." *Sociological Methods and Research* 1 (November): 187–242.

———. 1973. "On Urban Alienations and Anomie: Powerlessness and Social Isolation." *American Sociological Review* 38 (June): 311–26.

———, 1975a. "Toward a Subcultural Theory of Urbanism." *American Journal of Sociology* 80 (May): 1319–41.

———. 1975b. "The City and Political Psychology." *American Political Science Review,* vol. 69 (June): 559–71.

Forrest, J. 1974. "Spatial Aspects of Urban Social Travel." *Urban Studies* 11 (October): 301–13.

Gans, H. J. 1967. *The Levittowners: Ways of Life and Politics in a New Suburban Community.* New York: Random House.

Gates, A. S., H. Stevens, and B. Wellman. 1973. "What Makes a 'Good Neighbor'?" Paper presented at the annual meeting of the American Sociological Association, New York, August.

Gillespie, D. L. 1971. "Who Has the Power? The Marital Struggle." *Journal of Marriage and the Family* 33 (August): 445–58.

Greer, S. (1962) 1972. "Dispersion and the Culture of Urban Man." Pp. 55–67 in *The Urbane View.* New York: Oxford University Press.

———. 1963. *Metropolitics.* New York: Wiley.

———. 1967. "Postscripts: Communication and Community." Pp. 245–70 in *The Community Press in an Urban Setting,* by M. Janowitz. 2d ed. Chicago: University of Chicago Press.

Fischer and Jackson

Greer, S., and E. Kube. (1959) 1972. "Urbanism and Social Structure: A Los Angeles Study." Pp. 34–54 in *The Urbane View*, edited by S. Greer. New York: Oxford University Press.

Greer, S., and P. Orleans. 1962. "The Mass Society and the Parapolitical Structure." *American Sociological Review* 27 (October): 643–46.

Guest, A. M. 1972. "Patterns of Family Location." *Demography* 9 (February): 159–71.

Hawley, A. H. 1971. *The Urban Society*. New York: Ronald.

Hawley, A. H., and B. G. Zimmer. 1970. *The Metropolitan Community: Its People and Government*. Beverly Hills, Calif.: Sage.

Jones, L. M. 1974. "The Labor Force Participation of Married Women." Master's thesis, University of California, Berkeley.

Kasarda, J. D. 1976. "The Changing Structure of Metropolitan America." Pp. 113–36 in *The Changing Face of the Suburbs*, edited by B. Schwartz. Chicago: University of Chicago Press.

Kasarda, J. D., and M. Janowitz. 1974. "Community Attachment in Mass Society." *American Sociological Review* 39 (June): 328–39.

Lansing, J. B., and G. Hedricks. 1967. *Living Patterns and Attitudes in the Detroit Region*. Report of the Detroit Regional Transportation Land Use Study. Detroit: Southeast Michigan Council of Governments.

Lansing, J. B., and E. Mueller. 1964. *Residential Location and Urban Mobility*. Ann Arbor: University of Michigan Survey Research Center.

Laumann, E. O. 1966. *Prestige and Association in an Urban Community*. Indianapolis: Bobbs-Merrill.

———. 1973. *Bonds of Pluralism*. New York: Wiley.

Lopata, H. Z. 1972. *Occupation: Housewife*. New York: Oxford University Press.

McGahan, P. 1973. "Urban Neighboring and the Hypothesis of Alternative Social Structures." Paper presented at the annual meeting of the American Sociological Association, New York, August.

Marans, R. W., and W. Rodgers. 1974. "Toward an Understanding of Community Satisfaction." Pp. 311–76 in *Metropolitan America: Papers on the State of Knowledge*, edited by A. H. Hawley and V. Rock. Washington, D.C.: National Academy of Sciences.

Marshall, H. 1973. "Suburban Life Styles: A Contribution to the Debate." Pp.123–48 in *The Urbanization of the Suburbs*, edited by L. H. Masotti and J. K. Hadden. Urban Affairs Annual Reviews, vol. 7. Beverly Hills, Calif.: Sage.

Martin, W. T. 1958. "The Structuring of Social Relationships Engendered by Suburban Residence." Pp. 95–103 in *The Suburban Community*, edited by W. M. Dobriner. New York: Putnam's.

Michelson, W. 1973a. "The Reconciliation of 'Subjective' and 'Objective' Data on Physical Environment in the Community." *Sociological Inquiry* 43 (3–4): 147–73.

———. 1973b. "Environmental Change." Interim Report. Research Paper no. 60. Toronto: Centre for Urban and Community Studies, University of Toronto.

Michelson, W., D. Belgue, and J. Stewart. 1973. "Intentions and Expectations in Differential Residential Selection." *Journal of Marriage and the Family* 35 (July): 189–96.

Perlman, J. 1975. *The Myth of Marginality: Migrants to Rio's Favelas*. Berkeley: University of California Press.

Prewitt, K., and H. Eulau. 1969. "Political Matrix and Political Representation." *American Political Science Review* 63 (June): 427–41.

Reimer, S., and J. McNamara. 1957. "Contact Patterns in the City." *Social Forces* 36 (December): 137–40.

Riesman, D. 1958. "The Suburban Sadness." Pp. 375–408 in *The Suburban Community*, edited by W. M. Dobriner. New York: Putnam's.

Roberts, B. R. 1973. *Organizing Strangers: Poor Families in Guatemala City*. Austin: University of Texas Press.

Roistacher, R. C. 1974. "A Microeconomic Model of Sociometric Choice." *Sociometry* 37 (June): 219–38.

Rossi, P. H. 1955. *Why Families Move.* Glencoe, Ill.: Free Press.

Simmons, J. W. 1968. "Changing Residence in the City." *Geographical Review* 58 (October): 622–51.

Smith, J., W. H. Form, and G. P. Stone. 1954. "Local Intimacy in a Middle-sized City." *American Journal of Sociology* 60 (November): 276–84.

Stegman, M. A. 1969. "Accessibility Models and Residential Location." *Journal of American Institute of Planners* 35 (January): 22–29.

Stewart, J. Q. 1948. "Demographic Gravitation: Evidence and Applications." *Sociometry* 11 (March): 31–58.

Stutz, F. P. 1973. "Distance and Network Effects on Urban Social Travel Fields." *Economic Geography* 49 (April): 134–44.

Sutcliffe, J. P., and B. D. Crabbe. 1963. "Incidence and Degrees of Friendship in Urban and Rural Areas." *Social Forces* 42 (October): 60–67.

Tallman, I. 1969. "Working-Class Wives in Suburbia: Fulfillment or Crises?" *Journal of Marriage and the Family* 31 (February): 65–72.

Tallman, I., and R. Morgner. 1970. "Life-Style Differences among Urban and Suburban Blue-Collar Families." *Social Forces* 48 (March): 334–48.

Tarr, J. A. 1973. "From City to Suburb: The 'Moral' Influence of Transportation and Technology." Pp. 202–12 in *American Urban History,* edited by A. B. Callow, Jr. 2d ed. New York: Oxford University Press.

Thibaut, J. W., and H. H. Kelley. 1959. *The Social Psychology of Groups.* New York: Wiley.

Tilly, C. 1974. "An Interactional Scheme for Analysis of Communities, Cities, and Urbanization." Mimeographed. Ann Arbor: University of Michigan.

Tomeh, A. K. 1964. "Informal Group Participation and Residential Patterns." *American Journal of Sociology* 70 (July): 28–35.

Verba, S., and N. H. Nie. 1972. *Participation in America.* New York: Harper & Row.

Verbrugge, L. M. 1973. "Adult Friendship Contact." Ph.D. dissertation, University of Michigan.

von Rosenbladt, B. 1972. "The Outdoor Activity System in an Urban Environment." Pp. 335–55 in *The Use of Time,* edited by A. Szalai. The Hague: Mouton.

Warner, S. B., Jr. 1969. *Streetcar Suburbs: The Process of Growth in Boston, 1870–1900.* New York: Atheneum.

Webber, M. M. 1968. "The Post-City Age." *Daedalus* 97 (Fall): 1091–1110.

Whyte, W. H., Jr. 1956. *The Organization Man.* New York: Simon & Schuster.

Wirt, F. M., B. Walter, F. F. Rabinovitz, and D. R. Hensler. 1972. *On the City's Rim: Politics and Policy in Suburbia.* Lexington, Mass.: Heath.

Wirth, L. 1938. "Urbanism as a Way of Life." *American Journal of Sociology* 44 (July): 3–24.

Young, M., and P. Willmott. 1957. *Family and Kinship in East London.* Baltimore: Penguin.

Zimmer, B. G. 1974. "The Urban Centrifugal Drift." Pp. 15–90 in *Metropolitan America: Papers on the State of Knowledge,* edited by A. H. Hawley and V. Rock. Washington, D.C.: National Academy of Sciences.

12   The Machines in Cheever's Garden

Scott Donaldson
College of William and Mary

Certainly, Lewis Coser is right that "the life of art illuminates the social life of man" (1972, pp. xv–xix). Certainly, one agrees with Paul Blumberg that literature does provide "a rich form of social documentation, illuminating the norms and values and entire culture of our own and previous eras" (1969, pp. 291–92). But the plain fact is that most classical 19th-century American literature qualifies rather better as romance than as realism, so that only in the 20th century, after the white whales were hunted down at sea and the demons exorcised from Puritan forests, have the nation's serious writers begun to supply the kind of picture of everyday, contemporary, middle-class society that has been the staple subject matter of the English novel for the last 200 years.

Following the lead of William Dean Howells in *Criticism and Fiction* (1891), however, American writers have moved in this century toward more realistic rendering of the surfaces of American life, particularly as it was lived in the city or small town. Curiously, however, very few of our best writers have concentrated their gaze on the suburbs, despite their burgeoning population. Still fewer have descended beneath the suburban surface to discover "the formative but largely submerged currents" in the life of this time, currents which go undetected by all but the most perceptive of artists (see Hoggart 1966, p. 279). This is the accomplishment of the novelist and short-story writer John Cheever (1912–   ),[1] who during the past two decades has sketched in his fiction an exceedingly disturbing portrait of what it is like to live in the postwar, upper-middle-class American suburb. Whether purposefully or not, Cheever has come to function as the Jeremiah of our suburban age.

To a substantial extent, Cheever's method has been one of implicit contrast among city, country, and suburb. Thus his earliest stories, such as the well-known "The Enormous Radio" (1953), brilliantly evoke "the corrosive effect of metropolitan life upon essentially decent people who are isolated, defeated, or deprived of their individuality in the vastness of the great city":[2] people afflicted, in short, by urban *anomie*. Then in Cheever's first novel,

---

[1] See Peden (1964), p. 46. Peden calls Cheever "perhaps the most distinguished" among recent "chroniclers of the non-exceptional."

[2] See Garrett (1964), p. 6. Garrett's is an exceptionally insightful and well-written essay.

The Wapshot Chronicle (1957), the scene shifts to the seaside town of St. Botolphs, Massachusetts, heavy with tradition and populated by eccentrics—the exhibitionist Uncle Peepee Marshmallow, Doris the male prostitute, even (on a more respectable plane) the peculiar Wapshots themselves—who are affectionately tolerated by their neighbors.

Clearly, the author's preference is for this small town of the past, since, as he asks in celebration (but with the final phrase undercutting the sentiment), "Where else in the world were there such stands of lilac, such lambent winds and brilliant skies, such fresh fish?"[3] One critic has objected that nobody's grandfather ever lived in a place so idealized as St. Botolphs.[4] However that may be, Cheever certainly realizes that his country town is an anachronism and underlines the point in the anecdote of the young girl who, having run away from home, finds herself among the carolers on the St. Botolphs village green on Christmas eve and calls home to wish her mother Merry Christmas. The carolers are singing "Good King Wenceslas," but, as Cheever comments, the voice of the girl, "with its prophecy of gas stations and motels, freeways and all-night supermarkets, has more to do with the world to come than the singing on the green" (Cheever 1963, p. 11).

Attractive though it is, St. Botolphs emits an air of sadness as well, "for while the ladies [of the town] admired the houses and the elms they knew that their sons would go away. Why did the young want to go away? Why did the young want to go away?" Off go the Wapshot boys, Moses and Coverly, to their separate suburban destinations, aiming to make what fortunes are unavailable in the country town of their youth and no more aware of the significance of their departure than the most temporary summer visitor: "We have all parted from simple places by train or boat at season's end with generations of yellow leaves spilling on the north wind as we spill our seed and the dogs and the children in the back of the car" (Cheever 1957, pp. 21, 92).

In effect, Cheever followed the young men of the Wapshot clan south to their Connecticut and Westchester suburbs, for his fiction since the mid-1950s has consistently been set in suburban communities, variously called Shady Hill, Proxmire Manor, Maple Dell, and Bullet Park. Cheever himself has lived for some years in the up-the-Hudson exurb of Ossining, New York (also the site, incidentally, of Sing Sing prison), and understands as well as anyone writing today the style of life that predominates in the upper-middle-class suburb. His reputation, in fact, has suffered because to some critical

---

[3] Greene (1971) demonstrates that this pattern, "the systolic pulse of sublime and prosaic juxtaposed," occurs frequently in Cheever's writing. The quotation is from Cheever (1963), p. 111.

[4] E.g., Ozick (1964), pp. 66–67.

eyes he appears to play the role of apologist for the suburbs, and because to others the milieu seems so bland as to be incapable of supplying the stuff of fiction.

Both charges are nonsensical. It is true, to be sure, that Johnny Hake glowingly invokes the joys of cooking meat outdoors, of looking down the front of his wife's dress as she salts the steaks, of growing roses and gazing at the lights in Heaven: "Shady Hill is, as I say, a *banlieue* and open to criticism by city planners, adventurers, and lyric poets, but if you work in the city and have children to raise, I can't think of a better place." But even as he reflects on the pleasures of suburban living, Hake is plotting to burglarize a neighbor's house in order to maintain his place among the expensive people (Cheever 1958*b*, pp. 3, 12). Similarly, Eliot Nailles in *Bullet Park* inveighs against those who are always "chopping at" the suburbs ("I can't see that playing golf and raising flowers is depraved"), but something surely has gone wrong in the suburb where he lives and whose commuting life he can face only by taking daily, massive doses of drugs (Cheever 1969, p. 66).

"It goes without saying," Cheever once remarked in an interview, "that the people in my stories and the things that happen to them could take place anywhere" (Waterman 1958, p. 33). People live and love and suffer and die in all locations, but one difference is that they try very hard, in the suburbs of Cheever's fiction, to ignore suffering and death. Proxmire Manor, he writes, "stood on three leafy hills north of the city, and was handsome and comfortable, and seemed to have eliminated, through adroit social pressures, the thorny side of human nature." It is known "up and down the suburban railroad line as the place where the lady got arrested." It is also the place where it is illegal to die in Zone B, so that it is necessary to take the body of "the old lady and put her into the car and drive her over to Chestnut Street, where Zone C begins" (Cheever 1966, pp. 682–84; 1961, pp. 10–11).

The town of St. Botolphs, though sometimes ridiculous, had at least evolved through the natural order of things which shaped it as an organic community. The inhabitants of Proxmire Manor, by way of contrast, do everything in their limited power to subvert nature, to create an artificial community surrounded by paper fences and legal boundaries. But they cannot legislate death away, or crime, or the peculiar boredom that afflicts the well-to-do suburban housewife. In "The Embarkment for Cythera," Jessica Coliver begins—and ends—a casual affair with her grocery boy principally out of boredom. "Loneliness was one thing," she muses, "and she knew herself how sweet it could make lights and company seem, but boredom was something else, and why, in this most prosperous and equitable world, should everyone seem so bored and disappointed?" (Cheever 1966, p. 685). Perhaps it is because they have no roots, no true home—only a house in Maple Dell where "the houses stand cheek by jowl, all of them built twenty years ago, and parked beside each was a car that seemed more substantial than the house itself, as if this were a fragment of some nomadic culture" (*Time* 1964, p. 69). But if the suburb has no future, its greater sin is in neglecting or repudiating the past, as in Shady Hill's "tacit claim that there had been no past, no war, that there was no danger or trouble in the world" (Bracher 1963, p. 75).

The consequences of so short-sighted an attitude Cheever has depicted in increasingly apocalyptic terms. As George Garrett has observed, Cheever's 1964 novel, *The Wapshot Scandal*, like many of his stories in the last 10 years, "moves inexorably toward the end of the world." Like Thoreau's mass of men, his suburbanites lead lives of quiet (because suffering is not to be acknowledged) desperation. There is laughter in Cheever, for he will not repudiate his gift of wit, but at the end the corners of the mouth turn down in dejection. A characteristic Cheever story thus begins with a credible, realistic situation, proceeds to farce or satire, and finally descends to nightmare. "It is," a critic has commented, "as if Marquand had suddenly been crossed with Kafka" (Garrett 1964, pp. 4, 8, 9–10).

In part, it is the dusky aspect of modernity itself which supplies the shadow side of Cheever's fiction. It is at first merely amusing when the housewife cannot cope with the formidable dials on her labor-saving appliances, but less funny when she gives up in despair, turns to drink and adultery, and finishes in suicide (his stories are full of suicides). Technological progress, he warns, has swept away all received values in its wake. Left with nothing to guide them, the young joylessly copulate on a double date at the drive-in movie near the Northern Expressway where, as Cheever comments, the young man's "sitting undressed in the back seat of a car might be accounted for by the fact that the music he danced to and the movies he watched dealt less and less with the heart and more and more with overt sexuality, as if the rose gardens and playing fields buried under the Expressway were enjoying a revenge" (Burhans 1969, pp. 194–95).

However, John Cheever does not write his tales out of sentimental nostalgia or latter-day Comstockism. Unlike Jay Gatsby, he is under no illusions about any man's ability to repeat or recapture the past, but "he is convinced that the identity and the values man lives by are rooted with him in that past." In his fiction he is warning us against ourselves, against the "catastrophic penalty" we may have to pay for what passes for progress (ibid., p. 197).[5]

The symbols which stand for such heedless progress in Cheever's fiction are almost invariably associated with transportation, a theme which links his concern with modern suburbia to a concern with modernity in general. One of his most famous stories, "The Angel of the Bridge," specifically focuses

---

[5] Burhans perceptively isolates a theme which Cheever had yet to elaborate in *Bullet Park* and *The World of Apples*.

on the relationship between modern means of travel and the dispiriting quality of contemporary existence. The story is built around three phobias. The first is that of the narrator's 74-year-old mother, who came from St. -Botolphs and who insists on skating on the Rockefeller Center rink at the lunch hour, "dressed like a hat-check girl." She used to skate in St. Botolphs, and she continues to waltz around the ice in New York City "as an expression of her attachment to the past." For all her seeming bravado, however, she panics and is utterly unable to board an airplane. The second phobia is that of the narrator's successful older brother, who because of his fear of elevators ("I'm afraid the building will fall down") is reduced to changing jobs and apartments. Finally, the narrator himself, who had felt superior to both his mother and his brother, finds that he is quite unable, because of an unreasonable, unshakable conviction that the bridge will collapse, to drive across the George Washington Bridge. On a trip to Los Angeles (for he does not mind flying), it comes to him that this

> terror of bridges was an expression of my clumsily concealed horror of what is becoming of the world. . . . The truth is, I hate freeways and Buffalo Burgers. Expatriated palm trees and monotonous housing developments depress me. The continuous music on special-fare trains exacerbates my feeling. I detest the destruction of familiar landmarks, I am deeply troubled by the misery and drunkenness I find among my friends, I abhor the dishonest practices. And it was at the highest point in the arc of a bridge that I became aware suddenly of the depth and bitterness of my feelings about modern life, and of the profoundness of my yearning for a more vivid, simple, and peaceable world.

His problem is resolved when a young girl hitchhiker, carrying a small harp, sings him across a bridge with "folk music, mostly." "I gave my love a cherry that had no stone," she sings, and he can once more negotiate the trip across the Hudson, the sweetness and innocence of the music from the past restoring him to "blue-sky courage, the high spirits of lustiness, and ecstatic sereneness" (Cheever 1964a, pp. 23–35).

In *Bullet Park* (1969), the novel in which Cheever most acutely dissects suburban life-styles, the principal characters seek a similar angel to restore them to spiritual and psychological health. Once more, the dominant symbol for their ills comes from the world of transportation. In letting railroads, airlines, and freeways—which shrink space, distort time, and confuse perceptions—stand for a deep psychological alienation, he uncovers a malaise inherent not only in modern life but more specifically in that portion of it lived in the commuting suburb. His contemporary suburbanites are terrified by the hurtling freeway automobiles, high-speed trains, and jet airplanes which make it possible for them to sleep in Bullet Park and work in New York or office in New York and fly across the continent on a business call.

This emphasis grows naturally out of Cheever's fictional concentration on the journey motif. The concept of life as journey is probably as old as the earliest legends, but in Cheever's work the theme is obsessive. His characters are forever in transit; the dominant metaphor of his fiction is that of the risky journey that modern man takes each day (Bracher 1964, p. 49). There are some—"the losers, the goners, the flops" that Cousin Honora Wapshot annually invites to Christmas dinner—who manage to miss the "planes, trains, boats and opportunities," but such derelicts are the exception (Garrett 1964, p. 10). Normally, the Cheever protagonist has, in the eyes of the world, "made it": the house in Bullet Park stands as emblem of his success, and so does the daily trip into the city and back.

But no one who lives that disconnected life, one foot on Madison Avenue and the other in Westchester or Connecticut, manages to stay happy for long. His daily commutation, by means of technologically wonderful highways or railbeds, only takes him on a fruitless circular voyage. He stays in motion, and goes nowhere but down. He comes home to roost, but can sink no roots. Neddy Merrill, in "The Swimmer," conceives of a Sunday voyage: he sets out to cross eight miles of suburban space by water—or, more specifically, by the swimming pools that dot the landscape. Neddy "seemed to see, with a cartographer's eye, that string of swimming pools, that quasi-subterranean stream that curved across the county." He decides to swim home by this stream, which he names after his wife Lucinda. Neddy's trip becomes to him a quest undertaken in the spirit of "a pilgrim, an explorer, a man with a destiny." But reality keeps intruding (the whistle of a train brings him back to reality, reminding him of the time), and when he finally reaches home, after being insulted and ignored and rejected en route, he discovers (what he had been trying to forget) that the house has been sold and his wife and four beautiful daughters have moved on (Cheever 1964*b*, pp. 61–76).

Though his voyaging is fanciful and his plight extreme, Neddy Merrill is symptomatic of the restless and rootless denizens who inhabit Cheever's fictional suburbs. "The people of Bullet Park," for instance, "intend not so much to have arrived there as to have been planted and grown there," but there is nothing organic or indigenous or lasting about their transplantation. The evenings call them back to "the blood-memory of travel and migration," and in due time they will be on their way once more, accompanied by "disorder, moving vans, bank loans at high interest, tears and desperation (Cheever 1969, pp. 4–5). They are, almost all of them, but temporary visitors, and they will find themselves, most of them, in the same boat (or commuter train) every morning.

To further underline the rootless quality of Bullet Park, the narrator adopts the pose of an anthropologist looking back on what is, in fact, current American society. Though it is not raining, Eliot Nailles turns on his windshield wipers. Why? "The reason for this was that (at the time of which I'm writing) society had become so automative and nomadic that nomadic signals or means of communication had been established by the use of headlights, parking lights, signal lights and windshield wipers." For the power of speech, for face-to-face communication, contemporary society substitutes mechanical symbols. One character in the book is convinced that her windshield wipers give her "sage and coherent advice" on the stock market; Nailles is urged by the diocesan bishop "to turn on [his] windshield wipers to communicate [his] faith in the resurrection of the dead and the life of the world to come" (ibid., pp. 21, 155).

The technology of rapid movement (which is both a cause and effect of the development of places like Bullet Park) attempts, in short, to provide a convenient, painless substitute for true affirmation of one's spiritual faith. So Lent passes with only Nailles himself remembering the terrible journey of Paul of Tarsus: "Thrice was I beaten with rods, once was I stoned, thrice I suffered shipwreck, a night and a day I have been in the deep; in journeyings often, in perils of waters, in perils of robbers, in perils by mine own countrymen, in perils by the heathen, in perils in the city, in perils in the wilderness, in perils in the sea, in perils among false brethren; in weariness and painfulness, in watchings often, in hunger and thirst, in fastings often, in cold and nakedness" (ibid., p. 39). But what possible analogy can be drawn between the trials of Paul and the seemingly placid surface of the life which Eliot and Nellie Nailles lead in Bullet Park?

Eliot Nailles, the principal figure in the novel, is a middle-aged businessman with a job he would rather not talk about: though educated as a chemist, he is now employed to merchandise a mouthwash called "Spang." He is kind, uxorious, a conventional family man old-fashioned in his values. If he had the talent, he would write poems celebrating his wife Nellie's thighs. He loves her, as he loves their only child Tony, possessively and protectively, his love seeming "like some limitless discharge of a clear amber fluid that would surround them, cover them, preserve them and leave them insulated but visible like the contents of an aspic." He thinks "of pain and suffering as a principality, lying somewhere beyond the legitimate borders of western Europe," and hardly expects any distressing foreign bodies to penetrate his protective fluid (ibid., pp. 25, 50).

But in suburbia there is only a false security: Neither Nailles nor Nellie nor their son Tony, a high school senior, can escape the ills of modern society. Nellie goes to New York to see a matinee in which a male actor casually displays his penis; outside the theater college-age youngsters are carrying placards which proclaim four-letter words; on the bus one young man kisses another on the ear. She returns from her disconcerting afternoon "bewildered and miserable." In an hour, she thinks during the train ride home, she will be herself again, "honest, conscientious, intelligent, chaste, etc. But if her composure depended upon shutting doors, wasn't her composure contemptible?" (ibid., pp. 30–33). She decides not to tell Nailles about her experience, and it is just as well; absolutely monogamous and faithful himself, he is shocked and disturbed by promiscuity or homosexuality.

Thus, nothing much to trouble Eliot Nailles comes of Nellie's day in the city. The case is quite different when Tony, suffering through a prolonged spell of depression, refuses to get out of bed or to eat normally. Physically, there is nothing wrong with the boy; psychologically, he is consumed by a sadness which remains impervious to the ministrations of the family doctor, the psychiatrist, and the specialist on somnambulatory phenomena. His is a radical instance of the more common "suburban sadness." After Tony has been in bed for 17 days and it begins to look as though he will not survive his depression, Nailles also cracks and finds himself unable to ride the commuter train into the city without a sedative.

The locomotive, screaming across the countryside, was the preeminent machine invading the 19th-century American Garden of Eden. We have constructed an Atropos, a fate which will soon slip beyond our control, Thoreau warned. Do we ride upon the railroad or the railroad upon us? Emerson wondered. Dickinson's seemingly playful iron horse stuffed itself on nature as it hooted its way, paradoxically "docile and omnipotent," to its stable door. And Hawthorne, in "The Celestial Railroad," made clear (as the folk song affirmed) that you can't get to heaven in a railroad car.[6]

Disturbing though it may have been in 1860, the railroad has been supplanted in the mid-20th century by other, still more frightening technological monsters. Take, for example, the jet airplane which enables one "to have supper in Paris and, God willing, breakfast at home, and here is a whole new creation of self-knowledge, new images for love and death and the insubstantiality and the importance of our affairs" (Burhans 1969, p. 190). This is no conventional paean to the wonders of progress, for "God willing" emphasizes the risk attendant upon jet travel, and if our "affairs" which cause us to hurtle across oceans and continents are truly insubstantial, without body, they are hardly important enough to justify the trip. Just how trivial these affairs are, in fact, is emphasized in Cheever's much anthologized "The Country Husband." In that story, Francis Weed survives a crash landing on the flight from Minneapolis to New York and that same evening attempts, unsuccessfully, to interest anyone—his wife, children, neighbors, friends— in what has happened. For nothing in his suburb of Shady Hill "was neglected; nothing had not been burnished" (Cheever 1958a)—and the residents want things to stay that way. They do not wish to hear of disasters, much less disasters narrowly averted; they shut tragedy, especially potential tragedy, out of their consciousness. Cheever's fiction, however, tries to wake

[6] For a brilliant analysis of this idea, see Marx (1964).

them up, to point to the thorns on the rosebushes, to call attention to the hazards of the journey.

The trains of today, by way of contrast, play a somewhat ambiguous role in Cheever's gallery of horrors. To the extent that they are reminiscent of a quieter past, they summon up a certain nostalgia. "Paint me a small railroad station then," *Bullet Park* begins, and by no accident, for the "setting seems to be in some way at the heart of the matter. We travel by plane, oftener than not, and yet the spirit of our country seems to have remained a country of railroads." The train mistily evokes loneliness and promise, loss and reassurance:

> You wake in a pullman bedroom at three a.m. in a city the name of which you do not know and may never discover. A man stands on the platform with a child on his shoulders. They are waving goodbye to some traveler, but what is the child doing up so late and why is the man crying? On a siding beyond the platform there is a lighted dining car where a waiter sits alone at a table, adding up his accounts. Beyond this is a water tower and beyond this a well-lighted and empty street. Then you think happily that this is your country—unique, mysterious and vast. One has no such feelings in airplanes, airports and the trains of other nations.

A romantic aura envelops any journey, by night, along the tracks of the continent. But in the small suburban railway station at Bullet Park, designed by an architect "with some sense of the erotic and romantic essence of travel," the windows have been broken, the clock face smashed, the waiting room transformed into a "warlike ruin" (Cheever 1969, pp. 3–4, 14).

The train trip is one thing; commutation is something else. The commuter station is the site of the sudden death, one perfectly normal morning, of Harry Shinglehouse, who is introduced on page 60 and disposed of on page 61 of the novel. Shinglehouse stands on the Bullet Park platform, like Nailles and Paul Hammer (who has determined, in his madness, to crucify Tony Nailles) waiting for the 7:56, when "down the tracks came the Chicago express, two hours behind schedule and going about ninety miles an hour." The express (a deadly product of technological progress) rips past, its noise and commotion like "the vortex of some dirty wind tunnel," and hells off into the distance. Then Nailles notices one "highly polished brown loafer" lying amid the cinders and realizes that Shinglehouse has been sucked under the train.

The next day, troubled by his memory of this incident and by Tony's refusal to get out of bed, Nailles misses his usual connection, takes a local which makes 22 stops between Bullet Park and Grand Central Station, and finds that he has to get off the train every few stops to summon up the courage to go on. "Nailles's sense of being alive was to bridge or link the disparate environments and rhythms of his world, and one of his principal bridges—that between his white house and his office—had collapsed." To restore this sense of continuity and to alleviate his commutation hysteria, Nailles starts taking a massive tranquilizer with his morning coffee, a drug which floats him into the city like Zeus upon a cloud. The day the pills run out, however, Nailles discovers that the doctor who prescribed them has been closed down by the county medical society and desperately turns to a pusher to get an illegal supply of the magic gray and yellow capsules. Even after Tony is miraculously restored to health by the unlikely angel of this novel, one Swami Rutuola, his father continues, each Monday morning, "to meet his pusher in the supermarket parking lot, the public toilet, the laundromat, and a variety of cemeteries." And even after Nailles, with the help of the Swami once more, manages to rescue Tony from crucifixion, "Tony went back to school on Monday [these are the final words of the novel] and Nailles—drugged—went off to work and everything was as wonderful, wonderful, wonderful as it had been" (ibid., pp. 60–65; 121–26; 142, 245).

Cheever's suburbanites drink and smoke and party a great deal, while their children stare fixedly at television. Clearly, they stay drugged to ward off reality. Having a few drinks with the neighbors ("You can look all over the world but you won't find neighbors as kind and thoughtful as the people in Bullet Park") who come to commiserate with her about her husband's suicide, Mrs. Heathcup "almost forgot what had happened. I mean it didn't seem as though anything had happened" (ibid., p. 12). On his way from Boston to Kitzbühl to see his mother, suburbanite Paul Hammer first loads up on martinis to cross the Atlantic in a drunken haze and then gets thoroughly stoned in a pub when he is delayed in London. He is a victim of the economy which his mad mother (once a militant socialist) characterizes, with wisdom characteristic of the Shakespearean fool, as having degenerated "into the manufacture of drugs and ways of life that make reflection—any sort of thoughtfulness or emotional depth—impossible." It is advertising, she maintains, that carries the pernicious message: "I see American magazines in the cafe and the bulk of their text is advertising for tobacco, alcohol and absurd motor cars that promise—quite literally promise—to enable you to forget the squalor, spiritual poverty and monotony of selfishness. Never, in the history of civilization, has one seen a great nation singlemindedly bent on drugging itself." If she were to go back to the States, she tells her son, she would crucify an advertising man in some place like Bullet Park in an attempt to "wake that world" (ibid., pp. 164–69). Hammer takes over her mission, changes his victim from Eliot Nailles to his son, and only fails because he pauses to smoke a calming cigarette before immolating Tony on the altar of Christ's Church. For Cheever, then, the step between the drug culture of youth and the drugged culture of suburbia is a short one.

Drugging also facilitates driving on the freeways and turnpikes which represent, in Cheever's fiction, the most damnable pathways of contemporary civilization. Among the machines in his garden, none has wrought so cruelly or so terrifyingly as the bulldozers and road builders which have gouged out unnatural and inhuman roads. Poor Dora Emmison, for example, cannot negotiate the New Jersey turnpike unless she's drunk: "That road and all the rest of the freeways and thruways were engineered for clowns and drunks. If you're not a nerveless clown then you have to get drunk. No sensitive or intelligent man or woman can drive on those roads. Why I have a friend in California who smokes pot before he goes on the freeway. He's a great driver, a marvelous driver, and if the traffic's bad he uses heroin. They ought to sell pot and bourbon at the gas stations. Then there wouldn't be so many accidents." Fifteen minutes after this speech, well fortified with bourbon, Dora is killed in a crash on the Jersey pike (ibid., pp. 193, 196–97).

The suicide rate aside, the most shocking statistic in Bullet Park has to do with casualties on the highway; these "averaged twenty-two a year because of a winding highway that seemed to have been drawn on the map by a child with a grease pencil" (ibid., p. 10). A brief story in Cheever's latest book, The World of Apples, vividly portrays the cost, to one particular woman, of the technological wonder of Route 64. One Saturday morning Marge Littleton loses her husband and children when on returning from a shopping trip their automobile is demolished by a gigantic car carrier. Next she campaigns, unsuccessfully, against widening Route 64 from four to eight lanes. Then, upon recovering from her bereavement, she marries a "handsome, witty, and substantial" Italian named Pietro Montani who is decapitated by a crane as he drives down 64 in his convertible. Subsequent to these tragedies, curious accidents begin to occur on the highway. "Three weeks after Pietro's death a twenty-four wheel, eighty-ton truck, northbound on Route 64 . . . veered into the southbound lane demolishing two cars and killing their four passengers." Then the truck caught on fire. Two weeks later another 24-wheeler "went out of control at the same place," struck an abutment, and although there was no fire this time, the two drivers "were so badly crushed by the collision that they had to be identified by their dental work." Twice more trucks swerve out of control at the same spot, and in the last case the truck comes to rest peacefully in a narrow valley. When the police get to the oversized vehicle, they discover that the driver has been shot dead, but they do not find out that Marge has done the shooting. Finally, in December "Marge married a rich widower and moved to North Salem, where there is only one two-lane highway and where the sound of traffic is as faint as the roaring of a shell" (ibid., pp. 132–37).

Marge Littleton's one-woman vendetta hardly provides the harried suburban traveler with a practical way of expressing his objections against heedless technological progress. Nor can he find much consolation in the prayers of a drunken priest, in yet another story, for "all those killed or cruelly wounded on thruways, expressways, freeways and turnpikes . . . for all those burned to death in faulty plane landings, mid-air collisions, and mountainside crashes . . . for all those wounded by rotary lawn-mowers, chain saws, electric hedge clippers, and other power tools" (Bracher 1964, p. 53).

Unless it is halted, Cheever's fiction suggests, progress will not only kill large numbers of human beings but will also destroy the quality of life for those who survive. The world which Moses and Coverly Wapshot leave St. Botolphs to conquer is symbolized by the vast Northern Expressway which takes them south, "engorging in its clover leaves and brilliantly engineered gradings the green playing fields, rose gardens, barns, farms, meadows, trout streams, forests, homesteads and churches of a golden past." Similarly, Bullet Park's Route 61, "one of the most dangerous and in appearance one of the most inhuman of the new highways," is a road which has "basically changed the nature of the Eastern landscape like some seismological disturbance," a freeway on which at least 50 men and women die each year. The simple Saturday drive on Route 61 becomes warlike, and Nailles fondly recalls the roads of his young manhood: "They followed the contours of the land. It was cool in the valleys, warm on the hilltops. One could measure distances with one's nose. There was the smell of eucalyptus, maples, sweet grass, manure from a cow barn and, as one got into the mountains, the smell of pine. . . . He remembered it all as intimate, human and pleasant, compared to this anxious wasteland through which one raced the barbarians" (Cheever 1969, pp. 228–29).

Significantly, it is the mountains that Nailles's son Tony inchoately longs for as he lies in deep depression. Nailles rouses him from bed one fine morning, takes him to the window, shows him how bright and beautiful it is outside, tells him that "everything's ahead of you. Everything. You'll go to college and get an interesting job and get married and have children." But Tony sinks to the floor and then howls out, "Give me back the mountains." What mountains? The White Mountains in New Hampshire that he and his father climbed together one summer? The Tirol where, Nailles later remembers, he had been awfully happy climbing "the Grand Kaiser and the Pengelstein" (ibid., pp. 59–60, 241)? Tony does not know (and will not know until Swami Rutuola comes to work his cure) that the mountains are symbolic.

The Swami had first discovered his ability as a healer while employed to clean the washrooms at Grand Central Station. There he had been accosted, very early one morning, by a desperate man certain that he was going to die momentarily. The Swami took him up to the concourse where they gazed together at the "great big colored picture that advertises cameras" and which showed a man and a woman and two children on a beach, "and behind them, way off in the distance, were all these mountains covered with snow." Then, Swami Rutuola tells Tony, he had asked the dying man "to look at the mountains to see if he could get his mind off his troubles," and the therapy had worked. As part of his treatment for Tony, Rutuola recites "cheers of place" for pleasant, unspoiled places: "I'm in a house by the sea at four in the afternoon and it's raining and I'm sitting in a ladderback chair with a book in my lap and I'm waiting for a girl I love who has gone on an errand but who will return" (ibid., pp. 133–34, 139–40). These cheers, and others, miraculously restore Tony to health.

In a malaise similar to Tony's, Paul Hammer is overtaken "on trains and planes" by a personal *cafard*, or carrier of blues, whom he can escape only by summoning up images that represent to him "the excellence and beauty" he has lost. The first and most frequent of such images which counterpoint the realities of Bullet Park is that of a perfect, snow-covered mountain, obviously Kilimanjaro. In attempting to ward off his *cafard*, Hammer also calls up a vision of a fortified medieval town which, "like the snow-covered mountain, seemed to represent beauty, enthusiasm and love." Occasionally he glimpses a river with grassy banks—the Elysian fields perhaps—though he finds them difficult to reach and though it seems "that a railroad track or a thruway [has] destroyed the beauty of the place" (ibid., pp. 174–75).

In Tony's malaise, in Rutuola's cheers, in Hammer's visions, Cheever indirectly expresses his yearning after unspoiled nature and his conviction that mankind can stand only so much technological progress. Now that the walls of the medieval town have been breached, the Elysian fields invaded by freeways, space obliterated and time brought very nearly to a stop, Cheever joins Mark Twain in lamentation that "there are no remotenesses, anymore" (Tanner 1964, p. 183).

The depiction of the machine—particularly the railroad locomotive—as villain was, as has been noted, a commonplace in mid-19th-century American literature. In the first half of this century the theme reemerged in such writers as Steinbeck, Hemingway, and Faulkner. The Joads, in *The Grapes of Wrath*, are driven from their land by the tractor and painfully make their way west via broken-down automobile; Robert Jordan and the Spanish guerrillas, in *For Whom the Bell Tolls*, face "mechanized doom" from the sophisticated aircraft of the Fascists; Ike McCaslin, in *Go Down, Moses*, watches despairingly as the wilderness he loves is transformed into "flashing neon, speeding automobiles, sheet iron, and hooting locomotives." In the world these writers contemplate, "not only life and dignity, but human moral, spiritual, and rational processes are opposed by unreasoning forces of anonymous brute mechanism."[7] So, as Kurt Vonnegut would say, it goes.

The theme, then, is hardly original with John Cheever. His unique contribution has been, first, to point to the engines of the transportation revolu-

---

[7] Though one could cite many other examples, for felicitously suggesting these I am indebted to Waldron (1972), pp. 271–72.

tion as the particular devil-machines in the contemporary garden, and next, to localize the issue in that place—the upper-middle-class suburb—whose inhabitants he knows and understands and whose dependence, for its very survival, upon thruways and commuter lines most aptly qualifies it to exemplify the rootlessness and artificiality of contemporary life. In his fiction, Cheever warns, Jeremiah-like, against the boredom and depression, drugs and suicide, that will surely follow the suburbanite on the cruel journey of commutation, unless. . . . But the answers he leaves to us.

REFERENCES

Blumberg, Paul. 1969. "Sociology and Social Literature: Work Alienation in the Plays of Arthur Miller." *American Quarterly* 21 (Summer): 291–310.

Bracher, Frederick. 1963. "John Cheever and Comedy." *Critique* 6 (Spring): 66–77.

———. 1964. "John Cheever: A Vision of the World." *Claremont Quarterly* 11 (Winter): 47–57.

Burhans, Clinton S. 1969. "John Cheever and the Grave of Social Coherence." *Twentieth Century Literature* 14 (January): 187–98.

Cheever, John. 1957. *The Wapshot Chronicle.* New York: Bantam.

———. 1958a. "The Country Husband." Pp. 48–83 in *"The Housebreaker of Shady Hill" and Other Stories.* New York: Harper.

———. 1958b. "The Housebreaker of Shady Hill." Pp. 3–31 in *"The Housebreaker of Shady Hill" and Other Stories.* New York: Harper.

———. 1961. "The Death of Justina." Pp. 1–19 in *Some People, Places and Things That Will Not Appear in My Next Novel.* New York: Harper.

———. 1963. *The Wapshot Scandal.* New York: Bantam.

———. 1964a. "The Angel of the Bridge." Pp. 23–35 in *The Brigadier and the Golf Widow.* New York: Harper & Row.

———. 1964b. "The Swimmer." Pp. 61–76 in *The Brigadier and the Golf Widow.* New York: Harper & Row.

———. 1966. "The Embarkment for Cythera." Pp. 682–705 in *First Prize Stories 1919–1966 from the O. Henry Memorial Awards,* with introduction by Harry Hansen. Garden City, N.Y.: Doubleday.

———. 1969. *Bullet Park.* New York: Knopf.

———. 1973. *The World of Apples.* New York: Knopf.

Coser, Lewis A. 1972. *Sociology through Literature.* Englewood Cliffs, N.J.: Prentice-Hall.

Garrett, George. 1964. "John Cheever and the Charms of Innocence: The Craft of *The Wapshot Scandal.*" *Hollins Critic* 1 (April): 1–12.

Greene, Beatrice. 1971. "Icarus at St. Botolphs: A Descent to 'Unwonted Otherness.' " *Style* 5 (Spring): 119–37.

Hoggart, Richard. 1966. "Literature and Society." *American Scholar* 25 (Spring): 277–89.

Marx, Leo. 1964. *The Machine in the Garden.* New York: Oxford University Press.

Ozick, Cynthia. 1964. "America Aglow." *Commentary* 38 (July): 66–67.

Peden, William. 1964. "Jane Austens of Metropolis and Suburbia." Pp. 45–85 in *The American Short Story: Front Line in the Defense of Literature.* Boston: Houghton Mifflin.

Tanner, Tony. 1964. *The Reign of Wonder.* New York: Harper & Row.

Time. 1964. "The Metamorphoses of John Cheever." (March 27).

Waldron, Randall H. 1972. "The Naked, the Dead, and the Machine: A New Look at Norman Mailer's First Novel." *PMLA* 87 (March): 271–72.

Waterman, Rollene. 1958. "Literary Horizons." *Saturday Review* (September 13).

Conclusion

Images of Suburbia:

Some Revisionist Commentary and Conclusions

Barry Schwartz
University of Chicago

This volume is a response to changes that have recently taken place in the American metropolis. It is an attempt to describe these changes, to make them intelligible, and to assess cautiously the future they embody.

The purpose of this commentary is not to summarize and integrate the efforts of the contributors to this volume but to identify the more general outlines of the picture which emerges from the volume as a whole. It is therefore inevitable that the conclusions I reach will be at variance with at least some of those drawn by my colleagues. It is also inevitable that my statement will be based on impression and judgment as well as fact, that it will draw more liberally on some facts than on others, and that it will apply them to a typical, rather than any particular, suburb.

As the title implies, this commentary is also an effort to resurrect a question which I think has been put to a premature rest. That question is whether the suburban community is to be understood as a bald ecological fact—a mere by-product of metropolitan growth—or whether it is culturally important and therefore alters, in significant ways, the modes of life that are brought to it. To me, the latter view is the more compelling. And there is much at stake in this. By arguing that age-related, familial, and class-cultural forms are dominant modes of life organization—and not merely statistically prominent aspects of suburbia—I am forced to take issue with the common view that the suburban landscape is destined to merge imperceptibly with that of the city. I must also deny the assumption that our pejorative visions of suburbia are no more than crude stereotypes based on a few misbegotten field studies. This two-sided argument is in keeping with a perspective that sees the metropolis as a meaningful, that is, moral, as well as an ecological and demographic, order. It is also in keeping with my editorial duties, for a volume devoted to metropolitan change is responsible not only for charting that transformation but also for pointing to its limits.

VISIONS OF SUBURBIA

Two mutually opposing models may be abstracted from the literature which has accumulated over the years on suburbs and their people. The first model, which took shape in the 1950s, finds in the suburbs a unique and compelling

Gemeinschaft-like[1] culture and life-style which inevitably transforms those who come into sustained contact with it. This point of view finds most notable, though by no means exclusive, expression in the work of Whyte (1956), Riesman (1957; 1964), Spectorsky (1955), Seeley, Sim, and Loosley (1956), Martin (1956), Fava (1956), and Mowrer (1958). I deem this work to be "classic" because one can derive from it the first coherent argument concerning the cultural significance of suburbanization. The second model, worked out later in opposition to the first, denies the import of suburbanization, holding it to be merely a selective spatial extension of existing modes of life of the city. According to this view, there can be nothing sociologically interesting about suburbanization as such. The notion of "suburbia" as an integral cultural entity is held to be a "myth." (See, e.g., Gans 1967, Dobriner 1963, Donaldson 1969, and Masotti and Hadden 1973. For the original and still most powerful statement in this tradition, see Berger 1971a.)

I was originally convinced by this second model, which seems in fact to be currently the more authoritative. Yet, as I re-read the early community studies and essays, I found it difficult to dismiss them entirely. Like most myths, the "suburban myth" of the 1950s seemed to have a ring of truth about it. In particular, it suggested to me intrinsic limits to the changes which suburbs have been and are even now undergoing. Accordingly, I decided to assess the contributions to this volume in terms of their consistency with or relevance to the "classical" and the "contemporary" models of suburbanization.

The presence or absence of a more or less distinct suburban culture is of interest to those concerned with the meaning of the ecological and institutional trends reported in this volume and elsewhere. Yet, the relationship between suburban culture and our perceptions of it is a very complicated one. Here is a problem which derives from the work of Strauss (1968) and recognizes that communities possess symbolic as well as demographic and structural properties. To their residents, communities furnish a way of life; to outsiders, visions of a way of life. But what is the connection between the two? There is, of course, no denying that images are intrinsically conequential inasmuch as people are attracted to and repelled by a culture, or subculture, according to what they think they will find in it. However, these conceptions are grounded in reality; they are not merely expressions of some arbitrary artistic or ideological fantasy. On the other hand, facts do not lie isolated in our minds but, rather, arrange themselves and sometimes congeal into imperfect representations of the whole from which they are drawn. The fewer the facts, or the less confidence we have in them, the more likely certain aspects of that whole will be accentuated, even distorted, through our

---

[1] I use the term "Gemeinschaft" rather loosely to refer to a vague process, best defined, perhaps, in terms of a search for, maintenance, and celebration of community.

biases. However, as a newer and more certain vision is gained, old conceptions should be replaced by fresh ones. To say, with Berger (1971*b*, p. 171), that myths are held regardless of newly discovered realities which contradict them is a bit too cynical. In this connection, however, one of the most notable aspects of recent work on the suburbs is that it has produced no new image to take the place of the one it so forcefully rejects. Old conceptions of suburbia do persist, then, in the face of a contemporary theoretical model which denies them. This raises a number of questions: What are the sources of these traditional conceptions? What explains their persistence? Are these images really distortions or do they reflect facts which the newer theory ignores? To get at these questions, we need to look directly into the *idea* of suburbia, as it was originally formulated.

The cultural dimensions of suburbanization found their most detailed expression in the popular and social science literature of the 1950s. During that period, suburbanization pointed to a new way of life and provided a new modal character to go along with it. The middle-class suburban development was, for Riesman, Whyte, and others, not only a *typical* feature of the metropolitan periphery but also *representative* of what would become the dominant life-style of a consumption-oriented, postindustrial society. This transformation could be indexed by a set of quaint symbols: the ranch house, lawn, barbecue, and two-car garage; modern and "functionally designed" churches, schools, and shopping centers. As I have said, these visions are compelling and consequential in their own right. But what is more relevant from a strictly objective standpoint are the activities so closely associated with them: massive long-distance commuting, transience of residence awkwardly joined to an intense obsession with the repair and appearance of the home, hysterical neighboring and joining, the kaffeeklatsch as an institution, not to mention lack of privacy and an attending intolerance of the offbeat. The church-going, child-centered, garden-loving, Republican suburb, as we were told, is homogeneous and transformative. We were also told that the culture which superintends these developments is without substance—that its recreations are shallow; its institutions, trivial; its purposes, self indulgent. Complacent, superficial, and tedious, the suburb becomes a Catskillization of the old-fashioned city neighborhood—its safe streets, the natural habitat of those who have no love for "action." The bureaucratization of work thus finds its parallel in the suburbanization of residence, insofar as both attract and favor society's least venturesome souls and are organized with a view to further standardization and suppression of "individualism." And so suburbia becomes the center of the family way, the home of the "other-directed," the stronghold of the new "Social Ethic."

In short, the classic theory of suburbia argues that those who move across a city's boundary must eventually come to treat one another in new ways and to create institutions which differ from those they built in the city. This transformation must be described as a process of "reverse urbanization" in that it brings about a revitalization of the family-centered life-style, a heightened sense of collective consciousness through intensified participation in institutional affairs, and a corresponding deepening and cultivation of neighborly relationships. Suburbanism is thus held to be a highly communal form of social organization which, by the 1950s, became increasingly conspicuous as a counterpoint to the more individualistic and often anomic ways of life of the city.

Some would deny this. It can be argued, for example, that in the suburban context, where communal solidarity and sociability become ends in themselves, the individual finds the same social pressures and forms his predecessors faced in city ghettoes: the "urban village" is simply transformed into a "suburban village," from which it differs in no significant way. Or so it seems. In fact there are important differences. Above all, the new solidarity—if I understand the classical viewpoint correctly—is not grounded in primordial ethnic ties but in a particular, that is, middle-class, subculture. What is important about the life-style of this culture is its universality and freedom from particular relationships and localities. Suburbia is in this sense the negation of the traditional community. Accordingly, it allows for (and is in some respects probably an adaptation to) residential transiency and temporary social bonds. The roots of the suburban community, then, do not sink very deep.[2] They are, as one might say, superficial. The result? Conformity without tradition; affluence without style; sociability without rootedness. It is the pathos of a modern, not an anachronistic, order which embitters the early visions of suburbia.

But there is another objection, which runs somewhat as follows: While early writers, like Whyte and Seeley, devoted themselves exclusively to middle-class residential suburbs, more current investigations show that the suburban ring is not homogeneous in this respect. It never was. There have always been upper-class, working-class, and black suburbs, and even suburban communities with an altogether industrial, rather than residential, character. The nature of suburban life is therefore distorted in the classical studies. But this too is an ill-conceived argument, for it implies of a number of very intelligent men a denial of the patently evident fact that not all suburbs are like the ones they knew best. Of course, the claim of homogeneity was never made (see, e.g., Riesman 1957, p. 124). It is nevertheless true that two decades ago the *typical* and *fastest growing* suburb was white, middle class, and residential. It still is.

---

[2] However, these roots are widespread. Thus, one can move geographically from one suburb to another but stay tied to the same culture. This is to say that suburbs are more interchangeable than cities. In function, tradition, and imagery, Chicago is one thing; Philadelphia, quite another. But Park Forest and Levittown are not so different. Distinct centers spawn like peripheries.

The latter statement is most pointedly confirmed in the group of papers which make up Part I of this volume. One cannot help but notice what they say collectively: Despite gross changes in the economic relationship between city and suburb, the social balance between them has not been altered. True, Kasarda can demonstrate the dramatic shift of occupational positions from city to suburb; but others can show that the suburbs are becoming industrialized *without* the bother of an industrial population. Farley, for example, demonstrates that the gap between the income and educational levels of cities and suburbs has remained quite stable over the past decade; Schnore and his associates show the same to be true over a much longer period of time for race. Berry and his associates show why the racial composition of the suburbs will continue to be resistant to change. Long and Glick prove that differences between city and suburb with regard to family structure are about the same today as they were a decade ago: suburbia remains the nursery of the republic. Redistribution of economic activity in the metropolis has therefore occurred within a political structure which has suppressed its demographic consequences. And so the suburbs remain virtually all white, more affluent, and more likely than the city to contain upwardly mobile families engaged in the process of child rearing.

There is another well-used objection, this directed against assertions of an exclusive life-style distribution. So far as I can tell, however, no writer ever suggested that domestic preoccupations and neo-Gemeinschaft forms are confined to the suburbs; the precise statement is that the structure of suburbia is more conducive to their development than is the makeup of the city.[3] A number of contributions to this volume seem to bear out that statement. Thus the Greers document (in perhaps too peripheral a manner) the higher level of political participation in suburbia; Fischer and Jackson, more neighboring and other informal contacts; and Newman, more extensive and diffuse involvement in church affairs.

The question, of course, is how we are to interpret these findings. And this raises an important issue. The latter two papers seem disposed to say that, if the suburban community is a "sociologically meaningful" entity, then suburban *residence* per se will affect social relationships and behavior independently of the characteristics of suburban *residents*. I disagree with this formulation, for it can only be construed to mean that a community's "direct" or "intrinsic" effects are its only salient properties. Very few of us, I think, would honor such a claim, for we all know that "recruitment mechanisms," that is, a community's method of attracting certain types of people

[3] One might put this differently by saying that residents' social and psychological investments in a community can never be total. In this sense, all communities are "communities of limited liability" (Janowitz 1962). However, these limits are quite variable and, according to the classical vision, expand as one moves toward the metropolitan periphery.

and repelling others, is one of its most important *constitutive* (rather than residual or incidental) features. To control for residents' characteristics (and so hold the element of recruitment constant) in an inquiry into the way a community shapes behavior is, therefore, to commit a "partialling fallacy" (Gordon 1968, pp. 592–95) and to underestimate the community's efficacy in this regard. This is precisely what has been done in much of the current literature (see Marshall's [1973] recent summary) and in the otherwise excellent papers by Newman and Fischer and Jackson, which adhere closely to the methodological tradition of that literature by seeking to isolate a causal "suburban factor" and to judge its effects independently of the social elements which compose the factor itself. On the other hand, "direct effect" parameters were emphatically not part of the classical model of suburbia. From that vantage point, the attraction and spatial distribution of age-related class cultures are not only central but also intrinsic to the process of suburbanization. This perspective rightly emphasizes the compositional and organizational features of the suburban community and deemphasizes its ecological properties[4] and their relatively limited, though by no means negligible, consequences.

STRUCTURAL BASES OF SUBURBAN CULTURE

Suburban communities maintain the ecological partition of values and lifestyles by defending their boundaries, which most are ready, willing, and encouraged by political tradition and authority to do. The American ideal of the autonomous local community (whose complex governmental ramifications are taken up by the Greers) is by no means an anachronism. As Zimmer shows, suburbs will no doubt continue successfully to oppose arrangements which would promote their accessibility to the institutions and people of other communities.

---

[4] "Disputes over variables left uncontrolled," writes Gordon (1968, p. 593), "result from absence of explicit theory. One party may define a variable globally, for example, 'urbanism,' so that it includes the variables typically correlated with living in a city, such as higher income and education, and therefore not control for the latter, whereas others may construe 'urbanism' as a state of mind independent of income and education. Failure of the first party adequately to define urbanism in his study will precipitate attacks by the others on his omission of 'obvious' controls. Actually, the entire dispute would be over a matter of definition entirely, and it should be conducted, if at all, on the semantic-esthetic-theoretical level and not on the methodological level. Fear of being so attacked serves as an incentive for controlling everything the investigator can lay hold of, whether appropriate or not, when the appropriate remedy would be for him to specify clearly the working theory that is guiding his research." These remarks on "urbanism" apply equally well to "suburbanism." Obviously, the classical writers define suburbanism globally, while contemporary investigators tend to take a more restricted view by confining themselves exclusively to its *ecological* dimension, namely, residence per se, to which all other variables are extraneous and therefore subject to control.

In addition to charting growth in the number of different types of administrative units in metropolitan areas over past decades, Zimmer explains how fragmentation presently inhibits and, in most cases, prevents the kinds of institutional consolidations that would make for more efficient distribution of metropolitan-wide services. We know, however, that such obstruction is selective, applying more to institutional changes which threaten social boundaries than to integration of utilities, which do not. More than any other type of arrangement, then, suburbanism regulates distance and closeness among groups (especially black and white groups [see Farley]) by its inherent ability to minimize social variation within communities and maximize differences among them.[5] For, the suburb's political autonomy brings with it the right not only to create and maintain its own resources and institutions, but also to make its own ordinances and so control the size and quality of its population. (In view of this arrangement, which lends to the organization of the outer metropolis an almost feudal quality, one cannot help but view as symptomatic the recent tendency for suburban developers to design and name their projects after medieval castles and estates.)

The interactional consequences of this arrangement are, at any rate, straightforward. The more socially homogeneous a community, the more likely is any one person to find within close residential or institutional proximity others whose interests and tastes are similar to his own. Life-style (as opposed to simple demographic) uniformity tends in this way to intensify the formation of social networks. It follows that in socially homogeneous communities a resident's characteristics are more likely to affect others' as well as his own behavior. Under the influence of this effect, middle-class people planted in territorially and institutionally encased middle-class communities may be expected to behave differently than middle-class people in communities less isolated from the more and less affluent and their respective life-styles. "The suburb," says Riesman (1957, p. 134), "is like a fraternity house at a small college . . . in which like-mindedness reverberates upon itself as the potentially various selves in each of us do not get evoked or recognized." The more general significance of this statement is that whatever the socioeconomic composition of the suburban ring, the political autonomy of its communities help structure social relations and life chances by reinforcing homogeneity of life-style within and heterogeneity among them.

The hyper-communal, Gemeinschaft style is promoted by another factor:

[5] This is not to say that any suburban community is totally homogeneous in any one regard, nor even that most social variation in the suburban ring is attributable to differences among communities. It is simply to suggest that the political organization of the suburban ring can suppress social differences within its communities and so amplify differences among them (on matters which are relevant to residents) to a greater extent than would be possible in city neighborhoods.

the relatively small populations enclosed within suburban boundaries. This contingency has several important consequences. First, the more units into which a population distributes itself (the 33 largest metropolitan areas contain an average of 200 suburban non–school system decision units [see Zimmer]), the lower the ratio between the institutions located in these units and the number of citizens they serve. There are more institutions for fewer people. Hence the relatively high proportion of suburbanties active in civic affairs—and the notion of suburbia as a "hotbed of participation."

The absolute number of persons within a suburban boundary also takes on significance through its effect on the development of institutions themselves. Above all, individual suburbs lack the "critical mass" to support the cultural and economic enterprises which, in the city, find their fullest and most diverse expression. The corresponding social circles are likewise more specialized in the city; this in contrast to that confusion of means and ends which makes for the diffuse sociability so characteristic of suburban life. In his paper on religion in the suburbs, for example, William Newman shows how the rudimentary development of suburban communities forces their churches to take on extra-religious, that is, "social," functions. "The fewer the number of social institutions in any social system," he writes, "the greater the number of functions each of them is likely to have. Given the emergence of new communities in which few of the accustomed institutions existed, religious institutions became the sponsors of everything from girl scouts and dancing clubs to bingo." Newman goes on to outline some of the consequences for the occupational role of the clergy. "The churches," in his view, "have had to produce their own version of the organization man."

Small populations impose limits on "illegitimate" as well as "legitimate" opportunity. Thus, the incredible variety of deviant subcultures which thrive in different parts of the city would find less institutional sustenance in socioeconomically comparable but smaller and politically insulated suburban communities. This is not to deny existing suburban subcultures, nor even their capacity for growth (the public record is clear on that—see Uniform Crime Reports, 1963–73); rather, it is to say that these subcultures are less elaborate and encompassing, and their growth subject to a lower ceiling, than they would be if situated in the city. If this is so, then the celebrated "conformity" of suburbia, its heroization of normality, is likely to persist into the foreseeable future.

Considerations such as these seem to me to constitute grounds for questioning the recent argument that whatever is different about the suburban ring is transitory, that is to say, diminishing with the "urbanization of the suburbs." This assertion fails to take into account the constraints which political boundaries and sheer numbers impose on institutional development and social networks. These limits cause us to at least entertain the notion that, in functional terms, the suburban ring will always be more or less different from the city, that is, that it will never lose its dominantly residential and communal character. The suburb, by its intrinsic nature, therefore, shares one of the essential properties of the small town: It may suffer from relatively few problems, but it cannot boast of many massive accomplishments. It is organized for neither.

SUBURBIA AS EPITHET

Viewed in the light of present knowledge, then, the classic work of the 1950s is not so inaccurate in its description of suburban tendencies. Notwithstanding the measure of its validity, however, I am struck by the distinctly negative character of the suburban image itself. I am also struck by its power. In these respects, no more compelling documentation is available than a recent statement by one of the most strident critics of the suburban sociology of the 1950s. In his preface to the 1971 edition of *Working Class Suburbs*, Bennett Berger admits, "Despite everything reasonable I have said about suburbs, I *know* that the fact that I unreasonably dislike them has been conditioned, *beyond the possibility of redemption by mere research*, by the fact that the myth of suburbia exists." The honesty of this statement has unfortunately nothing to do with the question of whether Berger is reacting to the *myth*, as he says he is, or to a *reality* which he does not recognize. The latter interpretation seems at least plausible in light of the statements made so far. On the other hand, these statements only affirm certain sociologically peculiar features of suburbia; they really do not explain its negative character. To understand this we need to approach the matter from a different point of view.

To begin, let us recognize that the classical image of the suburb is not an isolated construction; on the contrary, that model has been compulsively formulated in direct opposition to our long-settled images of the city. The so-called suburban myth is indeed a counterpoint to our vision of the city— the city accentuated, as it were, then turned inside out. However, these opposing constructions are based on real structural differences which, in my opinion, relate derectly to the disdain in which suburbs are typically held. I shall try to identify them.

Every metropolis has a binary structure: it contains an intense and dynamic, that is, "effervescent," center and a relatively dispersed and languid periphery. These divisions correspond to its "urban" and "sub-urban" spheres. However, the centrality of the city in metropolitan organization is not to be understood in ecological or functional terms; these perspectives are subordinate to the present one, which holds the center to be a "point of intersection" of seemingly irreconcilable cultural and institutional modes. It is as if all the oppositions, dilemmas, and contradictions which the variety of social life makes possible are brought together and resolved in the metropolis's core. Thus, while the city is the locus of immense cultural achievement, it is at the same time fertile ground for abundant and diverse forms of degeneracy. To which corresponds a level of anomie that has shocked generations of commentators—in face of the cohesive and persisting primordial solidarities which have surprised them. The city contains the means not only for unparalleled production but also for mass consumption and lethargy; its economy promotes, in addition, dizzying mania and upward mobility and, as well, despair and social failure. There are other contradictions. Within the center's boundaries there are shrines and monuments which give vivid expression to the authority of the past; there are also the antitheses of rationality and disturbing, often uncontrolled, innovation. The city, then, embodies at once the most sacred and most radically secular impulses of mankind. On another level, we find in the metropolis intense, passionate conflicts superimposed upon a cool and almost perfectly cooperative articulation of seemingly innumerable and independent activities. Finally, the primal conception of the city as a negation of the natural wilderness, a refuge from danger, finds its own negation in the evolution within the city of its own special kinds of predators.

These oppositions are grounded in a unique institutional destiny and recruitment principle. Even in the face of rapid movement of commerce and industry to the suburbs, the city continues to be the seat of society's most decisive enterprises (see Kasarda). Suburbs have, on the other hand, always been looked upon as places of retreat (Mumford 1961, pp. 482–96). This teleological dichotomy conditions the general correlation between productive and remissive modes within these two units: The inhabitant of the city lives near his work; his counterpart, the noncommuting suburbanite, it would seem, works where he lives. A basic functional relationship is reflected in this formula. The historical destiny of the city resides in its cultural, administrative, and creative activities, to which residence is secondary. In this sense, the city is inevitably "a good place to visit, but not to live" (see Gallup Opinion Index, cited in Fischer 1972, p. 8). In the suburb, however, productive capacity is merely instrumental to better and cheaper living and is usually subordinated to that end whenever it comes into conflict with it. Thus, the work of suburbia, claims Riesman (1957, 1964), is the celebration of peace and domesticity. In the place of occupational achievement there is a new measure of man, to be found in the cult of the House Beautiful and the dilettante amateurism of do-it-yourself: a cheap parody of Thoreauvian independence. And there is other work to be done: at home, scientific child rearing; away from the home, the need to "get involved" in local groups and organizations, that is, immersion in *civic* as opposed to serious *political* life. No wonder that male and female symbolism should distinguish city and suburb with such decisiveness. Not only to the gender of its daytime population does suburbia owe its essential femininity, but also to the domesticity which is its very *raison d'être,* and to its corresponding alienation from the "serious" work which has always taken place within the masculine province of the city.

Corresponding to the diverging institutional destinies of cities and suburbs are opposing recruitment principles. One may conceptualize them by entertaining a continuum bound at one end by the rule "All may reside and participate except those specifically prohibited from doing so," and, at the other, "All are excluded except those expressly invited." Few empirical realities correspond to either of these pure formulations; however, city and suburb distinguish themselves in terms of them. While each suburb admits of a specifically circumscribed, often narrow, life-style, and attracts and repels newcomers on the basis of it, the city draws upon and brings together the most varied assortment of humanity, in accordance with its inherent interest in seeking out and exploiting diverse occupational, as opposed to particular life-style, capacities. In the suburbs, then, one renounces, in favor of a more tranquil repose, the variety and contrasts which have made the city the locus of the most colossal enterprises and ironic reconciliations. The suburbs, in this sense, conform to the Freudian conception of femininity: passive, intellectually void, instinctually distractive—in short, anti-cultural. Slater (1970, p. 9) gives speculative voice to this same idea. "Living in a narrow age-graded and class-segregated society," he writes, "it is little wonder that suburban families have contributed so little to the national talent pool in proportion to their numbers, wealth, and other social advantages." Civilization, after all, has always been served by those caught up in the tensions and contradictions of their time. It is shaped, ultimately, by the hands of rebels. But, as Bensman and Rosenberg (1962, p. 269) put it, "Where in suburbia are we to expect rebellion?" Or, more precisely, what is there in suburbia that could provoke rebellion?[6]

The city's eternal role in reconciling opposing cultural, institutional, and behavioral trends finds very direct expression in its imagery. When Mumford (1961, pp. 114–18) gave voice to the "drama of the city," he was referring to *heroic* drama: excessive spectacle, violent emotion and conflict, bombastic issues, and epic personages (to whose charisma the city's monu-

---

[6] Suburban contentment is not universal. However, the disaffected young suburbanites of the 1960s came to the *city* to give vent to their fury against the suburban-based establishment, of which they were a part. "It is also conceivable," say Bensman and Rosenberg (1962, p. 270), "that expatriate suburbanites will move to vestigial bohemias in the city and come to terms with themselves through art. One can imagine a literature in which hostility to the suburbs will then be the most significant cultural outcome of suburban life, just as hostility to the town was the most significant cultural outcome of life in the American small town of several decades ago."

ments stand as sacred testaments). Suburbia, which is almost as old as the city, has, on the other hand, few heroes. Their absence brings to mind Riesman's (1957) "The Suburban Dislocation," in which the lack of dramatic consequence in suburban affairs is so deeply felt. Now activities can only be "dramatic" when there is something at stake in their outcome. Part of the anti-heroic character of suburbia becomes intelligible in this sense, in that the fervent intensity of its affairs—even their public dimension—is muted by the triviality of their content. His new-found "republic in miniature" (Wood 1958) allows the suburbanite to take part in the debate on whether to put a fence around the community tennis court. Society's central issues, on the other hand, seem distant. The autonomy of the suburb is in this respect a spurious independence, jealously guarded and perfected by practice in the administration of things which count little (see the Greers' discussion). Hence its "banality" and "superficial" character. In a dominantly urban society, the previous condemnation of the "idiocy of rural life" is reserved for the suburban provinces.

There is a related implication. Given its withdrawal from a central order, suburbia represents a form of massive social regression. It is as if the metropolis's peripheral elements, unmindful of their ties to the center, turned in unto themselves in a sort of (institutionally mediated) incestual communion. This is the structural variant of the theme of suburbanite as renegade. And there is value in this image, for it seems not so much of hostility toward the city that suburbia is accused but, rather, of indifference. It is a matter of "psychological reneging," of denying spiritual solidarity in the face of an obvious material interdependence. To outsiders, suburbia thus becomes "the center of those middle-brow, conformist, respectable [but] uninspiring members of society who are quite content to potter around in their own rather limited world" (Thorns 1972, p. 149). Fischer and Jackson document this inturning (or "localism," as they call it) in their contribution to this volume. Using quantitative measures, they show in a most convincing way that the natural tendency to select friends on the basis of propinquity is significantly exaggerated in the suburbs. It is suburbia's *social* isolation from the city which is the cause and, no doubt, the effect of this pattern. Donaldson, on the other hand, demonstrates that the *meaning* of localism is not clarified by observable patterns of interpersonal contacts. There seems, in fact, to be a defensive quality about it. Drawing on the work of novelist John Cheever, he points to the artificial character of suburbia,[7] whose solidarity is based on transient individual acquaintances and friendships; this he contrasts with what might be called the "organic" community, whose members are bound to one another through common roots in a collective tradi-

[7] This is an ironic statement in view of Donaldson's earlier work (1969) on the subject.

tion. Hence the need in suburbia for unnatural forms of exclusion: unpleasantness is zoned out; composure depends on doors closed to other people and worlds. Communities without depth, Cheever says, require walls.

Cheever (as Donaldson represents him) gives voice to his lament through a series of comparative community studies. Take a man from Saint Botolphs, plant him in suburban Bullet Park, and see what happens. What we have, then, is a man working in the tradition of Zola's "experimental novel." To what does the experimental treatment lead? Desperation and boredom, on the one hand; on the other, the commutation hysteria, which brings into focus all the ills of the technological age. The suburb is therefore contemptible because of its spiritual bleakness, its "shallow and despicable life-style," which transforms poetic dreams of pastoral bliss into the cheap prose of the 7:50 and the power mower. Cutting itself off from the more "natural" atmosphere of small town and city, then, suburbia organizes a life without meaning, whose logical indictment is death itself. Observe its anti-heroic forms. One resident of Bullet Park, tells Cheever, is sucked under the wheels of a west-bound express train; another, observing his freshly painted house—and looking forward to painting it again, and again—pauses long enough to blow his brains out. A third man perishes when his clothes are ignited at the barbeque during a backyard cookout. Such is the grand pathos of suburbia.

Such is also the context for the philistine conception of "suburban man." But he is surely a very curious type of philistine. Unlike Thomas's (1966), this one (depicted best, perhaps, by Cheever) is mobile, his prototype standing at the intersection of two social circles rather than at the center of one, whence the diffusion rather than concentration of his commitments. For his connection with the city omits the primordial linkage of residence; his attachment to suburbia, on the other hand, excludes the dynamic element of productivity. The importance of the commuter image (notwithstanding empirical patterns of commutation) in the construction of the suburban character stems from these considerations, which allow us to infer from the segmental and partial nature of his external ties affectlessness and superficiality in his inner life.

One is bound to ask why the neighborhoods of the cities, themselves bounded and compact "bedroom communities," are not popularly cast, along with their residents, in the same baneful mold. Such a question underestimates the importance of territory as an ascriptive characteristic. True, the masses of the city may find in their lives nothing but routine and monotony; but, as members of the center, they are part of a collective dynamism which colors and becomes part of their existence. They become the "city people," of whom rural and small-town lore has so much to tell. The suburbanite evokes no such wonderment; *he* is the faceless one. There must be some truth in this. After all, Archie Bunker is a romantic fellow because he lives in the heart of the city; plant him in suburbia and he becomes a common philistine.

Perhaps I am being a bit romantic myself. I think not. For, the primordial psychological impulse of identification with soil has always been central to evaluative character analysis. This is why those negative accounts of the suburbs which rely on the notion of a "haven" for "escapees" are, and always have been, wrong. It is true that city dwellers may move into the suburban periphery to avoid the growing presence of dark minorities and the increasingly predatory life-styles of neighbors. Guterbock's paper, on the other hand, suggests that these "push" factors may be the least important causes (not motives) of the city's depopulation. However this may be, one thing can be said for sure: Nothing disdainful inheres in movement from dangerous to safer zones as long as that movement is confined to a solidary unit. Only when one "moves out to the suburbs," that is, when he denies commitment to a community by crossing its boundary, is he castigated. That chastisement must in turn perform a social function; it must have meaning in its own right. And this can only be that the integrity of the city as a moral union is still secure. Even more, it must heighten the solidarity of that union. This is because social boundaries are firmed up by labeling those beyond them as outsiders. Disdain for suburbanites does for the integrity of the city what punishment does for the integration of society. But the relationship is not exactly as straightforward as that. There is in fact a distinct element of ambivalence. One must remember that the disparaging conception of the suburbanite crystallized during an era of growing attraction to the community in which he lived. Just as if the caricature, drawn by those who loved the city, was meant to protect its residents against their own impulses. The image of the suburbanite as an indecently dull and passionless being, and of suburbia as a colossally bland place, could only blunt those wishes (in some measure or other), and, in doing so, strengthen the bonds among those in whom they so uncomfortably reside.

If the above statements help make intelligible the distinctly negative evaluation of suburbanism (as well as the useless protests against that characterization by irate suburbanites [see, e.g., McGinley 1959]), then they must also give expression to the special structural complex in which suburbanism is grounded. Accordingly, I propose that only a sustained deconcentration of the productive and destructive forces of the city will render the anti-heroic truth of the suburban myth obsolete. As of now, the romantic division of the metropolis into a driving center and a languorous periphery continues to have empirical merit. Indeed, that division is institutionalized by formal boundaries and by political processes intent on its maintenance. However, several of the contributions to this volume (Kasarda's being the most dramatic) show that division to be in an early stage of decay, which is to say that the classic convergence between the concepts of "city" and "urban" is no longer entirely appropriate. For as the "friction" of space is overcome (see Tobin), the center loses its density; its effervescence becomes attenuated and is diffused throughout the peripheral sphere.[8] It does not follow, however, that cities and suburbs will one day be indistinguishable, as the title of one reader (Masotti and Hadden 1973) on the subject implies; on the contrary, the biconcentric differentiation of the metropolis is, in the senses indicated, one of its invariant features. Accordingly, we need not deny change and variation in metropolitan life to assert intrinsic limits to the present centrifugal trend. Indeed, the dominant image emerging from this book is a superimposition in the suburbs of drastic population and economic growth upon a stubbornly permanent sociopolitical base. We can therefore appreciate the sense in which the "face" of the suburb is changing without denying the sense in which its underlying structure—its "soul," so to speak—is not.

REFERENCES

Bensman, Joseph, and Bernard Rosenberg. 1962. "The Culture of the New Suburbia." *Dissent* 9 (Summer): 267–70.

Berger, Bennett M. 1971*a*. *Working-Class Suburb*. Berkeley: University of California Press.

———. 1971*b*. "Suburbs, Subcultures and Styles of Life." Pp. 165–87 in *Looking for America*. Englewood Cliffs, N.J.: Prentice-Hall.

Dobriner, William M. 1963. *Class in Suburbia*. Englewood Cliffs, N.J.: Prentice-Hall.

Donaldson, Scott. 1969. *The Suburban Myth*. New York: Columbia University Press.

Fava, Sylvia F. 1956. "Suburbanism as a Way of Life." *American Sociological Review* 21 (February): 34–38.

Fischer, Claude S. 1972. "The Metropolitan Experience." Paper prepared for panel on the Significance of Community in the Metropolitan Environment, National Research Council, National Academy of Sciences, Washington, D.C.

Gans, Herbert J. 1967. *The Levittowners: Ways of Life and Politics in a New Suburban Community*. New York: Random House.

Gordon, Robert A. 1968. "Issues in Multiple Regression." *American Journal of Sociology* 73 (March): 592–616.

Janowitz, Morris. 1962. *The Community Press in an Urban Setting*. Glencoe, Ill: Free Press.

McGinley, Phyllis. 1959. "Suburbia, of Thee I Sing." Pp. 121–33 in *The Province of the Heart*. New York: Viking.

Marshall, Harvey. 1973. "Suburban Life Styles: A Contribution to the Debate." Pp. 123–48 in *The Urbanization of the Suburbs*, edited by Louis H. Masotti and Jeffrey K. Hadden. Urban Affairs Annual Reviews, vol. 7. Beverly Hills, Calif.: Sage.

Martin, Walter T. 1956. "The Structuring of Social Relationships Engendered by Suburban Residence." *American Sociological Review* 21 (August): 446–53.

[8] This development evokes the vision of a "Post-City Age" (Webber 1968; see also Strauss 1968). However, the vision is extreme in that it takes a mere spatial tendency to be prophetic of the metropolis's social, economic, and political destinies.

Masotti, Louis H., and Jeffrey K. Hadden. 1973. *The Urbanization of the Suburbs*. Urban Affairs Annual Reviews, vol. 7. Beverly Hills, Calif.: Sage.

Mowrer, Ernest R. 1958. "The Family in Suburbia." Pp. 147–64 in *The Suburban Community*, edited by William M. Dobriner. New York: Putnam's.

Mumford, Lewis. 1961. *The City in History*. New York: Harcourt, Brace & World.

Riesman, David. 1957. "The Suburban Dislocation."*Annals of the American Academy of Political and Social Science* 314 (November): 123–46.

———. 1964. "Flight and Search in the New Suburbs." Pp. 258–69 in *Abundance for What?* Garden City, N.Y.: Doubleday.

Seeley, John R., R. A. Sim, and E. W. Loosley. 1956. *Crestwood Heights*. New York: Basic.

Slater, Philip E. 1970. *The Pursuit of Loneliness*. Boston: Beacon.

Spectorsky, A. C. 1955. *The Exurbanites*. New York: Berkley.

Strauss, Anselm L. 1968. "The Latest in Urban Imagery." Pp. 508–14 in *The American City*, edited by Anselm L. Strauss. Chicago: Aldine.

Thomas, W. I. 1966. "Social Personality: Organization of Attitudes." Pp. 11–36 in *W. I. Thomas on Social Organization and Social Personality*, edited by Morris Janowitz. Chicago: University of Chicago Press.

Thorns, David C. 1972. *Suburbia*. London: MacGibbon & Kee.

Webber, Melvin M. 1968. "The Post-City Age." *Daedalus* 97 (Fall): 1091–1110.

Whyte, William H. 1956. *The Organization Man*. Garden City, N.Y.: Doubleday.

Wood, Robert C. 1958. *Suburbia: Its People and Their Politics*. Boston: Houghton Mifflin.

Indexes

Name Index

Abrams, Charles, 169, 201, 247, 248, 249, 254, 263
Abramson, Harold J., 274, 275
Abu-Lughod, J., 283, 286, 287, 304
Allen, H. David, 274, 277
Alonso, William, 96, 109
André, Carolyn D., *69–94*
Angell, Robert Cooley, 145, 160
Armstrong, Regina B., 114, 114n, 135
Athanasiou, R., 281n, 283n, 304
Austin, Richard B., 243

Babbie, Earl, 270, 276
Bain, C. W., 188n, 201
Bakalis, Michael, 240
Baldassare, M., 283, 285, 298, 304
Banfield, Edward C., 27, 37, 210, 218
Bauer, Catherine, 250, 263
Becquart, Jeannette, 215n, 218
Belgue, D., 283, 306
Bell, Wendell, 209, 218, 283, 286, 304
Bellah, Robert N., 272, 273, 275
Bensman, Joseph, 210, 219, 335, 335n, 339
Berger, Bennett M., 203n, 213, 275, 285n, 286, 304, 326, 327, 333, 339
Berger, Peter L., 271, 272, 274, 275, 277
Berman, Michael H., 244
Berry, Brian J. L., 114, 114n, 135, 137n, 138, 141, 144, 160, 161, *221–64*, 264, 329
Beshers, James A., 249, 263
Black, G. S., 287, 304
Blalock, Hubert M., 246, 263
Blizzard, Samuel, 268, 275
Blumberg, Leonard, 70, 93
Blumberg, Paul, 309, 322
Bogue, Donald J., 104, 110
Bohrnstedt, George W., 160
Bolce, Harold, 101, 109
Bollens, John C., 188n, 201, 207, 218
Borgatta, Edgar F., 160
Bourg, C. J., 287, 301, 304
Bowles, Gladys K., 47, 55
Bracher, Frederick, 314, 320, 322
Bradburn, Norman M., 222, 263, 285n, 288, 305
Bradford, David F., 70, 93
Bressler, Marvin, 258, 259, 263, 275

Brown, A. Theodore, 95n, 109
Burch, Genevieve, 267, 276
Burgess, E. W., 171, 201
Burhans, Clinton S., 312, 316, 322
Burstein, Paul, 279n
Butler, Edgar W., 254, 263, 283, 304

Callow, Alexander B., Jr., 95n, 109, 307
Campbell, A. K., 171, 171n, 188, 190, 194n, 199, 201, 287, 305
Campbell, Thomas, 270, 276
Carlos, Serge, 266, 267, 271, 276
Carp, F. M., 287, 301, 305
Carpenter, David, 105, 110
Carrothers, G. A. P., 280n, 305
Carruth, Eleanor, 114, 114n, 135
Casson, Herbert N., 102, 109
Cheever, John, 309–22, 309n, 310n, 312n, 322, 336, 337

Chinitz, Benjamin, 114, 135
Clark, Colin, 141, 156, 160
Clark, Kenneth, 249, 263
Clark, S. D., 284, 284n, 286, 286n, 287, 305
Clarke, James W., 214, 218
Clawson, Marion, 92, 93
Coffin, Gregory, 234–35
Cohen, Y. S., 114, 114n, 135
Cole, L. M., 284n, 305
Cooper, C. C., 285, 305
Cornelius, W. A., 287, 305
Corzine, J., 180, 181n, 198n, 202
Coser, Lewis A., 309, 322
Cowan, Peter, 114, 135
Cox, K., 287, 305
Crabbe, B. D., 286n, 307
Cressey, P. F., 165, 201
Cuzzort, Ray P., 146, 160

Dahl, Robert, 213, 218
Danielson, Michael N., 171, 199, 200n, 201, 210, 218
Demerath, N. J., 270, 271, 276
Dickenson, Emily, 316
Dittes, James, 270, 276
Dobriner, William M., 37, 39, 55, 274, 275, 276, 277, 280, 286, 304, 305, 306, 326, 339, 340

Italicized figures represent inclusive pages for entire chapters.

Name Index

Subject Index

Subject Index

Cities
  education of residents in, 18–19, (table) 20
  effect of migration on, 8–14
  employment in, 121–22, (table) 125
  family patterns in, 39–67
  future of, 131
  growth of vs. suburbs, 165–70
  migration to and from by age, 9, (fig.) 12,
    47–55, (figs.) 57–67
  occupational structure of, 113–36
  political machines in, 209–10
  population of, 4–15, 72–83, (table) 170
  racial composition of, 72–83
  socioeconomic status of residents in, 15–19
  tax base erosion in, 115
City-County consolidation. *See* Government
    reorganization
"Civil religion" hypothesis, 272
Clergy, and role-conflict dilemmas in subur-
    ban churches, 268–69
Cleveland, Ohio
  age distribution of, 13, (table) 14
  education distribution in, (table) 20
  and education of migrants, (table) 25
  income distribution in, (table) 16, 17
  migration between city and suburbs in,
    (table) 23, 28
  population of, (table) 7
  population change by race in, (table) 11
  population growth of, (table) 7, 75, (fig.)
    76, 77
Commuting. *See also* Motor transportation.
  annexation adjustments for patterns of,
    132–34
  amount of, by occupation, (table) 130
  increase in, 127–30
Concentration, measurement of, 140–42, 155–
  57
Consolidation. *See* Government reorganiza-
    tion
Contextual effects model of localism, 279
Cook County, Illinois, white migration by
    age in, (fig.) 63
Cosmopolitanism, and attitudes toward inte-
    gration, 259–61. *See also* Metropoli-
    tanism
Counties, increase in number of, 1957–72, 172
Crime
  as a cause of suburbanization, 137–39,
    147–51, 154–55
  measurements of, 145–46
Cuyahoga County, Ohio, (fig.) 61

Dallas, Texas
  age distribution of, (table) 15
  education distribution of, (table) 21
  and education of migrants, (table) 26

income distribution of, (table) 17, 18
migration between city and suburbs in,
  (table) 24
population of, (table) 7
population change by race in, (table) 11
population growth in, (table) 7, 8
Decon (deconcentration) score
  defined, 145
  formulae for computing, 159
Deconcentration
  measures of, 139–40, 142–45, 159
  panel analysis of, 150–51, 159–60
  rate variation for cities, 154, 154n
DeKalb County, Georgia, (fig.) 65
Demonstration Cities and Metropolitan De-
    velopment Act (1966), 200
Denominationalism, 273
Detroit, Michigan
  age distribution of, (table) 14
  education distribution of, (table) 20
  and education of migrants, (table) 25,
    26–27
  income distribution of, (table) 16
  localism in suburbs of, 295–301
  map of rings in, (fig.) 84
  migration between city and suburbs in,
    (table) 23
  population of, (table) 6
  population change by race in, 8, 10
  population growth in, (table) 6
  population growth pattern of, 83–84
  racial composition of, 85–88
  residential segregation in 28–25, (table)
    29–30
Distance-cost model of localism, 280
  minimizing factors of, 284
Distance from central city
  and localism, 298–99, 301–2
  and population growth by race, 88
  and social access, 281–82
Double-count majority, defined, 189–90n
Double majority, defined, 190n
Drug use, and suburban life, 318–19
DuPage County, Illinois
  racial segregation in, 225
  white migration in, (fig.) 63

Eastgate Residents Association, 240–41
Ecological theories of localism, 279
Ecorse (Detroit), Michigan, 88
Education
  of city vs. suburban residents, 18–19,
    (table) 20–21, (fig.) 22
  of migrants by race, (table) 25, 27
  and residential segregation by race in
    Detroit, (table) 29, (table) 33
  and suburban localism, 292, 300

350

Subject Index

Transportation. *See also* Motor transportation.
  and suburbanization, 95–111
  and suburban life, 312–14
Travel time, 168–69
Trucks
  industrial use of, 101, 105
  production of, 101, 102, 104–5, 107
Trust, Political, and suburban politics, 215–17

Unemployment, 115, 115n
"Unigov" (Indianapolis), 208

Values and suburban growth, 95–96
Virginia, government reorganization in, 188

Washington, D.C.
  age distribution of, (table) 14
  education distribution of, (table) 20
  education of migrants, (table) 25
  income distribution of, (table) 16, 18
  migration between city and suburbs in, (table) 23, 26, 47–49, (fig.) 48
  migration from, 8

population of, (table) 6
population change by race in, (table) 10
population growth in, (table) 6
Wayne County, Michigan, 62
Westchester County, New York, 59
West Englewood (Chicago), 226–29
White-collar employees, 115, 123, 125, 126, 128
White-collar employment, 122–24
Whites
  distribution of residence and place of work for, (table) 129
  "flight" of, 154–55, 221–64
  migration of by age, 48, 57–67
  population decline of in central cities, 78–83
  population of in suburban rings, (table) 82
  reactions to integration of, in Chicago, 221–64
Women
  effects of suburban residence on, 286–87
  employment of, 43, 45–46, 293
  and localism, 293
Women's Christian Temperance Union, 233
Working wives, 43, 45–46, (table) 45, 293